Beware the Grey Widow-Maker

by Bernard Edwards

Brick Tower Press
New York

Bernard Edwards

CONTENTS

Page

Preface

7

DEDICATION

This book is dedicated to those who go down
to the sea in ships.

"Men of all professions, in lightning, in thunder, storms and tempests, with rain and snow, may shelter themselves in dry houses, by good fires, and good cheer; but those are the chief times that seamen must stand to their tacklings, and attend with all diligence their greatest labour upon the decks"

Captain John Smith—1627

Bernard Edwards

AUTHOR'S NOTE

This book follows the changing pattern of man's fortunes at sea, from the golden age of sail, through the proud years when steam reigned supreme, to the present day, when the flag of convenience rules the waves. It tells of triumphs and disasters, some recent, some long forgotten, and illustrates how, contrary to all expectations, the fine art of seamanship has withered and died with the advent of advanced technology.

Also by Bernard Edwards:

Masters Next to God

They Sank the Red Dragon

The Fighting Tramps

The Grey Widow Maker

Salvo!

SOS, Men Against the Sea

Return of the Coffin Ships

Attack & Sink

Blood & Bushido

Dönitz and the Wolf Packs

Beware Raiders

Widow-Maker

PREFACE

The Atlantic Ocean was first crossed by air in May 1919 by Lieutenant-Commander Albert C. Read and a crew of five in a Curtiss flying boat. The crossing, from New York to Plymouth, via Newfoundland, the Azores and Lisbon, took an agonising 53 hours and 58 minutes.

This historic event occurred at the close of a long period of upheaval at sea which had seen the birth of the steamship, the slow death of sail, and the progression of the sea voyage from an undertaking fraught with the most dreadful discomfort and danger to a relatively safe and tranquil interlude between ports.

Before the Merchant Shipping Act of 1875, pioneered by Samuel Plimsoll, it was possible for unscrupulous shipowners—and they were then legion—to send their ships to sea in a deplorable state. Rotten hulls and inadequate crews were the order of the day, and insurance was easily obtained, even when a ship was clearly unseaworthy. Not surprisingly, the premiums were commensurately high, and the underwriters were happy. The shipowner, on the other hand, was not too worried if his ship disappeared in mid-ocean. All too frequently, the only losers were the passengers and crew.

Overloading was commonplace, with many owners, aided by the willing connivance of their captains, so burdening their ships in the pursuit of extra freight that the decks were awash in the slightest chop. The introduction of the Plimsoll Line in 1876 did much to curb this practice, but for decades afterwards, until the institution of strict port controls, a Nelsonian eye was turned on the load line. As to the need for a correct distribution of cargo in the holds to ensure a stable ship and a comfortable passage, this was often regarded as a time-wasting irrelevance.

The continuous watertight bulkhead was another luxury not brought into common use until well into the 20th century. When a ship's hull was breached by stranding or collision, the sea swept right through her, and she usually foundered before those on board had a chance to take to the boats. In the rare event of there being the opportunity to abandon ship in the orthodox manner, there was invariably, especially in the case of passenger vessels, insufficient lifeboats for the number of persons on board. Unless the master was particularly far-seeing, those boats that were carried were not kept stocked with food and water, and often had no oars or sails. Regular lifeboat drills were unknown, so that any attempt to leave a sinking ship was doomed to be attended by chaos, and sometimes violent disorder. As to calling on other ships or the shore for help, before the advent of wireless telegraphy the choice of means was very limited. Rockets and flares cost money, and were not favoured by the parsimonious shipowner. That left only the time-honoured, but notoriously ineffective hoisting of the ensign upside down by day, and the burning of oil-soaked rags at night, supplemented, in the case of a steamer, by frantic blasts on the whistle.

Fire at sea in the 19th century was a horrific nightmare best not dwelt upon. Ships were woefully ill-equipped to deal with this emergency; a few canvas hoses, fed by a hand-cranked fire pump, and a crew totally untrained in fire-fighting being the only defence. The net result was a ship consumed by flames while her terrified passengers and crew cowered on the poop awaiting their fate.

The world's merchant fleet almost doubled in size between the 1830s and the 1850s, giving rise to a long-running shortage of trained seamen. In consequence, the masters and officers of many ships were of a poor standard, while the ratings were often the sweepings of the jails and dockland brothels, supplemented by a sprinkling of young hopefuls inspired by the sentimental ramblings of armchair sailors on shore. Accurate navigation involving the use of sextant and chronometer was, largely through ignorance, not widely practised. Too much reliance was placed on dead reckoning, which is no more than guesswork based on experience. A wrong allowance for the run of the current or tide, or an incorrect estimate of the ship's speed, could spell disaster. There was a great deal of drunkeness among both officers and ratings, and in the event of an emergency arising, it was not always 'women and children first'. To be fair, many officers acted with restraint and courage, but the men were frequently more interested in saving their own lives than those of the passengers. But, as those who served before the mast were little better than slave labour, what else could be expected of them?

During the second half of the 19th century and the first quarter of the 20th, some 60 million people emigrated from Europe to the Americas and the Antipodes. Much of the mass exodus from the old world to the new had its roots in the reign of terror that began as a popular revolution in France at the end of the 18th century. When the guillotine fell on Louis XVI in 1793, and the ambitious Napoleon Bonaparte gained power, the continent of Europe drifted into two decades of bloody war, which left many countries devastated, with their governments in political turmoil. For another thirty years after that, revolution and minor war stalked the land from the English Channel to the Black Sea, bringing nothing but famine and abject poverty to the masses of Europe.

Soon after the victory of Waterloo, Britain, strong and politically stable, moved into an industrial revolution, and so escaped the chaos on the other side of the Channel. Ireland, however, remained firmly wedded to its primitive agriculture, and when the potato crop, on which the peasants were wholly dependent, failed in 1846, a wave of mass emigration began that was to halve the population of the island in the years that followed.

Wars and famine were not the only reasons for the great movement across the seas in the 1800s. The discovery of gold in California in 1849, and in Australia two years later, caused another outflowing of Europe's poor and oppressed. Few of those who followed the gold trail made fortunes; the majority eventually achieved the independence and security they craved by working the land—which was what they did best. The vast, open spaces of America and Australia had room for them all.

The long sea voyage—3,500 miles to America and 12,000 miles to Australia—was the initial, and severest, trial the emigrants had to undergo. When sail gave way to steam, it considerably reduced the length of the voyage, but it did little to improve conditions on board ship. For those travelling in steerage—and they made up the vast majority—the passage out was only for the fit and stout of heart. With as many as 500 men, women and children crammed into the damp, poorly ventilated holds of a small ship for weeks or months on end, life was truly a living hell. When there was also cargo in the holds, a not uncommon occurrence, then it was required only to lay a rough wooden platform over the cargo, leaving a height of not less than 5-foot 6-inches under the main deck for the passengers. If the cargo happened to be dirty or foul smelling, then it can be imagined how the poor wretches living on top of it suffered. For those not stricken with the horrors of seasickness, a stomach-churning diet of Irish stew and porridge was served up day after day, week after week. Sanitation was an afterthought with, on average, only two lavatories for every 100 people. Little wonder disease was rampant and one in every ten died on the voyage.

The emigrants were not the only ones on the move. This was also the day of great empires overseas, with a steady stream of colonial officials and merchants flowing back and forth across the oceans. Then there were the *nouveau riche* of the industrial age escaping the boredom of their pampered lives, and the tired masses of manual workers seeking a chink of light in their dreary existence. The sea, knowing no class barriers, claimed them all. This was an age of ignorance and brutality, and sudden death was no stranger on the scene. But it was the callous manner in which the sea took its victims that, even now, retains its power to shock.

By the end of the 19th century, the conduct of shipping had moved into a new era of respectability. The majority of ships were by then conscientiously maintained and crewed by professionals—or, at the very least, by men whose interests extended beyond a bellyful of rum and the price of whores in the next port.

A number of important lessons were learned from the tragic loss of the *Titanic* in 1912, and thereafter safety at sea became paramount. The apogee was reached soon after the end of the Second World War, when all the technological spin-off from that long conflict became available even to the most impoverished tramp. Today, those who go down to the sea in ships should do so without undue risk. Modern ships are large, powerfully engined, and carry navigational equipment capable of accurate position-fixing in all weathers. Radio communication with the remotest shores and other ships is clear and instantaneous. And yet, accidents at sea have lately become ever more bizarre and destructive as the new flag-of-convenience sailors, dazzled by electronics and blinkered by ignorance, contemptuously underestimate the power of the sea. Their graves, and those of men and women that put their trust in them, lie scattered over the oceans, from the China Sea to the South Atlantic, from the Pacific to the Mediterranean.

1 The East Indiaman

Grosvenor - 1782

When Persian armies led by Nadir Shah swept into northern India in 1739, they captured and ransacked the ancient palace of the Moguls in Delhi, stripping the building clean of all its fabulous wealth. Among their plunder was the magnificent Peacock Throne, on which the Mogul emperors had sat. The throne, shaped like a bed, was moulded in solid gold, encrusted with diamonds, emeralds and rubies, and backed by two golden peacocks, also lavishly studded with precious stones, from which it took its name. This was treasure on which no man could put a value. Nadir Shah took the throne back to Persia, where it then disappeared from view. It is thought it may have been broken up and distributed amongst the Shah's followers, but whatever happened to the Peacock Throne, it was never to be seen again. The two golden peacocks, on the other hand, said to be worth a vast fortune on their own, came to light forty-three years later when, securely packed in an iron-studded chest, they were loaded aboard the East Indiaman *Grosvenor,* bound for Britain. Where the peacocks had lain hidden all those years, and who acquired them is to this day still a mystery.

For the Honourable East India Company, the year 1782 was not a happy one. In the first half of the year no less than five of its ships were lost. Of these, three were on their maiden voyages: the *Fortitude* taken by pirates off the Coromandel Coast, the *Earl of Dartmouth* wrecked on the Nicobar Islands, and the *Major* destroyed by fire on the Ganges. The Company was rich and could withstand such losses comfortably, but when news was received in November of that year that the *Grosvenor* was overdue and believed lost with all hands at sea, there was consternation in London.

The *Grosvenor*, 729 tons, commanded by Captain John Coxon, sailed from Trincomalee, on Ceylon's east coast, on 13 June 1782, bound for London. She was a well-found ship, with a highly trained crew and armed with twenty-eight 18-pounder guns. Her total complement of 135 passengers and crew included eighty Europeans, mostly British. Her cargo, apart from the usual Indian produce, included gold, precious stones and ivory to the value of £2 million. In her strongroom, a secret shared only by Captain Coxon and his chief officer, was a consignment worth more than the *Grosvenor* and her cargo put together. The golden peacocks of the Moguls were on their way to a new home.

Ahead of the *Grosvenor* lay a voyage of 11,000 miles, a voyage beset with many dangers. Foul weather, marauding pirates and patrolling Dutch men-of-war—Britain was at that time engaged in a bitter war with Holland—all lay in her path. But for the East Indiaman's passengers and crew, perhaps the greatest hardship to come was to be cooped up in this tiny ship (she was no more than 160 feet by 34 feet) for seven long months. Because of the war with Holland, there could be no call at Cape Town to re-provision, so it would be necessary to strictly ration food and water. Sanitation, of course, would be of the most rudimentary, and for the unfortunate passengers, many of them women and children, there would be the awful, morale destroying curse of sea-sickness. This was to be a voyage of endurance, but there was not one on board who doubted that it would be completed.

The passage south across the Indian Ocean could not have been worse. The south-west monsoon was at its height, and from the time of sailing from Trincomalee until she neared the Equator, the *Grosvenor* battled against adverse gale-force winds and heavy seas. There followed day after day lolling in the calms of the Doldrums under a blazing sun that melted the pitch in her deck seams and turned her accommodation into a living hell before, at last, the south-east trades began to fill her sails. But the belated progress she then made was short-lived. When south of Madagascar, the *Grosvenor* ran into the first of the south-westerly gales that ravage the South African coast in winter. The battle against the elements was resumed.

On 3 August the ship was fifty-one days on passage and in a position estimated to be some 700 miles east of the Cape of Good Hope. The skies had been overcast for two days past and it had not been possible to take sights to verify this position, but Captain Coxon was confident enough of his reckoning to assure his guests at dinner that night that all was well. The ship, he maintained, was at least a hundred miles off the land and would pass well south of the Cape as she sailed to the west.

Yet another gale blew up during the night, and the *Grosvenor* was forced to heave-to under shortened sail. At about 2 o'clock on the morning of the 4th, in a break in the rain, Second Officer Shaw, who had the watch on deck, sighted a flickering light right ahead. He was about to put this down to another ship on the same course when he saw first one, then two, then a line of dancing lights stretching right across the bow. Shaw had seen native fires on a darkened coastline many times before, and it seemed to him that, even though she should have been many miles from the land, the *Grosvenor* was about to run ashore. Without hesitation, and praying he was not too late, Shaw called all hands and began to put the ship about.

The shrilling of bosun's pipes and the stamp of hurrying feet brought Captain Coxon on deck. By this time, the rain had closed in again and the lights were no longer visible. Shaw tried to explain his fears, but Coxon would have none of it. As far as he was concerned, the ship was well clear of the land. He ordered Shaw to resume course and then retired to his cabin again.

Having, albeit reluctantly, put the ship back on her original course, Shaw resumed his pacing of the poop, trying hard to convince himself that the lights had been a figment of his overwrought imagination. It was a black and heavily overcast night; certainly a night on which a man's eyes might play strange tricks. The watch dragged on and the fears Shaw had harboured began to fade. Then, as one bell was struck to signify the last quarter hour of the watch, there was a frenzied shout from the lookout aloft: 'Breakers ahead!'

And so began the long nightmare. Coxon was called on deck and attempted to wear ship, but it was too late. Carried on the back of a huge, tumbling swell with her sails hanging limp, the *Grosvenor* was hurled ashore, the terrible grinding of her timbers on the rocks matched by the screaming of her passengers.

Held fast by rocks that had pierced her bottom and pounded by the angry waves, the East Indiaman began to break up within a short time of grounding. Distress signals were fired, but, although the ship appeared to be not more than 300 yards from the shore, no answer came. Coxon ordered the pumps to be started and the masts cut away, hoping this would lighten the ship and she would float off. Again the result was disappointing. The *Grosvenor*, cast up on an unknown and probably uninhabited shore, was doomed.

Coxon now turned to the problem of saving his passengers and crew. The ship's two boats were lowered, but they were immediately dashed to pieces against the ship's side, fortunately without loss of life. A raft was then constructed with the idea of floating a hawser ashore. This time the launching was successful, but the raft disintegrated in the raging surf just a few yards from the ship. Three men lost their lives. Three others, who were powerful swimmers, volunteered to swim ashore with a line. It was a fearful risk, but two of the three men reached the shore, the other being lost in the surf.

When the swimmers landed they were surrounded by a crowd of natives, who appeared to be friendly. With their help, a heavier line was hauled ashore from the *Grosvenor* and made fast to a rock. A few minutes later, the stricken ship broke in two, but the hawser held. Some men reached the shore hand over hand on the hawser, but fifteen fell to their deaths in the surf while attempting this perilous route.

The shock of seeing so many men lost put an end to all efforts to escape. Those left on board huddled together on the poop awaiting their fate, for they were sure the ship would not last until dawn. Then, miraculously it seemed, the stern half of the ship broke clear of the rocks holding it and drifted into shallow and sheltered water close to the shore. All 115 on board reached the safety of dry land.

Most of the survivors were in a pitiful condition when they landed. Wet, frightened, and exhausted by their ordeal, they had no idea of where they had come ashore. Of one thing they were certain, it was a wild and forbidding place. The rocky beach was backed by sand dunes, and beyond that, some three miles inland, stood a wall of dense, impenetrable forest. They were, in fact, in Pondoland, about a hundred miles south-west of what is now called Durban and near the mouth of the Lombazi River. But this was then largely unexplored country and they had no means of identifying their location. The Kaffirs, of course, spoke a language that was unintelligible to all, so they were of little help. Furthermore, they seemed to be showing an unhealthy interest in the few possessions the survivors had managed to bring ashore. Coxon decided it would be wise to move on as soon as possible. He knew that somewhere to the west lay the Dutch colony of the Cape, but he had no idea how far it was to the nearest settlement. It might be five days march, or it might be fifteen; certainly, the going would be hard.

Having collected some casks of provisions and tools washed ashore from the wreck, the survivors spent remainder of the night around a fire built on the beach by the Kaffirs. It must have occurred with some irony, both to Coxon and Shaw that they were probably sitting close to one of the fires the second officer had seen two hours before the *Grosvenor* struck.

When daylight came, Coxon sent men to scour the beach for anything else that might have come ashore, then the whole party set off to the west, carrying one of their number, who had been injured in the wreck. They had not gone far before the Kaffirs began to follow them in large numbers. At first, the natives kept their distance, although they had become decidedly unfriendly. As the day wore on, they grew bolder and moved in, first to touch, and then to steal the few possessions the *Grosvenor*'s survivors had. None of Coxon's party was armed so they could do little to deter their unwelcome escorts.

For several days the band of survivors struggled westwards along the inhospitable coast, keeping the foraging Kaffirs at bay by buying them off with trinkets, and when these ran out, by confrontation that stopped just short of violence. The hostile band surrounding them was swelling all the time, and Coxon, conscious that he had women and children with him, wished to avoid a fight at all costs. Their route was intersected by numerous rivers, and wild beasts roamed the edge of the forest, adding to the dangers they already faced. The women and children began to tire, slowing the progress of the party to a mere crawl.

Day followed day, and soon all food was exhausted and the survivors were reduced to living off shellfish and roots. The Kaffirs stole their only tinderbox and they were obliged to carry their fire with them in the form of burning torches. Many collapsed through malnutrition and exhaustion, others simply did not have the will to carry on. Eventually, it was decided that forty-three of the fittest men would go on ahead to find a settlement and bring help. Coxon and his officers stayed with the sick, the women and children, planning to strike north into the forest, and there make camp, secure, it was hoped, from the increasingly hostile Kaffirs.

Four months later, seven emaciated, half-crazed men walked into a Dutch farm in the Cape colony. They were the only survivors of the forty-three who had set out to find civilisation. The rest had died on the long trek, succumbing to hunger, thirst, wild beasts and the Kaffirs. Although the Dutch were at war with Britain, when the Governor of the colony heard of the arrival of the seven men, he sent out an expedition several hundred strong to search for Coxon and the others. Another three months passed and the search party returned with twelve more pitiful wretches, three white men, seven Lascars and two Indian ayahs. Of the remaining sixty, no trace could be found. To this day, their fate is unknown, but many years after the loss of the *Grosvenor*, there were reports of a strange tribe of light-skinned Kaffirs in the area where she came ashore. It could be that some of the white women survived and were taken into the native kraals.

The *Grosvenor*, her rotting hulk now buried deep in the sands, still lies thirty yards off the shore near Port Grosvenor, to which she gave her name. Numerous attempts have been made to salvage her fabulous treasure, but this is a dangerous coast, fringed by jagged rocks and pounded by a huge surf. A few guns, a handful of gold coins and odd items of personal effects have been recovered, but none of the gold bars, precious stones and ivory the ship was said to be carrying. As to the fabulous peacocks of the Moguls, they are lost forever, or at least until man's technology is equal to the might of the sea.

The East India Company's run of bad luck continued long after the *Grosvenor* went ashore. At the end of August that same year, the 703-ton *Brilliant* was lost on the Comoro Islands, and then, in October, yet another ship on her maiden voyage, the 758-ton *Earl of Hertford*, was sunk in a violent storm while alongside the quay in Madras. The year following, 1783, proved even more disastrous, the Company losing six more valuable ships, including the *Duke of Kingston*, which caught fire off Ceylon with the loss of sixty-five lives. There were those who murmured about the curse of the Moguls being on the Company. Perhaps they were right.

Bernard Edwards

2 The Hard Road to Botany Bay

The First Fleet - 1787

On 29 April, 1770, Captain **James** Cook, fresh from his circumnavigation of New Zealand, took his ship, the 370-ton barque HMS *Endeavour*, into an unexplored bay on the southwest coast of Australia. As the bay was sheltered from the great Pacific rollers and appeared green and pleasant, Cook marked it down as a place for a possible settlement and took possession in the name of the British Crown. Eight years later, when Cook met his untimely end at the hands of a band of irate Hawaiian islanders, Botany Bay, named for its profusion of unusual plants, was still untouched by the colonist's axe. It was perhaps just as well that Cook did not live to see the humiliation heaped upon his discovery in later years.

The uprising of the American colonists and the final defeat of British forces at Yorktown in 1781 did more than wound British pride; it caused a major upset in the penal system of the Mother Country. Hitherto, it had been the custom of the British courts to banish undesirable offenders to the Americas, thus relieving the pressure of the jails at home, and at the same time providing cheap labour for the sparsely populated colony. American independence put a stop to this convenient practice and forced the British government to look elsewhere for a dumping ground for the country's unruly elements. Captain Cook's report on his exploration of the coast of New South Wales was taken down from the shelf where it had been gathering dust, and the potential of Botany Bay was re-examined. The colonisation of Australia was about to begin.

The fleet which assembled in Portsmouth harbour in May 1787 was not an inspiring sight. The ships were a poor lot, as were their passengers. The 600-ton flagship *Sirius* was a cast-off from the Honourable East India Company, parsimoniously refitted, armed with twenty guns and taken into the King's service for the occasion. Her consort, the tiny, 170-ton *Supply*, should not really have contemplated venturing beyond the limits of the English Channel. In their charge, these two third-rate men-of-war had the transports *Alexander*, *Scarborough*, *Friendship*, *Prince of Wales*, *Charlotte* and *Lady Penrhyn*, a string of 300-tonners noted for their leaky hulls and poor sailing qualities. Completing this mediocre assembly were the small supply ships *Fishbourne*, *Golden Grove*, and one other whose name has disappeared into the mists of time. The First Fleet, as it was to become known, carried a total of 1,350 souls, made up of 570 seamen and marines, and 780 convicts in irons. The latter, men, women and children, were to be the first colonists of Australia, their destination Botany Bay.

Unfortunately, there were no journalists on hand to record the feelings of the poor wretches as they were herded aboard the superannuated transports to face months of hardship and deprivation on the high seas. They were a pathetic crowd, petty criminals mostly; sheep stealers, prostitutes, child pickpockets, many of them victims of the Industrial Revolution attracted to the towns, where the living was hard and the temptations legion. However, such were the horrors they had already endured at the hands of His Majesty's jailers. it is most likely they felt they had little else to lose, except their lives. Given the state of the ships and the perils of the voyage ahead, the latter seemed a distinct possibility.

The First Fleet set out on the first leg of its voyage, bound for Tenerife in the Canaries, on 13 May, five months later than planned. In command, and sailing in the *Sirius*, was Captain Arthur Phillip, a proven navigator, an honest and compassionate man. From the outset, he was determined to alleviate the sufferings of his convict passengers by all means in his power. His orders to the captains of the transports were that strict attention be paid to cleanliness and that convicts be given as much fresh air and exercise as was commensurate with good order. He further instructed that the women be kept separate from the men and food and water be fairly shared amongst all, convict and crew alike. As to offences committed on board ship during the voyage, Phillip made it quite clear that the responsibility for the judgement and punishment of major crimes should remain in his hands. There were those in the Fleet, particularly Major Ross, Commandant of Marines, and Captain Meridith of the *Friendship*, who regarded Phillip as being too lenient and were determined to handle things their way.

Despite Arthur Phillip's good intentions, there were difficulties right from the start. It had been agreed to issue all convicts with proper clothing before boarding the ships, but, owing to the incompetence or corruption of those ashore, most of the prisoners arrived as they had left their cells, half-naked and filthy. It was all Phillip could do to find enough clothes in the ships to cover the women. Before the fleet cleared the Channel, fever had broken out in the *Lady Penrhyn*, probably as a result of exposure. Aboard the *Friendship* there was trouble of a different kind, when her crew demanded extra meat rations. The crew of the *Scarborough* joined in the action and Phillip was obliged to act harshly and swiftly to prevent the mutiny spreading throughout the fleet. Land's End was not yet out of sight astern when, on the 15th, Corporal Baker of the Marines accidentally shot himself in the foot, the ball from his musket then ricocheting off a cask of salt beef to kill two precious geese long before their time had come. This was hardly an auspicious beginning to a voyage destined to last eight months.

Once clear of the Channel, it was a long, hard slog westwards, battling against the prevailing winds and blustery spring gales, until the longitude of 12° west was reached. The fleet then came round onto a south-westerly course to run across the mouth of the Bay of Biscay with the wind on the starboard beam. In the long Atlantic swell, the small ships rolled heavily and without let-up. Seasickness is a miserable and debilitating affliction at the best of times; aggravated by overcrowding and lack of sanitation, it made life a living hell for the convicts.

A week out of Portsmouth, and with Cape Finisterre astern, the ships came under the influence of the Portuguese trade winds, fresh north-easterlies, before which they could run as steady as any small sailing ship can ever be. The reduced motion, combined with the warmer air, eased the suffering of the miserable wretches below decks. But the improvement came too late for one of their number. On 28 May, Ishmael Coleman, unable to endure any more, gave up the struggle and died. On that same day, John Bennet, described as 'a young man but an old rogue', broke free of his chains and received eighty-seven lashes for his efforts. But it was not all gloom. Three days later, when passing Madeira, Isabella Lawson, transported for stealing from her employer, gave birth to a baby girl. Not to be outdone, the *Sirius*'s goat produced two healthy kids.

It was with some relief that, after twenty days at sea, the island of Tenerife was reached on 2 June. Here the fleet rested for a week and took on fresh provisions and water. The convicts were not allowed ashore, but, at least, they were free of the interminable rolling that had made their lives such a misery at sea. Green figs, onions and pumpkin added to their monotonous diet of salt beef and hard tack also gave a much-needed boost to their morale.

Having tasted the delights of the Canaries, the fleet sailed for the South Atlantic on 9 June. The north-east trades were blowing strong, and with the wind right astern, the ships made good speed. But, as they moved into the tropics, the weather became hot and humid. The female convicts, who, largely for their own safety, Phillip had ordered to be battened down below decks at night, suffered terribly in their airless, floating dungeons. As a passage of at least fifty days lay ahead of them, Phillip wisely rationed the fresh water from the start. Each man and woman, whether convict or crew, was allowed three pints a day for washing and drinking. Personal hygiene became an irrelevance, and in the *Alexander*, whose master paid little attention to cleanliness, a fever broke out which threatened to engulf the whole fleet.

Widow-Maker

South of the Cape Verde Islands, the trades petered out, and the agony was increased as the ships drifted into the Doldrums. Sails were constantly tended to catch every fitful breath of wind, but, for the most part, the ships wallowed helplessly in the long swell, and it seemed to those on board that they were doomed to wander forever in this windless sea. The sun was almost overhead, and shone down from a cloudless sky with no mercy for captor or captive. Inevitably, water began to run short and Phillip was forced to cut the ration. Thirst was added to all the miseries already being suffered.

At last the Equator was crossed, and then came the first of the south-east trades. Within a few days these blew with unexpected ferocity, but they were fair winds, bringing the blessed rain with them. Cramming on all possible sail, the ships surged southwards at a cracking pace, their lee gunwales awash. The miles were eaten up, but there was a price to pay for progress. The *Sirius* lost a topmast, one seaman went overboard to his death, and a woman convict was killed when a ship's boat broke loose and crushed her.

The fine natural harbour of Rio de Janeiro, the largest of its kind in the world, was entered on 1 August after fifty-three days at sea. In this sun-drenched land of plenty, while the ships were repaired and re-provisioned, Phillip and his officers were lavishly entertained by the ruling Portuguese. So taken were they by the delights of Rio that the fleet languished in the harbour for five weeks. As far as the convicts were concerned, apart from the lack of rolling and the blessing of fresh vegetables, they might just as well have been at sea. They were confined to the transports under guard and had no contact with the shore. The fleet chaplain, Richard Johnson, possibly for the want of something better to do, visited each ship in turn to preach to the captive congregations. It is unlikely that his ministrations were much appreciated.

The fleet finally left Rio on 5 September and set course east by south for Cape Town. The ships were now well stocked with fresh fruit and vegetables and all on board, including the convicts, had benefited from the long, idle days in port. But the euphoria generated by this pleasant sojourn was quickly dispelled when, two days after leaving port, a series of gales began which was to last almost without interruption for the whole of the 3,400-mile passage. Yet another man was lost overboard, dysentery reared its ugly head, and there was open mutiny in the crew of the *Alexander*, the master of which had by now proved himself to be thoroughly incompetent. Because of the foul weather, the convicts were kept below decks most of the time, resulting in a great deal of unrest in their ranks. There was an inevitable increase in the daily punishment round. The future citizens of Botany Bay had come to wish they had never left the comparative comfort of the Crown lodging houses.

There was still worse to come. When the bedraggled fleet anchored in the shadow of Table Mountain on 13 October, it received a chilly welcome from the Dutch, who were not on the best of terms with the British. At first, the Governor of Cape Town refused point blank to supply provisions. However, Phillip, having no other choice, refused to sail until his ships were re-stocked. The Governor relented, but the prices charged for the supplies were three times the normal. Some of the ships had been severely damaged in the bad weather of the South Atlantic and the necessary repairs took almost a month. It was 12 November before the fleet, with relations between the Dutch and British stretched to breaking point, finally bade a sailor's farewell to the Cape.

Now came the real test of the voyage, the 7,000-mile leg across the bottom of the world to the Antipodes. The fleet was obliged first to steer well south into the Roaring Forties in order to make maximum progress eastwards. Here, on the edge of the great Southern Ocean, where the malevolent westerlies blow without let or hindrance right around the world, and giant icebergs drift shrouded in fog, was the final proving ground for the aspiring colonists. As it was, conditions in the ships were already worse than they had been at any time in the voyage. With the needs of the new colony in mind, Phillip had shipped a large quantity of livestock in Cape Town. If the transports had been crowded before, then they were now bursting at the seams. Pigs, horses, cows, sheep, bales of fodder and extra barrels of water filled every available inch of deck space. Running before storm-force winds and angry tumbling seas, the tiny ships of the First Fleet were like paper boats carried along on a mountain torrent. With sickening regularity they were pooped, swamped or laid on their beam ends. There was not a dry spot anywhere, above or below decks. Animals and men were washed overboard or drowned where they slept; others just died of sheer exhaustion from the incessant pummelling they received at the hands of the elements. Christmas Day came and went unnoticed, except for a special grog issue for the hard-pressed seamen—the convicts were past caring. Three days later, the situation worsened—if such a thing was conceivably possible—when the dreaded scurvy made its appearance. The first day of 1788, ushered in at the height of a storm of demoniacal proportions, found the fleet 800 miles from Botany Bay and running short of food, water and fuel for the galley fires.

On 7 January, 1788, fifty-six days out of Table Bay, came the first sight of land, when the southern tip of Tasmania—or Van Diemen's Land as it was then known—came over the horizon. Eleven days later, after weathering more gales and a spell of dense fog, the battered fleet entered Botany Bay, only to find it, contrary to Captain Cook's glowing report, a barren place totally unsuited for a permanent settlement. Another eight days were to elapse before a boat party discovered a magnificent deep-water harbour a few miles to the north, in which, in Captain Arthur Phillip's words, 'a thousand sail of the line may ride in the most perfect security'. The ships moved into Port Jackson—so named from afar by Cook—and the birth of Australia became a reality.

The voyage of the First Fleet from Portsmouth to Botany Bay had taken eight months and one week. Of the 1,350 souls who set out in the ships, forty had died on the way. That the fleet reached Australia at all was a great tribute to the navigational prowess, professionalism and tenacity of Captain Arthur Phillip, who was to become the first Governor of the new colony of New South Wales.

Bernard Edwards

3   Day Trip to Wales

Rothesay Castle - 1831

A t the beginning of the 19th century sail still dominated the high seas. White-winged East Indiamen flogged their way around the Cape, Whitby collier brigs ruled the short-sea trade, and the ponderous 'wooden walls' of Nelson's day held the enemy at bay. But on the River Clyde a quiet revolution in commercial shipping was under way.

When, in 1765, James Watt produced the first workable steam engine, his efforts were directed towards powering Britain's industrial revolution—to drive the machines which produced the goods—sail would then transport to more backward lands across the seas. Enterprising shipbuilders, however, soon saw the possibility of adopting the new engine for use at sea. Various attempts were made on both sides of the Atlantic, but it was not until 1802 that the first successful commercial steamship appeared. She was the *Charlotte Dundas*, a small wooden ship with a steam engine driving a stern paddle wheel. On her first voyage, on the Forth and Clyde Canal, the *Charlotte Dundas*, with two barges in tow, covered 19 1/2 miles at a speed of 3 1/4 miles per hour. Unfortunately, the wash from her stern wheel damaged the banks of the canal and her career was very brief, but had shown the way forward.

In 1812, the year of Napoleon's disastrous retreat from Moscow, John and Charles Wood, of Port Glasgow, built the *Comet*, a forty-two-foot side-wheeler of twenty-five tons burthen. For eight years, until she was wrecked in 1820, her owner used her to carry passengers between Glasgow and his hotel at Helensburgh, twenty-two miles down river. Two years later came the *Industry*, built at Fairlie and employed to carry passenger's luggage from Glasgow to sailing ships waiting at anchor off Greenock. She performed this task faithfully and efficiently for the next forty-eight years, a magnificent tribute to her Scottish builders.

Also launched on the River Clyde in 1816 was the *Rothesay Castle*, built by A.M. MacLachlan, of Dumbarton. She was a wooden paddle steamer of seventy-five tons burthen, with a thirty-four horse power engine giving her a speed of ten knots. For four years she plied the Firth of Clyde, linking the lower reaches with Glasgow, and providing an invaluable service on this busy stretch of water both for travellers and holiday-makers.

The *Rothesay Castle* was sold in 1820 to the Liverpool & Beaumaris Packet Company for £800, and for the next eleven years her new owners used her to carry cargoes in the coastal trade. At this time there were few rules governing the operation and maintenance of ships, and there can be no doubt that, after fifteen years hard running, the little steamer was nearing the end of her useful life. It was said, in fact, that her hull was rotten, her engine worn out, and her general unseaworthiness a matter of common knowledge. It was certainly difficult to find a crew willing to sail in her. None of which daunted her owners, who at this point decided to break into the lucrative Liverpool to Anglesey holiday trade.

Britain was at this time well into her industrial revolution, and prospering accordingly. But there had been a price to pay for the change over from an agrarian society to one which was largely centred around manufacturing. Tall chimney stacks filled the air with sulphurous smoke, noxious waste proliferated, and large swathes of a once green and pleasant land disappeared under grimy bricks and mortar. Men, women and children slaved for long hours under dreadful conditions, and when a benevolent employer decreed a day's holiday, there was inevitably a rush for the open spaces, preferably by the sea.

The island of Anglesey, the Yns Môn of the Welsh, is separated from the mainland by the Menai Strait, only 1,500 yards wide, but in the 1800s unbridged. The isolated island was then a place of soft, undulating beauty, with a few sleepy hamlets, the ruins of a 13th century castle, and white sand beaches; a paradise waiting for the pale-faced slaves of the Lancashire cotton mills. The railway had not yet arrived, and the Menai Strait was almost a hundred miles overland from Liverpool, a journey of many days by road, but only fifty miles by sea. On a fine summer's day, the round trip by steamer from Liverpool's pier head to Beaumaris was a treat full of memories to brighten the dark hours of winter to come. Five hours at sea with the wind in your hair and the clean, salt air flushing out clogged lungs, a few carefree hours ashore, and then the return with the moon dappling the waves with silver and the lights of Liverpool beckoning across the bows. It was a dream to be snatched at when it came within reach, and few ever gave a thought to the hidden dangers involved.

Another fifty-five years would pass before Samuel Plimsoll was able to push his radical reforms through Parliament; meanwhile, in early 19th century Britain, merchant shipping was at a very low ebb. Following the end of the Napoleonic wars and the emergence of America as a powerful nation, there was increasing competition from foreign shipping, leading to inevitable economies being made. The regulations governing ships and their crews were few and rarely enforced with enthusiasm, and insurance was easily obtained—a sit-

Bernard Edwards

uation most shipowners took full advantage of. Ships were poorly maintained, if at all, frequently overloaded, and manned by incompetent and often drunken crews. This had the effect of branding British ships as a bad risk in the eyes of foreign merchants, and so more trade was lost. By 1830, British shipping was in a deplorable state.

At 9 o'clock on the morning of 18 August, 1831, the *Rothesay Castle* lay at George's Pier, in Liverpool, ready for sea. The steamer's threadbare flags snapped in a fresh north-north-westerly breeze, but the promise was for a fine, warm day. On the fore deck a small band played suitably maritime music, much to the delight of the 150 passengers crowding the deck. The majority of these were women and children unashamedly excited at the prospect of the day trip to Beaumaris. For many this was their first time afloat, and their first visit to a land where people spoke in a strange foreign tongue, and, it was said, the golden sands were washed by a sea as blue as any summer sky. Little wonder there was an air of carnival aboard the *Rothesay Castle* that made her obvious faults seem irrelevant.

On the open catwalk above her paddle-boxes that served as the steamer's navigation bridge, Captain Atkinson paced back and forth impatiently, completely oblivious to the high spirits on deck. Atkinson, late of His Majesty's Navy, was not accustomed to such chaos. His temper had not been improved when he learned a certain London gentleman was insisting that his horse and carriage be carried with him in the ship to Beaumaris. A delay was inevitable while the animal and rig were loaded, but the gentleman in question wielded considerable influence with the *Rothesay Castle's* owners, and his wishes could not be ignored. With a snort of disgust Atkinson halted his pacing and retired to his small cabin aft, where he was joined by the first mate. A bottle was produced, and the two men settled down to drink and lament the fate that had reduced them to sailing in the run-down old paddler.

Meanwhile, the *Rothesay Castle's* tall, rust-streaked funnel belched black smoke, waste steam hissed from her relief valve, and the confusion increased. With a total of 165 persons on board, including her fifteen-man crew, the ship, a mere 93 feet long and 16 feet in the beam, was already seriously overcrowded. The fitting of a skittish horse and its carriage into a space cleared amongst the heaving mass of humanity was not an easy task. In fact, the operation consumed two hours, and it was past 11 o'clock before the *Rothesay Castle* pulled away from the pier, her paddles threshing purposefully, and her band playing with new-found enthusiasm. Captain Atkinson and his mate were by this time well fortified for the voyage.

By the time the *Rothesay Castle* reached the Bar light float, sixteen miles out to sea, the wind had increased to near-gale, and the ship was plunging her bows into a short, steep sea and sending showers of spray over the foredeck. The band was silent, and the worried passengers were huddled miserably together on the open deck, wondering why their dream holiday had suddenly gone wrong.

Panic was not far below the surface when a delegation of passengers went to Atkinson's cabin and requested he turn back for Liverpool before the weather worsened further. The captain, now brimming with alcohol-inspired confidence, scoffed at their fears and assured them they would soon be safely in Beaumaris. What he did not tell them was that the tide had turned against the ship, and the *Rothesay Castle*'s puny, 34-horsepower engine was barely able to maintain headway against the wind and sea.

Three more hours passed, and the Bar light float was still in sight astern, proof that the vessel had made very little progress in the time. By now, dark, glowering clouds were turning day into night, and it was blowing a full gale from the north-west. The *Rothesay Castle* battled on, her motion growing ever more violent, her decks swept by rain and flying spray. For her wretched passengers, now thoroughly frightened and wracked by seasickness, the exciting day out they had looked forward to for so long was turning into a terrible nightmare. There were those among them who looked anxiously around for a means of ensuring their safety should the need arise. There was precious little on offer. The ship carried no lifejackets, no lifebuoys, no rafts, and only one lifeboat. The latter was really no more than a small skiff, used in the little steamer's days on the Clyde to ferry her crew ashore to the nearest hostelry. A closer inspection would have revealed that the boat had a hole in its bottom and was without oars, mast or sails. The *Rothesay Castle* was not a ship to sail in should a serious emergency arise.

Despite further pleas from his passengers, Atkinson drove his ship on, and by the time full darkness set in, at around 9 o'clock, the twinkling lights of Llandudno, nestling at the foot of Great Ormes Head, were visible to port. Since leaving Liverpool ten hours earlier, the *Rothesay Castle* had covered only thirty-eight miles. It was now too late to turn back, for the battering the ship had received at the hands of the sea had opened up her seams. Water was pouring into her hull at a rate faster than the pumps could cope with. Atkinson, by now aggressively drunk, as was his first mate, stubbornly refused to send up distress signals. In point of fact, the ship carried none— no rockets, no flares, no signal gun.

Fortunately, Atkinson was not too drunk to navigate his ship, and this he did, setting a course from Great Ormes Head into Conwy Bay and for Beaumaris, then only twelve miles off. If the *Rothesay Castle* succeeded in staying afloat for another hour or so, by which time she would be in the shelter of Puffin Island, there might be a chance of saving her. This conjecture was of little consolation to the 150 passengers entrusted to Atkinson's care, for he kept them in complete ignorance of the situation. And to add further to their suffering, he refused point blank to allow any lamps to be lit, other than that at the compass binnacle. The truth was there was no oil on board to fuel the few lamps the steamer carried.

Another two hours passed before the *Rothesay Castle* finally clawed her way under the lee of Puffin Island, which lies five miles north-east of Beaumaris. As she did so, the rising water in her stoke-hold reached her boiler furnaces and quenched them with a great hiss of steam. And that was the finish. The hard-pressed engine ground to a halt, and within a few minutes, ashes washed out from the dead fires had choked the suctions of the pumps. Completely helpless and with her main deck level with the sea, the *Rothesay Castle* drifted beam-on to the wind and waves, and at midnight drove onto Dutchman's Bank, a notorious shoal off Puffin Island.

The shock of the sudden grounding brought the ship's tall funnel crashing down onto the crowded deck, crushing the steward and his wife and a number of passengers on the starboard side. Immediate panic broke out, which gave way to hysteria as the waves began to break right over the ship. On the foredeck there was no shelter, and those unable to find a handhold were swept into the sea. As many as fifty went with the first wave, carried into a raging mael-strom from which there was no escape.

The remaining passengers sought the protection of the pad-dle-boxes, where they found Atkinson and the first mate, assisted by some of the crew, attempting to lower the ship's only lifeboat. It was assumed by the distraught passengers that they were being aban-doned to their fate, and a howl of rage went up. In the mêlée that fol-lowed Atkinson missed his footing and fell overboard—or so it was said. Eventually, the boat, loaded with nineteen passengers and crew, was lowered. It capsized as soon as it hit the water, drowning all on board.

Firmly in the grip of the shoal and battered unmercifully by the breaking waves, the *Rothesay Castle* held together for another hour. The end, when it came, was sudden, her rotten timbers falling apart. The poop deck broke off and floated away in one piece, carry-ing a number of people with it. They disappeared into the darkness of the savage night, their cries for help unheard.

While the rest of the ship broke up and drifted away, her iron engine casing remained on the bank and largely above water. On this nine passengers took refuge, and with the seas breaking over them, held on until daylight, when a boat put out from the shore to rescue them. Others, clinging to scraps of wreckage, also reached the shore.

In all, of the 165 souls on board the *Rothesay Castle* only twenty-three survived. Many more might have been saved if the steamer had been equipped with distress flares or rockets—or if she had not been in total darkness for the want of a few pints of lamp oil. When the ship first struck on Dutchman's Bank, her bell was rung long and loudly in the hope of attracting attention. Unknown to those on board, it did just that. Men on the deck of a schooner lying at anchor off Beaumaris heard the tolling of the bell and suspected a ship might be in trouble close by, but seeing no distress flares, and in the absence of any lights to guide them, they hesitated to venture out into the night.

At a court of inquiry held into the tragedy the *Rothesay Castle*'s owners, the Liverpool & Beaumaris Packet Company, were severely criticised for allowing an unsound vessel to proceed to sea. It was also made public that the steamer's captain and mate were drunk, and that she was otherwise improperly manned. No action was taken against the owners, though they were clearly responsible for the loss of 142 lives.

Some good did come out of the senseless loss of the *Rothesay Castle*. In the following year a lifeboat station was established at Penmon, the north-eastern extremity of Anglesey which overlooks Puffin Island, and five years later a lighthouse was erected nearby.

4   A Dog's Chance

Sirius - 1838

In a forgotten corner of the Hull Museum of Fisheries and Shipping stands the carved wooden figure of a mongrel dog, weathered by the sea and blackened by age. The dog's out-stretched paws once offered up a symbolic star, but this star is long gone, lost in the mists of time like the memory of the ship this quaint figurehead adorned; a ship which, accidentally caught up in the events of her day, inaugurated a golden age at sea that was to last for 120 years.

At the beginning of the 19th century, the vigorous new world of North America was poised to unleash its unprecedented brand of innovation and enterprise on the world. Much of the wealth and expertise to feed this bubbling revolution lay in Britain and passenger traffic back and forth across the North Atlantic was booming. However, the habitually stormy passage was hazardous, uncomfortable and, above all, dreadfully slow. Even the fastest sailing packets took up to thirty days, the slower ones often twice as long. For the entrepreneur in a hurry the North Atlantic crossing was a dreary, nail-biting ordeal. The steam engine, which had been in use in coastal and river vessels for a number of years, seemed the obvious answer to the dilemma but it was, as yet, notoriously unreliable. Atlantic crossings had been made with steam assisting sail, but never under steam only.

Junius Smith, an American trader living in London and a frequent commuter across the Atlantic, was one who had faith in steam. He was also acutely aware of the benefits a fast, reliable transatlantic service could bring. With the help of British money, Smith established the British & American Steam Navigation Company in 1836, and the keel of the company's first ship was laid in Macgregor Laird's Birkenhead yard that year. The *Royal Victoria*, a paddle steamer of 1,890 tons gross, was to be the largest and most luxurious steamer afloat; a fitting contender for the title of first across the Atlantic under steam only.

Not to be outdone, the restless genius Isambard Kingdom Brunel hastened to fulfil his dream of joining London to New York via the Great Western Railway and the port of Bristol. Funded by a

*The s.s.'*Great Western' *sets off for New York*
(Photo: National Maritime Museum)

group of West Country businessmen, the Great Western Steamship Company was set up and Brunel saw his brainchild, the *Great Western*, begin to take form on the stocks of a Bristol shipyard. The race was on.

Junius Smith's American inspired venture was the first to suffer a major setback. The Glasgow company building the *Royal Victoria*'s engines went bankrupt and Smith was left with a powerless hull on his hands at a time when Brunel's *Great Western* was nearing completion. Smith might have dropped the matter there and then, but what had begun as a friendly challenge had now developed into a much-looked-forward-to event involving considerable national pride. Smith was synonymous with America, Brunel with Britain, and large wagers on the outcome of the race were being laid on both sides of the Atlantic. Smith was obliged to find a substitute vessel to carry the flag of the British & American Steam Navigation Company.

The honour fell to the paddle steamer *Sirius*, owned by the St. George Steam Packet Company of Cork. Built in 1837 by Menzies of Leith, the 703-ton *Sirius* had hitherto been engaged exclusively in the coastal trade between Cork and London, her keel never having kissed the deep waters. She was a two-master with a tall funnel and, at 208 feet long and only 25 feet in the beam, she had a sleek look that was somewhat spoiled by the drabness of her green and black paintwork. Her engines developed a horsepower of 320, giving her, in fine weather, a speed of eight knots on twenty-four tons of coal a day. Like all steamers of her day, she carried a full set of sails. Her only distinguishing feature was a figurehead in the shape of a dog holding a star in its paws, representing the dog-star Sirius.

In comparison, Brunel's purpose-built transatlantic steamer was huge. Of 1,320 tons gross, the four-masted *Great Western* had an overall length of 236 feet and a beam of 35 feet. Luxury cabin accommodation was provided for 128 passengers, with a rather less luxurious twenty-berth dormitory for servants. Her great saloon, seventy-five feet long, twenty-one feet wide and nine feet high, was said to be the most lavishly appointed ever seen in a passenger ship. Below decks, more than half the space was taken up by two massive side-lever engines developing a horse power of 750, four iron boilers and vast coal bunkers capable of holding 800 tons.

At the end of March 1838, both ships were in the London river being fussed over like high-bred racehorses. The passenger accommodation aboard the *Sirius*, previously somewhat spartan, had been gutted and refurbished in a much grander style and an extra cabin had been built on her after deck. Yet, for all the refinements, she was still basically a coastal paddle steamer and the odds being offered against her being first across the Atlantic under steam only were high. On 28 March the two ships set off down the Thames, the *Great Western* to call at Bristol and the *Sirius* at Cork to embark passengers.

The *Great Western*, commanded by Captain James Hosken, ran into trouble even before she had cleared the river. Her boiler lagging caught fire and serious damage to her engines was only narrowly averted. In the confusion Brunel, who was on board for the passage to Bristol, fell eighteen feet into the engineroom and was badly injured. Captain Hosken had little option but to beach his ship off Southend, so that the fire could be extinguished and Brunel landed into hospital. The *Great Western* was floated off on the next high tide, but by this time the *Sirius*, her red-painted paddle wheels threshing the water determinedly, had a good twelve-hour lead.

When the *Sirius* arrived at Cork, Captain Richard Roberts, a local man, was appointed to command and no time was lost in preparing the little ship for her first ocean passage. Moored alongside Penrose Quay in the shadow of her owner's head office, she took on 454 tons of bunker coal, twenty tons of fresh water, a cargo of fifty-eight casks of resin and forty passengers and their baggage. It was just as well the introduction of the Plimsoll Line was some years away, for the *Sirius* was dangerously overloaded. Doubtless her passengers would have missed the significance of this, for the excitement was high, with thousands of well-wishers lining the shore to see the ship off. At ten o'clock on the morning of 4 April a gun was fired and the *Sirius* pulled away from the quay, her tall funnel belching black smoke and her flags snapping in the breeze. Ahead of her lay 2,897 miles of the most inhospitable ocean of all.

Widow-Maker

In Ireland that year it was as though winter would never end. Although spring flowers bloomed timorously in the hedgerows, the sky remained stubbornly overcast and the rain had an icy lash to it. The North Atlantic, beset by an unending procession of vigorous depressions, had been in a constant state of agitation for months. When the *Sirius* left the shelter of Cork harbour, she steamed straight into the mouth of Hell itself.

Captain Roberts, ever conscious of the spectre of the larger and more powerful *Great Western* lurking somewhere astern, did not flinch. He ordered his chief engineer to work his engines up to maximum revolutions and to keep them that way at all costs. The *Sirius* was soon burying her canine figurehead deep as she met and breasted the mountainous waves of the open Atlantic. In her stokehold, fighting to keep their feet on the heaving plates, gangs of sweating firemen bent their backs to hurl ton after ton of coal into her roaring furnaces.

If things were bad for the little steamer's hard-bitten firemen, they were even worse for her passengers battened down in the airless accommodation. Tossed from side to side by the violent motion of the ship, deafened by the awful cacophony of clanging pistons, hissing steam and thumping paddle blades, they suffered the horrors of confusion, seasickness and abject fear.

On the afternoon of the 7th, the *Sirius* was sighted by an inbound clipper 433 miles to the west of Cork having, in spite of the fearful weather, averaged just over six knots since leaving port. Dick Roberts, deaf to the pleadings of his passengers and the increasingly ominous rumblings amongst his crew, would conquer the Atlantic or drive his ship under in the attempt.

Although he was not aware of the fact, Roberts was wise to push his ship, for the very next morning, the *Great Western*, having repaired her fire damage, came thundering out of Bristol hell-bent on making up lost time. She carried in her splendid 128-berth accommodation only seven passengers, the rest having cried off after the accident in the Thames. As a commercial venture the maiden voyage of the *Great Western* was doomed and Captain Hosken's professional reputation was at stake. Only a record crossing and arrival ahead of the *Sirius* would save the day for both.

Meanwhile, deep in the Atlantic, the *Sirius*, lighter by more than a hundred tons of coal, continued to ride the seas successfully, but Roberts had a crisis on his hands. Terrified by the huge and unfamiliar waves, some of the crew of the steamer had mutinied and were demanding that Roberts turn back for Ireland. This mutiny was short-lived, for Roberts, like many a sailing-ship master before him, simply gathered his officers around him and drove the men back to their posts at gunpoint.

On the 12th, in mid-ocean, the *Sirius* ran into problems of another kind. After eight days of hard steaming through the stormy seas, a number of paddle blades had worked loose and were in danger of falling off, while the stuffing boxes around her thrusting pistons were spewing out so much steam Roberts feared his boilers would soon lose their pressure altogether. There was nothing for it but to heave-to while the blades were secured and the stuffing boxes repacked. With the ship stopped and rolling in the troughs, this was difficult and dangerous work for the *Sirius*'s engineers. But the task was accomplished and the ship was soon under way again, undamaged by the seas and little delayed. During the brief stop, Roberts took the opportunity to check his bunkers. He was not encouraged to find that, with 1,700 miles yet to steam, only 250 tons of coal remained.

Some 550 miles astern, the *Great Western* was also in trouble. Hosken, who had been pushing his ship every bit as hard as his rival, was in the midst of a confrontation with his firemen. Exhausted by their labours in the stokehold and unable to rest when off watch because of the shock-like motion of the ship as she slammed into the seas, many of them were near breaking point. Hosken had no sooner placated them than the larboard paddle wheel began to shake so badly it had to be stopped. Two bolts which were found to be missing were replaced and full speed resumed. An hour or two later, a burst waterpipe in the engineroom caused a further delay. Hosken now began to despair of catching the *Sirius*, even though he had a superiority of at least two knots over the British & American ship.

April 17th dawned like all the previous days for the *Sirius*. She was 350 miles to the south of Newfoundland and battling westwards against heavy seas and driving snow. To Roberts, as he haunted the tiny flying bridge for the thirteenth successive day, it seemed the nightmare would never end. Then, as the day wore on, the snow began to thin and the wind fell away. By late afternoon, the sombre canopy of cloud had drawn back and, as the sun went down, so did the sea. Just over a thousand miles ahead lay New York and Roberts was at last able to contemplate victory. At that point his chief engineer informed him that barely 140 tons of coal were left in the bunkers.

Fast coming up astern, but still burying her bows in green seas, the *Great Western* had fuel problems of her own, but not through any shortage. Hers was a problem of transportation. The coal remaining in her capacious bunkers, although ample to see the passage out, was all in the far ends of the ship and had to be wheeled in barrows to the stokehold amidships. It was a long haul and her weary trimmers, who often found themselves pushing their barrows uphill as the ship climbed the waves, simply could no longer cope. The furnaces, starved of fuel, cooled and, as the steam pressure in the boilers fell back, the *Great Western* began to lose speed.

On the night of the 21st, the *Sirius* was to the south of the Nantucket Shoals, less than 200 miles from the Hudson River. The weather was fine and calm and she was surging ahead at eight knots. But all was not as well as it seemed, for her bunkers were almost empty of coal. Once the last precious lumps were gone and the dust swept up, she would have to resort to her sails and the magnificent efforts of all on board would have been in vain. She must either complete the voyage under steam or fail. Dick Roberts had an answer for this, too. Out came the axes and saws and into the hungry boiler furnaces went first the *Sirius*'s spare yards, then one of her masts and, finally much of her expensive cabin furniture.

The *Sirius* limped into New York harbour on the night of 22 April, her tall funnel still belching smoke. Her momentous passage, made entirely under steam, had taken eighteen days and ten hours and she had achieved an average speed of 6.7 knots. She was followed in some twelve hours later by the *Great Western*, only fifteen days out of Bristol. Hers was the fastest crossing to date of the North Atlantic, but she had lost the race.

The name of the *Great Western* still lives on, her likeness adorning the Blue Riband trophy fought over for so many years by the crack transatlantic liners that followed in her wake. As for the *Sirius*, having done all Junius Smith asked of her, in that she was the first ship ever to cross the Atlantic—or any other great ocean for that matter—entirely under steam, she returned to the coastal trade and obscurity. Eight years later, she came to an ignominious end on the rocks of Ballycotton Bay and all that now recalls her triumph is the shabby figurehead in the Hull museum.

In 1938, one hundred years after the saga of the *Sirius* and *Great Western*, the 81,000-ton *Queen Mary* became the fastest merchant ship in the world by steaming from Cherbourg to New York in three days twenty-one hours forty-eight minutes at an average speed of 31.69 knots. She arrived in New York with all her cabin furniture intact.

5   Maiden Voyage

Amazon - 1852

As the second half of the 19th century got under way, the sailing ship, for all its obvious shortcomings, was still considered by the majority to be the safest and most reliable form of sea transport. Sail power, in one form or another, had been in use for almost 6,000 years, during which time it had undergone continuous refinement, until reaching a state of perfection only God and his elements were competent to challenge. Steam, on the other hand, was still struggling to establish real credibility, and was often regarded, with some justification, as a dirty, unreliable work of the Devil himself. However, when, on the afternoon of Friday 2 January, 1852, the Royal Mail Steam Packet Company's *Amazon* sailed from Southampton on her maiden voyage, there was a new confidence in the air. Accompanied by an armada of small craft, her twin funnels trailing long plumes of black smoke, the 2,851-ton paddle steamer presented a brave sight to the crowds cheering her on her way.

Built at Green & Money Wigram's yard on the Thames, birthplace of the legendary Blackwall frigates, the *Amazon* measured 300 feet long and 41 feet in the beam. She was powered by two Seaward & Capel 400 horsepower engines, driving two massive forty-one-foot diameter paddle wheels designed to give her a service speed of eleven knots. In keeping with the turbulent times into which she was born, the *Amazon* was strengthened to carry fourteen thirty-two-pounder guns, and as a gesture to the age she was leaving behind, she was fully-rigged on all three masts. In her bunkers she carried 1,050 tons of coal, more than enough to see her to her first port of call, St. Thomas, in the Virgin Islands.

For Royal Mail the maiden voyage of the *Amazon* was doubly important, for she was also inaugurating their new service to Panama. Passengers landed at Chagres, on the east coast of the isthmus, would, after a sixty-mile journey overland, join ships of the Pacific Steam Navigation Company for ports on the west coast of South America. The service was intended to satisfy the great demand by mining engineers and merchants for a fast passage to an area crying out for exploitation. The fifty-five passengers the *Amazon* carried on this first voyage were made up of both categories. Her cargo included £20,300 worth of specie, and mercury to the value of

Widow-Maker

£5,000 consigned to the silver mines of Mexico. She was commanded by one of Royal Mail's senior masters, Captain Symons, and
manned by a picked crew of 105.

Royal Mail was one of Britain's prestige shipping companies
and the *Amazon* was a prestige ship. Great things were expected of
her. No doubt, she would have obliged, had she not suffered from a
weakness inherited from the age of sail she hoped, once and for all,
to ring down the curtain on. The *Amazon* was built entirely of wood.

The short winter day was drawing to a close as the *Amazon*
made her way down the Solent towards the open sea. A falling
barometer and low cloud warned Captain Symons of bad weather
moving in from the Atlantic. In which case, he was anxious to make
all possible speed down Channel in order to clear the coast of
Brittany before the full force of the wind was felt. Although the
Amazon's engines were of the best, they were as yet untried, and
Symons, with a caution bred of his long years in sail, had no wish to
be caught on a lee shore. He passed the word to the engine-room to
increase revolutions.

When the order reached Chief Engineer Angus, hovering over
his gleaming pistons in the bowels of the ship, he was not pleased.
The new engines required a great deal of patient nursing before they
were ready to be pushed to their limits. Already, despite liberal
applications of grease, the bearings of the paddle shafts were running
hot. For Angus, the coming night promised to be long and full of
stress.

The sun went down unnoticed behind a thick layer of low cloud
and total darkness quickly closed around the *Amazon*. The wind was
freshening from the south-west, but the ship rode comfortably
enough, and in the grand saloon the passengers enjoyed an excellent
first dinner at sea. A few pessimists were of the opinion that to sail
on a Friday was to tempt Providence, but the majority were in good
spirits. The *Amazon* was a first class ship, manned by the best of seamen, and would carry them safely to the West Indies, and beyond.
The rapid beat of her powerful engines indicated that the passage
might well be a record one.

The first indication of trouble came at 9 o'clock that night,
when the *Amazon* was abeam of Portland Bill. Despite the protesta-
tions of Captain Symons, overheated paddle shaft bearings forced
Angus to stop his engines, and for the next hour the ship drifted
while the bearings were cooled with water. This procedure was
repeated again later on in the night, and yet again in the early hours
of next morning. Fortunately, these subsequent delays were of shorter duration, as the bearings were slowly running in, though not
without the expenditure of a great amount of grease.

By noon next day, the *Amazon* was forty-five miles south of the
Lizard and feeling the first of the long swells rolling in from the
Atlantic. She was steaming into a west-south-westerly wind that was

freshening by the hour, but Symons was confident of being well clear of any land by the time the full force of the gale was felt. However, he continued to press the engine-room for more speed.

The weather was fair enough for the more hardy passengers to be on the open deck taking the fresh air. Among them was Robert Neilson, an engineer by profession, on passage to Barbados, via St. Thomas. As Neilson strolled around the decks, he cast an expert eye over the ship's equipment. The *Amazon*'s life-saving gear immediately struck him as being of an unusually high standard. She carried no fewer than eight lifeboats, more than sufficient for all on board. However, the two largest boats, each capable of holding thirty-five persons, were stowed on the platform abaft the paddle boxes and lashed down in iron cradles bolted to the platform. While this was an admirably secure arrangement in the case of bad weather, it occurred to Neilson that launching them would be a slow operation. The heavy boats would first have to be lifted bodily out of their cradles, before being swung overside. In a serious emergency there might not be time.

The *Amazon*'s engine-room drew Neilson like a bee to honey. Here he was even more impressed. The twin, 400 horsepower engines, each fed by eight boilers, had huge, ninety-six-inch diameter cylinders with a stroke of nine feet, and were an engineer's dream of technical excellence. But it did not escape Neilson's critical eye that the engine-room store, containing large amounts of tallow and grease, was directly above the roaring furnaces of the forward boilers. This did not appear to be a particularly safe arrangement in a wooden ship.

At eight o'clock that night, Neilson, who, it must be said, was exceeding his privileges as passenger in the ship, again visited the engine-room. He found the engineer on watch worrying over shaft bearings running so hot that the contents of the grease cups were going up in smoke. Neilson advised the engineer to reduce speed, and when Chief Engineer Angus arrived on the scene a few minutes later, the engines were stopped. This brought an immediate protest from the bridge, but to no avail. For the next three hours the *Amazon* lay stopped while hoses were played on the bearings to cool them off.

It was eleven-thirty before the ship was once more under way and steaming at about eight knots. Neilson then came up on deck, where he found Symons anxiously pacing up and down. The barometer was falling steeply and the captain, who had anticipated outrunning the approaching gale, confided in Neilson that he was not pleased with the performance of the engines, and voiced the opinion that the ship might be better off under sail. The two men stood talking until midnight, then Symons went below. Neilson, still mulling over the problem of the hot bearings, continued to walk the deck for another half hour, when he again went to the engine-room. Finding that, with the engines on reduced revolutions, the shaft bearings were no longer overheating, he then went to his cabin reassured.

Second Officer Treweeke and Midshipman Vincent had the middle watch, midnight to 4 am, on deck, not a pleasant duty on a night rapidly turning foul. The *Amazon* was by then 110 miles west-south-west of the Scilly Isles and crossing the mouth of the Bay of Biscay, rolling sluggishly in a long beam swell. The wind was holding steady in the west-south-west and nearing gale force. A rough head sea from time to time erupted over the bows, sending a lash of icy spray across the open navigation bridge. For Treweeke and Vincent, protected only by their streaming oilskins, every minute that passed seemed like an hour.

At about one in the morning, Vincent went below to retard the ship's clocks to apparent time, this being dictated by the rate at which the *Amazon* crossed the meridians of longitude as she moved westward. Vincent was about to enter the main saloon when he saw flames shooting up from the hatchway of the forward stokehold. Without waiting to investigate, the midshipman ran for the bridge to inform Treweeke, who then sent him aft to call Captain Symons.

Below, in the engine-room, Fourth Engineer Stone, who was in charge of the watch, was working in the after part when he saw flames coming from the forward boiler space. With considerable presence of mind, Stone ran to stop the engines, but he was beaten back by an advancing wall of smoke and flames before he could reach the controls.

Neilson was half undressed and ready to turn in when he heard the clamour of the alarm bell, accompanied by shouts and the hysterical screams of female passengers. Without waiting to put on more clothes, he ran on deck, where an appalling scene met his eyes. The whole forward part of the ship was engulfed in a sea of flames, which was rapidly moving aft. Before it fled a panic-stricken mob of passengers, most of them in their night-clothes, and some of them already on fire and shrieking in agony.

In spite of the raging fire, it was bitterly cold on deck, and Neilson, ever logical, decided to return to his cabin for warm clothing. While he was below, the glass partition at the fore end of the accommodation shattered with a tremendous crash and flames came leaping through. It was time to go. Pausing only to snatch up his lifebelt, Neilson fought his way through the smoke and was caught up in a stampede of passengers, which carried him bodily back onto the deck.

On the open deck the scene had changed from panic to absolute chaos. The *Amazon*'s engines were still running, and with all access to the engine-room blocked by fire, nothing could be done to stop them. The ship was steaming into the teeth of a rising gale, which was driving the flames aft, consuming everything as they came. Half the crew were trapped in the fore part of the ship, on the other side of the wall of flame; dead or alive, nobody knew. The rest of the men, led by Symons and his officers, were fighting a valiant rearguard action against the fire with hoses and buckets. It was a hopeless task.

Symons now took the only course open to him and put the ship before the wind. In doing so, he knew he was signing the death warrant of those of his men still trapped forward. With the wind astern, the flames were momentarily checked, and then surged greedily towards the bows like a forest fire out of control. The screams of the dying men rose above the roar and crackle of burning timbers.

In putting the ship about, Symons had, for the time being at least, saved the lives of all those on the after deck, which included the passengers. It had also prevented the fire reaching the lifeboats, all of which were providentially stowed aft of the engine-room. But to what end? While the *Amazon* was still under way, and with the wind astern making in excess of twelve knots, any attempt to launch the boats was doomed to failure. Yet the only alternative was death by fire, for the flames were now creeping aft again. Reluctantly, Symons gave the order to launch the boats.

The after-most boat on the port side, with twenty-five people on board, was the first to be swung out. When the boat hit the water, the tackles were successfully slipped, but the sea was running high, and before the boat could pull clear of the burning ship's side, it was swamped, spilling all its occupants. It is doubtful whether any of the poor unfortunates survived more than a few minutes in the icy seas.

Next away was the pinnace, also stowed on the port side. When this reached the water, the after hook was slipped easily, but the boat surged up and down so violently in the heavy seas that the crew could not unhook the forward tackle. Consequently, the *Amazon* simply dragged the boat under as she steamed ahead unchecked. Not a man in the pinnace survived. And so it went on, with boat after boat coming to grief as it was launched.

Since returning to the upper deck, Neilson had remained on the port side of the poop watching the launching of the after boats and waiting for the opportune moment to save his own life. It was his intention to jump over the side and swim to one of the boats, but it soon became clear to him that survival did not lie in that direction. When he noticed a number of the crew struggling to launch one of the large lifeboats from the paddle-box platform, he decided to join them.

As Neilson had feared when he first looked around the decks soon after sailing, it was proving to be a labour of Hercules to lift the heavy boat out of its cradle. Until this was done the boat could not be swung out. Neilson added his weight to that of the sixteen men already hauling on the tackles, but their combined efforts failed. They were about to give up and look elsewhere for a means of escape, when the flames were seen to be licking at the deck under their feet. With one desperate heave born out of fear, the boat was raised sufficiently for it to be manhandled over the side and lowered to the water with a run. Neilson, one of the last to board, slid down the ropes of the after tackle into the tossing boat. As he did so, he saw the next boat astern crash to the water bow first, spilling all its occupants into the sea.

Neilson's boat survived only by virtue of the fact that it was manned mainly by seamen, although some of these had been badly burned in the hurried evacuation. Dragged through the water by the moving ship, and battered by the heavy seas, the boat was skilfully fended off, and, once clear of the ship's side, cut adrift. There was some delay in shipping the oars, but once they were in place, the men put their backs into it and the boat pulled away from the burning ship. When they were out of danger, they feathered their oars and looked back in horror at the carnage from which they had so narrowly escaped.

The *Amazon*, still under way and running headlong before the wind and sea, was ablaze from bowsprit to mainmast. In the light of the flames a terrified mob could be seen gathered on the poop with nowhere else to go. All the lifeboats were gone; either destroyed by fire or launched, mostly unsuccessfully, and it now only remained for the flames to reap their last harvest. Some were already leaping into the storm-lashed sea. For them, at least, the end would come quickly.

It was now blowing a full gale, and it was all the men at the oars could do to keep the boat's head into the wind and prevent her from being swamped. Then, they heard cries for help nearby, and despite their own predicament, searched around until they found the *Amazon*'s dinghy, manned by Midshipman Vincent, three seamen and one passenger. Waves were breaking right over the small craft, but Vincent successfully brought it alongside the larger boat, into which he and the others scrambled. It was decided not to cut the dinghy adrift and it was taken in tow in the hope that it might be the means of saving more. Vincent, being the only officer present, now took charge of the lifeboat.

And so began a long night filled with such savage violence that few in the boat expected to see the end of it. The sea, which before had only been gathering its strength, now unleashed its full fury. Seen in the eerie light of the burning ship, long ranks of angry, foam-topped waves marched in, each one rearing up over the boat before crashing down on it. There could be no thought of progress, all energy being directed towards bailing and preventing the boat broaching-to. However, the greatest danger came from an unexpected quarter. It was the empty dinghy towing astern on its short rope that broached-to, and riding up on the towline, smashed into the stern of the lifeboat, carrying away its rudder and all but swamping the boat.

For the twenty-one men in the lifeboat the prospects of survival, of even seeing out the night, were now very slim. Their boat was waterlogged, rudderless, they had no mast or sails, and no compass. And to compound an already hopeless situation, many of the men were half clothed, which on a freezing January night in the North Atlantic was inviting a quick death. Furthermore, there was no food in the boat, and the one small breaker of water had been stove in. In this miserable state they passed the rest of the night, with Neilson in the bows watching the advancing waves and directing Vincent, who was in the stern steering with an oar and holding the boat's head up into the wind.

At about four o'clock, three hours before dawn, they drifted close to the *Amazon* again. She was still burning fiercely, her funnels glowing red hot, but her engines had at last ground to a halt, and she was lying stopped, beam-on to the wind and sea. There was no sign of life on board. Suddenly, into the circle of light cast by the flames sailed a barque under reefed topsails. Moving in from the north-east, the stranger passed within 400 yards of the lifeboat, sending a great surge of hope through the survivors. They stood up in the heaving boat, shouting and waving, and to their great delight, the barque appeared to be shortening sail in preparation for picking them up. But it was not to be. After only the briefest of pauses, the barque shook out her sails again, passed around the *Amazon*'s stern, and disappeared out of the flickering light back into the darkness from whence it had come.

Whether the boat had been sighted or not, its occupants would never know, but the cruel disappointment they had suffered was enough to cast a pall over the boat that was blacker than the night itself. When it began to rain heavily, adding to their misery, the survivors slumped over their oars, all hope abandoned.

Although the rain was not welcome, it did herald a change in the weather—and for the better. The cold front of the depression was passing through, and as it did so, the wind veered to the north-west, became squally, and then eased. The slackening of the wind and the beat of the heavy rain combined to flatten the waves, and it was possible to bring the boat round onto an easterly course. This would take her towards the French coast, or, failing that, into the busy shipping lanes of the English Channel. Either way, the task ahead promised to be long and arduous. Even though the weather had moderated, the men were weak and demoralised, and no matter what encouragement Neilson and Vincent offered, the oars were dipped with a noticeable lack of enthusiasm. And as if to emphasise the hopelessness of their position, as they crossed the stern of the *Amazon* at a distance of about half a mile, she was torn apart by an explosion. The burning wreckage sank beneath the waves, taking with it the glow of light that for five hours past had been their only link with the other world. Now darkness, complete and absolute, descended on them. The darkest hour before the dawn was approaching.

Sunrise on Sunday, 4 January brought with it renewed hope, for the sky, washed clean by the rains of the night, was blue and without menace. The wind had lost most of its strength, and although the long Atlantic swell was ever present, the tumbling white horses did no more than give the boat's occupants an occasional playful wetting. But although the coming of a new day was bright and clear, it also revealed an empty horizon. If any other boats had been successfully launched from the *Amazon*, they had obviously not survived the night. They were alone on a vast and hostile ocean.

Vincent estimated the boat to be some 120 miles from the nearest land, the Brittany peninsular. Had they been blessed with a mast and sails, a day's easy sail might well have seen them on shore. Under oars only, assuming they could keep going, it might be five or six days before they reached land. This would be considered a hard row for fit men, but for the *Amazon*'s survivors, cold, tired and drained by a night of horror, without food and water, it was an impossibility. But it was either that or drift aimlessly until they all died. They put their backs to the oars.

After rowing steadily for three hours, the lookout in the bows of the boat sighted a sail ahead. Mindful of their heartbreaking experience with the unknown barque during the night, the survivors treated the sighting with caution, rather than jubilation. Soon it could be seen that the ship was a two-masted square-rigger and was heading to the south-west. Course was altered to close with her, and for two hours the men pulled hard. As they drew near the ship showed no sign of having seen them, nor did she answer their hails.

The wind was light, and the square-rigger moving only slowly, so Neilson and Vincent decided to run in on her, and, if necessary, board her by force, for another chance of rescue might not come their way. Fortunately, at that moment the ship suddenly backed her sails and hailed them to come alongside. Within half an hour, the twenty-one survivors were being helped aboard the brig *Marsden*, commanded by Captain Evans, and bound from London to California. Evans obligingly turned his ship about, and two days later the men were landed at Plymouth.

It was at first thought that the twenty-one were the only ones to come out of the disaster alive, but news came later of three other boats. The Dutch galliot *Gertruida* arrived in Brest with another twenty-five survivors. These had been picked up from two boats, which got away when the *Amazon* was losing steam and slowing down. Later still, the Dutch ketch *Hellechene* brought another thirteen into Plymouth, these from a boat found adrift in the Bay of Biscay. This was apparently the last boat to leave the *Amazon*, the launching of which had been supervised by Captain Symons with his clothes smouldering as the flames licked at his back.

Of a total of 161 souls on board the *Amazon*, no fewer than 102 perished, including Captain Symons and all his officers, except Midshipman Vincent. The cause of the fire that destroyed the ship was never established, but to put sixteen boilers with coal-fired furnaces into a wooden ship was a fearful risk. To also site a storeroom packed with highly inflammable materials over those boilers was one mistake too many. However, the loss of life cannot be blamed solely on the fire. It was the inability to stop the *Amazon*'s engines so that the boats might be lowered in safety that caused most of the casualties. As a result of this tragedy, the building of wooden steamers was stopped, and it became mandatory for all steamers to be fitted with a valve on deck, with which the engines could be stopped without entering the engine room.

Only a few bits of wreckage from the *Amazon* were ever found. By a strange twist of fate, one charred plank, positively identified as being from the ship, was washed ashore on a beach near Falmouth, just a few yards from the house in which Captain Symons was born.

6   The Point of Danger

HMS *Birkenhead* - 1852

One hundred and thirty six years ago South Africa was in much
the same state as it is now, with black fighting white for territory that historically belongs to neither. The 8th Kaffir
War, the latest in a seventy-year long series of frontier skirmishes was
at its height. Hordes of Bantu tribesmen, pushed southwards by
their old enemies, the Zulus, were pouring across the frontiers of the
Cape Colony into lands occupied by the British and their reluctant
allies, the Boers. British casualties were heavy and towards the close
of 1851 Sir Harry Smith, Governor and Commander-in-Chief of the
Cape, sent out a cry for help. This was to result in another of those
peculiarly British blunders, the dreadful consequences of which are
so often eclipsed by the sheer courage and fortitude of those involved.

London responded to Sir Harry's urgent call with uncharacter-
istic speed and, on 7 January 1852, Her Majesty's troopship
Birkenhead sailed from Cork, bound for the Cape. On board were
reinforcements consisting of 488 officers and men of no less than ten
different regiments, including the 74th Foot (Royal Highland
Fusiliers), the 91st Foot (Argyll & Sutherland Highlanders), the 6th
Foot (Royal Warwickshire Regt.) and the 60th Rifles (Royal
Greenjackets). In command of the troops for the voyage was Major
Alexander Sefton of the 74th, a 37-year-old Scot from Aberdeenshire.

While the replacement officers and NCOs were regular and
experienced members of the various regiments, the great majority of
the troops were young Irish recruits, who had willingly taken the
English Queen's shilling to escape from an Ireland still suffering
from the Great Potato Famine of 1846. Most of these boys—and they
were only mere boys of eighteen and nineteen—had never heard a
shot fired in practice, let alone in battle. Few had seen the sea before,
even fewer had set foot on a ship. To add to Major Sefton's temporary
responsibilities, the troopship also carried twenty-five women and
thirty-one children; wives and families of men serving in the Cape.

HMS *Birkenhead* was an iron-built paddle steamer of 1,400
tons, 210 feet long and 37 feet in the beam. She carried a crew of
129, including a detachment of six marines, and was commanded by
Master-Commander Robert Salmond, a most experienced seaman
and navigator whose naval ancestry went back to Elizabethan times.

Bernard Edwards

The *Birkenhead*'s builders claimed her to be a 'fast, comfortable, reliable and economical ship'. Captain Salmond and his crew would have it otherwise, and for good reasons. The ship had been built as a second-class frigate and shortly after completion had been found to be surplus to the fighting Navy's requirements and relegated to trooping. A forecastle and poop were added to her original flush deck and troop decks were created below by cutting large openings in her watertight bulkheads, thereby effectively defeating the primary object of these bulkheads. When fully loaded with troops, coal and stores, the *Birkenhead* floated two-feet below her original load waterline, giving her a freeboard of only five feet between her weather deck and the sea. In her new role she was slow, top-heavy and decidedly uncomfortable, if not unsafe.

It was blowing a full gale when the *Birkenhead* steamed out of Cork harbour on 7 January. She was to be dogged by foul weather for a full week until she was clear of the Bay of Biscay. With 673 souls crowded into such a small ship, conditions on board were appalling during those first days of the 6,000-mile voyage she had embarked on. Most of the recruits suffered the retching agonies of seasickness and were frightened to the point of panic by the violent movement of the ship. For the women the ordeal was even worse. Six were pregnant and went into premature labour brought on by the frenzied rolling and pitching. Three died with their stillborn babies, and another of their number succumbed to tuberculosis. Three infants survived to add their untried lungs to the screams, groans and curses that filled the tween decks of the storm-tossed trooper.

When Biscay was at last astern, the weather moderated and some semblance of order was restored to the ship as she progressed southwards into a warmer and more equitable climate. Major Sefton, aware that morale amongst the troops was at a very low ebb, lost no time in bringing them up on deck for regular exercises and drill. The remainder of the voyage provided the young Irishmen with a thorough grounding in the discipline of the British Army, a discipline that was to be put to the test far sooner than anyone on board anticipated.

After brief calls at Madeira, Sierra Leone and St. Helena for coal, water and provisions, the *Birkenhead* finally rounded the Cape of Good Hope on 23 February and dropped anchor off the naval base of Simonstown on that day. She had been six weeks and five days on passage.

Sir Harry Smith's needs must have been now even more acute, for, from the moment of arrival off Simonstown, the pressure was on Captain Salmond to sail again as quickly as possible. His orders were to take the troops to Algoa Bay and the Buffalo River, some 500 miles further up the coast. The ship was hurriedly re-fuelled and provisioned, horses were taken on for the officers of the regiments and most of the women and children were landed, leaving on board only seven women and thirteen children for the final stage of the voyage. When the *Birkenhead* was unceremoniously ushered out of Simonstown at 6 o'clock on the evening of the 25th, Captain Salmond and his crew had been working with little rest for almost forty-eight hours.

Fortunately, the notoriously fickle Cape weather was on its best behaviour. But it was a black night, lit only by the stars, which hung like clusters of diamond chips in a sky of deepest purple. The sea, undisturbed by even a cat's paw of wind, was an undulating mirror, occasionally reflecting back the twinkling of the brighter constellations. As she crossed the great expanse of False Bay, the measured thump of her engines loud in the silence of the night, the *Birkenhead* rolled easily in the long, lazy swell that came sweeping into the bay from the Southern Ocean. Two hours after sailing, with the lights of Simonstown dipping astern, Captain Salmond and his sailing master, Mr. Brodie, plotted the ship's position on the chart and set course for Cape Aghulas, ninety miles to the south-east. The two men waited until Cape Hangklip was cleared at 9.30 then, apparently satisfied the ship would come to no harm, left the officer of the watch in charge and retired for the night. Having shouldered much of the burden of the hasty turn-round at Simonstown, both men were very tired. This may be why they failed to take account of certain unseen but crucial outside influences at work on the ship.

At midnight, Mr. J.O. Davies, Second Master, took over the watch on the bridge. At the wheel was Able Seaman Thomas Coffin, while two lookouts were in the bow and a leadsman, Able Seaman Abel Stone, was stationed on the port paddle-box sounding at regular intervals. The *Birkenhead* was making a steady eight-knots on a course of south-south-east with the low outline of the land just visible at three to four points on the port bow. All seemed well with the middle watch.

Shortly before 2 o'clock on the morning of the 26th, Abel Stone cast his lead and was surprised to find bottom at twelve fathoms. He immediately reported this to the officer of the watch but Davies, either short on experience or long on fatigue, took no action to swing the ship away from the land, for she was obviously too close inshore. Ten minutes later, the *Birkenhead* ran headlong onto an isolated pinnacle of rock just over one mile off the aptly named Danger Point.

Captain Salmond was on the bridge within two minutes of the ship striking. Quickly assessing the situation, he ordered a bower anchor to be let go and the quarter boats swung out and lowered to the water. His next action, which was to ring for full astern on the engines, proved to be a fatal mistake.

At first the *Birkenhead*'s churning paddle wheels had no effect, then the ship began to draw slowly astern. The pinnacle of rock on which she was impaled sliced open her bottom like a can opener at work on a sardine tin. A great rush of water swept into her lower troop decks, surging through the openings in her once-watertight bulkheads and flooding compartment after compartment. The fetid air rang with the pitiful cries of more than a hundred men as they were drowned in their hammocks.

On deck, in the ghostly light of the blue distress flares set off by the ship's gunner, John Archbold, the surviving troops, many of them half-naked, lunged wild-eyed in all directions. Women and children screamed, horses neighed and kicked, and all the while the stricken ship swung to and fro, grinding horribly on the rock that held her transfixed. It seemed absolute panic was about to take hold, until Major Alexander Sefton drew his sword and stepped into the pages of the history books.

Calling on the troops to hold fast, Sefton, with the aid of his officers and NCOs, fell the men in on deck as though they were on a routine parade. Historians have long romanticised over this scene, portraying the troops in full uniform, drawn up in tight ranks and with fife and drum sounding defiance to the sea. In reality, the ranks were ragged, the men only partly clothed—some even naked—and all half-crazed with fear. Yet Sefton held them.

With order restored, Captain Salmond was able to begin the evacuation of the ship. First priority was given to the women and children, who were taken off in one of the quarter boats already in the water. The second quarter boat was then brought alongside and one of the gigs successfully launched. Within a matter of minutes, the three boats were pulling away from the ship carrying eighty survivors. The boats were heavily laden, but the sea was still calm and they were in no danger.

At this point the operation began to go seriously wrong. It was found that the davit pins of the two paddlebox lifeboats were rusted in and no amount of brawn could swing these boats out. The large boat the *Birkenhead* carried on deck amidships also proved useless, as there was no means of launching it. The second gig was swung out, but as it was being lowered, a tackle parted, the boat up-ended and was swamped. Of the seven lifeboats the troopship carried only three had got away.

The catastrophe gathered pace. In the midst of the futile battle to launch the remaining boats, the *Birkenhead* broke her back. As she did so, her tall funnel crashed down, killing many of those still heaving on the tackles of the starboard paddlebox boat, including the sailing master, Mr. Brodie. The whole fore part of the ship then broke off and sank, taking with it some sixty men who had been below manning the pumps in a hopeless bid to keep the sea at bay.

Those still alive retreated to the poop deck, the superb discipline of the troops continuing to hold. There was no more talk of lifeboats, for none remained. It would then have been easy for Sefton to give the word for every man to look to himself, but he feared that, in the ensuing fight to survive, the boat containing the women and

HMS 'Birkenhead' *founders off Danger Point*
(Photo: National Maritime Museum)

children might be overwhelmed. And so they stood, shoulder to shoulder, more than 350 strong, awaiting the end. This came soon. With an anguished scream of rending metal, the after part of the *Birkenhead* split again and began to sink bodily. Only twenty minutes had passed since the ship first struck the rock, which was forever after to bear her name.

Eight hours later, the British schooner *Lioness*, passing Danger Point on her way to Cape Town, sighted a boat inshore pulling towards her and signalling urgently. The *Lioness*, commanded by Captain Ramsden, stood in to investigate and soon learned of the awful tragedy of the night. She took thirty-seven survivors off the boat and them moved in towards the reported location of the wreck, on the way in coming upon the second lifeboat, which contained the *Birkenhead*'s women and children. Neither boat had been able to reach the shore owing to the heavy surf.

When Ramsden arrived off the wreck during the afternoon, he found forty-three men clinging to the spars and rigging of the *Birkenhead*'s main topmast, all that remained of the trooper above water. After a fruitless search of the surrounding waters, the *Lioness* then made all sail for Cape Town, having on board 117 survivors in all.

HMS 'Birkenhead' *breaking up off Danger Point*
(Photo: National Maritime Museum)

Early next day, Her Majesty's paddle sloop *Radamanthus* arrived off Danger Point and sent in boats to pick up sixty-eight men who had made it to the shore on improvised rafts and scraps of wreckage. Of the others who stood fast on the poop when the *Birkenhead* went down—an estimated 290 troops and seamen—there was no sign. The scores of sharks that attended the sinking had done their work well.

When the final reckoning was made, it was found that only 184 of the *Birkenhead*'s total complement of 638 had survived. Captain Robert Salmond had gone with sixty-seven of his crew, as had Major Alexander Sefton and 386 officers and men of the British Army.

There can be little argument on the primary reason for the grounding of the *Birkenhead*. Captain Salmond, under pressure to make a fast passage to Algoa Bay, had set his course close inshore in order to avoid the full strength of the Agulhas Current, which flows north-westwards at up to two knots in this area. He also hoped to take advantage of a counter-current setting in an east-south-easterly direction between Cape Hangklip and Cape Agulhas. Unfortunately, he failed to make sufficient allowance for the inshore component of this current and for the effect of the swell, which throughout the night was relentlessly pushing the ship in towards the shore.

As to the subsequent sinking of the ship and the resultant terrible loss of life, much of the blame must lie with those who sanctioned the wilful destruction of the *Birkenhead*'s watertight integrity by the convenient piercing of her bulkheads. When first built, her hull had been divided into eight watertight compartments, and had this still been so when she struck the rock, the outcome of that dreadful night would have been very different.

Today the once-lonely Birkenhead Rock is the scene of a great deal of unusual activity. The lure of a fortune in gold rumoured to have been in the *Birkenhead*'s strongroom when she went down has at last proved too much for the salvagemen. The stern section of the wreck has been located and divers are probing the mud around it. In the low sandhills of Danger Point, where many of the *Birkenhead*'s heroes still sleep, there is an uneasy stirring.

Wreckage of HMS 'Birkenhead' on sea bed off Danger Point
Photograph taken during salvage expedition, 1989
(Photo: E. Davies)

Bernard Edwards

7   The Gold Ship

Central America - 1857

Samuel Taylor Coleridge's Ancient Mariner's distrust of the wheeling albatross was born of an old seafaring superstition that endows these birds with supernatural powers. Each one, so it is said, carries on its wings the soul of a drowned sailor, and must be treated with the utmost respect, or no good will follow. Certainly, when the Ancient Mariner shot his albatross, he was drawn into a world full of the most terrible evil. Captain Johnson, master of the Norwegian barque *Ellen,* had a somewhat different experience.

On the afternoon of 12 September, 1857, the *Ellen* was off the coast of South Carolina, and heading on a course a little to the east of north-east. Captain Johnson, having been without observations for many days, was unsure of his ship's position and feared she might be running into shallow waters. As he paced the poop deck deep in thought, Johnson suddenly became aware of a strange sea bird, the like of which he had never seen before, flying in circles above his head. The bird appeared to be in a state of great agitation, and swooped low, several times grazing Johnson's shoulder with its wings. When the bird flew at his face, Johnson caught it and handed it over to his crew. At that the bird went berserk, slashing with its beak at anyone who approached it. Eventually, the bird had to be killed.

Johnson, like most seamen of his day, was intensely superstitious and regarded the visitation of this strange, hostile bird as an omen; a warning to him that he must change course, or run into danger. With only a moment's hesitation, Johnson put the helm over and sailed due east, away from the coast. In the early hours of the following morning, the *Ellen* sighted wreckage in the water, and when she closed on this, discovered forty-nine people clinging to it. They were survivors of the steamer *Central America*, and had been in the shark-infested water for eight hours. Without the change of course prompted by the strange bird's visitation, these people would most probably never have been found. Unlike the Ancient Mariner's albatross, the death of Johnson's bird brought nothing but good.

The United States mail ship *Central America* sailed from Havana, Cuba on 8 September, 1857, bound for New York. Owned by G. Law & Company, of that city, the 1,200-ton paddle steamer

Widow-Maker

The gold ship 'Central America'
(Photo: Numast*)*

was commanded by Captain Herndon and carried a crew of 101, in whose care were the Pacific mails, 491 passengers, and a strong-room full of gold. The gold, three tons of ingots and twenty-dollar Gold Eagles, worth an estimated one billion dollars at today's rates, was being rushed from California to New York to stave off a financial crisis.

The majority of the *Central America*'s passengers were gold miners and their families, returning north after years of hard work in the Californian diggings. They too carried gold, millions of dollars worth in their luggage. The men were hard, uncompromising individuals, and by nature of their chosen profession, inveterate gamblers and prodigious drinkers. Captain Herndon feared, with good cause, that there might be trouble below decks during the voyage.

When the *Central America* pulled out of Havana's inner harbour and steamed past the 16th century Castillo del Morro to the open sea, the weather was fine and warm, with a high, steady barometer. Her coal bunkers were full, her engines in first class condition. Herndon was confident she would maintain her usual twelve knots and cover the 1,167 miles to New York in a little over four days. However, the unpredictable weather of this unstable corner of the Atlantic was to decide otherwise.

For much of the year, the north-east trade winds dominate the seas around the West Indies. These are benign winds, bringing with them clear, blue skies and untroubled seas. The early Spanish explorers had good cause to name the area the 'Lady's Gulf'. In the months of August, September and October, when the sun has crossed the Equator on its journey south to Capricorn, the trade winds are at their lightest; no more than gentle zephyrs. It is then that malevo-

Bernard Edwards

lent outside forces move in to fill what has become a partial vacuum.

At this time of the year, there lies over the Cape Verde Islands, some 3,000 miles to the east of the West Indies, an area of great atmospheric instability; the ideal breeding ground for hurricanes. Beginning as a lazy circulation of warm, moist air, an embryo hurricane deepens as it moves west at the rate of 300 miles a day along the bottom edge of the North Atlantic high. Nearing the West Indies, still skirting the periphery of the high pressure, through which it cannot break, the now fully formed hurricane hauls more to the northward. By this time it is up to 500 miles in diameter, and with a barometric pressure in the centre, or eye, of as little as 920 millibars. Some hurricanes sweep across the Bahamas into the Gulf of Mexico, but the majority spiral up the east-coast of America, to veer back into the Atlantic as higher latitudes are reached. The typical North Atlantic hurricane, like the typhoon of the China Seas and the cyclone of the Indian and Pacific oceans, is a freak of nature possessed of awesome destructive powers. More than half the hurricanes that approach the West Indies during an average year occur in the months of August and September.

The *Central America* was twenty-four hours out of Havana and at the northern end of the Florida Strait, when the first signs of impending bad weather became evident. At first it was only a small fall in the barometer, but in an area where, allowing for the diurnal range, the barometer stays unchanged for months on end, this was enough to alert Captain Herndon. Within the hour, the wind had freshened and dark banks of cloud were massing ominously on the horizon. When, during the night, the ship moved clear of the shelter of Grand Bahama Island, a long swell came rolling in from the open Atlantic. By morning, it was blowing a full gale, and the glass was dropping rapidly.

It was now clear to Herndon, that, somewhere to the east, perhaps three or four hundred miles out to sea, a full-blown hurricane was trundling in towards the coast, and the *Central America* was in its path. If the hurricane maintained a westerly course, and headed straight into the Gulf of Mexico, it would pass astern of the ship. On the other hand, should it run true to form and curve to the north as it neared the coast, then the *Central America* was on a collision course with a monster on the rampage. Being in constricted waters, Herndon had little option but to try to outrun the monster. He sent for his chief engineer, Mr Ashby, and asked for all possible speed. Ashby recognised the urgency of the situation and doubled up the firemen on the furnaces. With the powerful, north-flowing Gulf Stream behind her, the *Central America* fought her way through the rising gale, racing against time and the barometer.

At daylight on the 10th, after a dark, uncomfortable night, Herndon knew the race was lost. The wind, which had been in the north-west, was backing steadily to the west, a sure sign that the hurricane was passing ahead of the ship. But already it was too late to turn back, for the *Central America* was in danger of being overwhelmed by the mountainous seas. In order to avoid serious damage to his ship, Herndon had been forced to reduce speed so that the paddles were turning just sufficiently to maintain steerage way. Riding the waves with the wind and sea on the port bow, she would still take a beating, but, so long as the engines kept turning, she had a fair chance of survival.

As the day progressed, so the wind climbed up the Beaufort scale, until by nightfall, it was force twelve and gusting up to a hundred knots. Thunder rolled and lightning flashed, illuminating the great overhanging seas that filled the air with flying spray and spume. It was nature gone wild. Those manning the flimsy bridge of the ship marvelled at her tenacity as she plunged into each dark valley and then, with her decks streaming water, climbed valiantly to meet the next oncoming mountain of water with her slender bows. There were times when her paddles thrashed at thin air as the sea fell away from them, but she held her own.

Below decks, the *Central America*'s unfortunate passengers were in the midst of a hideous nightmare. The dreadful curse of sea-sickness visited upon most of them was bad enough, but the wild gyrations of the ship, the crash of the waves, the screech of the wind, and the cannonade of thunder put the fear of God into them. Women screamed, children whimpered, and even the hard-case miners, toughened in the fire of the Californian gold fields, were near to breaking point. They took refuge in drink.

For those working below in the engine-room, engineers, firemen and trimmers—and especially for the latter—what had always been a difficult and thankless job had become a foretaste of Hades itself. In order to keep the paddles turning the hungry boiler furnaces must be adequately fed. This involved, apart from the non-stop wielding of heavy shovels, the transfer by wheelbarrow from the bunkers to the stokehold of almost two tons of coal an hour. This was the work of the trimmers, and undoubtedly one of the most gruelling tasks ever invented by man. For four hours without a break, stripped to the waist, with the sweat cutting rivulets through the coal dust blackening their bodies, the trimmers trundled their heavy wheelbarrows between bunker and stokehold like a human conveyor belt. In a ship on an even keel in fine weather it was backbreaking work, in the *Central America*, riding the switchback of a hurricane, it was a near impossibility. Men staggered and slipped, wheelbarrows were overturned, and the air was filled with curses, but somehow the coal got through. Without it the *Central America* could not hope to survive.

The eye of the hurricane passed ahead of the ship during the night, and by daylight on the 11th there was a perceptible slackening of the wind. It was still blowing in excess of storm force, and the seas were dangerously high, but it seemed safe to assume the worst was over. Herndon was on the point of leaving the bridge for the first time in thirty-six hours, when Ashby reported to him that the ship was making water in the coal bunkers. The manhandling she had received at the hands of the hurricane had sprung her plates.

Herdon immediately ordered the pumps to be started, and for a while it seemed the situation was in hand. But two feet of water running amok in the bunkers proved to be the final straw for the *Central America*'s trimmers, already near the limit of their endurance. The supply of coal to the stokehold slowed, and, despite all the efforts of Chief Engineer Ashby, eventually ceased altogether. Starved of fuel, the furnaces died, the boilers lost their steam pressure, and the engines which had for so long defied the might of the hurricane, ground to a halt. Without her churning paddles to hold her up into the wind, the *Central America*'s head fell off, and she broached-to.

Rolling helplessly in the trough of the waves, the steamer was now in an extremely dangerous position. Her pumps, driven by steam from the main boilers, were without power, and the level of the water in her hull rose unchecked. Within minutes, through the action of the violent rolling, water began to come in through the lee side paddle shafts and deadlights. Efforts were made to raise steam on the donkey boiler, situated on the upper deck in order to restart the pumps, but to no avail. The seas were now washing right over the ship, making any movement on the open deck almost impossible. An attempt to dump cargo overboard to lighten the ship also failed. The *Central America* was sinking and nothing could be done to help her.

But the ship did not accept her fate easily. Throughout the remainder of that day and during the long night that followed, she lay helpless, beam on to wind and sea, rolling heavily and all the time sinking lower in the water. Her passengers had by now given up all hope of survival, and had lapsed into a state of apathy. Many of the men were hopelessly drunk, while the women and children cowered in their berths awaiting the end. Herndon and his crew, to their great credit, exerted a steadying influence on these poor people, but could do no more. The *Central America* was well equipped with lifeboats, but to attempt to launch them in the tempest that still raged around her would have served no useful purpose.

Being caught in the powerful grip of the Gulf Stream, the drifting *Central America was* carried in a north-easterly direction, parallel to the coast of South Carolina. She was thus held within the shipping lanes, and on the afternoon of the 12th, was sighted by the brig *Marine*, commanded by Captain Burt and out of Boston. The sea was still running very high, and the wind near to gale force, but in a remarkable rescue operation using boats from both ships, the women and children, 121 in all, were taken off the sinking ship.

The rescue would have gone on, but when the last boat carrying the women and children had pulled away, the *Central America* was rolled over on her beam ends by a huge sea. The poor ship, weighed down by the great volume of water in her hull, failed to recover, and slipped beneath the waves to her final resting place.

It appears that most of the crew, who were below decks engaged in a futile attempt to bail the ship out by hand, went down with her. Others, including the majority of the male passengers, either dived overboard before she went down, or came to the surface again after being sucked down with the ship. By this time it was completely dark, with low, scudding cloud obscuring the stars. When the lightning flashed it revealed a sea of wreckage, amongst which bobbed hundreds of heads.

The survivors shouted in vain for the *Marine* to come to their aid, but she was some distance off and Captain Burt was not aware that the *Central America* had gone down. Later, when he became suspicious and searched the area, he could find no-one.

The several hundred men who were in the water, borne on the swift flowing Gulf Stream, had drifted out of sight of the *Marine*. Most of them wore lifejackets and there was ample wreckage for them to cling to, but the sea was still rough and they began to drown through the effect of the waves continually dashing in their faces. The sea was warm, near to 80°F, but inevitably hypothermia set in amongst the survivors. And then there were the sharks. By the time the *Ellen*, commanded by the superstitious Captain Johnson, found them at two o'clock on the morning of the 13th, only forty-nine remained alive.

The story of the *Central America* did not end there. Sixteen days later, the barque *Laura*, inbound from Bremen, arrived in New York with three more survivors on board. The tale these men had to tell was not a pleasant one.

Second Engineer John Tice stayed with the *Central America* until her dying moments, and then, clasping a heavy plank of timber, launched himself overboard. He had left his escape very late, for the sinking ship took him down with her, and only released him when his lungs were about to burst. Still keeping a tight hold on his plank, Tice shot to the surface, only to find himself alone on a dark and stormy sea. For three days he drifted on his plank without a sight of a ship, or another human being. He was near the end of his tether when, on the morning of the 16th, he spotted an empty lifeboat. Summoning up the last of his strength, he swam to the boat and heaved himself aboard. It turned out to be one of the *Central America*'s lifeboats, which must have broken free when she went down. Unfortunately, there was no food or water in the boat, but Tice's chance of survival had improved immensely.

Next day, Tice drifted close to a waterlogged raft on which there were four men. Three of the men at once left the raft and swam towards the boat. Only one of them, Alexander Grant, a fireman in the *Central America*, reached the boat, the others were drowned. Tice and Grant then rowed the boat across to the raft, which turned out to be the remains of the *Central America*'s bridge deck, and picked up the fourth man, G.W. Dawson, a passenger in the ship.

When Dawson was safely in the boat, Grant related how, after the ship went down, he found himself clinging to the shattered bridge deck along with eleven others, six of whom were passengers. No other survivors were visible in the sea around them. On the second day, Dawson, a coloured man, drifted up on a plank and tried to join them on the makeshift raft. The flimsy wooden deck was already awash with the weight of the twelve men and the others refused to allow Dawson to board. He bided his time, clinging to the edge of the deck while, one by one, those on board died, most of them through drinking sea water, and were pushed or fell off. When it was safe, Dawson took his place on the deck. Soon, only he and three others remained alive, and two of them were to perish in the bid to reach the lifeboat.

Tice, Grant and Dawson made an effort to row the boat in the direction of the land, but they were so weak that they only succeeded in threshing the water ineffectually with the oars. However, some good did come of their efforts. One of the oars struck and killed a large dogfish, which was immediately hauled on board and eaten raw. After five days without food the men were ravenous.

They had no more sustenance for the next three days, and all three were very near to death. Fortunately, on the night of the 20th, it rained heavily, and they were able to drink their fill. Otherwise, they would not have been alive when, on 21 October, nine days after the sinking of the *Central America,* they were picked up by the Scottish brig *Mary.* The three men had drifted on the Gulf Stream a distance of 576 miles in a northerly direction since their ship sank. They were fortunate that the *Mary* came upon them when she did, for at that point the current veers away from the coast and sweeps out into the North Atlantic. Unseen, Tice, Grant and Dawson, or their shrivelled corpses, would have embarked on a long voyage into obscurity. As it was, the *Mary*, bound from Cardenas, Cuba to Cork, transferred them to the barque *Laura* in mid-Atlantic, and so they reached New York.

Figures from different sources vary, but a fair estimate is that of the 592 passengers and crew on board the *Central America*, at least 420 lost their lives. When news of the disaster reached Wall Street, there was panic, until the insurance companies concerned made it known that they would pay out in full on the gold lost. There was no compensation, however, for the gold that went down with the ship's passengers. Many, it was said, carried so much gold in their money belts that even cork lifejackets could not keep them afloat.

In 1990, the wreck of the *Central America* was located in 8,000 feet of water 150 miles off the coast of South Carolina by the Columbus-America Discovery Group. Now, having spent ten years and fifteen million dollars finding the wreck and salvaging the 1.05 billion dollars in gold, Columbus-America finds itself engaged in a bitter wrangle over who owns the treasure. The British and American insurance companies who underwrote the ship and her cargo 136 years ago, are laying claim to the gold. As they fulfilled their obligations in 1857 by paying all claims in full, they may well win their case in court. If that happens, Columbus-America has threatened to return the gold to the sea.

THE LOSS OF THE CENTRAL AMERICA.

LIVERPOOL, SATURDAY.

The following items respecting the loss of the steamship Central America are extracted from the details of the catastrophe published in the papers brought by the Europa :—

"Of the 23 children who were saved the greater part were babies. The stewardess of the steamer was a stout negro woman. She had collected the money thrown away by the passengers, it was supposed, and buckled it around the body. The weight of this money was the cause of her death when she was hoisted into the Marine, where she died from having too much gold about her loins. One of the ladies placed her canary bird in her bosom on leaving the steamer and preserved its life.

"Mr. George, who went down with the vessel, says :— He heard no shriek, nothing but the seething rush and hiss of waters that closed above her as she hurried, almost with the speed of an arrow, to her ocean bed. Night had closed in before the vessel sank, and he was sucked in, by the whirlpool caused by her swift descent, to a depth that in its seeming was unfathomable, and into a darkness that he had never dreamt of. Compared with it the blackest night, without moon or star, was as the broad noonday. He was rather stunned than stifled, and his sensations on coming to the surface were almost as painful, from their reaction, as those which he endured at the greatest depth to which he sank. When he became conscious, after the lapse of a minute or two, he could distinguish every object around him for a considerable distance. The waves, as they rose and fell, revealed a crowd of human heads. Those unfortunates who had lost their life-preservers or planks while under water, owing to the force of the whirlpool, were frantically snatching at the broken pieces of the wreck, which, breaking from the ship as she continued to descend, leapt above the surface and fell back with a heavy splash. Their cries arose thus mingled into one inarticulate wail, and then the lustier and less terrified shouted for assistance to the bark Marine, which was far beyond hailing distance. The waves dashed them one against another at first, but speedily they began to separate, and the last farewells were taken. One man called to another in our informant's hearing, ' If you are saved, Frank, send my love to my dear wife ;' but the friend ap-

fact that a few gave l..g the steamer from example of that few standing the constan officers that everythi worked faithfully 's serious disadvantage refreshments.'

"Mrs. Small an Herndon, of whom was handed into th very firm. ' Mrs. 8c not to get you home away.

"Mr. Payne states for his life. I wa before I went, and I said, ' Thank God, we are strong.' He ' You take the next he requested me t watch and chain, ar Said he, ' Tell her deep emotion, and changed it by say of the company, M communicate with t

"After saying th and sat down on a parently overcome. moments, and then boat from the brig

"The conduct of condemned, and so ' lynching ' him. engine-room long be charged against him vacant, and a pers instant Ashby, w the women and and raising as. if to get out. H near, and the m pushed off, Ashby j a cry was heard, 'S

An extract from The Times of London, Monday, October 5, 1857
Reporting on the loss of the 'Central America'

Bernard Edwards

8   The Transatlantic Trade

Austria - 1858

B y the late 1840s, the mass exodus from Europe to America, brought on by war, revolution and famine, showed no signs of slowing. Emigration from Germany alone had reached the half million mark, and the demand for shipping to accommodate this continuing shift of population was enormous. It was to this end that, in 1847, the Hamburg Amerikanische Packetfahrt Actien Gesellschaft was formed. Hamburg America Line, as it later became popularly known, entered the transatlantic service with the sailing packet *Deutschland,* and immediately began to prosper. Its first steamship, the *Borussia* sailed for New York on its maiden voyage on 1 June, 1856. By this time, British, French and American companies were vying with each other for the cream of the passenger trade, offering ever better accommodation and competing fiercely for the Blue Riband of the Atlantic. The first holder of this, as yet mythical award, Cunard Line's *Acadia,* had crossed from New York to Liverpool in thirteen days in 1840. In 1856, that same company's *Persia* crossed in nine days four hours and fifteen minutes. So keen had the competition become that, on a voyage of 3,000 miles, even the minutes were being counted.

Hamburg America, until then content to make a living from the emigrant trade, which required only very basic accommodation and a modest speed, now realised it was being left behind in the transatlantic trade. It feared that when the emigrants dried up—and they must surely do so—it would be in no state to compete with its competitors. This led, in 1857, to the building of the *Austria.*

The 2,383-ton *Austria* was a steam clipper, fully rigged for sail, and having the fine lines of a clipper ship, but equipped with a screw driven by a 800 horsepower engine. Built on the Clyde by Caird & Company, she was 320 feet long, 40 feet in the beam, and had accommodation for cabin passengers and emigrants of a high standard for the day. With a top speed of only twelve knots, she could not hope to match the passage time of her foreign rivals, but the *Austria* was to offer a call at Southampton. Although Southampton had good overland communications with London, at the time it had no direct sailings to New York, and Hamburg America hoped to establish a lucrative trade in first class passengers and mails. Unfortunately, the

Widow-Maker

Austria was a ship dogged by bad fortune from the day of her launch.

At about the same time as the *Austria*'s keel plates were being laid on the Clyde, the British Army introduced into India the new .577 Enfield percussion rifle. This was a muzzle-loader using cartridges wrapped in greased paper, and was said to be the best of its kind. However, Indian nationalists, always on the lookout for a spark to light the fire of rebellion against the British Raj, spread the word that the Enfield's cartridges were greased with a mixture of cow's fat and hog's lard. There was no truth in this allegation, but it was enough to create serious unrest among the Indian sepoys. The Muslims in their ranks regarded the pig as unclean, while the Hindus venerated the cow. Both groups refused to handle the cartridges, and out of this was born the infamous Indian Mutiny.

The mutiny resulted in an urgent call for ships to carry troops to the troubled sub-continent. The *Austria* was chartered by the British Government as soon as she left her fitting-out yard, and thus started her life as a troopship. Coincidentally, this was a godsend for Hamburg America as freights were temporarily depressed following the end of the Crimea War and they were glad to have their ship taken up. Unfortunately, the *Austria* did not distinguish herself as a trooper. She made only two voyages to India, each time spending many months out of service due to engine problems. The British were relieved to see the back of her.

When the *Austria* was handed back to her owners in the early summer of 1858, the North Atlantic trade was again booming, and after a hurried refit, she was rushed into service. Her long-delayed maiden voyage under the German flag began on 2 September, when she sailed from Hamburg under the command of Captain Hedytmann, and with a crew of 102. She carried 68 passengers in her first class cabins, 111 in second class, and 241 in steerage. The latter were poor German and Hungarian emigrants seeking a better life in the promised land across the water.

After an uneventful passage across the North Sea and through the English Channel, the *Austria* reached Southampton on the morning of the 4th. Here she picked up a further fifteen cabin passengers and a small quantity of mail, sailing again at 5 pm on the same day, having on board a total of 538 passengers and crew. Soon after leaving Southampton she ran into fog, and despite Captain Hedytmann's anxiety to gain the open sea as soon as possible, was forced to anchor in the Solent. The fog cleared a little before dawn on the 5th, and Hedytmann ordered the anchor to be weighed at once.

Although she was a modern steamer in other respects, the *Austria*'s anchor windlass was straight out of the days of sail, an old style capstan turned by the muscle and sweat of deck crew. The raising of an anchor by hand was a slow, laborious operation prone to accidents. On this occasion it proved to be fatal. The weight of the anchor was great, the decks were wet, and it was half-light. A man slipped, the capstan ran out of control, its flailing bars hurling men in all directions. One man was flung overboard into the cold, grey waters of the Solent and was never seen again; two others were seriously injured. It was very late that day before Heydtmann, having landed the injured men, was able to set sail.

Eighteen days later, the *Austria,* being six days overdue at New York, was posted missing. Ominous reports of a derelict ship answering her description having been sighted drifting in mid-Atlantic led to speculation that some terrible disaster had overtaken the ship. This proved to be only too true.

The *Austria* met with bad weather as soon as she cleared Land's End, running into strong head winds and rough seas. For the next seven days she fought a ceaseless battle with the elements for every mile of westerly progress made. Her once unreliable engine performed faultlessly, but she was never able to achieve more than nine knots. No records would be set on this maiden voyage.

On the 12th, when the *Austria* was 1,500 miles deep into the North Atlantic, the weather at last began to relent. By noon on the 13th, she was making a steady eleven knots, with Hedytmann confidently predicting arrival at New York on the 18th. The time and the place were now opportune to carry out one of the more irksome tasks of the passage—the fumigation of the steerage accommodation.

The emigrants the *Austria* carried below decks were, as might be expected, not only poor and hungry but unacquainted with the finer virtues of hygiene and sanitation. They were, in the main, ignorant peasants, who took to sea with them colonies of lice, and whose eating habits in the confined space of the steerage provided ample food for fast-breeding rats and cockroaches. All emigrant ships were thus, and the United States immigration authorities, with good cause, insisted on a thorough fumigation of all steerage decks before arrival in a US port. For this purpose, it was recommended that tar be heated in a bucket until it gave off thick, sulphurous smoke, guaranteed to asphyxiate the hardiest of bugs and vermin, and which left behind a strong odour of apparent cleanliness.

As soon as the midday meal was over, and after consulting the ship's surgeon, Heydtmann cleared the steerage of all passengers and instructed the fourth officer and the boatswain to begin the fumigation. The two men heated a length of small link chain on the galley fire and took this below with a bucket of tar, their intention being to plunge the red hot chain into the tar, and thus generate the cleansing smoke. It was a well-tried procedure and should have been perfectly safe. Unhappily, the law that governs all silly accidents chose that moment to come into play. The glowing chain slipped from the boatswain's grasp and fell to the wooden deck, which immediately caught fire. In the confusion that followed, the tar bucket was overturned and the tar went up in flames. There was no water at hand to douse the fire, and within minutes, the tinder-dry bunks and their straw mattresses were alight.

A little after two o'clock, Charles Brews, a first class passenger, was pacing the quarterdeck enjoying the sunshine and fresh air. Brews, a senior official of the Irish Constabulary, who boarded the *Austria* at Southampton, was on his way to British Columbia, where he was to set up the province's first police force. The crossing to New York was only the first leg of a long and difficult journey ahead of Brews. The days of the great transcontinental railways of the New World had not yet arrived, and the 3,000-mile trek overland through territory as yet largely unexplored was out of the question. The only feasible route to western Canada lay by sea, by packet boat from New York to the Caribbean, across the isthmus of Panama on horseback to the Pacific, and then north again by sea. It was an undertaking fraught with many hazards and likely to take anything up to five weeks.

A woman's scream and a rush of feet brought an end to Brews' contemplation of his immediate future. He swung around and saw dense black smoke pouring out from the entrance to the steerage accommodation. At the same time, the steady beat of the *Austria*'s engines slowed and an agitated woman passenger reached the quarter deck with the news that the ship was on fire.

By nature of his calling, Brews was not one to walk away from an emergency, and although the woman's cry had been taken up by others pouring aft, he went forward to investigate. He soon discovered the gathering panic was justified. The whole of the ship's amidship's accommodation was ablaze, smoke and flames pouring from every opening. Screams coming from the fore part of the ship indicated that a number of people were cut off.

The *Austria* was still under way at about half speed, and steaming into a headwind that was fanning the flames aft. Brews was no seaman, but he was intelligent enough to realise that the ship must be stopped and put beam-on to the wind in order to check the spread of the fire. He ran aft to the quarterdeck, now crowded with passengers fleeing from the flames, and looked around for an officer. There was not one to be seen.

The situation was far worse than Brews realised. Soon after the fire broke out, the *Austria*'s engine-room, situated directly abaft the steerage, had quickly filled with toxic smoke, overcoming the men on duty. Several attempts were made to enter the compartment from the deck, but each time the men were beaten back by smoke and flames. Meanwhile, the engine continued to turn. Hoses were rigged, but the sea intake pipes for the fire hydrants, which ran through the engine-room, were of lead and soon melted. With the fire out of control and access to her engine-room impossible, the Austria seemed destined to continue steaming into the wind until her boiler fires died and the steam pressure fell.

Fighting his way through the frightened mob of passengers

choking the quarter deck, Brews reached the wheelhouse, where he found the helmsman alone, and in the absence of orders to the contrary, still holding the ship on course—dead into the wind. Brews pleaded with him to put the ship off the wind, but the man shrugged and carried on steering, for he did not understand a word of English. Eventually, Brews found an English-speaking German passenger, and together they convinced the helmsman of the necessity for a change of course.

With the wind on the beam, and the smoke and flames blowing overside, conditions improved on the quarterdeck, and it was possible to rescue some passengers trapped in the second class cabins. But there was still a great deal of panic and confusion, and a total lack of leadership from the ship's officers. Captain Hedytmann, who appeared to have lost all control of himself and his men, was making efforts to launch the port quarter lifeboat with the help of the fourth officer. This was a foolhardy thing to do with the ship still under way, and it ended with the boat being swamped as soon as it hit the water. The fourth officer, who was in the boat, cut the falls, but the boat was sucked into the *Austria*'s threshing propeller and smashed. In the excitement, Heydtmann fell from the deck of the ship into the sea and disappeared.

Brews gave a hand with lowering the starboard quarter boat, an operation that proved to be an even greater disaster. So many people rushed forward and crowded into the boat as it was being launched, that the falls ran away, and the boat fell twenty-feet from the deck into the sea fully loaded. All on board, with the exception of one man, were drowned, and Brews counted himself lucky to have remained on deck.

All the other lifeboats were cut off by the fire so those left on the quarterdeck, the majority being first and second class passengers, had no avenue of escape. To make matters worse, the helmsman had deserted his post, and the ship, as all ships will when rudderless, had put her head back into the wind. Within minutes, flames were licking at the quarterdeck. As the flames moved relentlessly towards them, the crowd became hysterical. Men and women milled around like frightened cattle, husbands looking for wives, wives seeking husbands, mothers calling for their children. As the flames advanced, so they retreated further and further aft along the deck, until they reached the stern rails and there was nowhere else to go. Brews, who had climbed on to the empty lifeboat davits on the starboard quarter, watched in horror as men, women and children hurled themselves into the sea to escape the flames. But there was no escape for them in the sea. The waves were running high, and those who did not drown right away were sucked in by the *Austria*'s still turning propeller and suffered a worse fate.

The heat and smoke was becoming intolerable, and Brews feared he too would soon be faced by the choice of death by fire or water. Then, he saw below him a waterlogged boat, still made fast to the ship, and being dragged along in her wake. This was his last chance to live, and he took it without hesitation, going hand over hand down a rope hanging over the ship's side. With great difficulty, for there was already one man clinging to the rope rigid with fear, Brews reached the boat and jumped in. Fortunately, he carried a penknife, and he used this to saw through the rope holding the boat. The boat at once began to drop astern as the ship moved on, and although Brews tried to fend off, the boat was drawn inexorably into the *Austria*'s propeller. There was a bang, the boat capsized, and Brews was catapulted into the sea.

He dived deep into the cold, dark water, hearing the thump, thump of the screw as its sharp blades passed within inches of his body. When he came to the surface again, he found himself alongside the upturned boat. By putting all his weight on one side, and with the assistance of a convenient wave, he righted the boat and heaved himself over the gunwale. When he looked for the ship, she was a quarter of a mile off, a blazing pyre, moving away at a good seven or eight knots. People were still visible on the poop, some of them with their clothes on fire, and as he watched, they began to hurl themselves into the sea one by one. Moments later, the *Austria* was torn apart by an explosion as her magazine went up, and there was a final mass exodus over her rails. Brews, up to his waist in water in the swamped boat, was sickened by the slaughter he was witnessing.

When, half an hour later, the awful drama drew to a close, and there was no more movement on the burning ship, Brews looked to his own predicament. The oars had been lost when the boat capsized, but he found a broken plank, and used this to paddle towards the *Austria.* He had no clear object in mind, but the burning ship drew him like a beacon of hope. Soon, he came alongside a German passenger swimming strongly in the same direction, and hauled him into the boat. Another plank was found, and the two men joined forces in an effort to reach the ship. Their efforts seemed doomed to failure, for the *Austria* was still pulling away from them. Then, at around five o'clock, they saw a sail approaching the steamer. Two hours later, with darkness closing in, they were picked up by the French barque *Maurice.*

The *Maurice*, commanded by Captain Ernest Renaud, and bound from Newfoundland to the Isle of Bourbon with a cargo of fish, had already rescued forty survivors from the *Austria*. Most of these had been taken from the doomed steamer's bowsprit, where they had sought a last refuge from the fire. Throughout the night the *Maurice* searched the area and a further twenty-five were picked up from the sea. When daylight came on the 14th the barque had on board a total of sixty survivors. Many were badly burned, and all were suffering from shock and exposure. Captain Reynaud, who showed considerable tenacity in the long rescue operation, was equally generous in his care of the survivors.

At seven o'clock that morning, having satisfied himself that no one else remained alive in the water, Renaud set sail for Fayal, in the Azores, to land his unexpected passengers. However, that afternoon, the *Maurice* came up with the barque *Lotus*, bound from Liverpool to Halifax, which agreed to take off some of the survivors and carry them to Nova Scotia. Among them was Charles Brews, who landed in Halifax on 23 September, bringing the first news of the tragic loss of the *Austria*. It must have been with some trepidation that Brews faced his long sea passages to the other side of the continent.

It was later learned that a Norwegian barque had picked up seven more survivors from the *Austria*, bringing the total saved to sixty-seven. Out of the 538 passengers and crew who left Southampton in the steamer, 471 had lost their lives, a great many of them women and children, and all in the interests of a clean ship.

9   The Record Breaker

Indian Queen - 1859

As the 1850s drew to a close, few ships on the North Atlantic run, steam or sail, were much over 2,000 tons gross, and suffered greatly at the hands of that turbulent ocean. But when offered the choice between a ten-day pounding on a steamer and a month imprisoned on a lurching, wave-swept sailing packet, it is not hard to imagine which the prospective passenger would settle for. So far as the North Atlantic was concerned, then, the steamers had firmly established their supremacy over sail by the time the decade came to an end.

On the long run to Australia, via the Cape of Good Hope, it was a different matter. No steamer of the day could carry enough coal for the passage, and it was necessary to set up and supply a string of coaling stations on the route. The Peninsular and Oriental Steam Navigation Company alone employed 170 sailing ships to carry coal to its steamers on the Indian Ocean service, a very costly operation. On the road to the Southern Cross, economics dictated that the clipper ships would hold sway for many years to come. With their audaciously raked stems, distinctive counter sterns, and billowing press of white sail, they were built to be pushed to their utmost limits—and they were. Their high freeboard enabled them to run before the towering seas of the Roaring Forties, often logging in excess of 350 miles in a day. In the Doldrums they suffered a temporary disadvantage, but God's wind that powered them was free, and they could not fail to be economical on a long voyage.

When Captain James Cook, blown off course by heavy weather, stumbled upon Australia in April, 1770, he found this vast land uninhabited, except for a handful of black hunters of indeterminate origin. By 1850, thanks to the policies of the British Government, the colony was home to 100,000 convicts, their attendant gaolers, pimps and prostitutes, cast-offs from the English gentry and 30,000 sheep. In all, apart from the poor, bewildered Aborigines, who had retired to the hinterland, this huge sub-continent of three million square miles, twenty-five times the size of the British Isles, then supported a mere 400,000 people. Its commerce was non-existent, its agriculture in a shambles. By all standards of the day, the future of Australia looked very bleak indeed. Then, in March, 1851, gold was discovered at Bathurst, in New South Wales, and later that year, at Ballarat and Bendigo, in Victoria. A rerun of the great Californian gold rush of 1849 followed. The yield of the Australian gold fields was prodigious, as much as 65,000 ounces a week, and was the making of the colony. Within eight years the population had risen to over one million, and the balance of trade with Britain had turned in Australia's favour. Gold was still the most valuable export, but the sheep population stood at twenty-million, and wool production was 2,000 tons a month, all of which was readily absorbed by the mills of the mother country. The demand for fast ships to move people and goods between Britain and Australia became greater than ever.

In the forefront of the Australian sea trade was James Baines, whose legendary Black Ball Line operated eighty-six cargo/passenger ships and employed 300 officers and 3,000 seamen. A Black Ball clipper, with its distinctive black hull and white masts with black yards, sailed from Liverpool on the fifth of every month without fail. The ships were under contract to the Government to carry the mails and make the outward passage within sixty-five days, or suffer a penalty. It was inevitable then, that in a world of fast sailing clippers, James Baines' were the hardest driven, yet they offered a surprising degree of comfort to their passengers. Games and music were provided above and below decks, a cow was carried to give milk, and there were baths for all classes of passengers; little enough by today's standards, but for the 1850s, unimaginable luxury.

The 1,050-ton *Indian Queen* was one of the Black Ball Line's best. Built at Miramichi, New Brunswick in 1852, her hull was of hackmatack and birch sheathed with yellow metal, and she rated A1 at Lloyd's. She was a handsome three-decker, with accommodation for cabin and steerage passengers said to be the finest ever seen on the Australian run. On her first voyage, with Captain Jobson in command, she made the round trip to Melbourne in six months and eleven days, including time in port. While she was not as fast as her sister ship, the famous *Marco Polo*, she was nevertheless a credit to her builders and owners.

On 13 March, 1859, the *Indian Queen* sailed from Melbourne, bound for Liverpool with a full cargo of wool, forty passengers and a strongroom crammed with bags of gold dust. In command was Captain Brewer, who had under him a crew of thirty-two, included in which was his own son, an apprentice in the ship. Ahead of them lay a voyage of some 15,000 miles, stretching, perhaps, to as much as three months. Winter was approaching in the Southern Hemisphere, and they would face hardship and danger in plenty, but their greatest enemy would be boredom. For seventy-three people, including three women and seven children, to be confined together in a vessel 200 feet long by 35 feet in the beam, on strict water rationing and a monotonous diet, was to test the tolerance of human nature to destruction. The majority of the *Indian Queen*'s passengers were gold miners returning home with their spoils; a rough lot, hard drinking and foul mouthed, but no more so than her crew. These were clipper-ship-men, the toughest of a tough breed, pushed to their absolute limits in the service of a ship that would tolerate no half measures. During the long voyage, grudges would emerge, arguments run fierce, and fighting follow as day follows night. Captain Brewer, for his own peace of mind, must seek out the quickest route to the east and north, so that not one unnecessary day was spent at sea.

Contrary to popular belief and the presentation of most maps and charts, the shortest distance between two points on the globe does not lie in a straight line, but in a curve following the invisible camber of the earth from horizon to horizon. It is not, however, possible to sail a ship exactly along a curved track without alterations of course being so frequent as to be a ridiculous burden. The compromise used by the mariner is to follow a great circle track, which involves altering course at a number of predetermined points, ten degrees of longitude apart. In this way, by making a small course correction every twenty-four hours or so, the ship keeps as nearly as can be expected to the curvature of the earth's surface. On a short passage, and on or near the Equator, a great circle track will show little gain, but on a long run in high latitudes the distance saved is considerable.

After leaving Melbourne, Captain Brewer, being a man in a hurry, decided to steer a great circle course once clear of the south island of New Zealand. This would take the *Indian Queen* down as far as sixty degrees south latitude, thus ensuring that, on the 6,000-mile leg to Cape Horn, she gained maximum advantage from the permanent westerlies of the Roaring Forties. The passage promised not be comfortable, for, running before the great tumbling seas that thundered unchecked around the bottom of the world, the clipper's decks, and often her accommodation, must be ever awash. The miles would fly by all right, but tearing blindly along through the blizzards, rainstorms and fog that haunted the region involved awesome risks. This was the time when the Antarctic ice field was at its furthest north, bringing with it drifting icebergs, some of them up to twenty miles long, and several hundred feet high.

Initially, the weather was as favourable as it can ever be in these waters, and eight days out of Melbourne the *Indian Queen* passed the lonely outpost of Campbell Island, 350 miles south of New Zealand, and shaped her course more to the east. Ahead lay 4,500 miles of empty ocean, with the frozen continent of Antarctica 900 miles to starboard. The thermometer had fallen like a stone, and the cold ate into the bones, but with the wind and sea acting with unusual restraint and the visibility remaining good, life on board the clipper was more than tolerable.

The fair weather stayed with the *Indian Queen* for another six days, enabling her to make excellent progress. Then, on 27 March, when halfway to the Horn, there was a sudden change of mood. The wind went around to the north-west and climbed to gale force; at the same time the visibility began to fall. By the morning of the 31st, when the ship was in 58° South, 151° West, and logging a steady twelve knots, she ran into patchy fog. In view of the uncertain visibility, it would now have been prudent to shorten sail, but Brewer, sensing he might be within reach of a record homeward passage, would have none of this. The *Indian Queen* pressed on under full sail.

The fog had turned to a drizzling rain when Second Mate Leyvret took over the watch at midnight that night. It was a black night, full of menace, with the cloud down to mast-top height, and the following seas flashing red and green in the glow of the sidelights as they galloped along on each side of the ship. The air was filled with the deep-throated, melancholy roar of the wind, the drumming of the sails and the sighing of the rigging, creating a booming Wagnerian chorus that matched the mood of the weather.

Standing with his feet well apart to meet the roll of the ship, oilskins gleaming wet in the light of the binnacle lamp, Leyvret cursed his lot as the first day of April moved into its opening hours. But the resentment at being dragged from a warm bunk to stand watch on such a night was little compared with the unease he felt at crashing along under all sail in limited visibility. It might be that the *Indian Queen* was in open waters a thousand miles from the nearest land, but she was also passing through the cruising grounds of the Antarctic icebergs. He could not but dwell on how, only four years earlier, Millar & Thompson's *Guiding Star* had met a brutal end in these waters on her second voyage.

One morning in March, 1855, just as dawn broke, the 2,013-ton *Guiding Star* found herself sailing straight into a deep bay in a vast berg sixty miles long, forty miles across and three-hundred feet high. Two other ships, which had been keeping company with the big four-master, also entered the bay, but by a series of short and desperate tacks, succeeded in escaping from the icy trap. The *Guiding Star*, being less manoeuvrable than the smaller ships, found herself caught on a lee shore and crashed headlong into the precipitous cliffs of gleaming ice. She capsized and foundered, taking with her all of her crew of forty and one-hundred-sixty passengers.

Depressed by his thoughts, cold and miserable, Leyvret became more and more apprehensive as the watch dragged on. There were times when, straining his eyes to pierce the darkness ahead, he thought he heard above the cacophony of the ship and storm in conflict, strange noises resembling the far off rumble of thunder. Leyvret was familiar with the sound of breakers, but he could not bring himself to believe his ears, until, as four bells rang out to mark the end of the second hour of the watch, he heard a startled cry from the lookout in the bows.

Leyvret ran to the fore end of the poop, and there stood gripping the rail, unable to see any danger, and uncertain of what action he should take. Then, as the curtain of rain slowly drew apart, there was the glint of ice on the port bow. For only a brief moment Leyvret stood transfixed, then he was running aft again, shouting for the quartermaster to put the helm down, and calling for all hands on deck.

The second mate's action was too late. As the *Indian Queen* began to swing slowly to starboard in answer to the helm, she struck the berg broadside-on and slid to an abrupt halt, jarring every timber in her stout hull. There was a tremendous crash as her tall mainmast snapped off at the deck and went over the side, bringing blocks, spars, rigging and shards of ice raining down on the heads of the men beneath.

What followed was all confusion. Captain Brewer rushed up on deck and, instead of taking charge of the situation, flew into a blind panic, and with the first mate and fifteen other crew members, swung out the port lifeboat and abandoned ship. When the first of the passengers, aroused from their sleep by the shock of the collision, arrived on the poop, they were met by a scene of indescribable chaos. The *Indian Queen* was lying beached at the foot of a huge iceberg and listing heavily to starboard. Her masts, sails and rigging were in a shambles, and her decks piled high with debris and ice. The port lifeboat was missing, the helm deserted, and there was no sign of the crew.

Fortunately, before absolute panic took hold, Leyvret and the ship's carpenter, Thomas Howard, appeared on the poop. The two men did their best to restore order, but they had little reassurance to offer. Their hurried inspection of the damage showed the bowsprit and mainmast, still suspended by their rigging, were hanging over the side, and all the upper sails and yards were damaged beyond repair. However, Howard's soundings of the bilges showed the ship was not making water. The other crew members remaining on board were the doctor, the purser, the boatswain, two able seamen, one ordinary seaman, two apprentices, one of them Captain Brewer's son, and the cooks and stewards; a total of fifteen men in all.

Leyvret, being the senior officer, took command, and divided the seamen and male passengers into watches. Young Brewer was sent to the wheel, while the others set about cutting away the mast and bowsprit, and clearing the decks of the debris. It was a Herculean task, but Leyvret was a driver, and by the time the first pale fingers of dawn touched the sky, the decks showed a semblance of order.

The *Indian Queen* was still lying with her port side aground on the iceberg, and the next priority was to ease her off. The crossjack, the lowest sail on the mizzenmast, and the spanker were still intact, and these were hauled around to catch the wind. As this operation was nearing completion, faint cries for help were heard. In the growing light, the missing lifeboat containing Captain Brewer and the others was seen close by. There was a big sea running, and the boat appeared to be without oars, for the occupants, other than appealing for help, made no effort to regain the ship. The cries grew fainter as the boat was swept past the ship and was swallowed up in the surrounding murk. This was the last ever seen of Captain Brewer and the sixteen men who had deserted the *Indian Queen* when she needed them most.

There was no time for those on board to dwell on what horrible fate would overcome Brewer and his men. Under the influence of the backed crossjack and spanker, the ship began to slide astern, and finally drifted clear of the berg. Howard once again sounded the bilges, and again they were dry, indicating that the hull was not breached. It was by now fully light—or as light as it would ever be in this grey world of fog and drizzle—and Leyvret turned his attention to the broken mainmast. The mast and the main yard were still attached to the ship by the rigging and dragging in the water on the starboard side. Before any effort could be made to make sail, this mess would have to be cut away.

Passengers and crew turned to willingly, and the axes rang out clearly in the cold air. An hour passed, and the wreckage was almost clear, when another huge berg loomed up out of the murk on the starboard quarter. The ship was drifting directly towards this new danger, and there was a rush to trim what sails remained aloft. The action was taken only just in time, and after ten minutes, that passed like ten hours, the *Indian Queen* slowly began to move ahead, still dragging the wreckage of the collision with her. She missed colliding with the second iceberg by less than a hundred yards, but the strain of the manoeuvre brought down her foremast, which fell on the longboat, reducing it to matchwood. This was the last remaining lifeboat; Brewer and the others having taken one, and the others smashed by gear falling from aloft. There was now no means of escape from the crippled *Indian Queen.*

Over the next forty-eight hours, led by Leyvret, passengers and crew worked in watches around the clock to clear away the wreckage hampering the ship. This was achieved by the morning of the 3 April, when the wind came away from the south, and with and assortment of improvised sails rigged, course was set in the general direction of Valpariso, 3,800 miles to the north-east. The wind was on the quarter, and the *Indian Queen* worked up to a speed of about four knots, but her progress was erratic, for she was still surrounded by ice, and great care was needed. At one stage she again narrowly avoided destruction when passing close to a huge tabular berg, which suddenly split in two. One half of the berg charged at the ship but fortunately came to a halt before a collision occurred. The clipper escaped with little more than wet decks, caused by the tidal wave created by the runaway berg.

It was 7 April, in latitude 49° South, before they saw the last of the ice. More sails were then rigged, and course shaped directly for Valpariso. The *Indian Queen* was soon making a steady five knots, and for the next thirty days, battered by an unending procession of gales, she fought her way to the north. On 7 May, she fell in with the New Bedford whaler *La Fayette* whose master boarded them and offered assistance. Having come thus far, Leyvret declined a tow, but as his chronometer had been smashed in the collision, he was pleased to compare positions with the whaler. The *Indian Queen's* longitude proved to be three degrees in error. Next day, the French warship *Constantine* appeared on the scene, and escorted the clipper towards port.

On 9 April, land was sighted twenty miles south of Valpariso, and the *Constantine* went on ahead to carry news of the *Indian Queen's* arrival. Next morning, as the clipper approached Valpariso, boats from HMS *Ganges*, which was visiting the port, came out and towed her into the roads. There, forty days after colliding with the iceberg in 60°South, the *Indian Queen* came to anchor. It was some months before word reached James Baines in Liverpool of the disaster that had befallen his ship and the loss of Captain Brewer and sixteen men.

Bernard Edwards

10   China Clipper

Flora Temple - 1859

On the first day of January, 1808, thanks largely to the efforts of William Wilberforce, the British Government outlawed the slave trade within its jurisdiction. It then brought its considerable weight to bear on other countries to do the same. However, this was the first serious attempt to lift a dark shadow that had hung over mankind for many centuries, and it was not a change that would take place overnight.

Twelve years later, in 1820, slavery was still very much alive in East Africa, as Captain Moresby, commanding a cruiser of the Cape anti-slavery squadron, would bear witness. He wrote:

The Arab dhows are largely unwieldy open boats without a deck. In these vessels temporary platforms of bamboos are erected, leaving a narrow passage in the centre. The Negroes are then stowed, in the literal sense of the word, in bulk, the first along the floor of the vessel, two adults side by side, with a boy or girl resting between them, until the tier is complete. Over them the first platform is laid, supported an inch or two clear of their bodies, when a second tier is stowed, and so on until they reach above the gunwale of the vessel. The voyage, they expect, will not exceed 24 or 48 hours; but it often happens that a calm or unexpected land breeze delays their progress. In this case a few hours are sufficient to decide the fate of the cargo. Those of the lower portion of the cargo that die cannot be removed. They remain until the upper part are dead and thrown over. And from a cargo of from 200 to 400 stowed in this way, it has been known that not a dozen at the expiration of ten days have reached Zanzibar.

Another six years were to pass before it could be claimed that all slaves in the British colonies were free men. In other countries, notably the Spanish and Portuguese possessions overseas, the curse of slavery lingered on for another twenty-five years or so. But thanks to the work of Captain Moresby and his fellow officers of the Royal Navy, fresh slaves were exceedingly hard to come by in those years.

When, in the wake of Christopher Columbus, the Spaniards conquered the Caribbean island of Cuba, they found a land of hot sunshine, frequent rains, and a rich red soil of amazing fertility. Cuba was, in fact, an ideal place to grow sugar and tobacco, and this the

Spaniards did with considerable success. Such crops, however, require a great deal of labour, a commodity then in short supply on the island. Many of the native Indians had been put to the sword during the conquest, and most of the survivors took refuge in the forests and mountains. White men, even if enough were available, could not, and would not take on hard physical labour in such a climate, so an alternative had to be found. The first consignment of slaves arrived in Cuba from the Gulf of Guinea in 1521, and from then on the island never lacked for labour. As the expendable negroes died of hard work, disease, or sheer brutality—and they did so in their thousands—so ships were employed bringing a steady stream of replacements over from Africa. That was until Wilberforce began his crusade. By the mid-1800s, the Spanish slave masters found themselves with a rapidly declining workforce and looked around for an alternative supply of bodies.

Nine thousand miles due west of Cuba, in the South China Sea lay the Sikiang Valley, where sugar cane had been cultivated for hundreds of years. Coincidentally, by the 1850s the population of the valley had grown to such an extent that, for all its great fertility, the land could not support all those who lived and worked there. There was, therefore, in this province of China, a surplus of labour highly skilled in the growing of sugar, a ready-made workforce, of which the Spanish landowners of Cuba were quick to take advantage. Under an agreement signed with the Chinese Government, coolies were indentured to an estate for five years, on completion of which they would have the option of re-engaging as free labourers. After ten years in Cuba, they would qualify for a free passage back to China, or ten acres of land on which to settle in the island. For poor Chinese peasants with no future other than a life of hard work and poverty in their own land, Cuba offered an attractive alternative.

The system was intended to be closely supervised by both governments, but in reality, if became just another form of slavery. The contracts signed were worthless, and unscrupulous officials sold the coolies to the Cuban planters for 400 dollars apiece. When they reached the island, the poor ignorant wretches found they were contracted to work for eight years at the starvation wage of four dollars a month. At the end of this term, they were usually so heavily in debt to their masters that they were obliged to stay in Cuba until they could work no more. Even then there was no free passage back to China, and they were then turned out into the forests to fend for themselves. Yet, so desperate was the situation in the Sikiang Valley that there was never a shortage of recruits converging on the Portuguese trading station of Macao, at the mouth of the Sikiang River, all eager to take ship for Cuba.

Throughout history, man's insatiable search for gold has taken him down into the depths of depravity, but at the same time has resulted in some of his most spectacular technological advances.

Bernard Edwards

When, in December, 1848, James W. Marshall discovered gold at Sutter's sawmill, in the foothills of California's Sierra Nevadas, there was an immediate demand for fast transport from New York to the West Coast. The journey overland, on horseback or by stagecoach, was a dangerous gamble that few could win. The only alternative route was by sea, and the demand for ships to service this route became so great in so short a time that it was impossible to meet. Freight rates from New York to San Francisco rocketed to sixty dollars a ton, and a new ship could pay for herself in one round voyage. And so the clipper ship was born; not to carry maximum cargo with maximum economy, as had always been the golden rule, but to reel off the miles as had never been done before.

As might be expected, the American clipper was the best; the sleekest, the fastest, the envy of the maritime world. Shipyards from New Brunswick to Baltimore churned them out as fast suitable timber could be found and cut. For almost ten years they carried the cream of the cargoes; the gold, the opium, the tea, and the flood of emigrants out of a troubled Europe to the new worlds overseas. Then, as so often happens, the boom came to an unforeseen and abrupt end. In 1857, America ran into a severe economic depression that was to lead to civil war four years later, and overnight there were too many ships on the market. Freight rates plummeted, and the proud Yankee clippers, which once carried only the best, found themselves scouring the ports of the world for whatever cargo was on offer. The *Flora Temple* was among their ranks.

Built at Baltimore in 1853, and owned by Abraham & Oshcroft, of that port, the *Flora Temple* was a wood-built clipper of 1,915 tons, commanded by Captain Johnson, and carrying a crew of fifty. On the morning of 8 October, 1859, she sailed from Macao with 850 Chinese contract labourers on board, bound for Havana. She was embarking on a voyage that would take her the length of the South China Sea, through the Sunda Strait into the Indian Ocean, around the Cape of Good Hope, and north-westwards through the South Atlantic to the Caribbean. The distance to cover was in excess of 14,000 miles, and, depending on the weather experienced, Captain Johnson expected to be at sea for anything up to a hundred days.

In contemplating such a long voyage with 850 Chinese peasants cooped up on board, Johnson knew he was courting trouble, for his crew would at all times be greatly outnumbered. Before sailing from Macao, therefore, he had a stout barrier erected across the mid-part of the ship from bulwark to bulwark. In this way, the Chinese passengers were confined to the fore part of the vessel, while his crew had free movement aft of the barrier. Two locked gates gave access to the foredeck, so that the anchors and sails might be tended as and when needed.

The South China Sea, even for the modern ship equipped with

sophisticated navigational aids, is an area of great hazard. The skies are frequently overcast, typhoons come barrelling in from the far reaches of the Pacific, and currents are unpredictable. Scattered in the path of the shipping lanes are hundreds of tiny, low-lying islands, submerged reefs and coral heads, on which many a fine ship has come to grief. Ferocious sharks haunt the depths, while on the surface piracy still lives on. In the 19th century, when most maritime commerce was carried by sail in this region, and position fixing depended on the sun and stars, the South China Sea was a navigator's nightmare.

When the *Flora Temple* cleared Macao harbour the weather was set fair, with a gentle north-east monsoon blowing; hardly enough wind to belly her sails. It was the height of the typhoon season, and the modest eight knots the clipper settled down to was not to the liking of Captain Johnson. He was anxious to press on southwards before the inevitable tropical storm came tracking across from the east.

Macclesfield Bank, a large area of submerged coral reefs lying 370 miles south of Macao, was safely rounded on the night of the 10th, with the weather continuing fine and the barometer steady. Contrary to expectations, the Chinese coolies seemed quite content with their lot. This may have had a lot to do with the weather being warm and dry, allowing them to move about freely on the foredeck. Additionally, the men were well fed by their own cooks, and their leaders exercised a tight control over them. But Johnson was not prepared to take risks, and the gates in the barricade were kept locked at night, and open during the day, but watched over by armed guards. No matter how docile the Chinese appeared, they still outnumbered his crew by seventeen to one.

Tuesday the 11th dawned fine and clear, with the *Flora Temple* on a south-westerly course and running free before a light wind. The sun came up with tropical suddenness, and began its climb to the zenith in a sky of flawless blue. Startled by the clipper's creaming bow-wave, shoals of tiny flying fish broke the surface and skimmed across a rippled sea of pure indigo in which early-morning dolphins played and not a shark dare show its ugly snout. It had the promise of an idyllic day to come. The gates in the barricades were opened, and the watch on deck moved freely amongst the coolies, who were up in large numbers, apparently enjoying the warm sunshine.

The scene was so full of innocence and normality that, at seven o'clock, the guard at the port-side gate of the barricade felt it safe to leave his post. He headed towards the galley, from which emanated the tantalising smell of freshly brewed coffee. The man had not been gone more than a few minutes when pandemonium broke out on the forecastle head, where a group of coolies were seen to be milling about in apparent panic. Smoke was seen issuing from a hatchway, and the cry of 'Fire!' was heard.

In any ship at sea, fire is a danger not to be ignored, and the

Flora Temple's watch on deck lost no time in running forward to investigate. The panicking Chinese indicated the fire was in the steerage accommodation, and the sailors disappeared below.

There was no fire, of course, and while the watch was occupied below, the coolies poured through the open gates of the barricade. The guard on the starboard gate was hacked to death with his own cutlass, and the mob, armed with axes, belaying pins and marlin spikes, made a rush for the after cabin. Fortunately, at that moment Captain Johnson appeared on the poop. He immediately gave the alarm and ran to his cabin for his revolver. The ship's surgeon, Dr Childs, and Captain Johnson's brother, a passenger on board, also armed themselves, and the three men fired over the heads of the advancing horde. This stopped the Chinese in their tracks, and faced by another fusillade, they retreated behind the barricade, but not before they had killed another seaman and wounded several others.

When order had been restored, the wounded attended to, and the dead buried, Johnson held an investigation into the outbreak of violence. Some of the Chinese were questioned, and they revealed that a plot to take over the ship had been hatched soon after leaving Macao. The apparent good behaviour of the coolies was a deliberate ploy to lull the *Flora Temple*'s crew into a false sense of security—and it had worked. The cook's meat axes were stolen from the galley on the night before the attack, and the plan was to murder all the white men. Only the prompt action by Johnson and his brother, and the surgeon, had foiled the attempt.

The mutiny was a frightening reminder to Johnson that he and his men were very heavily outnumbered by the Chinese, and the situation would be thus for at least another three months, during which things could only get worse. It was suggested that the coolies be confined below decks for the rest of the voyage, but Johnson rejected this as impracticable. Neither could the gates in the barricade be kept locked at all times, for the crew must have access to the foredeck in order to tend the sails and rigging. In which case the ship would continue to be vulnerable. There only remained to exercise extreme vigilance. Johnson armed all his officers with revolvers, shared out all available cutlasses amongst the crew, and prayed for a miracle.

The miracle, although it was perhaps not recognised as such, came very quickly. During the rest of that day, the barometer fell rapidly, the wind veered, and a long swell rolled in from the north. To Johnson's experienced eye this suggested a typhoon passing to the north, probably not close enough to be of great danger to the ship, but it was sure to make its presence known. The captain's appreciation of the weather was correct. The next dawn came in complete contrast to the one before, with heavily overcast skies, and the wind around to the south-west and blowing a full gale. By noon, the *Flora Temple* was hove-to with the wind ahead, and plunging her bowsprit into angry seas that swept her fore-deck from end to end. The 850

Widow-Maker

Chinese passengers, most of whom had never seen the sea before they boarded this ship—let alone a sea in such a vindictive mood—were both frightened and seasick. They disappeared below decks and stayed there.

For forty-eight hours, the clipper, with minimum sail set, rode out the gale, battered by fierce rain squalls that reduced the visibility to a matter of yards. Her crew, fully occupied in ensuring the ship's survival, had little time to dwell on the threat their passengers posed.

When, on the morning of the 14th, the wind at last eased, Johnson was reluctant to make more sail, for having been without sights for two days, he was unsure of the ship's position. He was unable to calculate what progress she had made to the south and west, if any, while riding out the gale, nor how the current had been running during that time. By dead reckoning, he judged her to be somewhere off the northern end of the extensive area of dangerous reefs that runs parallel to Borneo's northern coast for some 500 miles. How close he was to these reefs, he could not tell, but his instinct told him to take great care. The reefs were steep-to, and soundings would give no indication of danger. Johnson posted extra lookouts in the rigging and warned his officers to exercise extreme vigilance. He could do no more.

The sun did not show again that day, but when night came without even a sight of discoloured water, Johnson felt able to relax, and left the poop for his first real meal of the day. When, just before seven-thirty, he returned on deck, his first move was to send the officer of the watch forward to check if the lookout at the topsail yard had anything to report. The officer was not halfway along the deck when the man aloft cried out that breakers were in sight on the port bow.

Johnson heard the warning, and immediately put the helm hard up and ordered the spanker to be lowered. The sail came down with a run and the *Flora Temple* began to swing quickly to starboard. As she canted, the officer of the watch ran aft, calling for the helm to put down. He had seen more breakers on the starboard bow.

The boom of the breakers now became audible, and soon a necklace of foaming surf was seen stretching from three points on the port bow to four points to starboard. The clipper was rushing headlong into a crescent-shaped trap. Urged on by Johnson and his officers, the hands worked like men possessed to bring the ship about, but, in the room available, this was an impossibility.

The *Flora Temple* struck lightly at first, and it seemed she might run over the reef into deep water, then, with a jarring crash, she came to a complete halt, listing heavily to port. Splintered timbers coming to the surface on the port side told their own story.

Within minutes, the dark, overcast night was full of terror. The stricken ship lay over on her side with the seas breaking right over her, and water pouring into her broken hull. From forward came a spine-chilling chorus of anguish as the water entered the crowded steerage accommodation. And it was this, more than the grounding of the ship, which struck fear into the hearts of the *Flora Temple*'s crew. It reminded them that the clipper carried only five lifeboats, sufficient to take a maximum of 100 of the 900 persons on board. Should the Chinese decide to rush the boats there could be only one result.

As yet, Johnson had no intention of abandoning the ship, but at 10 o'clock, in order to calm the fears of his men, he ordered the two quarter boats to be lowered. With an officer and five men in each, these were ordered to stand off and be ready to move in and take the rest of the crew off, should the situation warrant it. Unpredictably, the Chinese made no move to come aft, nor did they even appear on deck.

At midnight, when the ship began to show signs of breaking up, two more boats were lowered, and all the crew, with the exception of Captain Johnson and fourteen men, left the ship. The remaining boat, the longboat, was proving difficult to launch, and at the same time, Johnson was reluctant to leave his ship. It was four hours later before the longboat was finally manhandled over the side, and Johnson, having accepted the inevitable, went with her. Soon after daybreak, the five boats passed through the breakers, leaving the *Flora Temple* to her fate. Lying fast on the reef with her back broken and the seas making a clear breach over her starboard quarter, she was a pitiful sight, more so for the hundreds of bewildered Chinese crowding her decks, left to the mercy of the sea.

Not long after the boats left the ship they ran into a heavy gale and were separated. A week later, the French warship *Gironde* came across the longboat, and picked up Captain Johnson and fourteen of his crew. They were landed in French Indo China, where Johnson, to his credit, made strong representations to the authorities to mount a rescue mission to look for other survivors. His request was granted, and within a few hours, the *Gironde* left port again, with Johnson, his brother and Dr Childs on board.

No trace was found of the *Flora Temple*'s other lifeboats, and it was assumed they must have foundered in the gale encountered soon after leaving the ship. When, on 2 November, the *Gironde* reached the wreck, only part of the clipper's bows remained above water. Of the 850 Chinese contract labourers there was no sign. Their grave is to this day marked as a tiny dot on the South China sea chart called Flora Temple Reef.

11   East to the Horn

General Grant - 1866

The longest day's run ever logged by any sailing ship was 465 nautical miles in twenty-three hours seventeen minutes by the Liverpool ship *Champion of the Seas,* commanded by Captain Alex Newlands. Running before a north-westerly gale in the South Indian Ocean, she averaged 19.97 knots, a speed to challenge any modern container ship powered by turbocharged diesels and burning two-hundred tons of oil a day.

When she made this record run, the *Champion of the Seas* was, as would be expected, making her easting through the Roaring Forties, that 600-mile-wide corridor of open water that spans the bottom of the world between the southern continents and the Antarctic pack ice. It was here, in the heyday of sail, that ship and men were tested to the absolute limits of endurance, ever running before the monstrous seas in the pursuit of commercial gain. Those deep, cold waters are littered with the bones of those who tried and failed; those who took just one risk too many and paid the ultimate price.

Captain William Loughlin was a man not averse to a calculated risk, and when, on 4 May 1866, he took the *General Grant* out of Melbourne, he was looking for a record passage to Land's End. Owned by Boyes, Richardson & Company, of Boston, Massachusetts, the 1,103-ton *General Grant* was manned by a crew of thirty-seven, and carried forty-five cabin class passengers, the usual mix of miners, merchants and military. She had a full cargo of wool in her holds, plus nine tons of zinc concentrates.

With the help of two steam tugs, the *General Grant* was eased off her berth in Melbourne and towed out into Port Phillip Bay. As soon as the ship was clear of shallow waters, Loughlin dismissed the tugs and set all sail, anxious to reach the open sea. Luck was not on his side. The wind was light and variable, and it was next morning before the *General Grant* had crossed the forty-mile deep bay and escaped through the headlands. It was not a promising start to a long voyage.

Grudgingly, the light winds blowing off the coast of Victoria gave way to a strong easterly, and the *General Grant* was clear of the island of Tasmania by the morning of the 6th. From then on, with the easterlies persisting and increasing to gale force, the clipper was forced to fight hard for every mile she gained on her 6,000-mile run to Cape Horn. Close-hauled on the port tack, pitching and rolling heavily, and with her decks and much of the accommodation awash, life was difficult for her crew, and sheer purgatory for her passengers. The wind was the reciprocal of that normally prevailing in the area, but Loughlin was confident the strong westerlies would soon arrive. Meanwhile, he shaped his course to pass midway between the southern tip of New Zealand and the Auckland Islands, 200 miles further south, and revised his original estimate of rounding the Horn by the end of the month.

The easterly gales continued to blow until the morning of the 13th, and Loughlin's confidence in the Roaring Forties began to wane. Then, later on in the day, the wind suddenly dropped, and with hardly a pause, came away strongly from the west. This, at last, was the following wind he had been waiting for, and Loughlin took full advantage of it. Every stitch of canvas was crammed on, and the *General Grant* flew headlong before the wind, showing a clean pair of heels to the seas that came rolling in astern of her like galloping white-maned horses. As time went on, the seas grew larger and wilder, gaining on the ship and lifting her stern high in the air as they passed under her. Loughlin was courting danger, for if the *General Grant* faltered in her stride and was pooped by one of these waves she would broach-to with disastrous consequences.

Since leaving Tasmania astern the skies had been heavily overcast with no opportunity for sights, so Loughlin was navigating by dead reckoning. His calculations, based on guesswork more than anything else, put the ship midway between the south island of New Zealand and the Aucklands. A cold drizzle was falling, and the visibility was not good, but with a hundred miles of clear water on either side of the ship, or so he thought, Loughlin deemed it safe to press on at all possible speed. In doing so, he committed a grave error of seamanship.

Soon after dark that evening, the wind suddenly fell away, but borne on the crests of the following seas, the *General Grant* coasted on into the gathering gloom. A sixth sense warned Loughlin that something was wrong, but he could see nothing and hear nothing. Only minutes later his worst fears were realised when breakers were sighted right ahead. It was at first assumed there was ice, possibly a berg, ahead, then, to the horror of those on deck it became apparent that the waves were breaking on a line of jagged rocks. And beyond them, rising sheer out of the sea for almost 400 feet, was a wall of precipitous black cliffs. The *General Grant*, swept off her course by more than one hundred miles, had found the Aucklands.

The Auckland Islands, discovered by Captain Abraham Bristow in the whaler *Sarah* in 1806, lie in latitude 51° South and 200 miles south-south-west of New Zealand. Made up of one large island, twenty miles by fifteen and rising to a maximum height of 1,325 feet, and several smaller islands and isolated rocks, the Aucklands stand square in the path of the Roaring Forties. All the islands are steep-to on their western coasts, the rocky cliffs rising out of the sea to a height of 750 feet in places. For much of the year, these inhospitable shores are shrouded in rain, snow or fog, and in the 19th century many ships met an untimely end here. The Aucklands were the outer ramparts of the infamous Cape Horn itself, forbidding, brooding; lying in wait to destroy those who would dare to take up the challenge of the Great Southern Ocean. A whaling station was set up on the main island in 1850, which it was hoped would become a permanent settlement, but was doomed to early failure. Covered only with coarse grass and scrub; cold, damp and swept by an endless procession of westerly gales, the Aucklands are not for human habitation. After stoically enduring two years of the dreadful weather—they saw only two fine days in this time—a disappointing catch, and supplies so irregular that they often came near to starvation, the whalemen bowed to nature and left for good.

As soon as the breakers were sighted, Loughlin tried to go about, but without wind to fill her sails, the clipper was dead to the helm. It was that old, recurring nightmare that haunts all seamen suddenly become reality. The helpless ship, carried on the back of a great surging ground swell, was lifted clean over the rocks and hurled at the precipitous cliff face.

The *General Grant* hit the cliff head-on, the impact being taken by her seventy-foot jib boom, which crumpled and snapped off at the stem. The ship bounced back off the cliff and was swept stern first by the current for half a mile southwards, before being brought up by rocks. This time her spanker boom and rudder went. Released of all restraint, the wheel spun viciously, caving in the frightened helmsman's ribs, a hail of debris fell from aloft, and the ship, caught by the stern, pivoted on the rocks. A dreadful grinding noise rose above the boom of the breakers.

Just when it seemed the clipper was hard and fast, she broke free of the rocks. The current took hold of her, canted her around until her bows were once again facing the land, and another big swell launched her at the cliff face. The men on her decks saw death coming and screamed in horror. Clinging to rails, stanchions and the rigging, they braced themselves for the crash that would mean the end, but it did not come. The *General Grant* appeared to sail straight through the cliff and came slowly to a halt, afloat, upright, and apparently unharmed.

The darkness was total; black as the depths of Hell itself. Loughlin ordered flares to be lit, and it soon became clear that, by an amazing stroke of luck, the ship had sailed through an unseen fissure in the cliffs, and into an enormous cavern. The harsh light of the flares revealed the cavern to be about 250 yards long and so high that the *General Grant*'s 150-foot-high mainmast disappeared into the darkness overhead. Soundings taken at the stern showed twenty-five fathoms of water under the ship.

The relief felt by those in the *General Grant* at their apparent deliverance was short-lived. The ground swell that had driven the clipper into this incredible trap continued to surge at the mouth of the cavern, its residual energy pushing the ship deeper and deeper into the unknown darkness. Then the truck of her foremast scraped against the roof, and large pieces of rock showered down on her foredeck, stoving in the forecastle head. It was only a matter of seconds before the mast carried away, and with all its attendant sails and rigging, came crashing down. The main topgallant mast followed, bringing down another fall of rock accompanied by broken spars and rigging. Men buried under the rubble screamed and died, adding a new horror to this fearful chain of events.

Throughout the rest of that night, long terror-filled hours, the *General Grant* laboured in the grip of the incoming swell, dashing herself against the walls of her prison, while her remaining masts rammed into the roof of the cavern each time she lifted. And all the while, outside in the world to which she would never return, the wind howled mournfully and the breaking sea boomed, adding to the terror of those entombed with her. Towards dawn, the inevitable happened; on a particularly big swell, the clipper reared upward, her forty-inch diameter mainmast rammed the roof of the cavern, and was driven clean through her bottom. The *General Grant* began to sink.

Up to this point, because of the darkness and the confusion on board, Captain Loughlin had made no attempt to lower any boats. But with the ship now going down under them, and a faint, grey light beginning to creep into the cave, he turned his mind to saving the lives of his passengers and crew. Only three boats remained undamaged, insufficient to take all the survivors. This problem was easily solved, for when the boats were launched, many of the passengers were too frightened to leave the ship. Loughlin, as befitted his command, elected to stay with them, telling the boats to return later to take them off.

The three boats pulled for the mouth of the cavern, fear lending prodigious strength to the arms of the men at the oars. One boat capsized in the breakers at the entrance, and all its occupants were lost. The other two broke free into the open sea, and as they did so, the *General Grant*, battered and holed, gave up her long struggle and sank, taking all those on board with her. Some hours later, the two boats, containing between them only fifteen men, all that was left of the eighty-three people on board the ship, succeeded in landing on an island six miles further down the coast.

On the following day, the fifteen survivors, still not fully recovered from their distressing ordeal, explored the island—and suffered a crushing disappointment. They would not want for water, as the rain was unending, but the island was totally barren. They could find no animals, no fruits, no berries, no food of any kind, not even edible roots. It seemed bitterly ironical that after all they had been through, and come out alive, they were now doomed to die of starvation. But the very fact that these fifteen men had survived, while sixty-eight others died, proved that they were tough and resourceful. One of their number, an Irishman named Jack Teer, emerged as a leader, and under his direction, shellfish were collected, which sustained them until they managed to kill an old seal on the beach. Later, wild goats were discovered on the other side of the island, and the cooking pots were kept filled.

After four weeks on the island, which in view of their original impression, the survivors named Disappointment Island, they were forced to come to terms with the reality that their stay might be a very long one. A regular procession of ships bound from Australia around Cape Horn passed the Aucklands, but due to the constant bad weather, they normally gave the islands a wide berth. When, months later, the *General Grant* was posted missing, ships would be asked to keep a lookout for her, but there would be no organised search. Certainly no ship would call at the Aucklands, except in a case of emergency. A handful of survivors from the topsail schooner *Grafton*, wrecked on the islands in January 1864, had waited nineteen months before being rescued. In May of that same year, the 888-ton square-rigger *Invercauld* came to grief on the north side of the main island, and only three of her crew were still alive a year later. They were rescued by a Portugeuse ship that had anchored off for repairs after springing a leak. It was later realised that the survivors from both the *Grafton* and the *Invercauld* were together on the islands for some months, and yet were not aware of each other's presence. Such was the total isolation of the Auckland Islands.

Thanks to the discovery of the wild goats, the *General Grant*'s survivors would not want for food, but with only a few sheath knives between them, they were in desperate need of tools to build a shelter. It was known that the *Grafton* had gone ashore on Adams Island, which lies to the south of the main island, and Jack Teer volunteered to lead a foraging party to look for any implements left behind. Taking advantage of a rare break in the weather Teer and his party sailed one of the *General Grant*'s boats the seventeen miles to Adams Island, but their rewards were not great. After an extensive search of the island, they came across a tumble-down wooden hut, probably built by the whalers in the 1850s. This yielded only a rusty shovel, a file and a flint. When they returned to Disappointment Island, the file was used to fashion a number of crude miniature boats, which were launched carrying messages it was thought someone in the outside world might find. It was a pathetic, futile gesture, but the fifteen men marooned at the bottom of the world desperately needed something to hope for.

Winter turned to summer, and then back to winter again, although the passing of the seasons showed very little variation in the foul weather. At last, in September 1867, having been on the island for sixteen months, the men finally accepted that no rescue ship would come. It was then decided to make an attempt to reach New Zealand. One of the boats was fitted out as best as possible and First Mate Brown and three others set out to cross the 200 miles of stormy water to Invercargill. They were never seen again, and it is presumed their boat capsized and they were drowned.

Soon after the boat left Disappointment Island, scurvy struck the camp. This loathsome disease, brought on by a prolonged lack of fresh fruit and vegetables, was the scourge of the sea in the eighteenth century, sometimes killing half a ship's crew on a long voyage. The progression of scurvy is swift and terrible. Its victims become weak in body and mind. Their gums become swollen and suppurating; their teeth fall out; they are wracked by aches and pains; limbs swell and constant haemorrhaging occurs, resulting in death. Yet, deadly though the disease is, it is easily treatable, the patient requiring only vitamin C to bring about a complete and rapid recovery. There was no vitamin C in any form on the Aucklands, but Jack Teer, again a tower of strength in a crisis, fought off the disease by the simple expedient of not allowing the men to become inactive, using a whip on them when necessary. Only one man died.

In November, 1867, the New Zealand brig *Amherst*, commanded by Captain Gilroy, was cruising in the seas around the Auckland Islands looking for whales, when she picked up one of the miniature boats launched by the castaways more than a year earlier. The message, giving the location of the men, was still readable, but the *Amherst* spent nearly three weeks combing the islands, before the smoke from a campfire on Disappointment Island led her to the right spot. The ten men were taken off on 21 November, but did not reach Melbourne until March, 1868, almost two years after they sailed from that port.

And that, it would seem, was the end of the *General Grant*. There was no call for a search to be made for her last resting place, for she was just another entry in the catalogue of hundreds of ships lost annually in the days of sail. Her bones, and the bones of those who went down with her, were destined to lie forever undisturbed in their hidden grave on the western coast of Auckland Island. Then, many years later, it was realised that no zinc ore was mined in Australia until twenty-two years after the *General Grant* was lost, and questions were asked regarding the nine tons of zinc said to be in her cargo. It did not take long for records to be found showing the so-called zinc concentrates to be gold from the mines at Ballarat; nine tons of it, worth an incredible amount at today's rates. There was probably more, for many of her passengers were miners, and they will almost inevitably have been carrying small personal fortunes in gold dust or nuggets in their baggage.

The race was soon on to find the *General Grant*'s gold. Over the years that followed, a number of salvage expeditions were mounted, some small, some large. However, the survivors all died without revealing the exact location of the wreck, and the unceasing gales that assault the western side of Auckland Island have frustrated all efforts to find the cavern that holds the *General Grant* fast.

Ironically, in 1866, after the wreck of the *Invercauld* and the *Grafton*, HM Colonial steamship *Victoria* had visited the Aucklands and set up a depot containing provisions for the use of shipwrecked mariners. The survivors of the *General Grant* were unaware of the existence of this depot.

Bernard Edwards

12   The Long Haul

The Tea Clippers - 1866

In the mid-1850s, with the Californian gold rush in full swing, hordes of fortune hunters, drawn from all parts of the world, thronged the city of New York. Their aim was to secure the fastest possible transportation to the Pacific coast. The trans-America railway was still some twenty years away and overland travel was often a dangerous gamble, sometimes ending in death by violence, starvation or thirst. The only route which offered these men a reasonable chance of survival lay on the sea, via Cape Horn. It was to this end the first clipper ships were built. Their success was immediate.

The record time for the passage from New York to San Francisco was set up in 1851 by the Californian clipper *Flying Cloud*, built by the celebrated Donald Mackay of Boston. With every scrap of sail in her locker set, masts vibrating and sleek hull crashing through the water at speeds sometimes in excess of twenty knots, the *Flying Cloud* covered the 14,500 miles in question in eighty-nine days twenty-one hours.

In their day the clippers, and in particular those engaged in the China tea trade, were the subject of enormous publicity, sending the press into convulsions each time a sail was unfurled in earnest. Their evocative names were constantly on the lips of an admiring public on both sides of the Atlantic, and often in the four-corners of the globe. The annual races from Foochow and Hong Kong to London were looked forward to with as much anticipation as the top sporting events of today. It was a poor man indeed who would not risk a wager, however small, on his favourite clipper ship.

Of course, it was easy for those safe on shore to endow the clippers with a romance all of their own. The clean lines and billowing white sails of these ships were enough to set the blood pumping in the stoniest of hearts. For the seamen involved it was another matter. On the long voyages—and they were always long—the food was monotonous in the extreme and often too rotten for a starving man to eat. Such was the low freeboard of the clippers and so hard were they driven, that the decks and accommodation were rarely dry, making life on and off watch a nightmare of dampness and discomfort. But all the hardships endured on deck paled into insignificance when a man went aloft. Here, on the swaying yards 150 feet above the sea, where the snapping canvas ran riot, it was an unending fight for survival—a fight which men lost with frightening regularity. Yet, despite all the hardships and dangers, there was immense prestige to be won, and few clipper men would have it otherwise.

The men who commanded the clippers were an elite, the likes of which the world may never see again. Speed was their god, on the altar of which they were prepared to sacrifice all human comfort, dignity and, when necessary, life itself. Obsessed with the need to pile on ever more and more sail, they would do so until it seemed the ship must drive herself under or, at the very least, lose her masts. But with a foresight borne of long experience, they knew just how far to push their ship and the elements. Their mode of discipline was often so harsh as to be completely outside the law, even in those unenlightened days. They used fists, clubs, and sometimes the gun, to back up their orders. They were respected and cosseted by their owners, feared and hated by their crews, but admired by all for their sheer, audacious professionalism.

The heyday of these 'wooden ships and iron men' was in the summer of 1866. In late May of that year, nine of Britain's finest clipper ships lay in the port of Foochow, on China's east coast, loading the first of the season's tea for the London market. The scene at the Pagoda Anchorage, eleven miles from the town and twenty-two from the sea, resembled a gathering of the clans, for eight of the tall ships were out of Scottish shipyards and no less than five were wholly Scottish owned.

Once loaded, the clippers would match canvas and cunning in a 16,000-mile race across the oceans, the object of which was to be the first ship into London Docks with the new season's tea. The successful captain would receive a personal bonus of £100, and his owners a premium of 10 shillings per ton on the cargo. In a day when many men counted their wealth in pennies, this was no mean inducement, but there was more at stake than mere gold. The men who sailed home the winning ship, from captain down to lowly cabin boy, would forever sit at the right hand of Poseidon, lord and master of the sea.

The race began on the evening of 29 May, when the *Ariel*, owned by Shaw, Lowther & Maxton of London, left Pagoda Anchorage in tow of the steam paddle tug *Island Queen*. Commanded by Captain John Keay, a man noted for his iron discipline, the 853-ton, 197-foot long *Ariel* carried 25,451 square feet of canvas and had such fine lines she was reputed to be able to glide through the water without a breath of wind to urge her on. Being the newest and largest of the clippers in the anchorage, she was the natural favourite with those placing money on the race in China and Britain. Loaded to her tropical marks with 14,000 chests of the finest teas, she looked set to cross the Min River bar at least twelve hours before her nearest challenger.

Activity in the anchorage increased to a fever pitch when the *Ariel* was seen pointing her long bowsprit downstream, for four other clippers were also very near to completion of loading. They were Scotland's best, the *Taeping*, 767 tons, owned by Alexander Rodger of Glasgow, the *Taitsing*, 815 tons, owned by Findlay & Longmuir of Greenock, the *Serica*, 708 tons, owned by James Findlay of Greenock and the *Fiery Cross*, 689 tons, owned by John Campbell of Glasgow. The tension was high as the last of the tea-chests were manhandled into the hatch coamings of these ships. The *Fiery Cross* was the first to ship her hatchboards and tarpaulins, and so consumed with the need to get away was her master, Captain Richard Robinson, that he sailed without signing the bills of lading for his cargo.

Meanwhile, twenty miles downriver, the much-fancied *Ariel* had run out of luck. Her tug was not powerful enough to tow her across the bar and she had been forced to anchor to await a slackening of the tide. Some hours later the *Fiery Cross*, in tow of a first-rate tug, glided past the anchored *Ariel* and headed out to sea. The night air rang loud with Captain Keay's bellows of frustration.

The *Ariel* finally reached the open sea fourteen hours later, in the forenoon of the 30th. By then, the *Taeping*, commanded by Captain MacKinnon, and the *Serica*, Captain G. Innes, were snapping at her heels. The *Taitsing*, with Captain Daniel Knutsford in command, was the last of the vanguard to sail, crossing the Min River bar on the 31st.

The 16,000-mile race was now on in earnest, with the four Scots, *Fiery Cross*, *Serica*, *Taeping* and *Taitsing* all determined to show their sterns to the lone English contender and favourite, the *Ariel*. The ships would follow a well-tried route down the South China Sea, passing first to the north and east of Formosa, and then on a dog's-leg course across to the coast of Indochina and south to the Sunda Strait, gateway to the Indian Ocean. The South China Sea was, and still is, a most hazardous area, often cursed with poor visibility and dotted with low islands, sunken reefs and hidden shoals. In the nineteenth century it was poorly surveyed and accurate charts were hard to come by. The many wrecks on its reefs were stark memorials to those who had been foolish enough to ignore the old seafaring rule of 'lead, log and lookout'.

Running free before a fresh north-easterly wind, the *Fiery Cross* led the way through the Bashi Channel, which runs between Formosa and the Philippines, and by 3 June was passing to the north of the Paracels, an extensive group of low coral islands and reefs 180 miles to the east of what is now Vietnam. Holding his south-westerly course until within fifty miles of the coast, Robinson brought the *Fiery Cross* around to head due south for the Natuna Islands, which lie to the north-west of Borneo and guard the approaches to the Sunda Strait. The wind was now in the south-west and freshening.

'Taeping' with the 'Fiery Cross' in hot pursuit.
(Photo: National Maritime Museum)

On 7 June, when to the east of Saigon, Robinson had the first sight of his pursuers since leaving the Min River, when a large full-rigged ship appeared briefly on the horizon astern. This was the *Ariel*, with the formidable Captain Keay using all his considerable skills in an effort to overtake his Scottish rival. The other clippers, although out of sight, were close behind.

At the Sunda Strait, the narrow passage between Java and Sumatra, the ships were once again well strung-out. *Fiery Cross* slipped past the doomed island of Krakatoa on the 18th, the *Ariel* and *Taeping* on the 20th and the *Serica*, with the *Taitsing* close in her wake, on the 22nd.

With strong south-easterly winds blowing in the Indian Ocean, all five ships made good time, the *Ariel* on one occasion logging 330 miles in a day and the *Fiery Cross* 328. The Scottish ship crossed to the south of Mauritius on 30 June, with the *Ariel* still lagging two days behind. At the Cape of Good Hope, which the *Fiery Cross* rounded on 15 July, the *Ariel* had gained a day and was pushing hard. Their nearest challenger, the *Serica*, was six days astern.

Once in the South Atlantic, despite the favourable run of the Benguela Current and strong south-east trades, the race lost its momentum. The *Fiery Cross* did not reach the Equator until sunset on 4 August, having averaged only 160 miles a day from the Cape. A few days later, she hit the Doldrums and came to an abrupt halt. On the 9th, while Robinson still fumed and trimmed his sails to tempt every passing cat's paw of wind, MacKinnon's *Taeping* clawed her way over the southern horizon. Sailing fitfully, the two ships kept company for the next eight days. During this time, there was no sight or sound of the others. Robinson and MacKinnon now assumed the outcome of the race would be decided between them. They were to be proved wrong.

By 17 August, the *Fiery Cross* and the *Taeping* had reached the furthest point west in their long, curving sweep out into the Atlantic. They were a thousand miles west of the Canaries and sniffing at the southern edge of the north-east trades, when the *Taeping* caught a favourable wind and, lifting her skirts, disappeared over the horizon. With the *Fiery Cross* still becalmed, it was Robinson's turn to taste bitter disappointment.

A further dramatic change of fortune occurred at the Azores. For the first time since her ill-fated attempt to be first across the Min River bar some three months earlier, the London-registered *Ariel* went into the lead. The *Taeping*, *Fiery Cross* and *Serica* were in hot pursuit, all four ships passing Flores on the same day. The *Taitsing* was three days behind and fighting to make up lost ground. With 1,500 miles to go and all ships running free before the prevailing south-westerly winds, it was still anyone's race, but the *Ariel*, with her greater sail area, had a slight advantage. Much would now depend on the individual sailing skills of the clipper masters.

As dawn broke off the Lizard on 5 September, the *Ariel* was alone and confidently in the lead when, to Captain Keay's amazement and chagrin, the *Taeping* loomed up out of the haze astern. MacKinnon, on the *Taeping*, was no less surprised, for the two ships had not seen each other for more than seventy days. Keay and MacKinnon were old rivals, both having at one time commanded the legendary *Ellen Rodger*, one of the fastest clippers ever to grace the China trade. The two men now prepared to do battle on a personal basis, the England/Scotland factor taking second place.

Crowding on every available stitch of canvas, the *Ariel* and *Taeping* raced up Channel side by side, running their gunwales under before a stiff west-south-westerly. At daybreak on the 6th, they picked up their pilots off Dungeness within minutes of each other and thundered on up through the Straits of Dover to the Downs. Here they were taken in tow by tugs and continued into the Thames Estuary. Unknown to them the *Serica* was a bare four hours astern.

Once more, as at Foochow, the balance of this great sailing race was tipped by steam. The *Taeping* had secured the best tug and she docked in London at 9.45 that night, just short of ninety-nine days on passage. Captain Keay, with his blood pressure at boiling point, brought the *Ariel* to her berth half an hour later, while the *Serica* locked in at 11.30 on the last of the tide. The unfortunate *Fiery Cross* did not reach the Downs until the 7th, and was there forced to anchor to ride out a gale. She berthed at 8 o'clock on the morning of the 8th. The back-marker in the race, the *Taitsing*, arrived in the river on the 11th.

Officially, the Scottish *Taeping* took the honours by a bowsprit, but there were no real winners in the race of 1866. With so many clippers arriving in the port within the space of a few days, the London market found itself with several million pounds of new tea on its hands—half a year's consumption for the whole of Britain, in fact. Prices fell heavily and, from then on, it was decided to discontinue the cargo premium for the first ship home. The annual clipper races still went on, but they were never the same again.

The gruelling clipper trade was the ultimate test of man and ship; the perfect marriage of human tenacity and skill with the products of the world's finest shipyards. But the sacrifices called for and the risks taken inevitably exacted a heavy toll. Men grew old before their time, died before their time; ships were lost when they should not have been lost. Captain MacKinnon, of the victorius *Taeping*, died in Cape Town on his next voyage, worn out at forty-one. Five years later, the *Taeping* was lost when she ran onto Ladd's Reef in the South China Sea, while on a voyage from Amoy to New York. Captain Innes died in the *Serica* with all but one of his crew, when she was wrecked on the Paracels in 1872. In that same year, the gallant *Ariel* also met her end, pooped while running her easting down in the Roaring Forties. Only the *Taitsing* and the *Fiery Cross* lived on into old age. The *Taitsing* was lost off the coast of Zanzibar in 1883 and the once-proud *Fiery Cross* came to a sad end in 1889, when she sank in the River Medway with her cargo of coal on fire. So the mighty fell, but they will never be forgotten.

Bernard Edwards

13   Disaster at Shadwan

Carnatic - 1869

The history of the Suez Canal goes back nearly 4,000 years before the French diplomat and engineer Vicomte Ferdinand Marie de Lesseps arrived on the scene. In the 12th Egyptian Dynasty, King Sesostris ordered a canal to be dug linking the Red Sea with the Nile, and traces of that construction are said to be still visible today. In 609 BC, more than a thousand years after Sesostris, another enterprising monarch, Necho, began a more ambitious project. His canal took ninety years to complete, during which time 120,000 labourers engaged on the task lost their lives. De Lesseps built his canal in under ten years, and with infinitely less loss of life. When completed, this canal ran from Port Said in the north to Suez in the south, a total of 103 miles. It had a depth of 26-feet 3-inches, a bottom width of 72-feet 2-inches, and was more than large enough to accommodate any ship of the day. The Suez Canal opened on 17 November, 1869, just three months too late for the Peninsular & Oriental Steam Navigation Company's steamer *Venetian* to take advantage of it. Certainly, the thirty-seven passengers who sailed in the ship from Southampton would have been spared a great deal of discomfort and danger, had the canal then been in operation.

The *Venetian* left Southampton on 28 August, 1869, and apart from a few summer storms, her voyage to Alexandria, via Marseilles, passed pleasantly enough. At Alexandria, a flyblown, noisome place made bearable only by the occasional sea breeze, the steamer, having reached the eastern limits of the landlocked Mediterranean, would turn around and retrace her steps back to northern waters. For her passengers, who were mainly army personnel and civil servants bound for India, the real trial was about to begin. They were to be taken overland by rail, first to Cairo and then to Suez, where they would join another ship. As the distance from Alexandria to Suez was a mere 200 miles the journey should have been a short and agreeable interlude in the sea voyage; an opportunity to become acclimatised to the ways of the East. In reality, it was a long-drawn-out ordeal that even the most seasoned traveller would not wish to repeat. Although the railway was only six years old, the engines were in an appalling state and constantly breaking down, the carriages dirty and dilapidated, the food atrocious and the officialdom of the Egyptian authorities unbelievable. Travelling only by day, and with an overnight stop in Cairo, the journey dragged out over three excruciating days, at the end of which the passengers were exhausted and thoroughly demoralised.

Arriving at Suez, which was hot, dusty, and, if anything even less inviting than Alexandria, the long-suffering travellers were greatly relieved at the first sight of the ship that was to take them on to Bombay. Seen from the quayside, the P & O steamer *Carnatic* represented an oasis of order in a land of chaos. Her paintwork was immaculate, her awnings scrubbed white and the uniformed figures on her decks had an air of benign authority and efficiency.

The 1,776-ton *Carnatic* built in 1862 by Samuda Brothers of London, was a typical ship of this age of upheaval at sea. With a sharply raked stem, complete with bowsprit and figurehead, tall masts and long, tapering yards fully rigged for sail, she was a direct descendent of the old East Indiamen. Her only visible concession to the new era was an ugly, black funnel conspicuous between her masts. Below that, and out of sight—and here was the difference—were two inverted compound engines, geared to a single propeller, and developing 884 initial horsepower. These gave her a service speed of twelve knots, and with the latest patent hydraulic steering gear installed, the *Carnatic* was a very superior ship. She carried British officers and petty officers, and Indian ratings; a total crew of eighty, under the command of Captain P.B. Jones, RNR, one of P & O's most senior masters.

The *Carnatic* had already loaded a full general cargo ex-Liverpool, also carried overland from Alexandria, and in her strong-groom—although this was not made public—was specie to the value of £40,000. As soon as her passengers, thirty-two men, three women, one child and a native servant, were aboard she was ready to sail for Bombay. But the wheels of Egyptian bureaucracy were turning at their usual slow pace, and another night was to pass before clearance to sail was obtained. At 10 o'clock on the morning of 12 September, with an impatient blast on her steam whistle, the *Carnatic* weighed anchor, shook off a small fleet of bumboats and official launches, and steamed out of Suez Bay. Ahead lay the Red Sea, and perhaps the most testing time of the voyage.

Separating North Africa from Arabia, the Red Sea is a 1,200-mile-long projecting arm of the Indian Ocean, flanked by barren, mountainous lands, where no rain falls, and the arid desert merges with the sand of the seashore. In this great flooded valley, formed when the continents moved apart 200 million years ago, the mercury in the thermometer boils by day and simmers at night. In the days before air-conditioning, to be incarcerated within the bulkheads of a coal-fired steamer for the four-day passage was to sample purgatory itself. The temperature on board was often in excess of 120°F, and the relative humidity as much as 95 percent, so that any physical activity by day was an impossible burden, and the nights were long, sleep-less hours spent tossing and turning in sweat soaked sheets. Heatstroke and heat exhaustion were common complaints, especial-ly among the engine-room crew, some of whom went mad and jumped overboard to be devoured by the sharks. For others, burial parties on the poop were a regular feature of the passage. The lucky ones—if they could be so judged—were those passengers who wield-ed sufficient influence with the shipping company to obtain cabins on the port side on the outward voyage, and on the starboard side homeward bound. These cabins escaped the full heat of the afternoon sun, and were thus the most habitable at night. It was from this arrangement, *Port Out, Starboard Home,* that the word *posh* was coined, for only the upper classes could command the best.

On the first leg of the outward passage, the 170-mile run down the narrow Gulf of Suez, Captain Jones was occupied by matters far more pressing than the sun and its effects on his passengers. His course lay though waters strewn with unmarked coral reefs and shoals, culminating in the Jubal Strait, a bottleneck five miles wide containing numerous rocky islets and hidden reefs. This was the final gauntlet to run before breaking out into the Red Sea, and one that is best navigated by daylight. Jones was not to be blessed with such good fortune.

The *Carnatic* began her approach to the northern end of the Jubal Strait at 11 o'clock that night. It was very dark, with no moon, the only light being cast by a myriad of twinkling stars hanging motionless in a sky of blackest velvet. This was just sufficient to show up in silhouette the shoreline to starboard, but it was difficult to identify the salient points. Captain Jones was on the bridge with the officer of the watch, the two men tense, alert, but in full com-mand of the situation. They both heaved a sigh of relief when, at 11.30, the flashing light on Ashrafi Island, the only lighthouse in the strait, was sighted fine on the starboard bow. Now they had a known point with which to fix the ship's position and maintain a safe distance off the land. For the next hour bearings were taken of the light, until it was abeam, and then dropping astern on the quarter. By 12.45, the light had dipped out of sight below the horizon, and ahead lay only darkness. The narrowest part of the strait was behind the *Carnatic*, but she still had a number of unlit islands and reefs to edge past before entering the Red Sea, and the currents were strong and unpredictable.

At one o'clock in the morning, judging the ship to be off the northern end of Shadwan Island, the last obstacle in the Jubal Strait, Jones made a small alteration of course to port, in order to give the unseen island a wider berth. It was too little, and too late. Unknown to Jones, over the preceding half an hour an exceptionally strong west-going current had been sweeping the *Carnatic* in towards the Egyptian coast.

Widow-Maker

Ten minutes later, breakers were sighted on the starboard bow, and Jones immediately ordered the helm hard over. The hydraulic steering gear brought the rudder round smartly, but the move was futile, for the white water now stretched right across the bow and far out to port. The engines were put to full astern, but before the propeller had time to stop and reverse, the *Carnatic* was ashore. There was a loud, agonised screech as her keel ploughed into the coral, and she came to a shuddering halt.

Throughout what remained of that traumatic night every effort was made to refloat the ship by pumping out ballast and using full astern power on the engines, but she remained hard and fast. Until daylight came and it was possible to fully assess the situation, Jones could do no more. As the *Carnatic* was not making water, and apparently in no immediate danger, he advised his passengers and crew to get some rest.

When it was fully light, it was seen that the ship was not aground on Shadwan Island, as Jones had suspected, but on a reef two miles to the north of the island, and ten miles from the Egyptian mainland. Soundings taken around the ship showed eleven feet of water under the bows, twelve feet abreast the funnel, sixty feet at the gangway and eighty-four feet under the stern. This meant that she was aground from the funnel forward, while her after part was in deep water. The sea was calm and the weather fair, but balanced as she was, the *Carnatic* was in grave danger of breaking her back.

There was another unwelcome development when, at around eight o'clock, as the tide rose, the steamer began to take in water at an alarming rate. By noon, the level of water in the forward holds was such that the pumps were having great difficulty in containing it. Plainly, the *Carnatic* was badly holed, and might well sink if she came off the reef. Jones therefore decided it would be the lesser of two evils to keep her firmly aground. To this end, he let go both bower anchors and set the engines going ahead at dead slow speed. The after hatches were then opened and cargo dumped overboard to lighten that end of the ship. As a precautionary measure, the lifeboats were lowered to the water and tied up alongside. A light breeze sprang up during the afternoon, but the *Carnatic* remained upright and steady.

At six o'clock, with darkness coming in again, Jones called a muster of the passengers and gave them a completely frank account of the situation. He assured them that the worst of the danger was over, and barring a gale—highly unlikely at that time of year—the *Carnatic* was safe for another night. During the course of the next day he informed them two of the company's ships, the *Nerra* and the *Sumatra*, were due to pass through the Jubal Strait, one of which would take them off. Faced with the alternatives of staying with the ship or taking to the boats to await rescue, the passengers unanimously voted for the former.

Although he had reassured his passengers, Jones was far from convinced himself that the ship was safe and he did not leave the deck that night. At midnight, soundings showed that, while the pumps were keeping the water in the forward holds in check, the after holds were now flooding. An hour later, the water was lapping over the propeller shaft tunnel, and by three o'clock had entered the stokehold. Before long, the boiler fires were quenched, and, without steam, the *Carnatic*'s engines stopped, and so did her bilge pumps. The water did not rise appreciably, but, as a precaution, Jones moved everyone into the fore part of the ship.

The rising sun brought with it a moderate breeze, but the weather remained fine. With no engine to hold the ship on the reef, Jones resorted to his redundant sails, hoisting the fore topsail, foresail and jib. The heavy sheet anchor was then swung out and dropped under the bows. Thus secured, the ship showed no movement, but she was clearly in great danger, and, anticipating the worst, the lifeboats were provisioned and manned.

Jones anxiously watched the water rising in the after holds, and by 10 o'clock, with no other ships in sight, realised he could delay the inevitable no longer. Quietly, he gave the order to abandon ship.

The sea being calm, and the behaviour of the *Carnatic*'s crew impeccable, the evacuation was carried out in an orderly manner and with the minimum of fuss. Captain Jones, supervising the operation from the forward gangway, ordered his officers to take the boats through the surf to Shadwan, and there set up a temporary camp until the *Nerra* or *Sumatra* hove in sight.

All passengers were off the ship and in the boats by 10.45, and Jones was about to order those crew members still on board to leave, when the disaster he feared suddenly occurred. The hundreds of tons of water pouring into the after part of the ship, which was unsupported and suspended over deep water, finally reached the point where gravity could no longer be denied. Strong though the *Carnatic*'s iron hull might be, it was not built to stand such a powerful bending moment, and, with a screech of rending metal, she broke her back. The after part of the 294-foot steamer tilted, and then broke off abaft the funnel and slid under, creating a wave that capsized one of the boats standing off and threatened to swamp the others.

Captain Jones was thrown off the gangway into the sea, but was quickly picked up by one of the lifeboats. His first thought on being rescued was for those of his crew still on board the ship, and he took the boats to an exposed part of the reef, where the passengers were landed. The empty boats then went back to the ship to take off the survivors. When all had been ferried to safety, no mean accomplishment in view of the heavy surf on the reef, the boats were reloaded and they set off for Shadwan Island.

It was close to sunset when the last boat was drawn up on a narrow strip of shingle at the north end of the island. Jones then called a muster, which revealed the full extent of the tragedy. All the passengers were safe, except five men, missing, presumed drowned when their boat capsized. The *Carnatic*'s crew had not fared so well. Nine officers, including her surgeon, purser and chief engineer, and fifteen Chinese ratings were unaccounted for and assumed to have gone down with the after part of the ship. In all, the wreck of the liner had cost the lives of twenty-eight men.

The island on which the survivors landed was not an inviting refuge for men and women who had already gone through a most unpleasant forty-eight hours. Measuring eight miles by two miles, Shadwan is totally devoid of vegetation, except for the occasional stunted cactus. There is no fresh water on its rocky surface, and it is home to many species of sand snakes, some of them large and very poisonous. So far as the castaways were concerned, the island's only redeeming attribute being its close proximity to the shipping lanes. All ships passing in and out of the Gulf of Suez are obliged to pass within a mile or so of Shadwan's eastern shore, and it was assumed that rescue would not be long in coming. Certainly, eighty-nine people, including three women and a young child, without shelter from the sun, and having only a limited supply of food and water, could not hope to survive long on this barren island. Jones was pinning his hopes on either the *Nerra* or the *Sumatra,* the former southbound and the latter bound north, passing within a few hours, and he was determined to stop one of them. Lookouts were posted, signal fires built from driftwood, and a boat was made ready to lie off the island during the night.

Shortly before 8 pm, when the boat was about to set off, the lights of a northbound steamer were sighted. The signal fires were lit, and the boat, under the command of the *Carnatic*'s chief officer, pulled out into the strait to intercept the ship. She proved to be, as Jones had anticipated, P & O's *Sumatra,* inbound from Bombay for Suez. She dropped anchor off Shadwan and at once sent boats ashore. Jones put his passengers in the *Sumatra*'s boats, but decided that he and the surviving members of his crew would maintain a degree of respect by rowing out to the rescue ship in their own boats.

It was unfortunate that the normally placid Red Sea weather chose that moment to deteriorate. A near-gale blew up, piling up a heavy surf on the beach, and despite repeated attempts throughout the night, it proved impossible to launch the *Carnatic*'s boats. By first light, the survivors were exhausted and all their boats damaged in one way or another. In the end, Jones and his men suffered the final indignity of being dragged through the surf by lifelines floated ashore from the *Sumatra*'s boats.

The *Sumatra* landed the eighty-nine survivors in Suez in the early hours of the morning of 16 September. Within hours of their landing, the dramatic news of the loss of the *Carnatic* reached P & O's office in London, and the sad business of assessing the final cost to the company was set in motion. Salvage experts and divers were dispatched to Suez on the next ship, but their reports, when they came, were not encouraging. The *Carnatic*'s cargo was judged to be a total loss, although the mails and specie, being in the forward part of the ship, might be saved.

Over the next six months, the salvage team recovered the *Carnatic*'s mails and most of her specie before, in March 1870, a storm interrupted the operation. While the work was suspended, the wreck was washed off the reef and joined its other half in deep water, taking an estimated £8,000 of gold with it—and there it lies to this day.

The opening of the Suez Canal in November 1869, and the resultant massive increase in traffic through the Jubal Strait, led to the erection of a lighthouse on lonely Shadwan Island. It stands as a fitting monument to the men whose bones lie interred in the remains of the *Carnatic*.

14   In the Lee of Dungeness

Northfleet - 1873

It is unlikely that the inhabitants of the Hampshire village of Tichborne were much disturbed when, in the summer of 1854, they heard of the death of the heir to the Tichborne estates. Sir Roger Charles Tichborne, described as 'a slender, delicate, somewhat feeble young man of fair, though not finished, education', was reported lost in the ship *Bella* off the coast of Brazil, and soon forgotten. When the tenth baronet, Sir James Tichborne died, the next son in line assumed the baronetcy and the estates, and life in the village went on. However, twelve years later, like the proverbial bad penny, Roger Tichborne came back from the dead.

The resurrected Tichborne was a man of about the right age, but grossly fat, ignorant and uncouth, a far cry from the young fop presumed to have gone down with the *Bella* in 1854. Strangely enough, he was accepted by many of the family, including Sir Roger's mother, Lady Tichborne, but when he laid claim to the estates, the incumbent baronet refused to step down. The case went to court and dragged on for seven years. Finally, in January, 1873, the Tichborne claimant, otherwise Arthur Orton, alias Thomas Castro, an English butcher who had emigrated to Australia in 1852, was sent to trial accused of perjury and attempted fraud. One of the witnesses called for the prosecution was Captain Oates, said to be the last person to see Sir Roger Tichborne alive before the latter left Rio de Janeiro in the ill-fated *Bella.* When Oates was presented with the subpoena to attend the Tichborne Trial, he was aboard his ship, the *Northfleet,* in London's East India Dock and ready to sail on the tide.

The 951-ton, three-masted barque *Northfleet* took her name from the Kentish village where she was built in 1853 for Dent & Company who were in the China trade. At an early age she came under the well-known flag of Duncan Dunbar, and held her own with the best of the clippers in the Far East for a number of years. Inevitably, with the passage of time, she lost her ability to compete in this the most glamorous of all trades, and passed to John Patton & Company of Liverpool and London, who were in the business of carrying emigrants. In January 1873, then twenty years old but still sound, she was chartered by Edwin Clark, Punchard & Company for service to the Tasmanian Main Line Railway.

Bernard Edwards

Tasmania, an island 200 miles south of the Australian mainland, was discovered in 1642 by the Dutch explorer Abel Janszoon Tasman. It was briefly visited by Tobias Furneaux in 1773, but lay unexploited until a penal settlement was established on the island in 1804. For the next fifty years Tasmania served as a dumping ground for the worst elements of the convict population of New South Wales, the prison at Port Arthur acquiring a reputation as a place of unrestrained brutality. Some forty percent of all convicts transported to Australia eventually ended up on the island. Only when it was discovered to be rich in copper, tin, silver, lead and coal did Tasmania throw off its penal image and move into the gentler world of commerce. At that time, internal transportation was based on horses and bullocks, and the roads were so bad that the creaking bullock carts frequently progressed at no more than three or four miles in a day. The cost of transport per ton miles consequently became astronomical, surpassing even that of shipping goods from Europe to Tasmania by sea. This ludicrous situation led to the setting up of the Tasmanian Main Line Railway Company, and the work of laying the track was begun in 1871.

The subpoena to appear as a witness at the Tichborne Trial was served on Captain Oates by a Treasury official on board the *Northfleet* on the afternoon of 12 January, 1873, thus presenting the ship's owners with a quandary. By law, Oates could not refuse to attend the trial, which would require his presence in London for an unknown number of days, yet, at that very moment, the *Northfleet* was ready for sea. No ship ever earned money lying idle in port, so Patton & Company had little option but to replace Captain Oates. Fortunately, the *Northfleet*'s chief officer, William Knowles, although quite young, was an extremely competent and experienced officer, so the command was passed to him. This suited Knowles eminently, for he had only recently been married and, as master of the ship, would be allowed to take his new wife with him on the voyage. A somewhat breathless Fredericka Knowles unpacked her belongings in the master's cabin next day as the *Northfleet* moved out of the East India Dock.

Under the tow of a steam tug, the *Northfleet* moved down river to Gravesend, where she was secured to a buoy by four o'clock that afternoon. She already had on board her cargo, 450 tons of railway iron stowed in her lower holds, and she now awaited the primary reason for her charter. They started to arrive on board next morning, 257 navvies, hired to feed the insatiable demand for labour in Tasmania as the railways expanded. Some of the men brought their families with them, thirty-nine women and sixty-three children, bringing the *Northfleet*'s passenger list up to a total of 359. They were poor, unsophisticated people, but even to them the accommodation they were offered in the ship must have seemed less than salubrious. They were assigned to the ship's tween decks, in which crude wooden bunks had been erected and fitted with straw mattresses. There was no heating, very little ventilation and no sanitation. And in such surroundings they were expected to spend the next four, perhaps five months. That these people boarded willingly spoke volumes for the awful deprivation of the working class England from which they were escaping.

The early morning mist was still clinging to the river when, at 6 o'clock on 17 January, Trinity House pilot George Brack boarded the *Northfleet* at Gravesend to take her down Channel. The wind was light, the weather settled, if cold and grey, and Brack looked forward with confidence to a trouble-free passage. When the steam tug *Middlesex* had passed her towrope, the *Northfleet* cast off from her buoy and moved out into the river, her next port of call Hobart, Tasmania. Including her crew of thirty-four, she had on board a total of 393 persons.

George Brack's expectations of a fair passage were short-lived. When, twelve hours later, the *Northfleet* reached Dungeness Roads and discharged her tug, a moderate south-west wind had sprung up. It was foolish to try and beat down Channel against this adverse wind, and, after consultation with Brack, Captain Knowles decided to anchor in the roads to wait an improvement. But the wind held stubbornly in the south-west, and during the night increased to gale force. There being little shelter from a south-wester off Dungeness, Knowles decided to return to the Downs, where a temporary refuge might be found in the lee of the South Foreland.

With the wind at her heels, the *Northfleet* arrived at the Downs at noon on the 18th, only to find every square foot of the anchorage occupied by a fleet of ships of all sizes and nationalities. There was no room in the lee of the headland for the barque. Brack suggested an anchorage close to the Goodwin Sands, but Knowles, not surprisingly, was not prepared to take the risk of being blown ashore on these treacherous banks. He continued northwards and, late that afternoon, the *Northfleet* eventually found a suitable anchorage in Margate Roads, close under the North Foreland.

It was the early hours of the 21st before the wind moderated and veered to the north-west. By this time Knowles was impatient to get on with the voyage, and gave orders to weigh anchor at once. By 4 o'clock that morning, the *Northfleet* was abeam of Folkestone and looked set to clear the narrows of the Straits of Dover without further delays. Then the wind suddenly backed again to the south-west and freshened. Once again, Knowles found himself fighting a losing battle against the wind. He carried on, in the teeth of a rising gale, until off Hastings, by which time his ship was taking such a battering that he was again forced to admit defeat. Once more the *Northfleet* went about and returned to Dungeness Roads to seek shelter. She anchored at sunset in company with a number of other vessels.

For Knowles, on his first voyage in command, this was a crushing humiliation. The *Northfleet* had been at sea for more than five days, had covered over 200 sea miles, and yet she was little further into her 12,000-mile voyage than if she had spent the time languishing at her buoy off Gravesend. The strain on Knowles and his crew had been enormous; long, arduous and sleepless nights, and on top of all that, the soul-destroying frustration of being constantly outwitted by the wind and sea. As for the *Northfleet*'s passengers, their introduction to the delights of sea travel had turned into a bad dream. Even when the ship was at anchor, she had never been still for a moment. Frightened, perplexed, and reduced to a state of abject misery by seasickness, most of them were more than ready to abandon their hopes of a new life in Tasmania for a swift return to dry land.

The promontory of Dungeness, which juts out into the Dover Strait twelve miles south-west of Folkestone, is really only the seaward end of Romney Marsh. It stands only a few feet above sea level, but is high enough to take the sting out of any wind in the west. The holding ground in the shelter of the low headland is good, consisting of a layer of sand over clay and mud. Anchored two miles off shore in eleven fathoms, and with sixty fathoms of cable out, the *Northfleet* lay quietly, despite the south-westerly gale raging. When the winter darkness closed in, the bright, unwavering beam of Dungeness lighthouse showed in line with the bowsprit, while the lights of Folkestone glowed reassuringly on the starboard quarter. Far out to sea, on the port quarter, the Varne lightship blinked red every twenty seconds, a blood-red warning of the dangerous shoals it marked. The occasional steamer passed up or down Channel between the *Northfleet* and the Varne, but the barque, her riding lights burning brightly, was anchored well out of the way.

At 8 o'clock, a watch of two seamen and a petty officer was set on deck, and the ship settled down for the night. She was lying comparatively quietly, and the passengers and the rest of the crew wasted no time in turning in. Soon, the ship was quiet, except for the creaking of her timbers and the fitful cry of a child awakened in the darkness. Captain Knowles and the pilot, George Brack, walked the deck for a while, discussing the chances of a clear run down Channel in the morning, but they too soon retired. Knowles went to his cabin and Brack to a comfortable armchair in the saloon.

The next two hours passed peacefully, with the watch sheltering from the icy wind in the lee of the main cabin, a heavily oilskined figure taking a turn around the decks at regular intervals. It was 10.30 when the seaman who had gone aft to strike the bells noticed the lights of a large steamer bearing down on the *Northfleet*'s starboard quarter. She was between the barque and the shore and closing at an alarming rate. It was obvious to the man that a collision was inevitable, and his first reaction was to hail the ship. This, of course, produced no result, for he was forgetting that, while a sailing ship glides along in comparative silence, the steamer surrounds itself with a battery of noise difficult to penetrate from outside. He ran to the poop bell and hammered on it, sending its brassy tones ringing across the water, but it was too late.

The shock of the collision was described by some witnessed as being like the concussion of a very powerful cannon, others felt and heard nothing. The watch on deck told of how the steamer, her bows towering above the *Northfleet*'s bulwarks, struck her just forward of the main hatchway, biting deep into her hull. Almost immediately, the steamer went full astern on her engines and backed away. Men were seen on her forecastle head hastily draping a tarpaulin over her port bow, in a blatant, and successful, attempt to hide her name. She continued on her course, and was soon swallowed up in the darkness. There can be no doubt that those on board the steamer must have been aware that they had been in collision, and the other ship had suffered major damage. Yet no attempt was made to contact the *Northfleet,* or to offer assistance, as is firmly enshrined in the law of the sea.

Knowles and Brack reached the deck within seconds of each other and just in time to see the stern light of the unknown steamer making off down Channel. By the light of a hurricane lamp they saw that the stranger's bows had smashed into the barque's starboard side, slicing her open from the main deck to below the waterline. The sea was pouring into her main hold, and she was settling rapidly.

Knowles ordered the pumps to be set to work, but it soon became clear they were having little effect on the rising water in the hold. Nothing could save the *Northfleet*, and Knowles turned his thoughts to her passengers and crew. There were several ships anchored close by, including the clipper *Corona*, which was only 300 yards off, and it was reasonable to assume that the collision had been seen and boats were already being lowered. Nothing could have been further from the truth.

The *Northfleet*'s signal gun was run out and loaded, but the touch-hole was found to be blocked, and the gun could not be fired. But the ship was well supplied with distress rockets, and these were sent soaring into the night sky, while brilliant flares were burned at deck level. It seemed inconceivable that the barque's plight should now go unnoticed, yet there was no response from the shore or the nearby ships.

Until the rockets went up, the *Northfleet*'s passengers, ignorant of the ways of a ship and befuddled by sleep, had no real understanding of the danger they faced. When it dawned on them that the ship was sinking, blind panic broke out.

Captain Knowles, having accepted that his ship would not last long, had by this time ordered the boats to be swung out. As was the common practice of the day, the *Northfleet* carried nothing like enough boats to take all those on board, but Knowles hoped to at least get the women and children away before the ship went down. But now, at a time when he most needed them, some of his seamen let him down by making a rush for the boats, intent on saving their own lives. Many of the male passengers followed their lead, and a shameful and undignified scramble for self-preservation ensued. The women and children, most of them shivering in their nightclothes, were pushed roughly aside; wives and families were abandoned as the hard-bitten men fought for places in the boats.

Knowles and his officers, struggling to restore order, were brushed aside with the women and children, and Knowles, fearful of the dire consequences of the riot, ran to his cabin for his revolver. When he returned, he threatened to shoot the first man to board a boat before the women and children. The men stepped back, but one seaman, Biddies by name, decided to challenge Knowles and moved towards one of the quarter boats. For his foolishness, he received a bullet in the knee, and collapsed to the deck screaming in agony.

The decisive action by the captain won a brief respite, and the boatswain, John Ember, began loading women and children into the starboard lifeboat, careful to see that the young Fredericka Knowles was among them. When the men realised what was afoot, they made a rush for the boat, but Ember cut the falls and the boat went down with only himself, Mrs Knowles, a twelve-year-old girl, a baby of three months, and eight navvies. In the confusion, the boat was badly damaged as it went over the rail, but Ember took it away from the ship's side as fast as possible.

The two quarter boats were lowered, crowded with panicking men, but both were swamped on reaching the water and their occupants swept away. And they were the last to leave, for at that point the *Northfleet* gave up the ghost and sank. George Brack, who had been at Knowles' side throughout the turmoil, went into the rigging with ten other men and reached the mizzentop crosstrees, which remained above the water when the ship sank. Knowles was last seen standing alone on the poop; a forlorn figure, his first command having lasted only ten days. He went down with his ship.

Only then, too late, did other ships at the anchorage realise the tragic drama being acted out within hailing distance. The steam tug *City of London* was the first to arrive, picking up the occupants of Ember's waterlogged boat, and then, in the course of the next few hours, rescuing twenty-two men from the sea. The Kingstown lugger *Mary* also picked up thirty men. Lastly, some two hours later, the Dover pilot cutter *Princess* saved a further twenty-one, among them George Brack and the others, plucked from the mizzentop crosstrees.

Of the 393 souls on board the *Northfleet*, only eighty-five survived the night of her destruction. They were the now widowed Fredericka Knowles, twelve-year-old Lucy Sturgeon and the baby of three months, Harriet Maria Taplin, both of them orphaned by the sinking, Trinity House pilot George Brack, Boatswain John Ember, ten seamen and seventy male passengers. Captain William Knowles, in the finest tradition of the sea, gave his life in attempting to save those in his care.

The steamer responsible for the loss of the *Northfleet* had been recognised as a Spaniard, but although the steam tug *Fiery Dragon* was dispatched down Channel to search for her, she could not be found. It was not until nine months later that the culprit was identified as the 3,000-ton *Murillo* and arrested as she passed Dover. An Admiralty court severely censored her master, Captain Berrute, and his officers, but due to lack of co-operation by the Spanish authorities, they escaped punishment. However, the *Murillo* was seized and sold to provide compensation for the *Northfleet*'s owners. Mrs Fredericka Knowles, married and widowed in just over one month, received a Civil List pension in recognition of her husband's bravery and self-sacrifice.

After a trial, which lasted 188 days, Arthur Orton, alias Thomas Castro, impersonator of Sir Roger Tichborne, was found guilty of perjury and fraud, and sentenced to fourteen years penal servitude. Captain Oates, sometime master of the *Northfleet*, would remember his name with gratitude.

Bernard Edwards

15   FIRESHIP

Cospatrick - 1874

Following his discovery in November 1642 of the island that now bears his name, Abel Tasman sailed on eastwards. On 13 December, he came to a 'high mountainous country', and thinking this to be part of South America, called it Staaten Landt, later to become known as Nieu Zealande. Bad weather and the fierce hostility of the natives prevented Tasman from landing in New Zealand, but Captain Cook's re-discovery of the islands, 127 years later, was attended by better fortune. Not only did he land and establish contact with the inhabitants, but carried out a very comprehensive survey of the whole of the coastline. The first missionaries and traders arrived in the early part of the 19th century and gold was discovered in 1861, the latter bringing the usual rush of new settlers. A few made fortunes but the majority, soon disillusioned, turned to the land.   Ten years later a million acres were under crops and ten million cattle and sheep roamed the lush Canterbury plains.

As with Tasmania, the need for a network of railways joining the interior of New Zealand to the coast now became pressing. Money was borrowed in London, and the call went out for men willing to wield the pick and shovel. But New Zealand was an alien world far distant from the British Isles, and a heavy inducement was needed. To this end, six million acres of land alongside the proposed railways were set aside, to be sold off cheaply to the immigrant labourers and their families when the work was completed. This was a carrot on a stick impoverished Britons found hard to resist, and they took to the sea in their thousands.

The invention of the compound steam engine and the opening of the Suez Canal in 1869 enabled the steamship to offer a fast, economical service from Europe to India and China, but the long haul to Australia and New Zealand was another matter. Here the sailing ship still held sway, carrying emigrants and general cargo out via the Cape of Good Hope, returning round the Horn with grain and wool. One of the leaders in this trade was Shaw Savill & Company of London, who despatched their first ship south in 1850, and played a leading role in the opening up of New Zealand.

Shaw Savill, who operated fifteen sailings a year to New Zealand, had a reputation for reliable, well-found ships, and their latest acquisition in the summer of 1873, the 1,220-ton *Cospatrick* was no exception. Bought from the Duncan Dunbar stable for £10,000, she was a three-masted Blackwall frigate, built of teak at Moulmein in 1856 for Dunbar's London-Cape Town passenger service. At seventeen years old, the *Cospatrick* was no flyer, but her timbers were sound and her passenger accommodation, while not luxurious, was clean and adequate. Her master, Captain A. Elmslie, a seaman of considerable experience, came over with her from Duncan Dunbar.

The frigate 'Cospatrick'
(Photo: National Maritime Museum)

On her second voyage to New Zealand under Shaw, Savill's colours, the *Cospatrick* completed loading a general cargo for New Zealand in the East India Dock on 10 September, 1874. That evening, manned by a crew of forty-two under Captain Elmslie, who also had his wife on board, she moved to Gravesend and took on her passengers. Comprising 177 men, 125 women and 127 children, they were young Irish farm labourers and their families wooed by the promise of land in New Zealand in return for a few years hard work on the railways.

Bernard Edwards

The emigrants, naive and full of hope, were very much impressed by the great ship—the *Cospatrick* was only 190 feet long and 34 feet in the beam—that was to carry them over 15,000 miles of hostile ocean to their new home. When, shortly before sailing, a fire drill was held on board to demonstrate the newly-installed fire engine, they regarded this as yet another proof that no expense was being spared to ensure their safety on the voyage. Fortunately for their peace of mind, they were not aware of the real reason for the fitting of this very costly piece of equipment. Stowed in the *Cospatrick's* after hold was 400 tons of gunpowder, an essential requirement of the railway constructors.

The opening phase of the *Cospatrick's* voyage was not encouraging. Sailing from Gravesend on the morning of the 11th, she ran into strong adverse winds soon after she cast off her steam tug at the South Foreland. Three wretched days followed, during which, in atrocious weather, she was forced to tack back and forth between the English and French coasts, fighting hard for every mile of westing gained. It was late on the 14th before she finally cleared Start Point and moved out into the open waters of the North Atlantic. By this time, most of her 429 passengers were regretting their enthusiasm for a new life overseas. And there was worse to come. Twenty-four hours later, the *Cospatrick* was deep into the Bay of Biscay and rolling her scuppers under in the long Atlantic swell. Many were the 'Hail Marys' said over the next forty-eight hours.

Cape Finisterre drew abeam on the morning of the 16th and the agony came to a sudden end. The sun shone, the Portuguese trades blew gently from astern, and the *Cospatrick* remained mercifully steady. One by one, her passengers appeared on deck, sheepishly testing their new-found sea legs as they were transported south to the tropics.

Picking up the north-east trades, the *Cospatrick*, making good speed, passed the Canaries on the 27th and sighted St. Vincent, the westernmost of the Cape Verde Islands on 4 October. Then she ran into the Doldrums. The sun, which had been welcomed with such enthusiasm only a few days before, now rode high in the sky, as the ship drifted aimlessly, her sails hanging slack and the pitch in her decks bubbling in the heat. The crowded steerage accommodation, dark and airless, became unbearable. Children whined and fretted, their parents quarrelled openly. Water was short, and the food growing ever more rancid by the hour.

After seventy-two tortured hours, the wind relented and returned to fill the *Cospatrick's* sails again. On the 12th, the guano-shrouded pinnacles of the lonely St. Pauls Rocks were sighted, and soon the first of the south-east trades were felt. A landfall was made off the Brazilian coast, near Bahia, on the 20th, and the ship's head was hauled around to make the long reach across the empty wastes of the South Atlantic to the Cape of Good Hope.

Widow-Maker

Passing ships were spoken with on the 18th and 28th, and the tall peaks of Tristan da Cunha briefly smudged the horizon on 8 November, otherwise, the crossing was without incident. By noon on the 17th, two months and one week out of Gravesend, the *Cospatrick* was 450 miles south-west of the Cape and eating up the miles on the wings of a fresh westerly wind. The weather was cool and invigorating, magically soothing away all the tensions and frustrations of the past weeks. Although New Zealand still lay 8,000 miles away, the halfway point in the voyage had been passed, and there was a new air of optimism on board.

That evening, the wind died away, leaving the *Cospatrick* rolling easily in a surprisingly calm sea, and making little forward progress. Captain Elmslie grumbled, but his passengers and crew were in good spirits, for this was the night of the ship's concert. Held on deck, under a star-studded sky the concert was a great success. The performance finished a little before midnight, when passengers and crew went to their respective berths in good spirits, leaving the ship in the hands of the watch and the fire patrol. The latter was recruited from among the male passengers, and charged with enforcing the no smoking rule below decks, and checking the locked lanterns in the alleyways.

Second Officer Henry Macdonald, keeping the 8 to 12 watch on the poop, had been obliged to listen to the concert from afar, but when he also turned in after midnight, he went to sleep content that all was well with the voyage. Two hours later, he was rudely awoken by the urgent shrilling of whistles and the clatter of running feet. When he heard the cry of 'Fire!' rise above the commotion, he tumbled out of his bunk, already wide awake.

Without stopping to dress, Macdonald rushed on deck to find dense clouds of smoke pouring from the fore end of the ship. Captain Elmslie and the chief officer were both on deck and organising a party to man the fire engine. The fire was located in the boatswain's store, under the forecastle head, which contained a highly inflammable mix of ropes, paints, oils, cotton waste and tar. Now was the time for the new fire engine to prove its worth.

The canvas hoses were run out, and willing hands cranked the handles of the engine. Unfortunately, the machine did not perform as it had done in the quiet waters of Gravesend Reach. A moderate swell had come up since midnight, and the ship was rolling awkwardly. At each roll the suction pipe of the fire engine came out of the water, and not a drop was reaching the hoses on deck.

A bucket chain was formed, but even with the male passengers pressed into service, this proved woefully inadequate. The movement of the ship made it almost impossible to fill buckets from the sea, and the space under the forecastle head was so restricted that no effective attack could be mounted on the fire. It was not long before the dense clouds of smoke billowing out of the boatswain's store

Bernard Edwards

drove the fire fighters back.

It might still have been possible to contain the fire, had other factors not chosen to intervene. Being a typical round-bowed Blackwall frigate, the *Cospatrick* was, at the best of times, difficult to steer; now, with her main sails furled to prevent them catching fire, she flew up into the wind and it was impossible to bring her back on course again. Although the wind was light, it was blowing from ahead, and was sufficient to fan the flames and drive them aft. At this point, the chief officer suggested lowering boats to tow the ship's head off the wind, but Elmslie was reluctant to do this. He feared the launching of boats would cause the passengers to panic.

Elmslie's caution was misplaced. Aided by the wind, the flames swept aft through the tween decks, reached the main deck, and leapt into the rigging. Within the space of half an hour, the *Cospatrick* was like a gigantic torch, her dry timbers, tarred rigging and salt-bleached canvas all burning furiously. She was doomed, and her passengers sensed this. They were frightened and helpless, and it was not long before the panic Elmslie had sought to avoid broke out.

The *Cospatrick* carried only seven boats, two cutters, two quarter-boats, one longboat and two small lifeboats, sufficient to take a maximum of 230 people. Had the ship's crew been allowed to launch these boats in an orderly manner, the weather was such that most of the women and children might have got away. But this was not to be. Driven on by the flames licking at their heels, the passengers surged aft demanding to be saved. In a belated attempt to restore order, Elmslie drew his revolver, but hesitated to fire, and was brushed aside by the mob.

The two bigger boats were stowed amidships, bottom up and on chocks. No hoisting tackle was handy, and, even if it had been, one of the boats was rotten and the other holed by falling spars. Regardless of this, the mob fell on the boats and tried to heave them bodily off the chocks. As they struggled, the flames enveloped both boats and men.

Meanwhile, Elmslie had conceded that he must abandon ship and sent his men to launch the quarter-boats. The starboard quarter-boat was swung out and lowered to the water, but was immediately swamped by sheer weight of numbers as a swarm of demented passengers slid down the ship's side. The boat capsized and more than eighty people were drowned.

The port quarter-boat was already on fire, and the longboat caught alight as it was being swung out. That left only the two small lifeboats, which hung in davits right aft, ready for launching in case of a man overboard. Some semblance of order had now been restored, and these last two boats were lowered without mishap, one with forty-two passengers and three crew under the command of Second Officer Henry Macdonald, and the other with thirty-nine passengers and crew in the charge of the chief officer.

Widow-Maker

Mindful of what had happened to the starboard quarter-boat, the two heavily laden lifeboats quickly pulled clear of the burning ship and lay off to await events. Over the following thirty-six hours, the lucky survivors, powerless to intervene, watched the agonisingly slow death of their ship and all left on board. Crowded together on the after end of the *Cospatrick*'s poop, with no escape left from the advancing flames, the doomed wretches were so paralysed by fear that they made no effort to construct rafts, which might have meant salvation. Their pitiful cries for help drifted over the water, moving those in the boats to tears, but if they wished to save their own lives, they must keep away from the ship.

It seemed that the end had finally come when, that night after dark, the burning ship's main and mizzen masts toppled and crashed to the deck with a shower of sparks. The mizzen mast fell on the poop, and many of the terrified people huddled there must have been killed or injured. Yet, when daylight came on the 19th, the *Cospatrick* was still afloat, and there was still movement to be seen on her poop.

The inevitable happened late that afternoon, when the flames reached the 400 tons of gunpowder stowed in the after hold, and the blackened hulk was rent apart by a violent explosion that reverberated from horizon to horizon. Minutes later, those still alive were seen to jump overboard, Captain Elmslie and his wife being last to leave. The smouldering remains of the *Cospatrick* sank with the setting sun, a cloud of steam rising from the sea as she went under. The onlookers in the boats could do nothing to help those left in the water, and the sharks soon moved in to finish the work begun by the fire.

When it was all over, and the horror had receded from their minds, the survivors took stock of their own situation, which was far from ideal. The nearest land, the southern tip of Africa, lay 380 miles to the north, and as neither boat had food, water or mast and sails, this was beyond reach. They were in a shipping lane, but this was a wide ocean and the possibility of being sighted by a passing ship was very remote. It would be months before the *Cospatrick* was considered overdue and reported missing; even then, there was no guarantee that anyone would come looking for them.

Over the next two days, the two boats kept together, drifting in calm conditions and undecided whether to make a bid for the land. On the night of the 21st the weather took a hand. The wind and sea got up and during the darkness they lost sight of each other. The chief officer's boat, with its forty occupants, was never seen again.

The plight of Henry Macdonald and the forty-five men crammed into the second boat was as bad as it could possibly be. They had nothing to eat or drink, no mast or sails, and only one oar. Such had been the urgency to abandon ship that they were all wearing thin night-clothes. By day the sun blistered their skin, and by night they shivered in the cold wind. On the 22nd, one man fell overboard, and so far gone were the others that they made no attempt to save him. Later in the day, three men, who had been driven to drinking seawater, went mad and died. Their bodies were thrown overboard with no thought other than their going would make more room in the boat.

On the 23rd the wind rose to gale force and before long seas were breaking over the boat, adding to the miserable state of the survivors. Macdonald rigged a sea anchor, and for a while they rode the waves in reasonable comfort, those who were able using a variety of makeshift bailers to clear the boat of water. Then the sea anchor carried away, and shortly afterwards their only oar was lost. Providentially, the wind then eased, but not before four more men had died. This time, before the bodies were thrown overboard, the living drank their blood and ate their livers.

The respite from the weather was short-lived. On the morning of the 24th the wind again rose to gale force, and although another sea anchor was rigged, the boat was soon awash up to her gunwales. The men were too far gone to care about bailing, and sat, up to their waists in water, waiting for the end. Six more slipped away during the day, their deaths providing sustenance for those left behind. The cruel torture was intensified next day, when the sun beat down remorselessly out of a cloudless sky, accelerating the process of dehydration. By the end of the day, only Henry Macdonald and seven others, three of these already mad, were left alive.

Just when it seemed all was finished, an hour before dawn on the 26th, a ship was sighted close by. But although the survivors shouted at the tops of their voices, the ship passed within fifty yards of the boat, apparently unaware of their presence. Another man died, and the cruel disappointment was momentarily forgotten while they satisfied their hunger.

There was hope again on the 27th as rainsqualls gathered all around. The seven men remaining, their emaciated bodies caked with salt and shrivelled by the sun and wind, waited with eager anticipation for the blessed rain to come lashing down on them. Not a drop fell on the boat. Two more men gave up the hopeless fight and went quietly to join their Maker.

Now only five remained; Macdonald, three seamen and one passenger. They lay in the stern of the boat hovering between life and death. All had drunk some seawater, the passenger a great deal, and he was mad. Even Macdonald, a man of great physical and mental strength, had finally given up hope of survival and drifted into an exhausted sleep, from which he hoped not to awake.

And this was how, on 27th November, the Liverpool barque *British Sceptre*, bound from Calcutta to Dundee, found them. Since abandoning the *Cospatrick* nine days earlier, they had drifted in an easterly direction for 540 miles into the loneliest stretch of the South Indian Ocean. Ahead lay another 5,000 miles of emptiness, into which, had it not been for a keen-eyed lookout on the *British Sceptre*, they would have disappeared forever.

The mad passenger and one of the seamen died two days after rescue. Only Henry Macdonald and the two other seamen recovered and were landed at St Helena fifteen days later. They were the only survivors of the 473 who sailed from Gravesend in the *Cospatrick* in September, 1874.

Bernard Edwards

16   Collision Course

Princess Alice & Bywell Castle - 1878

In 1878 Europe, for the first time in more than sixty years, was in a state of peace, transient though it might be. The marauding armies of Napoleon Bonaparte had receded into history and Prussian expansionism was, as yet, only a faint whisper on the breeze. In Britain, Queen Victoria was in the forty-first year of her long reign, and the industrial revolution, which had transformed the lives of her subjects, was at its height. Stability and prosperity for all was just over the horizon.

For the vast majority of the population of London's East End, the great Queen's supremacy and the nation's permanence were unquestionable. As for the prosperity their callused hands and bowed backs had helped to create, the evidence was less tangible. Crowded together in grim terraced houses, lacking proper sanitation, and breathing air fouled by thousands of smoking chimneys, life for the common man and his family was a drab, wearying round. Little wonder that, whenever the rare opportunity presented itself for an escape into more attractive surroundings, the opportunity was eagerly grasped.

There were no cheap package tours to the sunny Mediterranean, but the River Thames offered an affordable way out of the perpetual twilight of the East End. Throughout the summer months, fleets of paddle steamers plied the river crammed with day-trippers bound to and from the seaside resorts of Southend, Sheerness and Margate. The round trip, a full day out, was an unforgettable foray into another world; a world of grassy river banks where cows meandered at the water's edge, great ships hurried past to and from the far corners of the Empire, and the smell of the open sea was like wine in the nostrils. And, at the end, there were beaches where the sand was like warm gold dust and the sun shone all day.

It was with the promise of such a memorable day that, at 10 o'clock on the morning of 3 September, 1878, the *Princess Alice* left Woolwich landing stage. Packed with more than 800 trippers, mostly women and children, she was bound for Gravesend and Sheerness. It was a perfect late summer's day, with fluffy, cotton wool clouds drifting lazily in a clear blue sky, and the sun already hot enough to encourage bare arms. The crowd, complete with picnic baskets and crates of ale, was in high spirits.

The *Princess Alice*, owned by the London Steamboat Company, was a paddle steamer of 251 tons, the largest in the company's fleet, and certified to carry 899 passengers. Built in 1865, she was typical of her breed, being long and narrow, with two tall funnels and spacious saloons forward and aft. Her 140 horsepower engines, well maintained over the years, gave her a consistent speed of twelve knots. Her master, Captain William Grinstead, was a river man of long experience, and was licensed to navigate the Thames without the help of a pilot. Also on board the *Princess Alice* on the day in question was the London Steamboat Company's superintendent, Mr Towse, who, combining work with pleasure, had brought his wife and five children for the day out on the river.

At the time the *Princess Alice* left her berth, a few miles further up river the 1,376-ton collier *Bywell Castle* lay alongside discharging cargo under less idyllic circumstances. Submerged under a cloud of coal dust that threatened to block out the sun, her steam winches clanked furiously, and her derricks groaned as the heavily laden tubs of coal were lifted out of her holds and swung ashore. In his cabin below the bridge of the collier, Captain Thomas Harrison sweated and cursed the insidious black dust that penetrated tightly closed doors and ports into every nook and cranny of the ship, even forming a gritty coating on his teeth as he waded through the paperwork littering his desk. A hard, practical seaman, Harrison despised paperwork, and longed for the time when the last tub of coal was ashore and he could be on his way down-river again. As always, another cargo of coal awaited the *Bywell Castle* on the north-east coast, but in between was a blessed thirty-six hours at sea. Time then to wash down the ship, to breathe the clean, salt-laden air of the North Sea, and to see again horizons not marred by grimy houses and smoking chimneys. All of which would soon be within reach, for the collier was expected to finish cargo and sail before dark that day.

With the ebb tide behind her, the *Princess Alice* reached Gravesend, twenty miles down river, at 11.30 that morning. She lay alongside the pier of the busy market town just long enough for a few passengers to disembark and for others to board in their place. At around 1.30, she arrived at Sheerness and there was a general exodus ashore to stroll the promenade, or paddle in the none too warm water that lapped at the sand and shingle beach. For those so inclined, there was time to explore the historic old dockyard town, where Samuel Pepys once lived and worked; to stand on the hallowed spot where Lord Nelson's body was landed after Trafalgar. Then, all too soon, it was time to return on board.

The *Princess Alice* left Sheerness at about 3.30, arriving back at Gravesend shortly after 5 o'clock. Again, some passengers were landed and others came aboard. When she sailed at 6 o'clock, it is believed the steamer had on board a total of 900, including her crew, perhaps more. Although fares were collected diligently, no record of numbers was kept. Certainly, the *Princess Alice* must then have been carrying the maximum number permitted, if not more. But then, she was in the river with the land in sight on both sides; it promised to be a fine, clear night, and journey's end was only twenty miles away. Surely nothing could go wrong. Mr Towse, the company's superintendent had no fears, for having business to conduct in Gravesend, he stayed ashore, leaving his family on board to complete the trip alone.

It was half an hour before sunset when the *Princess Alice* pulled away from Gravesend pier and began the final leg of her journey up-river, now steaming against an ebbing tide. An hour later, with darkness setting in, she was in the Erith Reach, with ten miles to go to Woolwich. As anticipated, it was a fine night, with a brilliant moon just beginning its climb into a star-filled sky. It was the perfect ending to a perfect day. But it had been a long day and the children were fretful, their mothers exhausted and not a few fathers had more ale in them than they could cope with. It was time to go home.

Captain Grinstead, having spent most of the day on the steamer's open bridge, was as tired as any of his passengers, yet for him the most difficult part of the trip was to come. The river was narrowing, the tide strengthening, and despite the bright moonlight, the darkness would add to his burden.

George Long, first mate of the *Princess Alice*, surveyed the crowded decks from the top of the forward saloon and reflected that his day would not end with the docking at North Woolwich pier. Before he went ashore, it was his responsibility to see the ship's decks cleaned from end to end in preparation for the next morning's sailing. In the saloon below, the chief steward, Joseph Freeman, contemplated an even more daunting task, namely returning the accommodation to its normal state of cleanliness after the boisterous East Enders had gone ashore.

While the *Princess Alice's* voyage was drawing to a close, twelve miles up river, another voyage was just beginning. The last tub of coal had been dumped ashore from the *Bywell Castle,* hatches were being battened down, and the black dust that crunched underfoot and covered every exposed surface was under attack by high-pressure hoses. On the collier's bridge, Captain Harrison waited impatiently for the arrival of the river pilot. He did not have long to wait, for, alerted by shore officials, the pilot, Mr Dicke, was at that moment hurrying along the quay. Within twenty minutes, the *Bywell Castle* cast off her moorings and headed down river. She was riding high out of the water, having on board just sufficient ballast to submerge her propeller. Later, in the lower reaches of the Thames, more ballast would be run in to bring the ship down to a reasonable sea-going draught.

The tide was at two hours ebb and running strongly, and by 7.45 the collier was in Gallions Reach with the lights of Woolwich

Artist's impression of the collision between
'Princess Alice' *and* 'Bywell Castle'

(Photo: Cassell)

sliding past on her starboard side. Ahead lay Tripcock Point, where the river bends sharply back on itself; a blind corner for the mariner. Harrison prudently reduced speed and moved out into the middle of the reach. Having done so, he saw the red port sidelight and white masthead lights of a ship approaching the bend, bound up river. The notorious Murphy's Law prevails in all such cases, and the two ships, on opposing courses, were fated to meet at the apex of the bend. Cool heads were needed on both bridges.

The general rule of river navigation is that ships pass port to port, each keeping to her starboard side of the fairway. Accordingly, Harrison altered course slightly to starboard, moving over towards Tripcock Point in order to give the approaching ship more room. He was relieved to see her also follow the correct procedure by altering to starboard. The *Bywell Castle* was then free to pass under her stern.

Then, as the two ships drew closer, the unforgivable happened. The inbound ship's red light slowly changed to green, indicating she was altering to port. At the last minute, she was swinging right across the collier's bows.

A collision was clearly unavoidable, but Thomas Harrison did not lose his nerve. He rang for emergency full speed astern on the engine and gave a long warning blast on the *Bywell Castle*'s whistle. His hand was still on the whistle lanyard when the full horror of the situation was revealed to him. In opening up her starboard side, the other ship showed a mass of deck lights, and faintly across the water came the sound of music and voices raised in song. She was an excursion steamer!

Stopping a ship under way is not a simple matter of slamming on the brakes. A ship has no brakes, as such. First the propeller must be brought to rest, then reverse gear engaged, and the engine speeded up until the propeller is running full astern. Even then, the forward momentum of the ship must be overcome before she begins to move astern. In the case of the *Bywell Castle*, a mass of some 1,800 tons, under way for a almost an hour, and running before a strong ebb tide, a powerful braking force was needed to bring her up short. But flying light, and with her propeller barely submerged and unable to get a good grip on the water, this was not forthcoming. The collier ploughed on, her speed unchecked.

As for the *Princess Alice*, she had no opportunity to take avoiding action, and the oncoming bows of the *Bywell Castle* struck her squarely amidships, in way of her starboard paddle box, biting deep into her hull.

Apart from those on the bridge of the *Princess Alice*, no one on board had the slightest inkling of the disaster about to overtake them. The end of the trip was very near, and the familiar sights and smells of home were beckoning. Mothers gathered their squabbling children about them, and drowsy fathers lolled against the rails, sadly contemplating tomorrow's return to work. When the bows of the *Bywell Castle* suddenly reared up out of the darkness, and the terrible crash came, followed by the screams of the injured and dying, pandemonium broke out. Terror-stricken passengers milled around like stampeding animals, few aware of what had happened, none with any clear idea of what to do.

The life-saving equipment of the *Princess Alice* consisted of only a dozen cork lifejackets and four lifeboats, totally inadequate for the 900-plus people on board. Even so, determined efforts were made to save lives. Second Mate Ralph Wilkinson was on the starboard sponson making ready the ropes for mooring when the bows of the *Bywell Castle* slammed into the ship only feet away from him. As soon as he had recovered from the shock, he ran aft, and with the help of other crew members, swung out one of the lifeboats. As the boat went down the ship's side it was overwhelmed by a mob of screaming passengers, and capsized and sank when it reached the water. On the other side of the ship, George Long, the first mate, launched a boat single-handed, but it went away with only one person on board. Such was the confusion.

William Law, second steward of the *Princess Alice*, was in the forward saloon when the crash came. Above the ensuing confusion he heard the unmistakable sound of water pouring into the ship, and at once began to shepherd people out of the saloon onto the deck. As he was so engaged, the forward half of the ship broke away and sank, taking many of those still in the saloon with it. Law feared that the rest of the ship would follow, and looked around for his fiancé, who was on board for the trip. The young girl could not swim, so Law took her over his shoulder and jumped into the water. The shore was no more than 150 yards away, and although Law was a powerful swimmer, the swift-flowing river plucked the girl from his grasp and whirled her away. Law reached the bank, rescuing another man on the way, but his wife-to-be was lost to him forever.

Captain Harrison, of the *Bywell Castle* reacted to the disaster with commendable speed. The bows of his ship were still embedded in the paddle steamer and he ran forward to organise ropes and ladders to be thrown down on to the deck of the doomed ship. While his men were hauling survivors aboard, Harrison hurried aft to supervise the launching of the *Bywell Castle*'s three lifeboats, which he sent away to the aid of the people struggling for survival in the water. He then returned to the bridge, for his ship was drifting at the mercy of the tide and in danger of running ashore.

As Harrison reached the bridge, some five minutes after the collision, the tide prised the two ships apart, and the remaining after part of the *Princess Alice* capsized and sank in deep water. The majority of those still on board jumped, or were thrown into the water, others, trapped in the saloon, went down with the ship.

When the *Princess Alice* had gone she left hundreds of those who, only minutes before had been tiredly contemplating the end of a perfect day, dying in the cold, murky waters of Gallions Reach. Most of them could not swim, they had no lifejackets, so they lingered for a while, and then died. Boats from the shore, alerted by the screech of the *Bywell Castle*'s steam whistle, rowed out, but they were mainly one-man dinghies, able to pick up only two or three people at a time. Providentially, the *Duke of Teck,* sister ship to the *Princess Alice,* had been following her up-river, and she now reached Gallions Reach and at once lowered her boats.

The people of London's East End, as they have always done in the face of adversity, rallied around the survivors of the *Princess Alice* on that awful night. Plumstead Workhouse was taken over as a temporary refuge, hot soup and warm clothing were provided at Becton Gasworks, people threw open their homes, and cabs were pressed into service to rush the injured to hospital. There was no shortage of volunteers and no lack of compassion.

The rescue work went on throughout the night, and into the next day, but much of this was concerned with the grisly work of pulling bodies from the river and its muddy banks. At first, the boardroom of the London Steamboat Company was used as a mortuary, when this was full, the town hall, then a local factory, and still the bodies kept coming. When the final reckoning was made, it was clear that only 200 passengers and one crew member, an engineer, had survived the loss of the *Princess Alice.* Of the others, it was estimated that around 700 had lost their lives, among them the wife and five children of the company's superintendent, Mr Towse. Captain William Grinstead, the only man who might have been able to offer an explanation for the paddle steamer's suicidal, last minute swing across the bows of the *Bywell Castle,* took his secret with him.

In the early hours of the morning of 20 August, 1989, the forty-six-ton pleasure cruiser *Marchioness*, packed with young revellers, left Charing Cross pier, bound for Greenwich. Some twenty minutes later, having just cleared Southwark Bridge, she was run down and sunk by the 1,475-ton dredger *Bowbelle*. An immediate large-scale rescue operation was mounted but fifty of the 140 on board the *Marchioness* died. Once again, it was a fine, warm summer's night, without a hint of danger in the air, and yet the unthinkable happened. Such is the fallibility of the human hand.

17   Fog in the North Sea

Cimbria & Sultan - 1883

It has been said that man has conquered every aspect of the weather except fog. Central heating keeps the cold at bay, air conditioning curbs the excesses of the sun, a stout umbrella gives shelter from the heaviest of rain. Even the most violent hurricane can be tracked, and if not subdued, certainly forewarned. Fog, on the other hand, despite the wizardry of modern technology, still has the power to close ports and airports, ruin sports fixtures and bring chaos to the motorways. For the mariner, even though he now enjoys the benefits of high-tech radar, navigating in restricted waters continues to hold fearful risks.

In the 19th century, when log and leadline were the only aids, the safety of a ship in fog depended entirely on the eyes and ears of her lookouts and the reflex actions of her master and officers. A fog signal not heard, a light not seen or wrongly identified, an incorrect alteration of course, and disaster might follow.

On a murky night in the North Sea, in January 1883, such mistakes were made, resulting in a collision between two ships the like of which had never before been seen in those waters. As to who was to blame for this catastrophe, it is difficult to judge, for there were no unbiased witnesses, and each ship gave a very different version of events.

The year 1882 had not been a very happy one for Hamburg America Line. In the summer, their steamer *Herder* drove ashore on rocks off Cape Race, Newfoundland and was abandoned, and the *Thuringia* disappeared without trace in mid-Atlantic in the autumn. As winter moved in, the *Gellert* lost two blades of her propeller and was towed into Plymouth, while the *Westphalia* was so damaged in a collision in the Channel that she made port only with great difficulty. When the first sailing of the new year, the *Cimbria,* set out to cross the Atlantic, it is certain there were some uneasy minds in Hamburg America's boardroom.

The 3,037-ton *Cimbria* was one of the stalwarts of Hamburg America's North Atlantic mail and passenger service. Built at John Caird's yard on the Clyde in 1867, she was 330 feet long, 40 feet in the beam and fitted with a compound engine that gave her a service speed of thirteen knots. Her accommodation was for 100 first class,

130 second class and 600 steerage passengers, and she carried an all-German crew of 110. She was chartered by the Russians for a short period in 1877 for trooping during the Russo-Turkish War. Otherwise, she had spent all her life on the North Atlantic run, sailing with clockwork regularity between Hamburg and New York, with an intermediate call at Plymouth or Le Havre on route.

On Thursday 18 January 1883, the *Cimbria,* commanded by Captain Hansen, sailed from Hamburg, bound for Le Havre and New York with 380 passengers. A handful of these were in cabin class, but the vast majority were poor Prussian, Hungarian and Russian emigrants, among them seventy-two women and eighty-seven children. Also on board were six Chippewa Indians, who had been touring Germany with a circus and fourteen French seamen returning to Le Havre. The Indians would have been aboard an earlier steamer, but their departure was delayed by the illness of one of their number. Including her crew, the *Cimbria* was carrying a total of 490 persons.

When, soon after midday, the liner pulled away from Hamburg's St. Pauli landing stage, the weather was fine and settled, although bitterly cold. A large anti-cyclone covered much of Western Europe and the North Sea, giving clear skies and light winds. This, much to the relief of her passengers, indicated a smooth passage, at least as far as Le Havre. Captain Hansen, on the other hand, would have settled for the promise of more wind.

It seemed that the jinx on Hamburg America Line was set to continue, for when the *Cimbria* reached the narrows of the River Elbe, she ran hard aground on a sandbank. She was then forced to endure the humiliation of being pulled off at high water by the tug *Hansa*, owned by North German Lloyd, Hamburg America's closest rival on the North Atlantic. The *Cimbria* suffered no damage, but Captain Hansen and his owners were not amused. As for the passengers, who lined the rails and cheered as the ship came off, they viewed the incident as an exciting beginning to the great adventure on which they were embarked.

Given continuing fair weather, Hansen had anticipated arriving off Le Havre at daylight on the 20th, in which case he would expect to sail again before dark on the same day. The unfortunate grounding put paid to that calculation. It was well after 8 o'clock that night before the *Cimbria* reached the mouth of the Elbe and dropped her pilot off Cuxhaven. She was then running six hours behind schedule, which would result in an overnight stay in Le Havre.

As the lights of Cuxhaven dropped astern, Hansen saw them disappear momentarily in a swirl of mist. He sniffed the cold night air and ran his hand along the bridge taffrail. The varnished woodwork was dripping moisture, a sure danger signal. However, the hours went by and the visibility remained good, with the flickering lights of the farmhouses on the low-lying East Friesian Islands showing up clearly to port. The *Cimbria* was not alone. There was a con-

Widow-Maker

Hamburg America's mail and passenger steamer 'Cimbria'
(Photo: Numast*)*

stant stream of other ships passing on their way in and out of the busy ports of the Elbe and Weser. Hansen resigned himself to remaining on the bridge until daylight, when the ship would be clear of the coast. He was no stranger to sleepless nights, and provided the visibility held up, he was content to get by with the help of endless cups of coffee.

Unknown to Hansen, his troubles were about to begin. The anti-cyclone was drawing in a bitterly cold north-easterly wind straight off the Russian Steppes, while the temperature of the sea over which it was passing was relatively warm. It required only another degree or so fall in the air temperature for the warm vapour rising off the water to condense out in the form of fog. This was not long in coming. By 1.15 in the morning, when the *Cimbria* was north of the mouth of the River Ems, the stars had disappeared, and it was becoming increasingly difficult to see the shore lights. Borkum Island, the last in the chain of the German Friesians, lay only nine miles on the port bow, yet its powerful lighthouse, normally visible at twenty miles, was not yet showing. From then on, the visibility continued to deteriorate, and by 1.30, the liner was running into fog thickening by the minute.

The paramount rule for vessels navigating in fog is, and always has been, to slow down, and to proceed with extreme caution. This is a rule that many have ignored at their peril. Hansen, however, was not of that school. As soon as the fog began to roll in, he rang for slow speed and posted extra lookouts. There were no other ships in close proximity, and being reasonably sure of his position in relation to the land, Hansen decided to carry on, feeling his way cautiously through the growing murk.

Fifteen minutes later, even the comforting glow of the *Cimbria*'s masthead lights had been swallowed up by the fog, and her red and green sidelights reflected back eerily from the opaque whiteness closing in around her. The silence, broken only by the muted beat of the engine and the periodic boom of the steam whistle, was nerve-wracking. Captain Hansen and his officers on the bridge spoke in whispers as they strained eyes and ears to detect the slightest hint of danger.

At 2.10 the first warning came, the mournful wail of another ship's whistle, the sound echoing around the hidden interfaces of the fog, so that there was no way of knowing from which direction it came. Adhering strictly to the rules, Hansen stopped his ship and allowed her to drift.

The visibility was then less than 150 feet in any direction, and with her whistle sounding a double blast to indicate she was stopped, the *Cimbria* waited for the stranger to pass clear. She did not. At 2.15 Hansen and his chief officer, who were in the port wing of the bridge, were horrified to see the lights of another ship suddenly loom up out of the fog on the *Cimbria*'s port quarter. She was fifty yards off and heading straight for them.

It was too late to use the helm and engines to escape the danger. The bows of the other vessel crashed into the *Cimbria*, splitting her open and laying her on her side. The unknown ship then went astern and disappeared back into the fog from whence she came. She made no attempt to communicate with the *Cimbria*. The Hamburg America ship, listing heavily to starboard, began to settle in the water.

The 1,025-ton cargo steamer *Sultan*, owned by Bailey & Leetham, sailed from the Humber shortly before midnight on 17 January, bound for the Elbe. Commanded by Captain Cuttill, she was a regular trader between Hull and Hamburg, usually completing the round trip in seven days. Her top speed was eight knots, giving a passage time between the two ports of forty-eight hours. On this occasion, urged on by a fair wind astern and favourable tidal streams, she crossed the North Sea at a smart ten knots, much to the surprise and delight of Captain Cuttill.

By 1 o'clock on the morning of the 19th, the *Sultan* was in sight of the Borkum Riff lightship, which lies just north of the island, and slicing through a flat calm sea in crisp, clear weather. Bearings taken of the lightship showed the ship to be well to the southward of her course, and Cuttill hauled her up a point to the north to make for the Elbe I lightship. There were no other ships in sight, which was unusual for this normally busy area. Then the fog came rolling in, providing an explanation.

The visibility fell from ten miles to a hundred yards in a few minutes, and Cuttill, who was on the bridge with his first mate, had no option but to reduce speed. Two lookouts were sent forward, and the whistle was set going. Almost immediately after entering the fog, the whistle of another ship was heard sounding somewhere to the north of the *Sultan*. Slowly, very slowly, the sound moved down the port side of the ship, and so close did it pass abeam that Cuttill imagined he could just make out a dark shadow in the fog. This was obviously a steamer outward bound from the Elbe.

Cuttill relaxed again as the signal faded astern and out of hearing. Then, suddenly, the bows of another ship loomed unannounced out of the fog on the *Sultan*'s starboard bow. She dwarfed the *Sultan*, and judging by her creaming bow-wave, she was under way at full speed. Happily, when her lights came though, she was showing green, being on a parallel and opposite course to the cargo steamer. She would pass clear, but it would be a close thing. Cuttill was angry, for here was a ship, contrary to all common sense and regulations, going at full speed in dense fog and not sounding her whistle. He reached for the megaphone, intending to give her master a piece of his mind.

The rebuke was never passed. Without warning, the approaching ship went hard to starboard and laid herself square across the *Sultan*'s bows. It was a suicidal move, and Cuttill was powerless to do anything other than to ring for full speed astern. Before the *Sultan*'s reversing propeller had a chance to grip the water, the other vessel smashed into her starboard bow, spinning the smaller ship right around. There was understandable confusion on the bridge of the *Sultan* but, even so, a sharp pair of eyes picked out the *Cimbria*'s name on her bow before she went back into the fog. Seconds later, Cuttill was stunned to see her coming at his ship again from the port bow, as though intent on finishing her off. Fortunately, by this time the *Sultan* was moving rapidly astern, and the *Cimbria* swept harmlessly across her bows and re-entered the fog.

Cuttill stopped his ship and sent his first mate forward to assess the damage. It was severe. The *Sultan*'s bows had been stove in with such force that her figurehead and anchor hawsepipes had been driven through the collision bulkhead into the forecastle. Water was pouring into the forward hold through a seven-foot gash in the starboard bow extending below the waterline. Luckily, the first mate had no casualties to report, but some of the crew, who were asleep in the forecastle, had missed death by inches.

With his hawsepipes carried away, Cuttill was unable to anchor his ship, and she drifted in the fog for the next five hours while temporary repairs were made to the collision bulkhead. Throughout this time, nothing was seen or heard of the *Cimbria*, and it was assumed she had gone on her way, leaving the *Sultan* to her fate. Cuttill resolved to see she was brought to book when he reached Hamburg.

The *Cimbria* had gone nowhere but to the bottom. While Cuttill listened to the report on the damage to his ship, the liner, hidden by the fog, was going through her death throes only a few hundred yards away. The *Sultan* had struck her amidships on her port side, slicing her open to the waterline, and with the sea pouring into her engine room she sank within fifteen minutes.

At the time of the collision, the majority of the *Cimbria*'s passengers and crew were sound asleep. The crash, the sudden heel of the ship, the shouts and pounding of feet on deck brought them awake and apprehensive. Apprehension quickly turned to fear, and when all the lights went out, a wave of terror swept through the ship.

Hansen and his officers made a determined effort to restore order, and succeeded in handing out lifejackets to all passengers. All seven lifeboats were swung out, but due to the heavy list on the ship, it was possible to launch only four. In the unavoidable confusion reigning these boats went away half empty, and one capsized soon after leaving the ship's side. The *Cimbria* had a number of spare yards and spars on deck, and these were cut loose so that they would float off when she went down. This she did at 2.30 that morning, first heaving herself upright then sinking bodily in ninety feet of water. The sea surrounding her last resting place was covered with men and women fighting for their lives in the icy waters of the North Sea. The *Cimbria* had gone and no one in the outside world knew of her passing.

It was not until the evening of 20 January, when the British barque *Theta*, commanded by Captain Clark, arrived at Cuxhaven with thirty-nine survivors, that the loss of the liner became known. The *Theta* had found two of the *Cimbria*'s boats drifting sixty miles east of Borkum Island.

The alarm being now raised, a fleet of vessels—ironically led by the same tug *Hansa* that had pulled the *Cimbria* off a sandbank forty-eight hours earlier—set out from Cuxhaven to search for more survivors. They returned empty handed, but a boat containing nine passengers was reported as landing on Borkum on the 21st. Twenty-four hours later, the British steamer *Diamant* reached Bremerhaven with sixteen passengers and one of the *Cimbria*'s crew on board. These were survivors from the lifeboat which capsized after launching, who had spent ten hours clinging to the topsail yards of the ship, which remained above water when she sank.

The loss of the *Cimbria* was a maritime disaster of a magnitude unknown in the annals of German history, and the casualty lists appearing in the newspapers were likened to reports from a major battlefield. At the final count, it was clear that only sixty-five had survived, twenty-two of these being crew members. Those lost numbered 425, and included nearly all the seventy-two women and eighty-seven children on board.

The exact circumstances of the *Cimbria/Sultan* collision were never clearly established, as the two key witnesses, Captain Hansen and his chief officer, both lost their lives. However, statements made by other witnesses aboard the *Cimbria* placed all the guilt on the *Sultan*. They claimed that she came out of the fog at full speed, slammed into the *Cimbria*'s port side, and then steamed off without any attempt to render assistance. The survivors who took refuge in the *Cimbria*'s rigging also stated that, although they could see the lights of the *Sultan* clearly, she ignored their cries for help and abandoned them to the sea. On the face of it, the *Sultan* acted in a disgraceful manner, an act unworthy of a British ship, and entirely contrary to the law of the sea.

Captain Cuttill and his first mate, who were arrested in Hamburg when the full extent of the calamity became apparent, gave a very different account of events in the early hours of the morning of 19 January. They stated categorically that the German liner was not sounding her fog signal and was steaming at full speed when she came out of the fog, and rammed the *Sultan*; not vice versa, as claimed by witnesses aboard the *Cimbria*.

The two officers also claimed the *Cimbria* made a second pass at their ship—and this is where the confusion arises, and also raises the possibility of another ship being involved.

Far from running away after the collision, Cuttill stated that, as the German liner was much larger than his ship, he assumed the *Sultan* to have come off worst in the collision, and he therefore gave no thought to going to her aid. There were some grounds for Cuttill's view, for it was later proved that another foot of water in the *Sultan*'s forward hold would have sunk her. Certainly, the situation must have appeared grave at the time, for Cuttill ordered all the ship's lifeboats to be lowered to the water, and kept them alongside throughout the five hours she was stopped for repairs. Had he been aware that the *Cimbria* had gone down, Cuttill stated, he would most certainly have sent these boats to pick up survivors.

The evidence given by both sides in the collision was totally conflicting, and it was never established beyond doubt who was to blame for the disaster. What did emerge, however, was that Captain Hansen, his officers and crew, behaved magnificently in the face of insurmountable odds, but even they could not prevent the loss of 425 lives, many of their own included. Not for the first, or last time, the silent fog had drawn its impenetrable veil around its victims, and condemned them to a lonely death.

Bernard Edwards

18   Behind the Reef

HMS *Calliope* - 1889

The islands of Samoa lie close to the International Date Line and roughly halfway between New Zealand and Hawaii. It was from here, so legend has it, that 2,000 years ago the Polynesians set out to conquer the Pacific. The Dutch navigator Jacob Roggeveen was the first European to sight the islands, in 1722, but he passed them by. Over the next seventy years, La Pérouse, Wallis, Bougainville, Cook and Bligh followed in Roggeveen's wake. La Pérouse was attacked and twelve of his men killed, and Bougainville thought it advisable not to land. The others spoke of Samoa as a pagan paradise of silver sand beaches, tumbling rivers and lush green valleys. They came back again and again.

The explorers inflicted no lasting harm on Samoa but when the whalers came, in about 1790, to be followed by bands of unscrupulous traders, escaped convicts from Australia and missionaries full of zeal, the decline began. By 1840 the naive islanders had been introduced to a host of previously unknown diseases, guns, alcohol and an alien religion, none of which did them any good.

In the meantime, far across the seas, even more momentous changes were taking place. The first railway engine ran from Stockton to Darlington, oil was discovered in Pennsylvania, and the arrival of the motorcar, the telephone and electricity ensured that the European would never again be content with anything but unending progress. The Samoan islander, on the other hand, so long as he had a roof over his head, a few pigs, a good wife and lots of healthy children, was happy to live the simple life. And he was left, more or less, to do just that, until it was discovered that the humble coconut, which grew so profusely on the islands, was a valuable source of oil for the manufacture of margarine and soap. Then the greedy hands of the colonialists reached out for the islands.

The chief contenders for supremacy in Samoa were Germany and the United States of America. Germany coveted Western Samoa, consisting of the islands of Savaii and Upolu, while the United States sought control of Tutuila and the Manua Group, some seventy miles to the east. In time, so much enmity arose between the two nations over the islands that they were almost on the point of war. Britain, although expressing an interest in Samoa, had so many commitments elsewhere that she was content to stand aside and let the other two powers settle the matter between them.

In March, 1889, largely due to the intrigues of the rival colonists, war broke out between tribal factions in Western Samoa, giving the excuse for a show of force. The German Government sent into Apia, capital of Western Samoa, the cruisers *Eber, Olga* and *Adler*, while the Americans, not to be outdone, ordered Rear Admiral L.A. Kimberly to take into the same port his ships *Nipsic, Vandalia* and *Trenton.* When the 2,770-ton third class cruiser HMS *Calliope,* commanded by Captain Henry Coey Kane, arrived in Apia to represent British interests, the harbour was reminiscent of Spithead on review day.

Apia lies on the sheltered northern side of Upolu Island. Its harbour is really a lagoon, formed by an indentation in the coastline, fenced in and protected by the coral reef that fringes the island. It is an enchanted lagoon off an enchanted island, and there were no protests from *Calliope*'s crew at the prospect of a long, lazy visit to this demi-paradise, of which Rupert Brooke wrote, 'It is sheer beauty, so pure it is difficult to breathe in it.'

Captain Henry Kane, when he brought the *Calliope* through the three-hundred yard wide gap in the reef did not share the sentiments of most of his crew. There were already twenty-eight other ships, including the six German and American warships, in the lagoon, and it seemed that every square foot of anchorage space was taken. It required no mean feat of seamanship to slot the cruiser into a vacant corner far too close to the reef for Kane's peace of mind. The bottom was hard coral, poor holding ground for an anchor if it came on to blow.

The weather prevailing when the *Calliope* dropped anchor was, as it is for much of the year in Western Samoa, idyllic; warm sunshine, tempered by a gentle trade wind. But Kane had been long enough in the Pacific not to be lulled into a false sense of security. There was an unusually heavy swell breaking on the reef, and the barometer was slipping. These were ominous signs.

Kane was well aware that the islands were in the hurricane belt, and that the season was at its height, but he also knew it was extremely rare for one of these storms to hit Western Samoa. The hurricanes of the South Pacific form to the north-east of the Fiji Islands, move first to the south-west, and when in about latitude 20° South, re-curve to the south-east, usually passing well to the south of Samoa. Even when, on the morning of the 14th, tell-tale streaks of high cirrus appeared in the sky, and the barometer continued to fall, the consensus of opinion, both afloat and ashore, was firm. A hurricane was in the offing, but it would cause no more than a strong blow in the islands, and that the ships would be perfectly safe anchored behind the reef.

As the day wore on, the glass plummeted and the sky became

more and more threatening. It was clear that this was the exception to the rule, and the hurricane was heading directly for Western Samoa. It was not too late for the ships to put to sea and ride out the storm in unrestricted waters, and sixteen of the merchant ships did just that. The naval ships of the great colonial powers, on the other hand, became involved in a ridiculous face-saving exercise. Rear-Admiral Kimberly, the senior naval officer present, was in the USS *Trenton* and anchored nearest to the opening in the reef. If Kimberly had left, it is most likely the others would have followed suit. But the *Trenton* stayed put, stubbornly ignoring the signals the weather was sending out. And so the other American ships stayed, as did the Germans, each side unwilling to damage their national pride by being the first to run from the storm. Under the circumstances, though much against his better judgement, Kane decided that the *Calliope* must not bring disgrace on the Royal Navy by being the only warship to leave the harbour, and she also stayed. As a compromise, Kane increased the ship's moorings to five widely spaced anchors.

Towards evening, dark, threatening clouds gathered around Apia. The barometer continued to fall, the wind had reached gale force, and the sea at the entrance to the lagoon was so rough that it was no longer possible for any ship to leave the harbour. By the early hours of the 15th a full hurricane was blowing and the barometer was reading 27.8 inches, the lowest Henry Kane had ever seen the mercury fall in all his long years at sea. The boom of the surf on the reef was like thunder, and the water inside the harbour resembled a boiling cauldron. The *Calliope* rolled and pitched, tugging at her cables like a tethered beast. Kane ordered the engines to be brought to immediate readiness and resigned himself to a long, sleepless night on the *Calliope*'s bridge.

As the first grey light of dawn broke through it revealed a world gone mad. The wind, in excess of one hundred knots, and howling like a soul in torment, was in the north and blowing directly into the harbour. Out to sea, great, white-topped rollers—some witnesses said they were seventy feet high—marched in to fling themselves on the protecting reef, exploding in a welter of spray and spume that was immediately snatched by the wind and hurled horizontally across the anchorage. All around the thunder rolled and lightning flashed, and in the midst of this maelstrom, blinded by the flying spray and spume, the ships remaining in the harbour fought to hold their position.

The German ship *Eber* was the first to break adrift. She lost her anchors and was swept bodily across the harbour to crash into the United States sloop *Nipsic*. The American ship, anticipating such a collision, had already rigged fenders, so she suffered little damage. The unfortunate *Eber*, completely out of control, cannoned off the *Nipsic* and slammed into one of her own, the *Olga*. The *Eber* was again fended off, but at that point the wind changed direction and she was hurled onto the reef, breaking her back. For a few minutes she remained sitting upright, then she rolled off the reef to sink in the deep water outside.

The death throes of the *Eber* went unnoticed by the other ships, for the clouds opened and torrential rain reduced visibility to a matter of yards, adding to the horror of the storm. The *Nipsic,* the grip of her anchors probably loosened by the collision with the *Eber,* was the next to drag. She also bounced off the *Olga* then slammed into the merchant schooner *Lily* before being driven ashore in front of the American Consulate. She lowered her boats, but they capsized as soon as they reached the water.

What happened thereafter is largely a matter for conjecture. Hidden in the driving rain and spray, ships were wrenched from their moorings and hurled around the anchorage. They smashed into each other, ran aground, and in the case of some of the small merchant ships, simply sank under the sheer weight of water coming aboard. There could be no thought of rescue, for every ship was fighting desperately for its own survival. Men in the water were left to fight their own lonely battle with slow death by drowning.

The *Calliope,* with five anchors down and her engines going ahead to ease the strain on the cables, was one of the few to hold her position. But as the hours went by and the hurricane continued to blow with undiminished fury, her plight worsened. One by one her cables snapped, until she was holding on to only one anchor, and that began to drag along the hard coral bottom. Kane tried to hold her with the engines, but the weight was too much and she broke free. Twice she was flung against the ship nearest to her, the USS *Vandalia*, and, in desperation, Kane debated whether to head deeper into the harbour and beach her on the soft sand of the foreshore. But there was now a tremendous sea running inside the lagoon, and it was clear the *Calliope* would break up as soon as she was beached. That left Kane with only one other option, and that was to make a bid to escape through the reef into the open sea. The wind had swung back to the north again, blowing directly into the entrance, through which huge, tumbling seas were running unchecked. It was a wild gamble, for although the *Calliope*'s engines were maintained to perfection and were capable of fifteen knots, she would be battling against a wind of indescribable strength. One mistake, one false move, and the ship would be finished. Kane made the decision and sent for Staff Engineer Burke.

The last remaining anchor cable was slipped and Kane rang for full ahead on the engines. Black smoke poured from the cruiser's funnel, her propellers threshed the water, but, in the teeth of the wind, with waves breaking over her forecastle head, she began to drift astern. Grim-faced, Kane rang for emergency full speed, and the beat of the engines mounted towards a noisy crescendo. For the next hour, vibrating so violently that it seemed every rivet in her hull must pop, and with her shaft bearings running so hot that Burke called for fire hoses to cool them, the *Calliope* held her own against the wind and sea. But she made not an inch of forward progress.

Just when Kane was about to accept he had made a grievous mistake in slipping his last anchor, the *Calliope* began slowly, almost imperceptibly, to make headway. At no time, even with her engines running at maximum revolutions, did she work up to more than half a knot, but she was moving. In order to hold her up into the wind the helm movements were many and violent, and the strain on her rudder was enormous. This eventually proved too much and one of the steering chains parted. Only quick action by a party of volunteers, three of whom went over the side to make the repair, saved the ship from broaching to.

As she fought her way towards the gap in the reef, a long streamer of black smoke trailing horizontally astern from her funnel and the waves breaking over her like a half-tide rock, the *Calliope* passed close to USS *Trenton*. Rear Admiral Kimberly's flagship was herself in dire peril, but her crew were so impressed with the *Calliope*'s brave fight for survival, that they forgot their own predicament and lined the rails to cheer the British ship.

At last, after what seemed like an age, the *Calliope* reached the gap in the reef and broke free into the open sea. There, she was still in danger from the ferocity of the hurricane, but she had sea room to ride out the storm and lick her wounds. In the collisions with the *Vandalia* and in her fight to clear the harbour, she had taken some hard knocks. Her foreyard was sprung, her bowsprit gone and all her boats but one were smashed, but, miraculously, only one man had been injured.

The hurricane, one of the worst ever known in the South Pacific, lasted for twenty-nine hours and left terrible destruction in its wake. In the town of Apia only a few of the more solidly built houses were left standing, and the coconut plantations around the town resembled a cornfield trampled by a herd of stampeding elephants. There was not a ship left afloat in the harbour. The *Eber* had disappeared under the overhang of the reef, the *Nipsic* and *Olga* were high and dry on the beach, the *Adler* sat on top of the reef with her back broken, and the *Trenton* and *Vandalia* were under water. The six merchant ships that had stayed with them were in a similar state.

The *Trenton* had been the last to go, swept from her moorings by seas breaking over the reef. Her boiler fires were out, her sails were in shreds, and she was blown across the harbour towards the wreck of the *Vandalia*. The crew of the *Vandalia* who had taken to the rigging, watched in horror as the other ship bore down on them. In a last ditch effort to save his ship, Lieutenant Brown, commander of the *Trenton*, sent two hundred of his crew into the rigging on the weather side, hoping the tightly packed mass of men would act as a sail. The plan worked, and the *Trenton*, instead of crashing into the wreck of the *Vandalia*, came gently alongside her. The *Vandalia*'s crew took the opportunity to save themselves by swarming down onto the *Trenton*'s decks. But all Lieutenant Brown's ingenuity could not save the *Trenton*, and she later tore her bottom out on the reef and sank. Happily, only one of her crew of 450 was lost, and all those taken off the *Vandalia* were saved.

Thus ended a great sea battle, fought to a draw without a shot being fired. The Germans and Americans each lost three of their best warships in the Pacific, and with them went 146 men. That HMS *Calliope* escaped was due to the initiative of Captain Henry Coey Kane and the great courage and dedication to duty of his crew. To commemorate the achievement the Admiralty struck a special medal which was presented to every man on board the *Calliope*.

When the chaos created by the hurricane was put to rights, the Samoan question was settled by allowing Germany to annex Western Samoa, while the United States took control of Tutuila and the Manua Group, which became known as American Samoa. Today, Western Samoa is an independent country and American Samoa is an unincorporated territory of the United States. The copra has gone and tourism has taken its place, and the average Samoan, little affected by a century of colonial interference, is still at peace with the world with a roof over his head, a few pigs, a good wife and lots of healthy children. Robert Louis Stevenson, master storyteller, lies at rest on Mount Vaea overlooking Apia harbour, where the rusting remains of the German ship Adler still sit astride the reef. To the west of Apia, under the warm sands of the Mulinuu Peninsular, traditional burial ground of Samoa's kings and queens, lie the bodies of the 146 German and American seamen who died in the hurricane of 15 March, 1889.

Bernard Edwards

19   Utopia Meets the Fleet

Utopia - 1891

In high summer, to spend weeks idling in Italian ports under a warm Mediterranean sun is many a seaman's dream of the good life. In late winter, with the sun hidden behind thick cloud and a chilly north-easterly blowing, the dream pales. It was therefore with some relief for her crew that the liner *Utopia*, having spent a dreary month on the coast, sailed out of the Bay of Naples on the evening of 12 March, 1891 and turned her bows towards the Straits of Gibraltar.

The 2,731-ton *Utopia*, owned by the Anchor Line of Glasgow, was on voyage to New York, calling at Gibraltar for coal bunkers. Built on the Clyde in 1874, the *Utopia* had, in her day, been a first-rate transatlantic liner, holding her own with the best on the Western Ocean. The passage of the years had taken their toll and she was eventually relegated to the humble, albeit highly lucrative, Italian emigrant trade. That is not to say she was in any way an inferior ship. She had been extensively refitted at a cost of £30,000, before sailing from the Clyde in November of the previous year, and her hull and engines were in good condition and her accommodation adequate.

However, the *Utopia*, only 350 feet long and 35 feet beam, was not designed to carry 827 Italian emigrants, the number she had on board on sailing from Naples. She was an overcrowded ship with all her utilities stretched to the absolute limits, and with a sixteen-day passage ahead of her. Faced with the inevitable sickness and unrest among the volatile Italians, it would not be an easy passage for the *Utopia*'s master, Captain John McKeague, and his fifty-nine man British crew. Despite the best efforts of the ship's surgeon, Dr Sellar, and Chief Officer James Thompson, chaos and squalor would always prevail in the cramped steerage quarters. The situation was not improved when, some hours after leaving Naples, three stowaways were discovered; three more hopefuls seeking a new life across the sea, who were even too poor to pay their way in steerage. Below decks, the *Utopia* had as full a quota of seething humanity as any ship might be expected to bear.

Above decks, in the first class accommodation, there lay another world. For the passage to New York the *Utopia* carried only three saloon passengers, Mr Charles G. Davies of Boston, and Mr & Mrs William D. Colbron of New York. In roomy, well furnished cabins with an excess of stewards to cater for their every whim, the trio of Americans were set to enjoy a very comfortable voyage. There would be no water shortage in first class, and the food would be only of the best. For the newly-wed Mr & Mrs Colbron, the trip was the conclusion of an extended honeymoon, and they delighted in their good fortune.

In all, when she sailed from Naples, the *Utopia* had on board a total of 893 persons, among them eighty-five women and sixty-seven children. She carried lifeboats for less than half that number.

When she came out of the builder's yard, the *Utopia* easily maintained a service speed of twelve knots. Seventeen years and many punishing North Atlantic crossings later, her triple expansion steam engines, although carefully nursed by her Glaswegian chief engineer, Herbert Cook, were capable of no more than eleven knots, given fair weather. At this speed Captain McKeague expected to reach Gibraltar before noon on the 16th, and allowing one full day for bunkering, arrive in New York by the end of the month. Unfortunately, the Mediterranean can be as fickle as any ocean at the equinox. Throughout the 980-mile passage westwards, dogged by adverse winds and currents, the *Utopia* was hard pressed to reach eight knots. It was therefore six o'clock on the evening of the 17th, a few minutes before sunset, before she neared Europa Point, the southern most tip of the 1,400-foot high, wedge-shaped promontory known to the Moors as Jebel Tariq, and to British seaman as The Rock.

Gibraltar, captured by British forces under the command of Admiral Sir George Rooke in 1704, sits astride the western entrance to the Mediterranean Sea. For more than a century it was the principal base and repair depot for ships of the Royal Navy. Then, with the building of larger and better dockyards at Malta in the 1830s, the strategic importance of Gibraltar went into steep decline, but the port did not become derelict. Its safe harbour was in a convenient position for merchant ships bound to and from the Cape of Good Hope and the East to replenish their coal bunkers. For the next hundred years, although naval ships still called, Gibraltar's main role was as a bunker and supply port for commercial shipping. British colliers discharged coal on to the moles, barges ferried it out to the anchorage, and Spanish labour, weather permitting, carried it up the ships' sides in baskets to tip into the bunkers. It was a slow, primitive process, but it was economical and it suited the pace of the day.

The weather had begun to deteriorate some hours before the *Utopia* sighted Gibraltar, and by the time she exchanged signals with the Admiralty signal station on Europa Point, it was blowing a gale from the south-west. The approach to Gibraltar harbour through Algeciras Bay is not a difficult one. However, darkness was now setting in, and with the wind blowing directly into the bay, McKeague would have been well advised to lie off, or anchor to the east of the Rock, to await daylight, or, at the very least, an improvement in the weather. It was most likely the gale blowing was the result of an Atlantic depression moving east across Spain into France, and would soon pass. But for reasons best known to himself McKeague stood on. It may be that after the frustratingly slow passage from Naples, he was unwilling to lose more time.

After rounding Europa Point, McKeague reduced to half speed and steamed north-north-west for the approach channel to Gibraltar harbour. Low, scudding clouds and a thick drizzle had hastened the onset of complete darkness, and a heavy quarterly swell made steering difficult. As a precaution, McKeague sent Chief Officer James Thompson and the carpenter, Hugh Taggart, forward to stand by the anchors. The lights of some ships at anchor in or near the entrance to the harbour were visible, but they did not appear to present any danger to the *Utopia.* Beyond that, McKeague had no idea of the true situation in the harbour.

In 1891, for once in its long and turbulent history, Europe was at peace with itself and the rest of the world, but, as ever, the pot was still bubbling and intrigue and rivalry still stalked the continent. The serf-like citizens of Russia were on the verge of bloody rebellion, and the irrepressible militarists of Germany, France, Italy and Austria were all flexing their muscles. As a result of the uncertainty, a large squadron of the British Channel Fleet, under Rear Admiral Jones, was showing the flag in Gibraltar. On that stormy night in March, as the *Utopia* approached to replenish her coal bunkers, Gibraltar harbour and its surrounding waters were crowded with naval ships at anchor, among their ranks the great battleships HMS *Anson* and HMS *Rodney.*

It was common practice at the time for ships equipped with electric generators to burn oil lights at night to save fuel, and the ships of the Channel Fleet were no exception. As they lay at anchor off Gibraltar, their oil lights were dim and their low silhouettes barely visible in the gloom. Coming in from seaward, McKeague formed the judgement that the ships he could see in the anchorage were small and few in number, and that he would have no difficulty in wending his way through them to reach the coaling berth. When he finally became aware that his course into the harbour was blocked by a large number of big ships swinging to their anchors, it was too late. The *Utopia*, urged on by a following wind and sea, was at the point of no return. The drizzle had now turned to blinding rain, but John McKeague, knowing full well the fearful risks he was taking, was obliged to carry on. His passengers, meanwhile, were blissfully unaware of the danger. Excited by the lights of the port, which for many was the first sight of a foreign land, the Italian emigrants lined the rails laughing and talking. Above them, on the empty promenade deck, the honeymooning Colbrons held hands and made plans for a trip ashore. The only other saloon passenger, Charles Davies, was in his cabin resting.

The men keeping harbour watch on the bridges of the anchored warships, who had been watching the approach of the *Utopia,* expected her to drop anchor before she reached the fleet. When they realised she was committed to passing through their lines, their eyes opened in horror. In broad daylight and with calm weather, she might just have got through safely; under the conditions prevailing, she was attempting the impossible.

Taking a snap judgement on the best option left open to him, McKeague decided there was just room to pass between the bows of one of the larger ships and the end of the New Mole. It would be a tight squeeze, but once past this ship, the way through the anchorage appeared to be clear. McKeague rang for full speed and took the gap at a run so as to avoid being swept down on the other ship by the wind and current.

It seemed that the merchant captain's strategy might work, then, when the *Utopia* was about to cross the bows of the other ship—she was the battleship *Anson*—the dim lights of another ship loomed up out of the rain right ahead. HMS *Curlew* was anchored two cables inside the *Anson*, and with her stern overlapping the battleship's bow. It was too late to take the way off the *Utopia* and McKeague was forced to throw the helm hard over in order to avoid a collision with the *Curlew.* The liner's bows came quickly round to starboard and her stern slewed to port, and for a moment it seemed that she would slip through between the two anchored ships. But in trying to thread the eye of the needle McKeague underestimated the force of the wind and waves. As she swung, the *Utopia* slid, broadside on, onto the bows of HMS *Anson.* Even then she might have cleared the danger—if only by a few precious inches—had it not been for an unseen menace hidden below the waves.

The main weapon of the fighting galleys of the Eastern Mediterranean in the heyday of Greece and Rome was the ram bow, a wicked, sharp pointed beak projecting underwater from the stem. This was used to great effect in battle, the classic manoeuvre being to circle an enemy until he presented his broadside, and then to dash in and punch a fatal hole in his side with the ram. With the advent of the heavy shipboard gun, this practice became fraught with risk, and the ram bow passed into history. Many centuries later, in the 1860s, when the first ironclad warships appeared, the ram bow was re-introduced, but for what reason is not clear. The range of naval guns was by this time measured in miles, and there was scarcely ever need for two adversaries to approach within ramming distance of each other. The Royal Navy's only experience of the ram bow in action was in the Irish sea in 1875, when the battleship *Vanguard* was accidentally rammed and sunk by her sister ship HMS *Iron Duke.*

However, for many years after that, an inflexible Admiralty insisted on all battleships being built with ram-bows, huge, bulbous underwater projections that made docking difficult and served no useful purpose. HMS *Anson* was so equipped.

The *Utopia* fell heavily against the *Anson*'s ram bow with a crash that brought the cacophony of the storm raging around her to a sudden crescendo and jarred every rivet in her hull. The armoured ram smashed into the liner's engine-room, and such was the forward momentum of the ship that the ram ripped open her underwater plates like a giant tin opener. When she came to rest, after a hundred yards or so, the *Utopia* had a hole in her side twenty-six feet long by fifteen feet wide. The sea poured into her engine-room and after holds, and she began to settle by the stern.

Captain McKeague, although as yet unaware that his ship had been sliced open, realised the gravity of his predicament and began sounding SOS on his steam whistle. This was taken up by the surrounding warships, who fired alarm guns and sounded whistles, filling the dark night with urgency. Those nearest to the *Utopia* turned their searchlights on the sinking ship, bathing her in brilliant light. It was a scene watchers on shore, only a quarter of a mile away, would never forget. As the guns boomed and the whistles blared, the stage came alight, and they found themselves witness to a human tragedy of dreadful proportions.

The unexpected horror of the collision, and the uproar that followed, was enough to send the *Utopia*'s steerage passengers into a blind panic. Many of them were on deck when the crash came, and their first reaction was to rush below to find their families and their personal belongings. Very soon, as those fighting to get below met with those equally determined to reach the deck, complete bedlam broke out. Men, women and children fought with fists, boots and knives in a hopeless, jumbled heap at each hatchway, so that all access to the ladders was blocked. It was a situation of stark terror, one which McKeague and his crew could not hope to control.

Those not engaged in the struggle at the hatchways rushed the lifeboats, and although the *Utopia*'s officers tried to halt the stampede, they were swept aside. McKeague gave orders that no boats were to be launched, for in the heavy sea running would clearly smash against the ship's side before they reached the water. And so the demented Italians sat in the boats and waited for rescue to come to them. The *Utopia*'s stern was already under water, and she had not long to go.

In spite of the horrendous weather conditions prevailing, help was already on the way. As soon as the seriousness of the *Utopia*'s plight was realised aboard the warships, the Royal Navy acted with characteristic efficiency. All ships in the immediate vicinity of the sinking liner launched boats, and within minutes a fleet of launches, pinnaces and cutters was battling through the storm-lashed darkness towards the *Utopia*. Boats from the Swedish warship *Freya* and the cable ship *Amber* also joined in. As the rescue boats drew near the *Utopia* they heard the pitiful cries for help from those on board, but they dared not approach too close for fear of being dashed against the liner's side. They were forced to lay off to leeward and await their opportunity.

The state of affairs on board the *Utopia* had degenerated into one of absolute confusion. Seeing no hope of containing the mob, McKeague had withdrawn his men to the bridge, where they would at least be safe from attack. On the deck, now being swept by waves, hundreds of terrified Italians screamed and fought each other as they retreated towards the forecastle head, which was still rode high out of the water. Many did not make it, being washed overboard by the seas, others took to the rigging, climbing over each other in their haste to escape from the waves. Soon the forecastle and the forward rigging were a heaving mass of frightened humanity.

For those who reached the forecastle, this provided only a very temporary refuge. At about 7.10 pm, fifteen minutes after she had impaled herself on the ram bow of the *Anson*, the *Utopia* succumbed to the massive inrush of water into her hull and sank. She went down in fifty-four feet of water, washing off all those clustered on the forecastle head and clinging to the lower rigging. Only those in the upper rigging held on and remained above water.

This was the signal for the waiting rescue boats to move in. They threaded their way through a sea of floating wreckage, in amongst which bobbed hundreds of heads, many of them disappearing as the boats approached. Some of the boat's crews, at great risk to themselves, dived into the raging sea to rescue drowning men. Those who had taken refuge in the upper rigging, numbering forty or fifty in all, were taken off alive by a steam pinnace, an operation lasting over four hours. Some, in the highest reaches, had to be prised out of the rigging and carried down on the backs of their rescuers.

The fight to save lives went on all night, and so did the storm. Several of the naval ships' boats were smashed, and the steam pinnace of the battleship *Immortalité* hit a rock and two of her crew were lost. Aboard the anchored warships, all those not actively engaged in the boat-work gave medical assistance and succour to the survivors as they were brought aboard.

The weather moderated with the arrival of daylight, and then it became clear for the first time that Gibraltar had witnessed a major disaster. Of the *Utopia*'s 830 Italian emigrant passengers, only 290 were safe. The absence of bodies in the water indicated that most of the others had gone down with the ship. This was confirmed a few days later by divers who examined the wreck. They found the hatchways to the steerage blocked by bodies, while hundreds of dead lay entombed below decks, among them most of the women and children on board.

Bernard Edwards

One of the *Utopia*'s three saloon passengers, Charles Davies, who was in his cabin at the time of the collision, went down with the ship. Mr & Mrs Colbron, who were on deck, jumped into the sea as the ship sank, and became separated. William Colbron was picked up by one of the rescue boats and landed into hospital, where he learned that his wife of a few months was missing, believed drowned. A few days later, when Colbron, totally grief-stricken, was wandering the streets of Gibraltar, he came face to face with the woman he thought he had lost forever. She had also been pulled from the water by the Royal Navy, but taken to a different hospital, and had been similarly grieving for her lost husband. The reunion of the Colbrons was one good thing to come out of the disaster.

In all, 578 people lost their lives on the night the *Utopia* went down, thirty-five of them crew members. Captain John McKeague, who survived, was later to face charges of negligence at a court of inquiry. As to the ship, she lay only 300 yards off the head of the New Mole with her masts and funnel above water, constituting a danger to navigation. It was decided that she must either be destroyed or raised, the latter being preferable. A Scottish engineer, Napier Armit, was given the task, and in a remarkable feat of salvage, which involved building a cofferdam around the wreck, the *Utopia* was raised in just over four months. In early June, 1891, she was looking for new owners.

It might have been thought that those poor, frightened Italians who survived the sinking would have been welcomed into America with open arms. They had lost everything they owned in the world, including in many cases, those nearest and dearest to them. But bureaucracy will have its way. A law was at that time going through the US Senate to prohibit the landing of destitute immigrants. As the 290 who survived the Utopia were truly destitute, their future became the subject of a long and distasteful legal wrangle.

20   The Cape Horners

King David & Pass of Melfort - 1905

When the *King David* sailed from Newport Mon., South Wales in February, 1905, her days were already numbered. She was of a dying breed, one of the last of the great square-riggers that had dominated the sea-lanes for over half a century. During those heady years the steamer was born, and defying all the predictions of the traditionalists, gained in reputation and reliability until it was poised to oust fickle wind power once and for all.

The *King David* was a steel ship of 2,240 tons gross, square rigged on all three masts. Clyde-built in 1894, she was owned by the Glasgow King Shipping Company, and commanded by Captain Pride. A few hours before she sailed from Newport on a blustery February morning in 1905 the ship was visited by the chaplain of the local Mission to Seamen, who delivered on board a box of bibles and hymn books. This was in an age when life at sea was so brutal and uncertain that few seamen, hard-bitten unbelievers though they might be at heart, dared to turn their back on religion.

The enormous risks to be faced on the voyage ahead of the *King David* must have alone been enough for her twenty-five-man crew to seek some form of life insurance, be it only in the form of a half-remembered hymn sung tunelessly in the topsail yards. Loaded with a full cargo of Welsh coal, fresh-mined and volatile, highly susceptible to spontaneous combustion, and liable at any time to consume the ship from within, she was bound for Salina Cruz, on the Pacific coast of Mexico. It was a mammoth voyage of 16,000 miles, during which the *King David* would be called upon to do battle with all the powerful battalions of the Atlantic and Pacific oceans. The ultimate test of ship and men would lie in the awesome challenge of rounding the infamous Cape Horn from east to west.

Cape Horn, first sighted in 1616 by the Dutch navigator Willem Schouten, is the most inhospitable headland ever to tax the skill of the professional seaman. Standing steep-browed and forbidding, the Horn—or Cape Stiff as the windjammer men called it—is the south-facing bluff of Herschell Island, southernmost constituent of the cold and desolate archipelago of Tierra del Fuego. At this point the Great Southern Ocean funnels into the comparatively narrow Drake Strait, which separates America from Antarctica. Trapped between the two continents, the westerly winds of the Roaring Forties, hitherto blowing unhindered around the circumference of the globe, reach hurricane force, heaping up regiments of sixty-foot-high waves that march resolutely from horizon to horizon. They are accompanied by sleet and snow squalls that come sweeping down from the Andes, and, to add to the dangers, dense fog often blankets the area, hiding the hungry rocks of Tierra del Fuego and the drifting icebergs of the Antarctic.

The ordeal for those under sail at the turn of the century usually began well to the northwards of the Horn, with days of completely overcast skies making navigation largely a matter of guesswork. Running into ever increasing winds and mounting seas, ships often approached Cape Horn uncertain of their position to within as much as fifty miles. North-setting currents and poor visibility resulted in many fine ships finding graves amongst the accumulation of rocks and islets that is Magellan's 'Land of the Fires'.

Fate was kind to the *King David*, and she weathered the Horn safely, but it was early August, five and a half months out of the Bristol Channel, when, battered and rust-streaked, she finally limped into Salina Cruz. The men who manned her likewise bore the scars of the ordeal. Gaunt and hungry—for there had been nothing to eat for the final two weeks but the rough porridge they called burgoo—faces burnt red by the wind and hands covered in calluses from the unceasing struggle with salt-stiffened canvas, they had been to Hell and back. Fortunately for their sanity, the long months at sea were soon forgotten in a haze of cheap Mexican gin and the pleasures of the whorehouses of Salina Cruz, but even for this there was a price to be paid.

Salina Cruz lies in the Gulf of Tehuantepec, where the isthmus of Central America swells out to become Mexico. It is a hot, unhealthy place, surrounded by lush forests and impenetrable swamps, where, even today, malaria and yellow fever still stalk, held in check only by the miracle of antibiotics. At the turn of the century, when medicine was young and sanitation of little account, life expectancy for the white man in the isthmus was often measured in days. The *King David*'s sojourn in the port was therefore not a happy one. Several of her crew, including Captain Pride, went down with one fever or another. When she sailed, Captain Davidson, previously the ship's chief officer, was in command.

As Davidson took the *King David* out of Salina Cruz, a thousand miles to the south-east, in the Gulf of Panama, the 2,346-ton *Pass of Melfort* was coming to an anchor off the port of Ancon. Commanded by Captain John Houston, and with a crew of thirty-four, the *Pass of Melfort* was a four-masted steel barque owned by Gibson & Clarke, of Glasgow. She too had originally sailed from Newport Mon., and had traded on the West Coast of America for some months before heading in to Ancon to discharge a cargo.

Widow-Maker

If Salina Cruz was a bad spot, then Ancon, lying seven degrees of latitude further south, was a veritable cesspit, sweltering under a merciless Equatorial sun. The Conquistadors, laden with stolen gold, came this way, Morgan's buccaneers wreaked their bloody havoc here, and now, within sight of the *Pass of Melfort*, work was in progress on a canal to join the Atlantic with the Pacific. De Lesseps had tried before, only to be defeated when disease carried off 20,000 of his labourers in a single year. Now, the new Canal Company had drained swamps, improved sanitation, and waged unrelenting war on the fever-bearing mosquito, but, as the *Pass of Melfort* was to experience, this war was far from won. During the five weeks she languished in Ancon, malaria struck hard, killing Captain Houston and filling the hospital beds with his men. When the barque finally sailed from the port, her crew consisted largely of replacements provided by the crimp houses of Panama. Among the few originals remaining was Chief Officer Harry Scougall, who like Davidson of the *King David*, now found himself in command. The *Pass of Melfort* was also bound in ballast for Puget Sound, thus completing the links joining these two Glasgow ships that were to last even unto death.

The direct route from Salina Cruz to Puget Sound is some 2,800 miles, no more than an eight-day passage for the modern cargo ship. For the *King David*, with the wind her only means of propulsion, the way was more complex. It involved a 1,600-mile-long tack out into the Pacific on the north-east trades, before she was positioned to come about for the Juan de Fuca Strait, which leads into Puget Sound. In all, the actual distance covered would be almost 4,000 miles, with a passage time, in Captain Davidson's estimation, of about thirty days.

As it turned out, Davidson's estimate was wildly in error, and the *King David*'s passage north developed into a long, wearying marathon with no apparent end in sight. The trades were light and variable, adverse winds blew and there were long periods of flat calm, during which the ship lay drifting aimlessly with her sails hanging slack. It was 8 December, nearly eighty days out of Salina Cruz, before observations showed they were nearing the coast of Oregon. By this time food and water were running short, and tempers even shorter. For Davidson, there was the added worry of knowing that his ship must have by now been posted overdue and the underwriters were contemplating heavy losses. But, with no means of communication with the shore, he could do nothing to allay their fears.

And then, just when Davidson thought the worst of the long ordeal was over, the weather played another cruel trick. On the night of the 9th, the wind came out of the south-east at gale force, bringing with it miserable, driving rain that reduced the visibility to less than a mile. Very soon, the rain turned to sleet, then to snow, and the *King David*, running before the wind, was isolated in a white world whose boundaries stretched no more than a few hundred yards on all sides. She was then abeam of the entrance to the Columbia River, 150 miles south of the Juan de Fuca Strait.

Davidson reduced sail as much as was compatible with steerage way, but the gale blowing from astern had been joined by a north-westerly running current, and the ship went careering on unchecked. Captain Davidson might then have been wise to haul off the coast and wait for an improvement in the visibility, but the pressing need to replenish his empty storerooms and water tanks drove him on. He decided to edge further in towards the coast in the hope of sighting the light on Cape Flattery, on the southern shore of Juan de Fuca Strait.

Dawn came on the 10th, with no let-up in the blizzard, and no sighting of Cape Flattery. By dead reckoning, the ship should have been off the entrance to Juan de Fuca by 7 o'clock that morning, but Davidson began to have doubts. He feared he may have overestimated the ship's speed, and she might in fact be a long way astern of his reckoning. With a man in the chains sounding the bottom and extra lookouts posted, the *King David* sailed on.

The hours passed, with nothing seen or heard but the blinding snow and the keening wind. By noon, Davidson was forced to concede that he had overrun Cape Flattery and was hopelessly lost. Yet he still continued to press north, hoping for a sight of the land.

Day turned to night again, and as it did, so the wind suddenly veered around to the west, thus putting the *King David* on a dead lee shore. At the same time, the snow eased and the horizon widened. At around 9 o'clock that night, with no land yet in sight, Davidson reluctantly concluded that he must go about and claw back out to sea. Unfortunately, he had left it too late. As the men ran to the braces, the lookout at the masthead reported breakers ahead and, moments later, also breakers to seaward.

It was fortunate that Davidson, in command for only a few short months, was a tough, resourceful seaman, for he was faced by the most terrible nightmare ever to haunt navigators down through the ages. The *King David* had unwittingly sailed into a trap, with rocks ahead and between her and the open sea. Driving his men aloft—for there was no time to lose—Davidson brought the ship up short and anchored her in eight fathoms.

For the next seventy-two hours, the *King David* and her men lived in a hellish world filled by the howl of the wind and the ominous boom of breaking seas all around. The snow still fell steadily and there was no sight of land, but it was assumed they were somewhere off the west coast of Vancouver Island. Even Davidson could only hazard a guess within a hundred miles of their position. So long as their anchors held they were safe, but if they did not they were doomed to die in this grim, unknown spot so far from their native land.

There was a welcome improvement on the afternoon of 13th,

when the wind relented and the snow cleared. But as the visibility slowly increased, so the full gravity of their predicament became apparent. The ship was close inshore, about 1 1|2 miles off a rock-strewn beach, and inside a line of reefs on which the long Pacific swells broke in a welter of spray and foam. Only to the south-east did there appear to be clear water. After some discussion with his officers, Davidson decided it might just be possible to work the ship back out into the open sea using anchors and sails. Men were sent aloft, while Chief Officer Wollstein took a party forward to tend the anchors. It was a delicate manoeuvre, requiring one anchor to be lifted and the other cable shortened so that the anchor would drag along the bottom and act as a brake when sail was set. In this way Davidson hoped to back the ship out through the gap to the south-east. The plan might have worked, but the gods were not on the side of *King David* that day. At a crucial moment, a fierce squall blew up out of the north-east, the anchor cable jumped the windlass, and the ship was thrown onto a reef.

The *King David* was badly holed, listing heavily and in danger of sinking if she should slide off the reef into deep water, so Davidson ordered his crew to abandon ship. Two boats were lowered on the lee side and all the men left, except Davidson and Wollstein. Once on shore, the others found some deserted Indian huts and made several trips between the wreck and the beach carrying gear and provisions. Davidson and Wollstein stayed with the *King David* for three more days, leaving only when she began to break up on the 16th.

Sextant observations taken when they were on shore established that they had landed at Bajo Point, Vancouver Island, close to the spot where Captain James Cook, the first Britisher to set foot on the island, came ashore in 1778. Had they been aware of this—and they most probably were not—it would have been of little consolation to the castaways. The area they found themselves in was plainly inhospitable, densely forested and slashed by deep gorges and fast running rivers. Wild animals abounded but, so far as scouting parties were able to penetrate, there was no sign of human habitation. Their charts indicated the nearest outpost of civilisation to be a hundred miles south, at Cape Beale. For men largely ignorant of the ways of the wilds, and already worn down by the trauma of losing their ship, reaching Cape Beale at the height of winter was a physical impossibility. Davidson concluded that their only hope lay in being seen by a passing ship, and to this end, bonfires were lit on the foreshore and kept burning day and night.

The bone-chilling cold proved to be the men's worst enemy, for they had no clothes for such weather. The derelict huts provided some protection, but soon an air of bitter hopelessness settled over the camp. It was ten months since the men had left their homes, and the spectres of the grieving widows and orphans they seemed doomed to leave behind moved in to haunt them. Unexpectedly, it was the oldest and most experienced man among them who was first to crack. On one dark and sombre night, sixty-year-old sailmaker Donald McLeod went mad and threw himself into a blazing bonfire. He was terribly burned, but did not die, lingering on to torment his companions with his pitiful moans.

On 21 December, eight days after the wreck, Davidson made up his mind to act before death became a daily ritual and called for volunteers to take a boat south to Cape Beale to bring help. Later that day, Wollstein and six others set sail from the beach and were soon out of sight behind the nearest headland. Given fair weather, as then prevailed, Wollstein estimated they would reach Cape Beale in three days at the most.

For the seventeen men left marooned on the beach at Bajo Point Christmas Day, 1905 was cold and cheerless. A howling blizzard had been blowing relentlessly for two days, and as they sheltered in their tumbledown huts, it seemed inconceivable that anyone else could be in a worse position. They were wrong.

Just seventy miles to the south, and caught in the same blizzard that lashed Bajo Point, the *Pass of Melfort*, two months out of Ancon, was in mortal danger. Captain Harry Scougall, as Captain Davidson had been before him, was hopelessly lost and searching for the entrance to Juan de Fuca Strait. Unknown to Scougall, he had already overshot the entrance and was sailing close in to the treacherous coast of Vancouver Island.

Late on that stormy Christmas night, the *Pass of Melfort* tore her bottom out on rocks off the tall cliffs of Amphitrite Point, seventeen miles north of Cape Beale. She broke up and sank within minutes and not a man was saved.

On 15 January, 1906, the steamer *Queen City,* bound from Victoria to Cape Scott, sighted signal fires onshore near Bajo Point and sent a boat in to investigate. The landing party found seventeen emaciated, frost-bitten scarecrows huddled together around one of the fires. Davidson and his men, now almost out of food, could not have lasted much longer. For poor, demented Donald McLeod, rescue came too late. He died on board the *Queen City* and was buried at Winter Harbour, where the steamer stopped on her way back to Victoria to land the others.

Nothing had been seen or heard of the seven men, led by Chief Officer Wollstein, who sailed south for Cape Beale, and it seemed certain they must have perished in the storm. Then, amongst the mass of wreckage washed ashore after the sinking of the *Pass of Melfort* was found a cork lifebuoy marked KING DAVID. The current on that coast runs to the north-west, and for some weeks the wind had been from the south-east, so it was impossible for the lifebuoy to have drifted down from Bajo Point. It was, therefore, concluded that the buoy had come from the *King David*'s lifeboat. Were Wollstein and his men picked up by the *Pass of Melfort* and, by a cruel twist of fate, subsequently perished with that ship?

Five months later, an Indian fisherman, while paddling his canoe northwards along the coast from Amphitrite Point, sighted the entrance to a cave he had not previously seen. He decided to investigate and swam inside the cave, which proved to be fifty feet high and two-hundred feet deep, with a large boulder blocking the entrance. The light was good inside, and the fisherman was horrified to find a ship's lifeboat manned by seven grinning skeletons. He lost no time in regaining his canoe, and reported his macabre find to the authorities as soon as he returned to his village. Within a few days an expedition had reached the cave, but all attempts to enter it were frustrated by a heavy surf. It was concluded that the Indian must have stumbled on the entrance to the cave at a freak turn of the tide, never to be repeated again. As to how the lifeboat ended up inside the cave, it was assumed that a combination of high tide and heavy seas had lifted it bodily over the boulder at the entrance. Once inside the boat could not escape, and so the men died of starvation and exposure. There were seven skeletons. Was it the *King David*'s boat?

In 1950, Alexander McDonald, of Victoria, reported: *'I once landed my surf boat on the spot where the fine four-masted barque* Pass of Melfort *lies - at the entrance to Barclay Sound, Vancouver Island. The day I landed there it was fine weather, with very clear and smooth water, and there below us was a mass of iron tubes - probably some of her masts and yards. I found some of her hatches in among the forest trees about 400 feet from the high water mark, which gives some indication of the sea that was piling on and over those cliffs when she drove ashore during a south-west gale and snow squalls on Christmas Day, 1905. I also saw some of her wire running gear hanging over the face of the cliffs, which showed that her masts must have fallen onto these high places when she struck. No one was saved from her. The bodies of two young boys were picked up and buried close to where they died, and a picket fence - which I once helped to paint - encloses their lonely graves.'*

21   The Scapegoat

Californian - 1912

After lying undisturbed in her grave 13,000 feet deep in the North Atlantic for seventy-six years, the *Titanic* has already felt the searching eye of the underwater camera and the scrape of the salvageman's probe.

There is treasure, so it is said, of up to £80 million in the sunken liner's safe, but more likely this is just a product of the imagination of certain journalists of her day. If successful, however, such a major feat of salvage would arouse intense excitement around the world, thus proving extremely lucrative for the participants, but it would be unlikely to answer many of the questions posed by the loss of the great ship. It would certainly do nothing to clear the name of the saddest victim of the *Titanic*'s sinking, Captain Stanley Lord, master of the British steamer *Californian*. Lord, it was alleged, stood by and watched as more than 1,500 people died without lifting a finger to help. In reality, Captain Lord was nothing more than a convenient scapegoat who was used to divert attention from the shame of the world's first 'unsinkable' liner, which went down so tragically on its maiden voyage.

The *Titanic*, at 46,238 tons and 883 feet long, was in 1912 the largest ship ever built; she was also the most luxurious liner afloat. Owned by the Oceanic Steam Navigation Company, popularly known as the White Star Line, she had a service speed of twenty-two knots and was certified by the Board of Trade to carry 3,547 passengers and crew. She was equipped with the new wireless telegraphy and her lifeboats were fitted with the latest Welin mechanical davit system, which was said to ensure fast and trouble-free launching of the boats in the event of an emergency. Not that any situation involving the abandonment of this grand vessel was ever envisaged. Her cellular double-bottom—another brilliant innovation—and fourteen watertight compartments made her unsinkable in the eyes of all associated with her. The *Titanic* was her own lifeboat.

The *Titanic* left Southampton on her maiden voyage at noon on 10 April, 1912, bound for New York. She made brief stops at Cherbourg and Queenstown, embarking at the latter port a contingent of Irish emigrants. When she sailed from Queenstown on the afternoon of the 11th, she had on board a total complement of 2,206,

Widow-Maker

made up of 898 crew and 1,308 passengers, less than half the number she was equipped to carry. Her first class passenger list included a number of millionaires, diplomats, and famous names in industry and commerce, among whom were John Jacob Astor, Sir Cosmo Duff Gordon, Baron von Drachstedt, Charles Melville Hayes, president of the Grand Trunk Railway, and J.P. Thayer, president of the Pennsylvania Railroad. They were all in good hands, for in command of the *Titanic* was fifty-nine-year-old Captain Edward Smith, a master mariner of great experience on his last voyage before retirement. Smith's senior navigating officers, Chief Officer H.F. Wilde and First Officer Murdoch, both held extra master's certificates and were also very experienced men. This being a maiden voyage, at Captain Smith's shoulder—and possibly peering over it all too often—were J. Bruce Ismay, chairman of the White Star Line, and Thomas Andrew, managing director of the ship's builders, Harland and Wolff of Belfast.

The weather in the North Atlantic was unusually fair, and it was hoped to complete the 3,100-mile crossing in just under six days, the liner being scheduled to reach New York on the 16th.

Having cleared Fastnet Rock at about 5 pm on the 11th, the *Titanic*'s engines were worked up to full speed and a course was set for New York which would take the liner to the south of the iceberg zone. If, in the North Atlantic, the uninterrupted raging of the wind and sea is the greatest danger facing the mariner in winter, then in spring and early summer it is the iceberg. Calved from the glaciers of Greenland, the Atlantic icebergs drift southwards, borne on the cold Labrador Current, which increases in velocity as the sun moves north from the Equator. During their long journey south these bergs, which may be up to 450 feet high and 1,500 feet long at the time of their birth, lose much of their bulk as they move into a warmer climate. The smaller bergs will melt away altogether, but the larger ones, floating with nine tenths of their mass below the surface, end up on the southern edge of the Grand Banks of Newfoundland. Keeping close company with these icebergs are fields of pack ice, often swarming with young seals, which were once much sought after by the sealing fleets of the world.

For transatlantic ships bound for New York, April is the month of greatest peril, as this is when the ice reaches furthest south before finding extinction in the warm waters of the Gulf Stream. In this respect, April of 1912 was a particularly bad month, with no less than 395 large icebergs recorded as having crossed to the south of latitude 48 degrees North. Had Captain Smith been privy to this knowledge at the time, the course of history might have been changed.

By noon on the 14th, the *Titanic* was just under halfway across the Atlantic and behind schedule. At twenty-two knots, as she had been averaging, she would not reach her berth in New York until well after dark on the 16th. From White Star Line's point of view this was most undesirable. A great deal of publicity had been laid on for the vessel's arrival, much of which would be wasted unless she steamed up the Hudson River in daylight. After conferring with Bruce Ismay and Thomas Andrew, Captain Smith instructed his chief engineer to increase speed. It was imperative that the *Titanic* arrive on her berth not later than 5 pm on the 16th.

During the afternoon, the liner's wireless operator John Phillips began to receive a stream of radio messages from other ships warning of the presence of icebergs. It soon became clear that an extensive ice-field located between latitudes 41° 25' N and 42° 00' N was drifting south into the *Titanic*'s path. The danger was sufficient to warrant an alteration of course to the south in order to avoid the bergs, but as this would add more miles to the passage, Captain Smith declined to do so. There is no evidence that Ismay brought any pressure to bear on him, but Smith was certainly determined to keep a daylight appointment with New York's newspapermen.

On the night of the 14th, the *Titanic* was passing to the south of the Grand Banks of Newfoundland and steaming at twenty-two knots under a clear, starlit sky. There was no moon, but the visibility was exceptional and the sea a flat, oily calm rarely seen in those latitudes. However, the air was bitterly cold and most passengers remained below decks whiling away the evening in the ship's sumptuously appointed saloons or, as in the case of the emigrants, huddled close in the steerage for warmth. All classes were agreed that the rock-like steadiness of the liner inspired confidence in even the poorest sailors amongst them.

High above the accommodation, on the *Titanic*'s bridge, the atmosphere was one of low-key vigilance as she sliced her way through the black water on that tranquil April night. Extra lookouts had been posted and the officers on watch spent a great deal of time scanning the horizon ahead through their night glasses. If there were icebergs about, it was assumed they would be seen in good time to alter course.

In the wireless office John Phillips had other things on his mind. With New York only two days away, the liner's millionaire passengers were again taking up the reins of their various business enterprises, and Phillips and his junior, Harold Bride, were inundated with messages to send to the shore station at Cape Race, Newfoundland. At 19.30, during a lull in the transmissions, Phillips listened to a warning broadcast by the 6,233-ton Leyland Line ship *Californian* reporting three large icebergs in sight five miles to the south of her. The position given was fifty miles ahead of the *Titanic* and directly in her path. Phillips apparently did not realise the significance of the warning and consequently delayed passing the message to the bridge for some time. Meanwhile the *Titanic* ploughed on through the night at maximum speed.

Widow-Maker

Soon after 21.30 Phillips heard the steamer *Mesaba* reporting the sighting of very heavy pack ice and numerous large bergs. Again the position given lay on the track being followed by the *Titanic*. At that moment, another clutch of messages to be sent arrived in the wireless office, and the *Mesaba*'s warning was put on file, to be delivered to the bridge when convenient.

The night moved on, and the messages to be sent piled up on Phillip's desk. He was now experiencing difficulty in raising Cape Race, and when, at 23.00, the *Califonian*'s operator, Cyril Evans, broke into his transmissions to report his ship stopped and surrounded by ice, a harassed Phillips told him to get off the air. Mildly annoyed at this rebuff, Evans, the *Californian*'s only operator, threw down his headphones and went off watch for the night.

At twenty minutes before midnight on 14 April, the lookout in the *Titanic*'s crow's nest, Able Seaman Frederick Fleet, became aware of a darker shadow on the horizon dead ahead of the ship. As he strained his eyes to pierce the blackness, the shadow grew larger and gained in substance at a frightening speed. With a sharp intake of breath the man lunged for the bridge telephone.

The urgent report from the crow's nest of an iceberg ahead seems to have been received on the liner's bridge with some scepticism, for many more precious seconds ticked by before avoiding action was taken. At last, under the influence of full helm, the *Titanic*'s bow swung slowly to port and a towering island of glistening ice slid down her starboard side. To those on the bridge it seemed that disaster had been narrowly averted, then the great liner rolled gently to port as she ripped open her bottom on the underwater shelf of the iceberg. The senior officer on the bridge, First Officer Murdoch, rang the engines to stop and then full astern before throwing the switch to close all watertight doors. The *Titanic* came to rest half a mile beyond the berg, which by then had been swallowed up by the darkness again.

Below decks, the impression was that the ship had been jostled by an unseen hand and, although some eyebrows were raised, few had any idea that a catastrophe had befallen them. Not until Captain Smith and his senior officers had made a hurried tour of the bowels of the ship was it realised there was a gash 300 feet long in the liner's bottom. Five of her watertight compartments were already flooded. The pumps were set going, but they were unable to deal with the ingress of water. The designers of this 'unsinkable' ship had omitted to carry her watertight bulkheads above D Deck, and as her bows sank lower, the sea spilled over into the next compartment aft, progressively flooding the hull as she settled in the water. The mighty *Titanic* was doomed.

Shortly after midnight, with the ship still deceptively upright, but with the sea pouring into her ruptured hull at an unstoppable rate, Smith ordered the lifeboats cleared away. Moments later, he

Bernard Edwards

passed the word for all passengers to don lifejackets and report to
their boat stations. This order failed to cause more than a general stir
of annoyance, for the majority of passengers refused to believe a serious emergency had arisen. To them, the thought of leaving the
warmth of the accommodation to line up on deck like sheep on such
a cold night seemed pointless, if not idiotic. Many went back to bed.

On the bridge, the full horror of the situation was all too apparent. Not only was the ship clearly doomed but, in view of her inadequate lifeboat capacity—a shortcoming not revealed to the passengers—it was certain that, unless help came quickly, more than half
her complement would have to go down with her.

In 1912 there were few rules governing life-saving equipment
in ships, and the number of lifeboats carried was left to the discre-
tion of the owners. Although the *Titanic* was certified for a maximum
compliment of 3,547, she had only eighteen lifeboats, with a total
capacity of a thousand persons. White Star was obviously of the opinion that only a token number of lifeboats was necessary for their new
liner, these serving merely to inspire confidence in the faint-hearted,
should there be any.

At 00.15 on the 15th, Captain Smith ordered John Phillips to
send out a distress. This was picked up by a number of ships, but all
were many hours steaming away. It was only by pure chance that at
00.30 Harold Cottam, wireless-operator of the Cunard liner
Carpathia, bound from New York to Gibraltar, decided to call the
Titanic before he retired to his bunk. Cottam was astonished when his
perfunctory call was immediately answered with an urgent burst of
morse. Phillips rapped out, 'SOS SOS. COME AT ONCE. WE
HAVE STRUCK BERG. POSITION 41°46'N 50°14'W. SOS'. This
was the first time the new distress signal 'SOS' had been used at sea.

The 13,603-ton *Carpathia*, commanded by Captain Arthur
Rostron, was at this time fifty-eight miles south-east of the *Titanic*.
Knowing the fearful risk he was running—the *Carpathia* had on
board 735 passengers and 300 crew—Rostron turned his ship about
and raced north-west at sixteen knots through the ice-strewn area,
praying that he would arrive in time.

Aboard the *Titanic*, Smith had given the order to swing out the
boats, and her officers were attempting to embark the women and
children, numbering 544 in all. The men, those who might be lucky
enough to find a place in the boats, would have to wait their turn.
Hopes were suddenly raised when, just before 01.00 on the 15th, the
lights of another ship were seen close by—between eight and ten
miles off those on the bridge of the *Titanic* estimated. Distress rockets were sent up and flares lit but, although at one time the other
ship seemed to be moving towards the liner, she did not answer her
signals and suddenly altered course and made off into the night.

And so the great drama being played out in mid-Atlantic drew
inexorably to its close. In the early hours of the morning of 15 April,

Widow-Maker

Captain Edward Smith found himself in command of a sinking ship, with sufficient boats to take off fewer than half those on board. This iniquity was compounded by the reluctance of passengers to leave the ship they had been assured was unsinkable, and the inability of many of the emigrants to find their way up on deck from the bowels of the ship where they were berthed. In the ensuing confusion, a number of boats went away only part-loaded; at least one sixty-man boat carried only twelve people, seven of whom were crew members. In all, only 336 women, 52 children and 315 men escaped the sinking ship in lifeboats. With the sea temperature at a lethal 28° F. those unfortunate enough to end up in the water would not survive for many minutes.

At 02.05 John Phillips sent his last message: 'COME AS QUICKLY AS POSSIBLE. ENGINE-ROOM FILLING UP TO BOILERS.' Fifteen minutes later, the 46,382-ton *Titanic* heaved her stern high in the air and slid bow-first to her last resting place beneath the waves. When the *Carpathia* arrived on the scene at 04.00 she found the sea littered with wreckage, amongst which floated the bodies of those who had stayed with the ship. From the lifeboats, found rowing in aimless circles, she took on board 703 souls, the only survivors out of the liner's total compliment of 2,201.

It cannot be disputed that the unshakeable belief of the *Titanic*'s builders, owners and captain in the liner's complete invulnerability was the primary cause of her loss. Over the intervening years, the myth of the 'unsinkable' ship has been well and truly exploded, but in 1912, when shipbuilding was in the throes of a new and exciting revolution, there seemed to be no end to man's growing ascendancy over the sea. The *Titanic*, with her double-skinned bottom and fourteen watertight compartments each capable of being isolated at the touch of a switch, was genuinely thought to be unsinkable. There can be no other explanation for Captain Smith's decision to press on through that black night at twenty-two knots when he had already received ample warning of icebergs in his path. It has been suggested, but never proved, that Smith—perhaps urged on by the line's chairman and the ship's builder—was attempting to make a record crossing on this maiden voyage. The weather throughout the crossing had been the best seen in the North Atlantic for many years and the temptation to go for a record must have been very strong. It is certain, however, that Smith was under pressure to make every attempt to berth in New York before dark on the 16th.

Tragically, while the *Titanic* was foundering, the 6,233-ton Leyland steamer *Californian*, commanded by 34-year-old Captain Stanley Lord, lay stopped just out of sight over the horizon. Owing to the presence of heavy ice, Captain Lord had stopped his ship at the onset of darkness on the 14th and was drifting awaiting daylight before proceeding. Her wireless-operator, Cyril Evans, who had tried unsuccessfully to warn the *Titanic* of the danger she faced, was sleeping soundly in his bunk. A little before 01.00 on the 15th, the *Californian's* officer of the watch saw rockets bursting low down on the horizon. He called Captain Lord, who by then had turned in for the night. It seems Lord accepted the report without concern and took no action

At the two subsequent courts of inquiry held into the disaster it was argued, and accepted, that the *Californian* must have been the ship seen by the *Titanic's* officers before they fired their distress rockets. On the evidence of the same officers it was also accepted that the *Californian* was only eight to ten miles off and must therefore have witnessed in full the sinking of the liner. Even though he produced his ship's log book, which gave the *Californian's* position as nineteen miles off the *Titanic*, and consequently below the visible horizon, Lord was already damned in the eyes of the world. As to the rockets seen by his officer of the watch, Lord said he had believed these to be signals between ships of the same line, or between fishing vessels in the area, both practices being common at the time. At the courts of inquiry, Lord was called only as a witness and no charges were laid against him, but it was made quite clear that the courts believed he had callously left more than 1,500 people to die on that night, and he was therefore the villain of the sad affair. The world's press took up the theme with relish and all the frustration and outrage generated by the loss of the 'unsinkable' ship was directed at a man who had not been given the chance to defend himself. The whitewash of the White Star fiasco was complete.

For many years, with the help of his professional association, Stanley Lord fought to clear his name, but without success. The stigma of the *Titanic* stayed with him until the day of his death, in January 1961. Ironically, shortly after he died evidence emerged which, had it been produced at the courts of inquiry, would most certainly have exonerated him. This was a statement made in 1912 by Henrik Naess, First Mate of the Norwegian sealer *Samson*, to the Norwegian consul in Iceland. Naess testified that, on the night of the 14/15 April 1912, the *Samson* had been illegally taking seals from the ice floes on the southern edge of the Grand Banks of Newfoundland. At some time after midnight, Naess and others saw rockets, flares and bright lights close by. It was assumed the pyrotechnics were signals between US naval vessels searching for seal poachers and the *Samson's* master, not wishing to be caught, recalled his boats and made off at speed. As the sealer had no radio, it was not until she reached Iceland that her crew heard of the loss of the *Titanic*. The *Samson's* master was, understandably, reluctant to make public his clandestine activities off the Grand Banks, but Henrik Naess, appalled by the magnitude of the disaster, felt compelled to speak out.

It has never been satisfactorily explained why the testimony of

Widow-Maker

Henrik Naess lay undisclosed for fifty years but, in view of this evidence, it seems almost certain the ship seen from the bridge of the *Titanic* was the *Samson* and not the *Californian*. Captain Stanley Lord may now rest easy in his grave; the same cannot be said for the *Titanic*.

Fortunately tragedies of the scale of the sinking of the *Titanic* invariably close stable doors which have been left open. In this case, an International Ice Patrol was set up, and new rules were introduced regarding life-saving appliances on all ships. The modern cruise liner is obliged to carry sufficient lifeboats and inflatable rafts to evacuate her total complement more than twice over.

Bernard Edwards

22   North Atlantic Rescue

Volturno - 1913

The Italian city of Bologna, fifty miles north of Florence, is renowned for its pasta, an abundance of Roman ruins and a university reputed to be the oldest in the world. It was here, in 1874, that a boy was born who was destined to change forever the progression of mankind.

Guglielmo Marconi was born of an Italian father and Irish mother, a genetic blending eminently suited to the production of genius. By the time he was twenty-one, Marconi had demonstrated successfully that it was possible to send signals through space using low frequency electromagnetic waves, and without the use of wires. And so wireless telegraphy was born; undoubtedly the greatest discovery since the wheel first made its appearance four thousand years ago.

A year later, Marconi went to London, where scientists at the Royal Institution encouraged him to push ahead with his work. Within months, he was able to show the enormous potential of his apparatus by transmitting signals across the Bristol Channel from Penarth Head to Brean Down, a distance of nine miles. In 1898, Marconi established wireless communication between England and France, sending a message across the English Channel from Boulogne to the shore near Dungeness. On this occasion the distance involved was twenty-four miles, but the two stations were still within sight of each other. The ultimate test came in 1901, when Marconi attempted, and was successful in sending a message over 2,000 miles of the Atlantic Ocean from Cornwall to Newfoundland. Wireless telegraphy, hitherto only a dream in a few restless minds, was now a proven and practical means of communication.

Even before Marconi spanned the Atlantic, his invention had been eagerly seized upon by shipowners, to whom good communications were a matter of great commercial importance. The first ocean-going ship to be equipped with wireless telegraphy was the Cunard liner *Lucania,* which sent its first radio signal winging across the empty ether in June 1900. By 1904, the number of ships so equipped was significant enough for the British Post Office to establish a shore station to communicate with them. Six years later there was hardly a big ship afloat not carrying wireless telegraphy.

Widow-Maker

The real value of wireless to ships at sea was not fully demonstrated until January 1909. On the 22nd of that month, the White Star liner *Republic,* bound from New York to Genoa with 761 passengers and crew, ran into dense fog when south of Nantucket Shoals. On an opposite course was Lloyd Italiano's *Florida*, carrying 830 emigrants from Naples to New York. The two ships collided and the *Republic* sank, but not before her wireless operator had set in train a rescue operation that resulted in the saving of all but three of the 1,391 people on board the two ships.

In the autumn of 1913 Europe was in ferment from the Channel to the Black Sea. The Triple Entente of Britain, France and Russia faced the Triple Alliance formed by Germany, Austria and Italy, each country with its own fears and aspirations. Britain felt her empire and trade to be threatened by the growing might of Germany's navy; Germany feared she was being encircled by her enemies; Russia was threatened by a socialist revolution; France was jealous of Germany's prosperity and Austria and Italy were at each other's throats. At any moment it seemed the whole continent might erupt into a full-scale bloody war, and, in consequence, emigration across the Atlantic to the Americas was in resurgence. The little people, the poor and disadvantaged, the ones who would be called upon to lay down their lives in a war, were getting out.

Among those on the move was Walter Trintepohl, a German employed by a firm of merchants in Barcelona. When the offer of a job in New York came his way, Trintepohl wasted no time in booking a passage across the Atlantic. He had visions of shipping out in one of the big passenger liners from Hamburg—with Hamburg Amerika, or Norddeutscher Lloyd, perhaps—but Trintepohl was not a rich man, and reality prevailed. Eventually, clutching a battered suitcase containing his most treasured possessions, he found himself being herded aboard the emigrant ship *Volturno* at Rotterdam.

The 3,602-ton *Volturno,* owned by the Canadian Northern Steamship Company, was a Glasgow-built ship, which came out of the Fairfield Yard in 1906. She was essentially a cargo ship, deep-framed and with good, solid bulkheads; a ship built to take all the hard knocks the sea and land would deal her over a lifetime extending perhaps to thirty years. She would never be an ocean greyhound, but her 324 horsepower, triple expansion steam engine would grow old with her, and given careful nursing, be relied upon to propel her at an economical speed until she reached the breaker's yard. It had never been envisaged the *Volturno* would ever carry more than a handful of passengers, but in 1913 the demand was there, and it would be a foolish shipowner who did not adjust to the trade.

When Walter Trintepohl boarded the *Volturno* in Rotterdam, he found himself one of 540 steerage passengers crammed into accommodation below decks that was basic, reasonably clean, but had no pretensions to comfort. His fellow passengers were mainly Polish, Rumanian and Serbian emigrants,—an unlikely mixture if there ever was one—with no common language and a deep-rooted suspicion of each other liable to erupt into open conflict at any time.

The *Volturno*, commanded by Captain Francis Inch, also carried twenty-four cabin passengers, and was manned by a crew of ninety-three, the latter being an unusual mix of British officers and German and Belgian ratings. In her holds were several thousand tons of general cargo, mainly high value, high freight manufactured goods, chemicals, textiles, wines and spirits. The only known hazardous commodity on board was a quantity of barium oxide, a chemical used in the manufacture of insecticides and paints, and liable to ignite if roughly handled. In view of its uncertain nature, the barium was stowed in the tween deck of No.1 hold, thus being well removed from the passenger accommodation. Stowed alongside and around the barium were bales of peat moss, bundles of rags and a quantity of straw bottle covers. Viewed in hindsight, this appears to be a very unwise mix.

The nature and stowage of the *Volturno*'s cargo were of little significance to Walter Trintepohl and his fellow passengers when, on the evening of 2 October 1913, the ship steamed out of Rotterdam docks. As they lined the ship's rails, they were more interested in a last, nostalgic sight of the grey world they were leaving behind for good. The low-lying, featureless banks of the River Maas, seen through the drizzling rain, were eminently symbolic of that world. Their future, which lay on the wide open prairies of Alberta, Saskatchewan and Manitoba, promised so much more. But first they must cross an ocean whose violent reputation filled them with apprehension.

Initially, it seemed that the fears of the emigrants were groundless, for although the skies were grey, the southern North Sea was unusually calm. Within ten hours of clearing the Hook of Holland, the *Volturno* was entering the narrows of the Dover Strait, with the sea still benign and a weak autumnal sun glinting on the famous white cliffs. And then, with one bound, they were free of the old world, out into the deeps of the English Channel, where the white horses frisked and seagulls wheeled overhead screeching a last farewell. The *Volturno*, the beat of her engines strong and re-assuring, was as steady as a rock. There were many who were naive enough to believe the North Atlantic held no fears for them.

It was not until the morning of the 4th, when with Land's End abeam to starboard the *Volturno* lifted her bows to meet the first of the long Atlantic swells, that the real power of the ocean was felt. A ripple of anticipation ran through the steerage decks, but there was no fear, for the sea remained calm, almost friendly. It was perhaps just as well that no one was aware of the real threat, which lay over the horizon, 2,000 miles out in the Atlantic. An area of low pressure, born several days earlier in the warm waters of the Caribbean, was deepening and moving east-north-eastwards. Near the centre of this depression winds were already up to gale force, generating a powerful swell, which, moving outwards concentrically like ripples made by a stone cast into a pond, was making its presence felt as far as the Western Approaches.

The *Volturno* was in mid-Atlantic before the weather showed signs of deterioration, and when the change came it was sudden and dramatic. On the morning of the 8th the sun came up into a sky veiled by high, ragged cirrus; by noon, with a steadily falling barometer, the wind was freshening from the south, and the sky heavily overcast with rain in the air. The wind veered to the west, and as night fell it was blowing a full gale, with rank upon rank of angry, white-topped seas advancing on the *Volturno* from the west. The heavily laden ship met the assault head-on, slamming her bows deep into each on-coming wave with a shock that shook her from stem to stern. Each time she slid into a trough her propellers raced madly, and when she climbed again to meet the next sea, she rolled sluggishly as thousands of tons of green water cascaded from her decks. Very soon, from below her hatches came ominous thumps as her cargo shifted under the continued onslaught. Captain Inch, wisely yielding to the superiority of the sea, reduced speed, but the storm increased in fury, until he was forced to heave-to in order to avoid damage to the ship and cargo. With the wind and sea fine on the bow, and just enough way on her to maintain steerage, the *Volturno* rode the seas awkwardly, like a mount under tight rein.

Walter Trintepohl, wedged tightly in his bunk in the depths of the steerage, passed a sleepless night filled with the hideous noise of the storm and the pitiful retching of the seasick souls all around him. At around 6 o'clock on the morning of the 9th, just as sheer exhaustion was about to give way to blessed sleep, he was jerked awake by a loud commotion. Word had come from the deck that the ship was on fire. Trintepohl threw on some clothes and followed the crowd up the ladder.

The *Volturno*'s British officers appeared to be in complete charge of the situation. They assured the nervous passengers that the fire was of a minor nature, but, as a precaution, they would be required to muster on the after deck until the blaze was out. Lifejackets were issued, and, as far as was possible under the circumstances, a semblance of good order reigned.

An outbreak of fire ashore is always a serious matter, but can usually be swiftly dealt with. Fire brigades, police and ambulance services, all highly trained and experienced in handling emergencies, are on call. Then, if all else fails, it is usually possible for those concerned to stand back and allow the fire to burn itself out. Heavy financial loss may result, but no lives are at risk.

A fire at sea is on a different plane altogether. There are no skilled emergency services at hand, no easy escape when things get out of hand. The ship's crew, with little or no serious fire-fighting training, must take up the hoses and do their best, retreating to the lifeboats when their best is not good enough. If the weather is reasonable, then they may save their lives and those of their passengers. In bad weather, and this is so often the case, they are caught between two deadly enemies and in mortal danger. A burning ship is something the seaman fears above all.

The fire in the *Volturno* was in her No.1 tween deck, where the barium oxide, thrown about by the violent gyrations of the ship, had ignited and set fire to the peat moss, rags and straw surrounding it. Smoke from the blaze was not seen issuing from the hatch until the first daylight came, by which time the fire was out of control and four seamen sleeping in the forecastle were already dead. Hoses were organised, but the ship was rolling and pitching so badly that the men handling them had difficulty in keeping their feet, and their efforts were largely ineffective. The fire began to spread aft.

It was not just an outbreak of fire Captain Inch had to deal with, serious though that might be. On board his ship were more than 500 men, women and children of mixed nationalities who were already demoralised and frightened by the power of the sea. The threat of panic breaking out among this unstable multitude, which outnumbered his crew by five to one, was too awful to contemplate. Already the women were near to tears and the men argumentative.

The *Volturno* was by this time in mid-Atlantic, and 870 miles from the nearest land, which was the east-coast of Newfoundland. Even if by some unforeseen miracle, the storm suddenly subsided, she would take seventy-two hours to reach port at her top speed of twelve knots—and it would still be too late. As an alternative to this unlikely event, there was the prospect of abandoning ship. The *Volturno* carried nineteen lifeboats, sufficient for all on board, but launching them in the terrible weather prevailing must be a last resort. The only real hope of salvation lay in a rescue by outside means. At 8 am, by which time the fire had spread aft to No.2 hold, Inch ordered his wireless operator to send out an SOS.

The 19,542-ton Cunard passenger liner *Carmania*, commanded by Captain Barr, was the first ship to answer the *Volturno*'s cry for help. The *Carmania*, bound from New York to Queenstown, was seventy-eight miles to the west of the burning ship. On receipt of the SOS, Captain Barr sent extra stokers to man the boiler fires and the liner was soon racing towards the *Volturno* at twenty knots, two knots in excess of her designed maximum speed. At the same time the *Carmania*'s wireless office sent out a general call for help, and before long nine other vessels were converging on the stricken ship, some from as far as two-hundred miles away.

On board the *Volturno*, the news that help was on the way and would reach them within four hours, changed the mood from one of hopeless resignation to wild optimism. Efforts to subdue the fire were redoubled, but they were to no avail. At 10 o'clock that morning, with much of the forward part of the ship ablaze, and the passengers assembled on the after deck, again bordering on hysteria, Inch reluctantly concluded that he must soon consider abandoning ship. The decision was taken out of his hands a few minutes later, when a violent explosion completely wrecked the foredeck and jammed the steering gear and engine-room telegraph. The *Volturno* slewed broadside on to the waves and lay helpless in the trough, rolling heavily.

As soon as Captain Inch gave the order to swing out the boats, all pretence of discipline broke down. It was to be feared the steerage passengers would panic, and Inch was prepared for that, but he did not expect some of his crew to join in the mêlée. The British officers stood firm, but the German and Belgian ratings, all thought of saving their ship gone, thrust the passengers aside and rushed for the boats.

In a last ditch attempt to salvage something from the chaos, the *Volturno*'s chief officer took charge of the first boat to be swung out and pleaded with the crew to allow women and children to board. He was ignored, and when the boat was lowered it was filled with seamen. Their selfishness brought them scant reward, however, for when the boat hit the water, it was thrown against the ship's side and smashed. All on board, including the unfortunate chief officer, were drowned.

In all, six boats were launched in a similar manner, and each one met the same fate, all its occupants, mainly crew members and male passengers being drowned. Determined to stop this senseless sacrifice of lives, Inch and his officers slashed the rope falls of the remaining boats, so that they could not be lowered. Those left on board the *Volturno* now had no choice but to wait for rescue.

The *Carmania* arrived on the scene at noon, having been steaming hard for four hours. By then, the *Volturno* was a grim sight. Flames and smoke engulfed her fore deck, and with her propellers fouled by the tangle of boat tackles hanging over her sides, she lay beam-on to the waves, rolling her bulwarks under. Her after deck swarmed with a seething mass of humanity, and as the *Carmania* drew near, pathetic cries for help could be plainly heard.

Captain Barr took his ship as close to the *Volturno* as safety would allow, and dropped a boat manned by First Officer Gardner and a volunteer crew. The distance between the two ships was not great, but the boat was small and the seas mountainous. After a two-hour battle to reach the *Volturno,* in which all but three of the oars were broken or lost, Gardner was forced to give up and return to the *Carmania.* His men were utterly exhausted, and it was only with great difficulty that the boat was hoisted back on board the liner.

It was clearly pointless to risk another boat, and Barr now

manoeuvred his ship to within one-hundred feet of the *Volturno's* stern with the intention of putting a line aboard. This was a magnificent feat of raw seamanship, for the huge Cunarder, rising and falling on the monstrous seas, completely dwarfed the 3,600-ton emigrant ship, and was constantly in danger of crashing down on her, with disastrous results for both ships. After several unsuccessful attempts to pass a line, Barr was forced to back off, with the cries of anguish of the poor souls huddled on the *Volturno's* stern ringing in his ears.

Other ships contacted by the *Carmania's* wireless operators now began to arrive. First, in late afternoon, came Norddeutscher Lloyd's *Grosser Kurfurst* and *Seydlitz*. They were soon joined by the International Mercantile Marine Company's *Kroonland*, Leyland Line's *Devonian*, Furness Withy's *Rappahannock*, the Atlantic Transport Company's *Minneapolis* and French Line's *La Touraine*. It was a truly international rescue fleet, British, German, Belgian, American and French, all gathered together by the magic of Marconi's wireless telegraphy.

For the rest of the afternoon, the ships circled the *Volturno* at a safe distance, with no one prepared to risk putting a boat in the water. Then, towards nightfall, the wind began to moderate, and, one by one, the rescue ships moved in to lower their boats. But there was still a heavy sea running, and each time a boat tried to pull alongside the burning ship it was beaten back. It was a dramatic sight; one that would be stamped on the memory of those there on that night forever. The eight great ships, each a blaze of lights, idled in a circle, at the centre of which the doomed *Volturno* burned fiercely, and within the circle, the flickering, dancing lights of the frail lifeboats, each one fighting a lonely battle with the cruel sea.

On board the *Volturno*, Captain Francis Inch waged his own battle on two separate fronts. When the *Carmania* first came in sight, his engine-room crew had rushed on deck, deserting the pumps and generators so vital to the ship's survival. Inch drove them below again at the point of his revolver, but they came back up minutes later when the fire broke through into the engine-room. Not even the threat of a bullet would persuade the men to go down again. The pumps stopped, the lights went out, and with them went all hope of survival. Soon, the heat on the bridge became unbearable, and Inch was forced to leave. Before he left, he ordered his wireless operator to send one last, poignant message. 'For God's sake, help us, or we perish!'

At 11 o'clock the flames burst through from the engine-room into the bunkers and there was a loud explosion. Distress rockets soared into the air and the other ships moved in, but they could do no more than drop lighted lifebuoys, in the hope that they might save someone. People were seen jumping overboard from the *Volturno* but although the *Carmania* turned her searchlights on the water, only one man was picked up. It was Walter Trintepohl.

Daybreak on the 10th saw the arrival of two more ships, the Russian Steam Navigation Company's *Czar* and the Anglo American Oil Company's tanker *Narragansett*. The sea had by now gone down considerably, and with the *Narragansett* lying to windward of the *Volturno* and pumping oil on the water, the boats of the other ships were at last able to go alongside the burning ship. Three hours later, all those remaining on board, 520 passengers and crew, had been taken off.

A total of 106 passengers and 30 crew died in the *Volturno* fire, most of them without good reason. The ship stayed afloat for another six days, and was finally scuttled by a boarding party from the Dutch ship *Charlois*. If there had been no panic, no rush for the boats, the loss of life might have been very small.

Bernard Edwards

23   The Curse of Fryatt's Gold Watch

Brussels - 1916

On the morning of 17 February 1917, the German submarine U-33 was fifty-five miles west of the Fastnet Rock and idling at periscope depth awaiting a suitable victim. When he sighted the old British collier trailing black smoke across the horizon, the commander of U-33 gave a grunt of satisfaction and laid his sights carefully. The torpedo struck the collier just abaft her engine room and exploded with a loud roar, sending a column of water and debris high in the air. Seen through the periscope, the scene aboard the doomed merchant ship followed a familiar pattern, her crew swarming like panic-stricken ants as they struggled to lower the boats before their ship sank under them.

Although the collier was noticeably lower in the water, she did not sink at once, and the impatient German commander brought the U-boat to the surface to administer the *coup de grace* by shellfire. The water was still streaming off her casings as her gun's crew raced forward to man the gun, but they were too late. Their innocent-looking victim opened her side ports, dropped her dummy deckhouses, and opened fire with five twelve-pounders, two six-pounders and a Maxim gun. His Majesty's Ship Q5, commanded by Lieutenant-Commander Gordon Campbell, sent U-33 spiralling to the bottom, leaving only two men in the water to be rescued. The curse of Fryatt's gold watch had been lifted.

Charles Fryatt, born in December 1872, went to sea in the North Sea ferries of the Great Eastern Railway Company as a young ordinary seaman. By the time he was forty, he had risen through the ranks to command the 1,380-ton *Brussels*, which plied regularly between Harwich and the Hook of Holland with passengers and freight. Built at Dundee in 1901, the *Brussels* was regarded as one of the best of her day. Fryatt, who was a dedicated, first-rate seaman, was proud to command her. The men who served under him did so with equal pride.

The outbreak of war in 1914 had little effect on the Great Eastern ferries, which continued to keep open the link between England and neutral Holland, much as they had done in times of peace. German U-boats were operating in the North Sea, but, under the international 'Cruiser Rules', they were constrained from sinking any merchant ship before she had been stopped, her papers examined and her crew allowed to take to the boats. Whether it suited the Germans to allow the Harwich-Hook route to continue, or the ferries were just too fast for the U-boats, has never been clear. Certainly, for many months after the outbreak of hostilities they left the Great Eastern ships well alone.

The situation took a dramatic turn for the worse when, in February 1915, Berlin issued a decree to the effect that all merchant ships found in British waters would be sunk on sight, regardless of their cargo. A few days later, Captain Fryatt received top secret orders from the Admiralty instructing him how best to act when threatened by a U-boat. The *Brussels*, like all British merchantmen at the time, was unarmed, and their Lordships advised, that when challenged her best course of action would be to steam straight at the U-boat, forcing her to dive. The order was, if not suicidal, certainly imprudent, for few merchant ships have bows strong enough to withstand ramming a submarine. However, Fryatt, with a twin-screw, fifteen-knot ship under his command, doubted he would ever find it necessary to take such drastic action. He was proved right when, on 3 March, the *Brussels* was threatened by a surfaced U-boat and he was able to avoid trouble simply by running away at top speed.

But escape was not always to be so easy. Three weeks later, on the afternoon of 28 March, when the *Brussels* was off the Maas light-

s.s. 'Brussels' *leaving port*

(Photo: A. Duncan)

ship and nearing the end of her regular crossing from Harwich, she ran into an ambush. Fryatt, who was on the bridge with Chief Officer Hartnell, was first to spot the submarine, on the surface and closing purposefully on the ferry's starboard bow. U-33, one of Germany's latest and most powerful submarines, commanded by Korvetten-Kapitan Gausser, was moving in to challenge.

Gausser signalled the *Brussels* to stop, but Fryatt, being only a few miles from Dutch territorial waters, had no intention of surren-dering his ship. Calmly, he called for maximum engine revolutions and altered course to starboard to pass astern of the submarine. Gausser countered by bringing U-33 sharply round to port, so that her bows pointed directly at the exposed port side of the British ship.

Fearful that the U-boat was manoeuvring to torpedo his ship, Fryatt decided the time had come to put the Admiralty's plan to the test. Instructing Hartnell to warn the engineroom, Fryatt altered course to port and put the submarine right ahead. The *Brussels* was by now making a good seventeen knots, and for a while it was touch and go for U-33. She only narrowly avoided being run down by exe-cuting an undignified crash dive. When an angry Gausser brought her back to the surface again, his intended victim was inside Dutch waters and out of his grasp.

The German Navy, humiliated by this apparently contemptu-ous treatment of one of their best submarines by an unarmed British merchant ship, was furious. Fryatt, who maintained he had not real-ly intended to ram the U-boat, was branded as a pirate and a poten-tial murderer. How Charles Fryatt, a peaceable, God-fearing master mariner going about his lawful business could be regarded as a pirate is beyond conception. His action in taking a run at the U-boat may have been prompted by the Admiralty's instruction, but it was also the instinctive action of a man intent on saving his own ship.

Their Lordships, on the other hand, were elated at this success-ful implementation of their policy and gave it maximum publicity. Fryatt and his officers received national acclaim, their defiance of the enemy was praised in the House of Commons, and Fryatt, his chief officer and chief engineer were presented with suitably inscribed gold watches by a grateful nation.

Charles Fryatt, fiercely proud of his gold hunter, carried it with him at all times. Friends and colleagues urged him to be careful, arguing that, if he were captured, the watch might prove provocative to the Germans. Fryatt would have none of this. Where he went, his watch went. It had become a talisman to him. His senior officers, on the other hand, preferred to leave their watches at home while they were at sea.

Meanwhile, all three continued to play their part in keeping open the tenuous link between Britain and the Netherlands. Unknown to them, the German naval authorities were quietly fum-ing at their disgrace, and the word had gone out that the *Brussels* must be brought to book, whatever the cost. Over the next twelve months, numerous attempts were made to sink or capture the ferry, but each time her speed and Fryatt's skilful seamanship enabled her to escape.

Late on the night of 22 June 1916, the *Brussels* sailed from the Hook of Holland, bound for Harwich with the usual passengers and cargo. As she was pulling away from the quay, those on her bridge were surprised to see a signal rocket curving skywards from the beach beyond the Hook. This was an unusual sight in wartime, even in these neutral waters, but Fryatt gave it only a moment's thought before he turned his attention to conning the ship down river.

The Maas lightship, its powerful beam sweeping the wave-tops four times in every twenty seconds, was passed just before midnight and the *Brussels* steamed out into the North Sea on a west-south-westerly course. It was a black night, and, as customary, the ferry was showing all her lights. An hour later, Fryatt, who might easily have taken the opportunity to go below, was still on the bridge with Chief Officer Hartnell. There was an uneasy tension on the bridge; even the dark outline of a fishing boat drifting past without lights had a sinister look to it. When the fisherman was abeam, a shaded signal lamp could be seen flashing seawards from her bridge and Fryatt's suspicions came to a head. Coincidence could not explain both the flaring rocket on sailing from the Hook and this idling drifter signalling their passing. He called to Hartnell to extinguish all lights and send the passengers below decks.

The *Brussels* continued on her course at full speed, with Fryatt and Hartnell sweeping the horizon ahead and to port and starboard with their night glasses. Soon, another darkened ship was seen approaching on a collision course and Fryatt was forced to switch on his navigation lights to warn her off. This was a move he lived to regret. Fifteen minutes later, the *Brussels* was surrounded by a flotilla of German destroyers, all with their guns manned and threatening to open fire if she did not heave-to. This time there could be no running away, and, mindful of the safety of his passengers, Fryatt had no alternative but to stop his ship.

At daybreak on 23 June, the *Brussels*, with the German ensign at her stern, was escorted into Zeebrugge, and then piloted up the canal to Bruges, some seven miles inland. Here she was secured and her passengers and crew taken ashore under guard. The passengers, many of them neutrals, were soon released for repatriation, but Fryatt and his crew were marched to the local jail. Next day, with the exception of Fryatt and Hartnell, the crew of the *Brussels*, which included six stewardesses, were sent to Germany for internment.

Fryatt, who had accepted the taking of his ship calmly, was not unduly disturbed when he was separated from Hartnell and put into solitary confinement. Again, when the long interrogation began and his treasured gold watch with its incriminating inscription was produced, he showed little surprise. He had guessed what the Germans were about. They were determined to make an example of him in return for the humiliation of U-33, and the watch was there to prove the case. Undeterred, he stuck to his story that he had merely taken a run at the U-boat to force her to dive, not to ram and sink her, as his interrogators would have it. Fryatt considered that, under international law, the very worst his captors could do would be to throw him into a prison camp for the rest of the war. But he underestimated the fury of the Germans.

On 28 July, Reuters in Amsterdam received the following official telegram from Berlin:

Captain Charles Fryatt. Executed at Bruges 27 July 1916 accused of attempting to ram a German U-boat

(Photo: Fryatt Memorial Fund)

On July 27, at Bruges, before the court martial of the Marine Corps, the trial took place of Capt. Charles Fryatt of the British steamer Brussels, which was brought in as a prize. The accused was condemned to death because, although he was not a member of a combatant force, he made an attempt on the afternoon of the 28th March 1915 to ram the German submarine U-33 near the Maas lightship. The accused, as well as the First Officer and Chief Engineer of the steamer received at the time from the British Admiralty a gold watch as a reward for his brave conduct on that occasion, and his action was mentioned with praise in the House of Commons. On the occasion in question, disregarding the U-boat's signal to stop and show his national flag, he turned at the critical moment at high speed on the submarine, which escaped the steamer by a few metres only by immediately diving. He confessed that in doing so he acted in accordance with the instructions of the Admiralty. The sentence was confirmed yesterday afternoon and carried out by shooting. One of the many nefarious 'franc tireur' proceedings of the British merchant marine against our war vessels has thus found a belated but merited expiation.

Widow-Maker

The news that Charles Fryatt had been taken out onto a piece of waste ground in the Bruges dockland and shot like a dog shocked the civilised world. Not since the execution of Nurse Edith Cavell in October 1915 had the international telegraph wires hummed so loud. Charles Fryatt did not, therefore, die in vain. His death evoked a great surge of world opinion against Germany, which was eventually to contribute to her defeat.

After the war, Fryatt's body was exhumed and brought back to England, to be finally laid to rest at Dovercourt, where he had lived with his wife and children, and overlooking the port of Harwich which had been journey's end to him for so many years. Today, Charles Fryatt is forgotten, his name living on only in an obscure fund set up in his memory by the Imperial Service Guild to bring succour to mariners incarcerated in foreign jails. It is not recorded what happened to the gold watch that sealed his fate.

Fryatt's ship, the *Brussels*, on the other hand, lived on into a somewhat undignified old age. For the remainder of the war she was used as a depot ship at Zeebrugge, ironically serving German submarines based at the port. When the end of the war was in sight, the Germans scuttled her before they retreated from Zeebrugge. It was August 1919 before she was raised by a British salvage team. Two years later, having been extensively repaired, she was sold to J. Gale & Company of Preston and spent the next seven and a half years running cattle between Dublin and Preston. When fully loaded, she was

'Brussels' *stranded at Felixstowe*

(Photo: National Maritime Museum)

Bernard Edwards

able to carry 600 cattle and 1,000 sheep, a far cry from her proud days on the Harwich—Hook run. In April 1929, then old, rusting and permeated with the smells of the farmyard, she ended her days in a breaker's yard on the River Clyde.

24   Twice Unlucky

Alnwick Castle - 1917

By January 1917, the great armies of Europe facing each other on the Western Front had fought themselves to a standstill. Their battlefield was a shell-churned waste of mud stretching from the Belgian coast, across France, to the Swiss frontier, and as winter tightened its grip both sides were so heavily dug in there was little to distinguish between the offensive and defensive. The artillery duels continued unabated, trenches changed hands—a few hundred yards gained here, a few hundred lost there—and overall lay the awful stench of death. The Great War was bogged down in a senseless quagmire of its own making.

In the opinion of the German Army, the only hope for victory lay in cutting off the steady stream of supplies flowing across the Atlantic from neutral America to Britain. To this end, the generals urged the Kaiser to declare unrestricted submarine warfare against all Allied merchant shipping.

On 20 October, 1914, when the first merchant ship fell to the U-boats, the sinking was a gentlemanly affair. The 866-ton British steamer *Glitra*, bound from Grangemouth to Stavanger with a cargo of coal, coke, iron plates and oil, was fourteen miles off the Norwegian coast when she was sighted by U-17, commanded by Kapitän-Leutnant Feldkirchner. Acting strictly in accordance with the International Cruiser Rules, Feldkirchner brought U-17 to the surface to challenge the *Glitra*, searched her, and then gave her crew time to abandon ship before sinking her with explosive charges. He then towed the lifeboats some distance towards the coast, so that they were easily picked up by a Norwegian pilot vessel.

With a few barbarous exceptions, other U-boat commanders continued to act much as Feldkirchner had done, until, in January 1917, the German High Command declared unrestricted submarine warfare against Allied shipping. Now the whole tenor of the war at sea changed, becoming a dirty, dishonourable business. The merchant ship became a cruelly exposed target, to be hunted and sunk without warning from beneath the cover of the waves. In February of that year, 230 Allied ships of 464,599 tons were sent to the bottom, an increase of almost fifty percent on January. Added to that, 300 neutral ships were tied up in British ports unwilling to take the risk of putting to sea. Now would have been the time to introduce convoys, but the Admiralty would have none of it. It feared that in bunching ships together they would make better targets for the U-boats. The merchant ship masters were of a similar opinion, and also claimed they would be unable to keep station in convoy, especially at night. The only concession made to organised action was for all ships to be given recommended routes for the approaches to the British Isles, so that the Royal Navy might keep an eye on their coming and going.

Up until then, the greatest danger from U-boats was thought to lie within a hundred miles of the coast, only fourteen ships having been sunk outside that distance, and only three at over two-hundred miles. When, on the morning of 18 March, the British collier *Trevose* reached a point 220 miles west-south-west of Land's End, her master felt it safe to assume she was out of danger. He was wrong. At precisely 11 am, a torpedo slammed into the engine-room of the 3,112-ton steamer, killing five of her firemen, and breaking her back. The *Trevose* went down a few minutes later, but not before the remaining twenty-five members of her crew had got away in two boats. Fortunately, the weather was fair, and being in one of the Admiralty's recommended shipping lanes, the men were confident of being picked up by a passing ship.

Some thirteen hours before the *Trevose* went down, the *Alnwick Castle* sailed from Plymouth, bound for Cape Town with a full general cargo, fourteen passengers and a number of head of cattle on deck. The 5,900-ton cargo/passenger liner, owned by the Union Castle Mail Steamship Company, was no stranger to war, having been requisitioned as a troopship in 1914. She served with distinction in the Gallipoli landings in the summer of 1915, before returning to the Cape run. Her master, forty-two-year-old Captain Benjamin Chave, RNR, was a very experienced officer.

By five o'clock on the evening of Sunday, the 18th, the *Alnwick Castle* was two-hundred miles west-south-west of Land's End, and steaming at 13 1|2 knots into a light westerly breeze. The sun was low on the horizon, and clear skies indicated a cold night ahead, but the mood on board was one of optimism. Having travelled thus far without a sight of the enemy, it was assumed the *Alnwick Castle* had left the war far in her wake. In twenty-four hours or so, she would be free to alter to the south and begin her long run down into the untroubled waters of the southern hemisphere. Ten minutes later, with only an hour to go to sunset, two ship's lifeboats were sighted, and by 5.30 all twenty-five survivors of the sinking of the *Trevose* had been picked up.

The news that the *Trevose* had been torpedoed only six hours earlier, and that the survivors had seen another ship sunk while they were in the boats, presumably by the same U-boat, brought about an abrupt change of atmosphere in the *Alnwick Castle*. So intent was

Captain Chave on clearing the area as soon as possible that he did not stop to lift on board the two lifeboats from the other ship. As the *Alnwick Castle*'s total complement was now 139, this was not altogether a wise move.

As soon as his ship was hidden in the darkness, Chave broke radio silence and reported the sinking of the *Trevose* to the Admiralty. During the night, he snatched a few hours sleep, and was back on the bridge at half an hour before dawn next morning. The sky was by then heavily overcast and the barometer falling, indicating bad weather ahead, but Chave was more concerned that the half-light of the coming day would provide good cover for an attacking U-boat. He instructed Chief Officer Blackman to begin a prearranged pattern of zig-zag courses and post extra lookouts. Two men went into the crow's nests, two into the foremast crosstrees and one to the upper bridge. In addition, two cadets were called to the bridge to act as extra eyes for the officer of the watch. As the *Alnwick Castle* was unarmed, Chave could do no more to ensure her safety.

At 6 o'clock, as the sun, hidden by the thick clouds, lifted over the eastern horizon, the captain's steward, Buckley, appeared on the bridge with a tray of coffee and toast. The ship was by then deep into the Atlantic, 330 miles west of Land's End, and far beyond the reported operating sphere of the U-boats. Captain Chave drank his coffee and surveyed the empty horizon with satisfaction. In two hours or so he would be justified in standing the lookouts down, so that his ship might return to her normal sea-going routine.

A few minutes later, at about 6.10, Chave was thrown off his feet when a torpedo struck the *Alnwick Castle* and exploded with a thunderous roar. A column of dirty water and debris shot sixty feet into the air from the foredeck, hung for a moment, then cascaded down on the bridge. The ship, her engines still driving her ahead at full speed, checked, and then lunged on with her forecastle visibly lower in the water. She had been hit in her No.2 hold and was making water fast.

Kicking aside the shattered remains of his coffee tray, Chave rang the engines to full astern to take the way off the ship, and sent Blackman down to clear away the boats. To Wireless Operator Carnaby, who had appeared at his elbow, he gave a hastily scribbled SOS message with instructions to keep sending until he received an acknowledgement.

Twenty minutes after the torpedo struck, the *Alnwick Castle*'s forecastle head was awash, and her stern lifting high out of the water. However, she remained upright, and as the sea was calm, all six lifeboats were launched without difficulty. It was now that Chave regretted not having picked up the *Trevose*'s boats. Two of his own boats were really only dinghies, normally used for painting ship or ferrying stores, and should not have been used for abandoning ship. However, with an extra twenty-five men to be saved, it was necessary to make use of them.

Although the ship was in imminent danger of sinking, Chave found time to go to his cabin for the weighted bags of Admiralty mail and secret codes books kept there. These he threw overboard and then returned to the bridge to collect Carnaby, who having received no answer to his repeated SOS transmissions, was still at his post. Both men then boarded a lifeboat and pulled away from the sinking ship.

Chave led the other boats to a safe distance off the ship, where they huddled in a small group to wait the end. It was a doubly harrowing moment for the *Trevose* survivors, who having had two ships blasted from under them in the space of less than twenty-four hours, were numb with shock.

As they watched, the sea boiled and the U-boat surfaced between them and the ship. Her deck gun was quickly manned and trained on the ship, but no shots were fired. At 6.45, in full view of victor and vanquished, the sixteen-year-old *Alnwick Castle* began her last journey. Proudly upright, and with her steam whistle sounding a long, mournful farewell, she slipped beneath the waves. When she was gone, the U-boat started her engines and made off towards the north-east, where a steamer was visible on the horizon, inward bound, and obviously unaware of the danger she was in. Some time later, there was a dull thump and a tall column of water soaring skywards told the *Alnwick Castle* survivors that any hope of immediate rescue was gone.

Chave now gathered the other boats around his and counted heads. He was greatly relieved to find that all passengers and crew were accounted for and uninjured. All the boats were overcrowded, with precious little freeboard, but he did his best to ease the situation by adjusting the number of people in each boat. Even so, the two small boats ended up with eleven men in each, a dangerous overload that might prove fatal in rough seas. For the moment, the weather was holding good.

Sails were hoisted, and with the wind still in the west, they set off in the general direction of the Channel. Keeping close company, they made steady progress throughout the rest of the day, but by sunset the wind had freshened enough to make steering difficult. By the time darkness closed in, the boats were scattered around the horizon. They were never to come together again.

In his lifeboat Chave had a total of twenty-nine people, consisting of the *Alnwick Castle's* chief engineer, doctor, purser, wireless operator, one cadet, twelve ratings, six passengers and five ratings from the *Trevose*. Unfortunately, most of the ratings were firemen or stewards, and, apart from Chave, only three others, Cadet Hemmings, Quartermaster Merrels and Able Seaman Morris, had any knowledge of boat handling.

The wind continued to freshen, and Chave was forced to reef

down. By the early hours of next morning, the 20th, it was blowing a full gale from the north-north-west. Steering an easterly course, the boat was beam-on to the weather, rolling heavily, and from time to time shipping seas. Without sufficient experienced men to assist him Chave feared the boat might capsize, and decided to heave-to. The sail was furled, the sea anchor streamed, and the boat came round to lay head-on to the wind and sea, pitching and yawing uncomfortably, but stable. The canvas boat cover was rigged to provide some protection from the weather, but the wind, laden with icy pellets of spray, seemed to be coming straight off the ice cap of the North Pole. And so they waited out the miserable hours until dawn.

Daylight revealed that both the sea anchor and the rudder had been carried away and the boat was once again beam-on to the seas. The wind, now round to the north, was too strong for the sail to be hoisted, so the oars were manned in an attempt to bring the bow up into the wind. While this was being done, Chave constructed a makeshift sea anchor by lashing two oars together. When streamed, the anchor was only partially effective, and throughout the day it was necessary to use the oars to prevent the boat broaching to. It was cold, demoralising work, yet they dared not give up.

The survivors were fortunate that their ship had been commanded by an experienced man like Benjamin Chave. Britain was entering her third year of war, and yet it was still not mandatory to stock lifeboats with the necessities for survival, other than the customary ten-gallon breaker of drinking water. But Chave, foreseeing the kind of situation he now faced, had made a practice of stocking each of the *Alnwick Castle*'s lifeboats with a case of condensed milk, a case of corned beef, two tins of ship's biscuits and a bundle of blankets. For twenty-nine men cast adrift for an unknown number of days this was not an abundance but it could mean the difference between life and death. Chave set a daily ration of four ounces of condensed milk, twenty-four ounces of corned beef and one dipper of water per man per day.

Late that night the wind eased, and it was possible to take in the sea anchor and set sail again. As before, course was set due east for the busy shipping lanes of the English Channel. Next morning, the wind veered more to the north-east and freshened, but the boat surged ahead riding the waves well—perhaps too well. Disaster struck that afternoon, when the mast step gave way under the strain, and mast and sail went crashing overboard. For the majority of the survivors this was the last straw, and they were ready to accept defeat, but Chave rallied them. The gear was dragged inboard, a new mast step improvised with the aid of an axe and a stout piece of wood, and the sail was again hoisted, but not for long. By 8 o'clock that night the wind had once more risen to gale force, and they were obliged to heave-to.

Having waged an unending battle against the sea for more than two days, the survivors were physically exhausted and mentally drained; they were hungry and thirsty, the latter being acute. Chave issued an extra ration of water for those worst affected, but he would not be able to repeat this, for the water was running out. During the night, the wind dropped away and a shower of hail fell. The hailstones were eagerly scooped up and swallowed, but they were not enough to assuage the men's raging thirst. When the hail turned to light rain the sail was spread to catch the rain, but there was not even enough moisture to wash the salt out of the canvas.

Early on the morning of the 22nd the wind came away from the north-east again, making it possible to set sail once more. But, as before, the fresh wind soon turned to a gale and the boat was soon making heavy weather of it and shipping spray overall. To add to the survivor's misery the boat began to leak badly, and continuous bailing was necessary if they were to stay afloat. Most of the men were nearing the end of their endurance, some of them half-crazed through drinking salt water, and they had no enthusiasm for bailing. Chave issued an extra ration of water mixed with condensed milk, but this had little effect. Kitcher, the foreman cattleman, died that afternoon.

It was a day without hope, most of it spent lying to a sea anchor at the mercy of an angry sea, and culminating after dark with the boat being swamped by a breaking wave. And that, it seemed, was the end. The boat was awash up to her gunwales, floating only on her buoyancy tanks, and its occupants had no will to do anything about it. Yet, exerting all his authority, Chave again put heart into them, and the buckets and bailers went to work. The boat was put before the wind by shifting the sea anchor to the stern, and slowly the level of water went down.

By midnight the boat was reasonably dry and the wind had dropped away, but the effort had been too much for the weakened men. Many of them collapsed, some lapsed into temporary insanity. Hopelessness turned to bitter recriminations and fighting broke out in the crowded boat. Chave was later to say, 'The horror of that night, together with the physical suffering, are beyond the powers of my description.'

Before dawn on the 23rd, with the help of the few men who had not given up, Chave set sail again. Allowing for the southerly drift caused by the wind, he estimated the boat to be in the Bay of Biscay. The water was almost finished, and his hold on the men becoming more tenuous by the hour. If they were not seen soon by a passing ship it would be all over. But, when full daylight came, the horizon remained as empty as ever. In answer to insistent demands, Chave made an issue of water. When the dipper had gone the rounds, the breaker contained sufficient for just one last share out.

They sailed eastwards throughout the morning, deeper into the bay. Most of the men had ceased to take any interest in their surroundings. Although a good deal of food remained, their throats were so parched that they could swallow nothing solid. Their lips were cracked, their limbs without feeling, their hands white and puckered through constant exposure to the sea.

Then they began to die. The first to slip away was Thomas, a fireman, followed soon afterwards by another fireman, Tribe. In the forenoon, Chave's faithful steward, Buckley died in his captain's arms, and on the stroke of noon a cattleman, whom Chave knew only as Peter, also passed away. The bodies remained in the boat, for there was not a man with sufficient strength left to tip them overboard.

That was how, two hours later, they were found by the *Venezia,* a French steamer commanded by Captain Paul Bonifacie. There was a heavy swell running, and although Chave and a few others made a gallant effort, they could not get alongside the French ship. It was left to Bonifacie, who with a display of magnificent seamanship, brought his ship alongside the boat without sinking it. The twenty-five survivors still alive were lifted on board the *Venezia* with ropes.

Five days later, Spanish fishermen off Cape Ortegal found Chief Officer Blackman's boat. Of the thirty-one originally on board, only twenty-one were still alive, and all of them near the point of insanity for lack of water. One man died as he was being lifted out of the boat, two others were so demented that they had to be dragged screaming from the boat. They had been adrift for nine days and had sailed a distance of 380 miles.

The *Alnwick Castle's* two small jolly boats, as Captain Chave had feared, were never seen again, but two other lifeboats were accounted for. In all, of the 139 on board the *Alnwick Castle,* forty died, including three of the crew of the *Trevose.*

Bernard Edwards

25   The U-Boats' Revenge

Belgian Prince - 1917

The western approaches to the British Isles became a graveyard of Allied and neutral merchant shipping. In March 1917, for the first time in the war, sinkings by German U-boats exceeded half a million tons. Yet the Admiralty, ignoring history, was still not convinced that convoys were the remedy needed. While the Admirals dithered, nine new U-boats were commissioned and let loose on the high seas, with the result that Britain's vital sea-lanes were soon all but severed. In that April alone the U-boats sent to the bottom 430 ships of 852,000 tons, and by the end of the month only six weeks supply of food remained in Britain's warehouses. The continued heavy fighting on the Western Front gravely exacerbated the situation. Many of the country's skilled shipyard workers had been conscripted into the Army, and were wasting their talents in the mud of Flanders, instead of building replacement ships. The total output from British yards for April 1917 was only 67,536 tons—and this when losses were approaching a million tons.

There were many influential voices, Admiral Jellicoe's among them, that said unless the balance at sea was redressed, Britain would be starved into submission by November. Ironically, it was Germany's declaration of unrestricted submarine warfare that really turned the tide. The sinking of unarmed merchant ships without warning and attacks on hospital ships, intentional or not, did much to sway opinion on the other side of the Atlantic, and on 6 April, America came into the war. It would be many months before her troops made their presence felt in France, but the immediate availability of thirty-five destroyers for escort duties certainly brought about a change of mind at the Admiralty. As from 10 May, all merchant ships sailed in convoy where possible. That month saw a dramatic reduction in the number of ships sunk, but this proved to be a false dawn. In June the U-boats disposed of 687,507 tons, 417,925 tons of this being British register—and all this for the loss of only two of their own number. The problem was that by this time the German submarine fleet numbered 132, of which sixty were at sea at any one time, forty of them concentrated in British home waters. However, the gathering together of merchant ships into convoys did at least make the U-boat commanders work harder for their Iron

Crosses. The easy targets, the single, unescorted ships, became increasingly hard to find. So thought Kapitän-Leutnant Paul Wagenfuhr, as, on the evening of 31 July, 1917, he stood in the conning tower of U-44 and scanned an empty horizon.

U-44 was one of Germany's latest and best. Manned by four officers and thirty-five ratings, she displaced 940 tons, had a top speed on the surface of 15.2 knots and a range of 4,800 miles. Her armament consisted of six tubes firing 50 cm torpedoes, a 105 mm deck gun and two machine guns. On this fine, calm summer's evening she was idling on the surface some seventy miles east-south-east of Rockall, square in the path of ships bound in and out of the North Channel, gateway to the busy ports of Glasgow and Liverpool.

When he first sighted the thin pencil of smoke on the eastern horizon, Wagenfuhr was both elated and on his guard. If this proved to be a lone merchantman, then his long days of waiting would be rewarded; if she turned out to be the leading ship of a convoy, then he must take care. Another two hours of daylight remained, which was time enough to mount an attack, or run away. Wagenfuhr cleared the conning tower and took the boat down to periscope depth to watch and wait.

Forty-eight hours out of Liverpool and bound for Newport News with a cargo of blue clay, the 4,765-ton cargo steamer *Belgian Prince* was alone, unarmed, and about to challenge the long Atlantic crossing. Built in 1901 and owned by Prince Line of London, she was commanded by Captain Hassan and carried a British crew of forty-three. Crossing the Atlantic unescorted was no new experience for any of these men, but they were well pleased to be clear of the dangers of the North-Western Approaches. They were cautiously relaxed as the night moved in to hide them in its cloak of darkness.

As he paced the scrubbed teakwood boards of the *Belgian Prince*'s boat deck on this fine summer's evening, Chief Engineer Thomas Bowman was particularly at ease with the world. The two weeks spent in dock in Liverpool had been put to good use by his engineers and shore fitters. The sixteen-year-old steamer's 492 horse-power, triple expansion engine had a new and vigorous beat to it. The *Belgian Prince* might never lay claim to be a crack transatlantic liner, but Bowman was confident she would comfortably maintain 10 1|2 knots on the passage.

At about ten minutes before 8 o'clock, with the sun almost tipping the horizon, Bowman decided to go below to supervise the change over of the watch. As he turned, he glanced to port and froze in mid-stride. The long swathe of bubbles streaking in towards the ship was unmistakably hostile.

The bridge must have seen the track at the same time, for the *Belgian Prince* heeled sharply as the helm was put hard to port in an attempt to swing the ship's stern away from the danger. It was too late. The torpedo struck in the after part of the engine-room and

Bernard Edwards

exploded with a muffled roar. Bowman was bowled over by the blast and lay on the deck half-stunned.

When he regained his wits Bowman got to his feet and ran for the engine-room. He swung open the heavy steel door, only to be driven back by clouds of steam and smoke billowing up from below. But, to his great relief, the watch, led by Second Engineer George Sileski, appeared out of the swirling mists, shaken but unharmed. The news they brought with them was not good. Sileski reported the *Belgian Prince*'s propeller shaft broken and her main engine and generator smashed beyond repair. She would never steam again.

When Bowman and the others reached the deck, the ship was listing heavily to port, and Captain Hassan had already given the order to abandon ship. As the boats went down, the U-boat surfaced close by and opened fire on the steamer's wireless aerials with her deck gun. This was quite unnecessary, for with the generator smashed by the explosion, and with no emergency battery power, the *Belgian Prince*'s wireless was already silent. There had been no time to send an SOS.

The three lifeboats containing all forty-four of the *Belgian Prince*'s crew pulled clear of the sinking ship, and when they were about two-hundred yards off, the occupants lay back on their oars to await the end. They watched helplessly as U-44 circled the ship, firing on her with a heavy machine-gun. What Wagenfuhr stood to gain from this is hard to tell, but it may have been that he suspected he had fallen in with a Q-ship and was testing her hidden defences. It was on a similar summer's evening in the Western Approaches that U-27 had accepted an innocent looking Allied merchantman at face value. The U-boat surfaced to challenge, and as she did so the steamer, otherwise HM Q-ship *Baralong,* dropped her shutters and opened fire with her six-pounder guns. U-27 went to the bottom, and those of her crew who escaped were shot under the most inhuman circumstances. This was an action most uncharacteristic of the Royal Navy, but it served to illustrate how bitter the war at sea had become.

To Thomas Bowman, in the stern of the starboard lifeboat, U-44's machine-gunning of a ship plainly beyond retaliation boded no good for the survivors. His fears were heightened when the submarine turned and motored towards the boats. The machine-gun in the conning tower was still manned and now trained on the boats. Bowman tensed himself to leap overboard when the bullets began to fly.

The machine-gun remained silent as the long, grey-painted submarine, casting a sinister shadow before it in the rays of the dying sun, glided to a halt within twenty yards of the small huddle of boats. They were ordered alongside, and when they touched, a voice called out in English for the captain of the ship to declare himself. Hassan, well aware of the German policy of carrying off into captivity the masters of ships sunk, had already removed his uniform jacket with its tell-tale gold braid. He stayed silent, and not a man in the boats betrayed him. Wagenfuhr repeated the order several times, impatience showing in his voice, but all he received in return was hostile stares. The machine-gun moved menacingly, and when Wagenfuhr rapped out an order in German, Hassan feared he was risking the lives of all his men by refusing to declare himself. He stood up, was ordered aboard the U-boat, and disappeared down the conning tower hatch to face the rest of the war in a German prison camp.

Having made a prisoner of their captain, the other survivors assumed that, at the very worst, the submarine would then make off, leaving them to their fate. They were mistaken. Wagenfuhr now ordered them all on board, and with the machine gun and a number of rifles levelled at them, they had no alternative but to comply. Standing on the submarine's casings, they were roughly handled by armed German seamen and subjected to a rigorous search. This they accepted with ill grace, but with resignation, for they had no alternative. It was only when the Germans took away their lifejackets and outer clothing that a ripple of fear ran through the British ranks. When their lifejackets were tossed overboard and the Germans set about wrecking the two larger lifeboats with axes, the survivors began to realise the stark horror of the situation facing them. Not even the youngest among them was naive enough to believe the U-boat commander was about to carry them all back to Germany as prisoners.

The smallest of the lifeboats had been left intact, and a party of five German sailors boarded this and rowed over to the *Belgian Prince*. They boarded her, and after ten minutes or so, signalled back to the submarine with a lamp, presumably reporting the state of the ship. The U-boat's engines then coughed into life, and she motored away, with the forty-three bewildered survivors clinging to her casings. When she was about two miles off the ship, she stopped and lay rolling gently in the swell.

The British seamen eyed each other nervously, wondering what to expect next. They were not left in suspense for long. The Germans disappeared from the conning tower, the hatch clanged shut, and there was a rush of escaping air as the ballast tanks were filled. The deck of the U-boat began to sink beneath their feet.

Bowman was the first to realise what was happening, and shouted to warn the others before jumping clear. In the water, he kicked out, swimming away to escape the powerful suction of the submerging submarine. When he looked back, she had gone, leaving perhaps a dozen men struggling in the welter of foam and bubbles. The rest had gone with her, sucked down into the vortex she created.

A lifejacket whirled past and Bowman instinctively grabbed at it and slipped it on. If nothing else, this scrap of cork and canvas would prolong his life by a few hours, but to what end? The outside world would know nothing of the attack on the *Belgian Prince,* and there would be no ships racing to their rescue. In three or four days, when she was judged to be overdue, a cursory search might be made, but by then only a few bloated corpses would remain.

It was now almost dark, and Bowman was tempted to throw off his lifejacket and slip beneath the waves to join the others. Then he heard a voice calling for help and he found the youngest member of the *Belgian Prince*'s crew, a sixteen-year-old apprentice, drifting near-by. The boy was wearing a lifejacket, but had swallowed a lot of water and was far gone. Bowman stayed with him, supporting and encouraging him, but, at around midnight, the boy died from exposure and shock. Bowman relieved him of his lifejacket and allowed the body to drift away· into the night.

In summer, daylight comes early in the high latitudes, and it was just after 3 o'clock on the morning of 1 August when Bowman, by then near the end of his tether, saw that the *Belgian Prince* was still afloat. A great surge of hope swept through him, chasing away the cold and misery, and he struck out for the ship, buoyed up by the two lifejackets. The distance was great and the engineer was weak, but he swam on, from time to time brushing against the bodies of men whom hours before had been his friends and shipmates. By about 5.30, an hour and a half after sunrise, he was almost there, when the *Belgian Prince* suddenly appeared to blow up and sank stern first.

While the ship was still there, Bowman had a goal to aim for, and this gave him heart. When she was gone, and all that was left was an empty sea strewn with wreckage, again he was tempted to end it all; to discard the lifejackets and join the others face down in the sea. But something, perhaps it was the thought of the grieving widow and orphans he would leave behind, drove him on, and he continued to swim. An hour later, still swimming, he was picked up by a British patrol boat. He had been in the water for eleven hours.

George Sileski, Bowman's Russian-born second engineer, also survived Wagenfuhr's callous mass execution. Although he had no lifejacket, he swam in the direction of the *Belgian Prince* throughout the night, and succeeding in boarding her at about 5 am. However, when he had been on the ship for about an hour, and had begun to construct a raft, he saw U-44 approaching the ship. He hid behind a deckhouse and watched as the submarine came alongside and a party of four armed men boarded. While they were searching the ship, Sileski scooped up a lifejacket, slipped over the side and swam quietly away. He had been in the water for about twenty minutes, when the U-boat opened fire on the *Belgian Prince* with her 105-mm deck gun, scoring two direct hits. The ship sank, and the U-boat moved away, but left behind the small boat used to board her on the previous night. Sileski reached the boat and was rescued from it half an hour later by the same patrol boat that had found Bowman.

The only other man to survive the sinking of the *Belgian Prince* was her American second cook, Willie Snell, who also spent all night swimming towards the ship. He was about a mile off her when she went down, and was not picked up by the patrol boat for another two and a half hours. Snell was by then very near to death.

Captain Hassan was released from a German prison camp at the end of the war. Thomas Bowman, George Sileski and Willie Snell lived on to sail another day. The others, thirty-nine unarmed, non-belligerent British merchant seamen, found unmarked graves one thousand fathoms deep in the cold Atlantic. When the war was over, nineteen German U-boat commanders were arrested as war criminals. Only three of their number were ever brought to trial. Kapitän-Leutnant Paul Wagenfuhr was not among them. The story of HMS *Baralong* and U-27 did not emerge until many years later, by which time the urge to punish those guilty of wartime atrocities had long faded.

Bernard Edwards

26   Home for New Year

HMS *Iolaire* - 1918

On 23 August, 1914, British troops met the advancing German Army for the first time in the ancient Belgian city of Mons. A fierce battle followed, at the culmination of which the British were forced to retreat almost to the gates of Paris. Four years, two months and nineteen days later, on 11 November, 1918, a battalion of Canadian troops finally recaptured what remained of Mons. And so ended the Great War, a conflict involving sixty-seven million fighting men; which left eight and a half million dead, twenty-one million wounded and half of Europe in ruins. It was a senseless, brutal war that achieved nothing but the destruction of the flower of a generation of young men.

Britain, one of the major participants, suffered 750,000 dead and more than two million wounded, many of whom would never recover in body and mind from the dreadful carnage of which they had been a part. When the last shot was fired, and on the eleventh hour of the eleventh day of the eleventh month of 1918, peace was declared, those who had come through unscathed offered up a quick prayer of thanks and prepared to go home.

At sea, the ending was more protracted. In late October, the German admirals decided they would take the Grand Fleet out into the North Sea to meet the enemy in one last glorious battle. It was a grand gesture certain to end in defeat, for the big ships of the Royal Nay outnumbered the Germans by two to one. Fortunately for both sides—for it would have been a very bloody fight—the ordinary German seaman had had enough of war. Mutiny broke out at Kiel on 3 November and quickly spread throughout the German ships, which remained firmly tied up in harbour. The ignominious end came on 21 November, when the Grand Fleet, consisting of sixteen battleships, eight light cruisers and fifty destroyers, steamed across the North Sea and entered Scapa Flow with their ensigns lowered. Only then was it possible for the men of the Royal Navy to secure their guns and turn their thoughts to home. For most of them, the final homecoming would be delayed until their ships were laid up or sent to the breaker's yard. Meanwhile, the season of goodwill was looming close, and for those lucky enough to be in home waters, leave was a certainty.

Widow-Maker

When in port, no ship of the Royal Navy is ever left without sufficient men on board to take her to sea in case of an emergency. And so, when Christmas and New Year come around and leave is granted, then it must be shared fairly amongst the ship's company. Traditionally, the English, Irish and Welsh have always been given the first option on Christmas leave, while to be at home for the New Year is the prerogative of the Scots. It is so now, and was so in 1918.

Kyle of Lochalsh, which lies a hundred miles north of Glasgow on the coast of Ross & Cromarty, was the old north-western terminus of the London, Midland & Scottish Railway. It was also the jumping off point for the Hebridean Islands, and in 1918 David MacBrayne ran a daily service across the wild Minches to Stornaway, the main port of Lewis, in the Outer Hebdrides.

In summer Kyle of Lochalsh is bleak, in winter it is a place of perpetual twilight, ravaged by Atlantic gales and gripped by the icy fingers of the Arctic. On New Year's Eve 1918, uncharacteristically, the small ferry port glowed with warmth and good cheer, thronged as it was with upwards of five-hundred blue-jacketed naval reservists, who had arrived by rail from Glasgow. They were all Lewis men, in high spirits and intent on seeing in the New Year at their own fire-side. Whether they would achieve their objective was very much in the balance. It was a six-hour passage by sea to Stornaway and the hours to midnight were ticking by. At 6 o'clock that evening, the MacBrayne steamer *Sheila* was full to capacity, and still the quay had not been cleared. For more than two-hundred men about to be left behind without a decent tot of whisky between them Hogmanay promised to be a miserable occasion. Then someone remembered the *Iolaire*.

The steam yacht *Iolaire*, built in 1896 for the millionaire Scottish shipowner Sir Donald Currie, had had a checkered career, spending more time in port than at sea, and changing her name and allegiance frequently at the stroke of a pen. She came off the slipway as the *Doris*, was the *Rione* in 1897, the *Iolaire* in 1899, the *Amalthaea* in 1907, then the *Celcelia*. She was under the last name, and owned by the executors of the late Sir Charles G. Asshetan Smith, when, in early November 1918, she was pressed into war service by the Admiralty. Once more named *Iolaire*, a name also borne by the naval shore establishment at Stornaway, she became the flagship of the Stornaway anti-submarine patrol.

HMS *Iolaire* had little time to prove herself in war, and on the night of 31 December, 1918, the 530-ton yacht, under the command of Captain Clement Cotter, and with a crew of twenty-three on board, was lying snug at her moorings at Kyle of Lochalsh awaiting demobilisation. It was a black, moonless night with the wind beginning to pipe in the rigging, and no doubt Cotter and his men were not over pleased when they were ordered to shift alongside the pier and take on passengers for Stornaway. But then this was the last night of the old year, the start of a new era of peace, and probably the last passage the old ship would make before going to the breaker's yard. It was time for a last good deed to be done.

The broad smiles on the faces of the naval reservists as they scrambled over the *Iolaire*'s rails with their kit was reward enough for the yacht's crew. When she left Kyle of Lochalsh at 8 pm, she was well down to her marks, having on board a total of 222 passengers and an unknown tonnage of personal effects. As the passage to Stornaway was just sixty-one miles, and the *Iolaire* had a top speed of eighteen knots, Cotter was confident he would be able to deliver his passengers before the witching hour of midnight

A fresh southerly breeze was blowing and the glass was falling when the *Iolaire* broke away from the pier and set course to pass between Longay and Eilean Mor. White horses were running on the dark waters of the Inner Sound, and out in the Minch, beyond the shelter of the mountains of Skye, which lay to port, Cotter assumed a full gale must be blowing. The crossing of the Minch promised to be a lively one, and he sent word below to secure all loose gear.

Forty-five minutes later, with Eilean Beag abeam to starboard, Cotter brought the *Iolaire* around on a northerly course. It was an hour after high water Dover and the tide was turning against them. The pilot book warned of a southerly flow of up to two knots, but it soon became obvious that the *Iolaire* was steaming against a run of in excess of three knots. It was now apparent she could not reach Stornaway harbour before one or two o'clock next morning. Captain Cotter had no heart to pass on this disappointing news to his passengers packed shoulder to shoulder on the yacht's deck. Despite flurries of snow borne on the freshening wind, the men were still in good spirits.

At 9.15 pm the *Iolaire* passed the northern end of Rona and moved out into the Minch. She was still in the lee of Skye, but the rollers were coming around the end of the island and she began to move uneasily. The movement aroused only howls of derision from the men on her decks. Most of them had fished these waters from a very young age in boats no bigger than the *Iolaire*'s lifeboats. When, three quarters of an hour later, the yacht ran clear of Skye and caught the full force of the southerly gale funnelling up the Minch, the reaction was more subdued.

The *Iolaire* now had thirty miles of open water to cross before she reached the shelter of Stornaway harbour, and the night had gone wild. A force nine wind, gusting to storm force ten in snow squalls, was blowing directly on the beam, whipping the tops off the advancing seas and hurling the stinging spray across the yacht's decks. As she steamed deeper into the Minch, she took on a shock-like roll, at times dipping her lee rails under. For those who were unable to find shelter below decks, which was the majority of her passengers, the

Widow-Maker

'quick trip across the water' they had anticipated was fast turning into a horrible nightmare.

The old year went out, and 1919 came in almost unnoticed, as the small ship fought her way across one of the world's most inhospitable stretches of water. Between snow showers, the visibility was excellent, and it was with some relief that, at thirty minutes after midnight, Cotter sighted the flashing white light on Arnish Point, at the entrance to Stornaway harbour. The light had an extreme range of thirteen miles, indicating the *Iolaire* was making good a speed of less than eight knots. The tide was still running against her, and with increased strength.

It was 1.50 on the morning of 1 January when the *Iolaire* began her approach to Stornaway harbour. On her open bridge, Captain Clement Cotter turned up the collar of his thick bridge coat and spread his legs wider against the awkward roll of the ship. He was cold and tired, and he would have preferred to be stemming the wind and sea, rather than running before them, but he had negotiated the entrance many times and his confidence was unshaken.

Stornaway, on the east coast of the island of Lewis, was founded by raiding Norsemen in the eleventh century. It is a fine natural harbour, two miles in length and with plenty of deep water. Entrance to the harbour is from the south-east between Arnish Point and Holm Head, an opening about six-hundred yards wide. Once abeam of Arnish Point, it is necessary to alter sharply to port to run into the harbour. Under most circumstances, given good visibility, it is not a difficult entrance, the only danger being a group of submerged rocks known as the Beasts of Holm, which lie off Holm Head. In order to give these rocks a wide berth, it is advisable to keep close up to Arnish Point when entering the harbour.

As the full force of the wind was blowing across the entrance, Cotter decided to round Arnish Point at full speed. Unfortunately, just as the *Iolaire* approached the point, she was caught by a fierce squall and driven sideways across the entrance towards Holm Head. Cotter ordered the helm hard to port and rang for emergency full speed, but he could not break the grip of the wind. The *Iolaire* was carried bodily onto the hidden Beasts of Holm, and she came to a halt with a jarring crash. She immediately took a heavy list to starboard, and the seas began to break over her.

The confusion on the decks of the yacht was absolute. Men, who moments before had been gathering their kit together ready for disembarking, were thrown into struggling heaps. Many were injured as they fell, some slid down the sloping deck and tumbled over the rails to meet death in the sea boiling around the stranded ship. Cotter and his crew tried to restore order, but when it was realised that the ship was only thirty yards from the shore, dozens of men jumped overboard. Not one survived the maelstrom to reach dry land. Two lifeboats were launched, but both were swamped as they hit the water. Of the occupants, only one man was saved.

Ten minutes later, with her bottom ripped open by the Beasts of Holm, the *Iolaire* was lifted clear of the rocks by the thundering surf and dragged seawards. Luckily for those still on board, the next big wave swung the yacht around and carried her past the Beasts of Holm to ground broadside on to the shore at the foot of Holm Head. Distress rockets were fired, in the light of which it could be seen that the ship's stern was no more than twenty feet from a cluster of rocks. Amidships she was within twenty yards of a possible landing place on the foreshore. Although the seas were breaking clean over the stern, the temptation to try and reach the rocks was very great. A number of men died in the attempt, their broken bodies tossed contemptuously ashore by the sea.

The *Iolaire* was breaking up just a stone's throw from the shore, but the impossibility of crossing those few yards of raging sea made prisoners of all on board. It seemed they must all soon die with the ship, until one of the passengers, Royal Navy carpenter John MacLeod, volunteered to swim ashore with a line. It was a last desperate gamble, but, biding his time until there was a temporary lull in the storm, MacLeod went over the starboard side and struck out for the shore. Twenty yards is no great distance, and MacLeod was a powerful swimmer, but he was up against a more powerful adversary. The sea tossed him around like so much driftwood, dragging him down, rolling him over and over, hammering at him until he felt he could take no more. And then, suddenly, he was free of the clutch of the surf and scrambling up the pebble beach to safety.

MacLeod signalled with the line and others on the ship attached a heavier hawser, which he hauled ashore and fastened to a rock. There was now a way of escape from the doomed *Iolaire*, albeit a perilous one, and soon men were coming ashore hand over hand. It was a frightening experience, for the rope dipped and swayed, plunging men into a raging sea that fought tooth and nail to bring them down. There were many who failed to make it to the shore.

When, some eight hours later, the gale blew itself out, one young reservist, Murdo Morrison, was found clinging to the *Iolaire*'s mast, battered and exhausted, but still alive. John MacLeod and thirty-nine others he had been instrumental in saving were found sheltering in a farmhouse on Holm Head. And they, forty-one men in all, were the only ones of the 246 on board the *Iolaire* who lived on into the year 1919. Captain Clement Cotter had gone, as had every one of his crew of twenty-three, and with them 205 naval seamen, who had survived a brutal and bloody war, only to die on their own doorstep. Scarcely a village on the island of Lewis was not affected by the sinking of the *Iolaire*, and the island's war dead was increased by twenty percent overnight.

At the Court of Inquiry held into the disaster, it was concluded that Captain Clement Cotter and his officers had not exercised sufficient caution in approaching Stornaway harbour. Furthermore, the court condemned the same men for not making sufficient efforts to save life. Judgement in hindsight is all very well, but not one of those sitting on the court were present on that wild January night when the Beasts of Holm claimed the *Iolaire*.

Nine years later, to the day, and almost to the hour, early on the morning of 1 January, 1927, the Minches also claimed the *Sheila*. The little MacBrayne steamer, twenty years on the Stornaway run, was inward bound to Kyle of Lochalsh when she made a wrong alteration of course and ran ashore in Cuaig Bay. On this occasion there was no loss of life, but it was the end for the *Sheila*.

Bernard Edwards

27   Crossing the Hard Way

Trevessa - 1923

Fresh from the bunkering berth, her once-smart paint-work blackened by coal dust, the British cargo vessel *Trevessa* slid clear of the breakwaters of the port of Freemantle, West Australia, and curtsied low as she felt the first push of the long Indian Ocean swell. It was Saturday 26 May, 1923. Ahead of the *Trevessa* lay a challenging voyage of 11,500 miles, to the other side of the world. She was bound for Antwerp, with only a brief stop at Durban to replenish her bunkers.

Built in Germany in 1909 and owned by the Hain Steamship Company of London, the 5,004-ton *Trevessa* was, like all things Germanic, substantially constructed and classed 100 A1 at Lloyd's, the highest registration class for a merchant ship. Her owners, part of the prestigious Peninsular & Oriental Group, had taken pains to see she was also equipped, maintained and manned to the best standards. Her master, thirty-six-year-old Captain Cecil Foster, was a seaman and navigator of considerable ability and experience. The *Trevessa* was, then, in the common parlance of her day, a 'well-found' ship in all respects. Yet, nine days after leaving Freemantle, she radioed that she was sinking in mid-Indian Ocean. Ships answering her SOS reached the spot two days later and found only scraps of wreckage and an upturned lifeboat. There was no sign of survivors.

Weeks passed with no news and Captain Foster and his men joined the long list of those of their calling posted as lost at sea without trace. In towns and villages up and down the United Kingdom wives, mothers and girl friends mourned and prepared to face a future suddenly made painfully empty. Then, on 27 June, twenty-three days after the *Trevessa*'s last plaintive message, from a lonely island in the South Indian Ocean came news of a miracle. A lifeboat containing Cecil Foster and seventeen of his crew had landed. These men, who had sailed a total of 1,700 miles in a twenty-six-foot boat, had a remarkable story to tell; a story of courage and endurance in the highest traditions of the British Merchant Navy.

When the *Trevessa* left Freemantle on 26 May, she was down to her maximum permissible marks with full bunkers, full fresh water and 6,500 tons of zinc concentrates in her holds. This cargo is loaded in a semi-liquid form, almost like wet cement, and is highly suscep-

Widow-Maker

Hain Steamship's 5004-ton 'Trevessa' *in ballast*

(Photo: Western Mail)

tible to shifting in heavy weather. Yet the possibility of the latter did not trouble Captain Foster unduly. If anything, he was more concerned with the state of his vessel's stability—that is her ability to return to the upright when inclined by an outside force. By virtue of the heavy weight of concentrates at the bottom of her holds, the *Trevessa* had an excess of stability. In a seaway, she would have a quick, jerky roll, which is not only extremely uncomfortable but, over a long period, guaranteed to search out any hidden weaknesses in the ship's structure. Foster judged that the 4,500-mile passage to Durban, much of the time beam-on to the long rollers of the South Indian Ocean, would put a severe strain on both ship and men. He was uneasy.

For the first twenty-four hours out of Freemantle, blustery but fine weather was experienced. Then, on the 27th, the sky clouded over and the wind freshened from the south-south-west, becoming progressively stronger as the day wore on. By nightfall, a full storm was raging and, for the next week, the *Trevessa* laboured in a heavy beam swell, her tall masts and funnel tracing quick, erratic arcs against the ragged clouds, with every rivet in her hull groaning in protest.

On the morning of 3 June, a mountainous sea rolled in and slammed into the port side of the ship, throwing spray high over the bridge. When the water receded, two of the *Trevessa's* four lifeboats lay in ruins.

At around ten o'clock that night, when the ship was hove-to and riding awkwardly with the wind and sea on the bow, she suddenly staggered as though she had run headlong into an unseen wall. Some said they heard an explosion and a ripple of fear ran through the ship, for the memories of the Great War were only five years old.

Bernard Edwards

Then the *Trevessa* recovered her stride and it was assumed she had merely taken a particularly heavy sea bow-on.

By midnight, it was obvious to Foster his ship was in serious trouble. The seas were sweeping right over her foredeck and, each time she dipped, she seemed more and more reluctant to rise again.

Able Seaman Michael Scully, clawing his way forward at the change of the watch, heard the ominous swish of water as he drew abreast of No.1 hold. A less experienced man might have dismissed this as just another voice in the awful cacophony of the storm. But Scully, a shrewd Liverpudlian in his sixties, was quick to sense danger. He reported to the bridge and Foster, accompanied by the chief engineer and carpenter, went forward to investigate.

It was as Scully had thought. No.1 hold was awash, with the water well above the height of the cargo. An inspection of the forepeak tank showed the collision bulkhead—the specially strengthened watertight bulkhead in the eyes of the ship—was bulging inwards and in imminent danger of giving way.

Foster returned to the bridge and put the ship's head off the wind to ease the strain on the damaged bulkhead, then ordered the pumps onto No.1 hold. His efforts at containment were in vain and, by one o'clock on the morning of the 4th, the seas were breaking green over the *Trevessa*'s forward hatches, as she settled slowly by the head. Fearing the worst, Foster issued lifejackets to all hands and ordered the two remaining lifeboats to be swung out ready for launching. At 01.16, he instructed his wireless operator to begin sending out an SOS.

The distress call was heard by at least three ships, Shaw Savill & Albion's *Runic* and two other Hain Line steamers, the *Trevean* and *Tregenna*. Unfortunately, the nearest of the three, the *Tregenna*, was 400 miles to the east and all were in heavy weather and unable to increase speed.

Meanwhile, in the shrieking darkness of that terrible night, the *Trevessa*'s pumps were running hot and able to make little impression on the rising water in her forward hold. She was so far down by the head that her propeller was almost out of the water and her foredeck was constantly awash. Foster knew it would only be a matter of time before her other watertight bulkheads collapsed and she went under, bow first.

The process of abandoning ship was not new to Cecil Foster. He had been twice torpedoed in the war, on the second occasion spending ten days in an open boat, suffering the agonies of thirst, hunger and exposure. He therefore laid his plans well, stocking the two lifeboats with extra water, cases of condensed milk, cigarettes, tobacco and sextants. At 02.15, he gave the order to abandon ship. The *Trevessa* was in position latitude 28° 27' S longitude 85° 25' E, roughly 1,500 miles from the west coast of Australia.

In spite of the high seas threatening to smash them against the ship's side, the lifeboats got away safely, the only casualty being the ship's black Persian cat which, having been put in one of the boats, jumped back on board the *Trevessa* and was lost. It may have been that her canine intuition warned her of the ordeal in prospect for those in the boats and she preferred to die with the ship.

Captain Foster was in charge of one lifeboat, having nineteen men with him, while Chief Officer John Stewart-Smith took the other boat with twenty-three men. Foster's boat nearly came to grief at the outset, when a huge wave lifted it right over the foredeck of the sinking ship. Luckily, the receding waters carried it back again with only slight damage.

At 02.45 on the morning of 4 June, the *Trevessa*'s crew, forty-four men crammed into two tiny, storm-tossed lifeboats, watched sadly as the ship they had come to regard as their home slipped beneath the waves.

Cecil Foster was now faced with what was perhaps the most difficult decision of his life, for the *Trevessa* had gone down at one of the loneliest crossroads of the Indian Ocean. Australia lay 1,500 miles to the east, while the nearest land to the west was the island of Rodriguez, a small dot in the ocean and 1,600 miles away. To the south, 670 miles off, were the equally small islands of Amsterdam and St. Paul; to the north there was nothing for 2,000 miles but the sweltering emptiness of the tropics.

The possibility of making for Amsterdam and St. Paul, Foster dismissed out of hand, for the islands were uninhabited and lay deep in the bitter cold and howling winds of the Roaring Forties. Likewise, he opted against sailing north, where the blazing sun would turn them into shrivelled corpses before land was reached. He could, of course, remain in the vicinity of the sinking and hope for rescue. But he knew this might take many days, during which the inactivity and cruel weather would destroy the morale of his men, eventually killing them as surely as if they had gone down with the ship. The temptation to try to make it back to Australia was very strong, but the wind and currents were against them. That left only Rodriguez, which they could possibly reach by taking advantage of the south-east trade winds and the westerly flowing Equatorial Current. If they missed Rodriguez—and there was a distinct possibility they might—the island of Mauritius was only three-hundred miles further west or, failing that, the shores of Madagascar lay beyond. To sail to the west was the only viable choice.

As a gesture to his would-be rescuers—if any—Foster held the boats riding to their sea anchors for the rest of that night and all next day. Except for the endless procession of angry waves, the horizon remained empty and, at sunset on the 4th, the *Trevessa*'s boats hoisted sail and set out to the west.

The plan of action, worked out jointly by Foster and Stewart-Smith, was to first make to the north until the south-east trades were reached in about latitude 23° 30' S, then north-west to latitude 19° 30' S—the latitude of Rodriguez—and then due west to the island. They were following the old sailing ship route, well trodden by their shellback forebears before them.

Due to the violent rolling and pitching of the small boats, the compasses proved useless but, steering by the sun and stars and checking their latitude by sextant whenever the opportunity occurred, they pushed northwards. Foster's boat, with a larger sail and lighter load, was by far the better sailer and, from time to time over the next five days he found himself forced to heave-to while Stewart-Smith's boat laboriously narrowed the gap. On the morning of the 9th, after a bad night in which the two boats had great difficulty in keeping in touch, Foster decided it would be more sensible to part company. It was agreed that whoever was first to reach land would send help for the others.

Without the slower boat holding him back, Foster made good progress despite the most appalling weather conditions, averaging about seventy miles a day. Then, on the 11th, the wind suddenly dropped away and for the next four days they were becalmed. Thanks to Foster's foresight, they still had a good supply of food and water but, ever conscious of the long voyage ahead, he had set the rations at a third of a cigarette tin of water, one biscuit and a few spoonfuls of condensed milk per day, per man. The men suffered most from thirst, even though, again benefiting from Foster's wartime experiences, they sucked buttons and pieces of coal to stimulate their saliva and kept their heads wet with salt water. The occasional shower of rain was a godsend, in which they bathed like excited children and collected water in tins and outstretched oilskins. But, so weakened were they by hunger and the long battle with the sea, their morale had fallen to its lowest ebb. And there was worse to come.

By alternately rowing and drifting, they reached the southern boundary of the south-east trades on the afternoon of the 15th. A north-westerly course was then set and, with the wind right astern and freshening all the time, the ungainly lifeboat seemed to fly like a bird before the curling waves. But the kindly trade wind, so revered by the old windjammer men, proved to be a curse for the men crouching in their frail craft only inches above the sea. Moaning like a demented soul, the wind piled up the seas astern until they became pursuing white-topped mountains, hell-bent on the destruction of the boat. This torture went on day after day without let-up. Twice the boat was pooped and the exhausted men were forced to bail for their lives.

Under the cover of darkness, in spite of Foster's warnings, some began to drink salt water and suffered the inevitable consequences. On 20 June, Fireman Jacob Ali died, to be followed next day on his long voyage to the unknown by his shipmate Mussim Nazi. Their committal to the deep made more room in the crowded boat, but this

Captain Foster's momentoes, including the ship's sextant, the spoon and comb used aboard lifeboat. Auctioned at Cardiff 1988
(Photo: Western Mail)

Captain Cecil Foster (left) & Chief Officer John Stewart-Smith of the 'Trevessa'
(Photo: Western Mail)

Bernard Edwards

Captain Cecil Foster of the 'Trevessa' *with his wife and Chief Officer*
John Stewart-Smith
(Photo: Western Mail)

was of little real comfort to those who remained. Foster was aware the
crucial stage in their ordeal had now been reached. As far as he could
tell from sun sights, the boat was then in latitude 19° 30' S and about
350 miles due east of Rodriguez. The consequences of missing the
tiny island he refused to contemplate. They must press on.

On the morning of the 26th, a tremendous sea reared up astern
and pounced on the boat, swamping it so that it sank to the gunwales. For the wretched survivors this final indignity must have
offered the temptation to surrender and die quietly, but again they
rallied and bailed. The reward for their efforts proved beyond price.
At 2.45 that afternoon, as the half-waterlogged boat rose sluggishly
on the crest of a wave, land was sighted. Five hours later, after narrowly escaping being wrecked on a reef, Foster and his men sailed
into Port Mathurin, Rodriguez. They had covered almost 1,700

miles in twenty-two days and eighteen hours.

The second miracle occurred three days later, when Chief Officer John Stewart-Smith brought his boat into Baie du Cap, at the southern end of the island of Mauritius. They had missed Rodriguez and sailed a total of 2,200 miles in twenty-five days. The cost of Stewart-Smith's achievement was high. Four Arab firemen had succumbed through drinking sea water, three Europeans, including one of the *Trevessa*'s young apprentices, had died of exposure, and Second Engineer David Mordecai had been lost overboard from the boat in a sudden squall.

The *Trevessa* lies in over 1,000 fathoms of water, and the cause of her loss will never be known. Did she, on that dark, storm-filled night in June 1923, strike a submerged object—an old wreck floating just below the surface, perhaps? Or was it a barnacle-covered mine, left over from the war and drifting unfulfilled in mid-ocean? This could account for the explosion said to have been heard. Or was it just the awesome power of the sea that smashed in the *Trevessa*'s bow and launched her crew on that long, hazardous voyage to the west?

Bernard Edwards

28　Winter North Atlantic

Ainderby - 1934

The power of the sea is absolute. Never has this been more dramatically shown than in the North Atlantic in the winter of 1934. This was a season of storms of unparalleled ferocity and duration in an ocean renowned throughout the ages for its vile weather.

It was still autumn in British waters when the 4,860-ton cargo steamer *Ainderby* left Swansea on 21 September. An area of high pressure was firmly established over Europe, giving cloudless skies and light winds, with only a hint of frost in the air presaging the approach of winter. The sea was calm as the *Ainderby* rounded Mumbles Head and pointed her bluff bows westwards. On the bridge her master, Captain Bestell, paced the freshly scrubbed boards sniffing at the clean air, at peace with the world. After years of recession, when shipowners had fought over disappearing cargoes like hungry wolves, and men with master's tickets stood in line for menial jobs on deck, British shipping was at last showing signs of sustained recovery. In consequence, the *Ainderby* was down to her marks with 8,000 tons of Welsh anthracite and bound for the Canadian port of Montreal. Admittedly, the freight on this cargo was not high, but to Bestell and his crew, many of whom had been on the beach in the bad days, the bulging holds spelled job security for many months to come.

Some two-hundred miles to the south-east, the equally heavily laden *Millpool* shouldered her way through the oily calm of the English Channel, also bound for Montreal. As he conned his ship past Beachy Head, its tall white cliffs shimmering in the coastal haze, Captain Newton, master of the *Millpool*, felt the tensions of the preceding four days slipping away. The passage from Danzig, where the *Millpool* had loaded a full cargo of grain, had been one fraught with all the dangers shallow and congested waters can bring to a deep-laden ship. Now, with the busy Straits of Dover safely astern, Newton was able to turn his mind to the 2,800-mile voyage ahead. He was well aware the long ocean crossing might prove a serious challenge, for the ageing *Millpool*, built in 1906, was sagging noticeably under her heavy load. On the other hand, he drew confidence from his long experience in the ways of the sea and the blessing of a first-class crew. The weather, apparently set fair for some time to come, was an added bonus.

Given the advantage of modern-day weather forecasting, the equanimity of the two master mariners might well have been profoundly disturbed on that fine September day. Unknown to them, the North Atlantic was already in the opening bars of a mighty overture to winter. Far to the west, pressure was falling rapidly over an area more than a thousand miles across, the isobars were packing in and, urged on by the rising wind, the surface of the great ocean had commenced to heave and roll with a ponderous movement that spoke of its awesome power.

The *Ainderby* and the 4,218-ton *Millpool* were first cousins, both out of the stable of Sir Robert Ropner & Company, of West Hartlepool. They were typical tramp steamers of their day, being small, under-powered and strictly functional. They might also be described as forerunners of the modern bulk carrier, specifically designed to carry coal, ores and grain to the maximum advantage. To this end, they had large, unobstructed holds, topped by an open shelter deck, which ran uninterrupted from forward to aft and, when piled with bulk cargo, acted as a gravity feeder for the holds below. The cost of manual trimming in port was therefore kept to a minimum, a very significant factor in those days of low freights. Additionally, all cargo stowed in the shelter deck was classed as being 'on deck' and attracted less in the way of tonnage dues. In reality, this open deck, although intended as an integral part of the ship's buoyancy, was an example of British design at its worst. The deck had only two watertight bulkheads, one at each end and forming part of the configuration of the well decks. They were, therefore, completely exposed to the sea. In heavy weather, the forward bulkhead inevitably took the full force of the seas breaking over the bows. As an economic expedient the principle behind these ships was sound; to the men who sailed in them, they were vulnerable ships, to be nursed with a firm but delicate hand.

The *Ainderby* was the first to feel the force of the gathering storm. Twenty-four hours out of Swansea, she ran into strong south-westerly winds, accompanied by heavy rain and rising seas. Soon, her massive stem-bar was slamming into each advancing wall of water with a force that threatened to shake loose every rivet in her hull. Captain Bestell had no alternative but to reduce speed.

For the next six days, the *Ainderby* struggled westwards, fighting the sea for every precious mile gained. On the 28th, she was 600 miles to the west of Ireland and nearing the mid-point in her ocean passage. To Bestell, his eyes heavy and face lined with fatigue, the worst seemed to be over. Then the Atlantic, which had really only been gathering its strength, struck with all the spiteful, pent-up fury of a frustrated Goliath. The wind came out of the west with hurricane force and mountainous seas thundered down on the *Ainderby*,

Bernard Edwards

slamming against her bows and filling her well decks with boiling foam. Only by the skilful use of helm and engines was Bestell able to prevent her broaching-to.

Later that morning, when Bestell had finally succeeded in heaving-to with the wind and sea on the bow, the enraged Atlantic claimed its first victim. Fifteen-year-old Apprentice Leonard Baxter was snatched from the deck by a wave and swept overboard.

Despite the danger of being caught beam-on to the sea, Bestell immediately put the ship about and, for three long hours searched the heaving wastes in the vicinity of the accident. His efforts were in vain. Leonard Baxter, youngest member of the *Ainderby*'s crew, was never seen again.

Bestell was deeply saddened by the loss of the young boy, but the professional code of the sea demanded he make every effort to continue his voyage. Throughout the next three days, the *Ainderby* lay bow-on to the wind and sea, barely making steerage way, and all the time weakening under the constant assaults of an ocean gone berserk.

On the morning of 1 October, hopes were raised by a gradual moderation in the weather and the battered tramp began to forge slowly ahead towards the coast of Newfoundland, now less than 500 miles off. Unfortunately, the respite was short-lived. By noon on the 2nd the storm clouds had re-gathered, the wind began to shriek again and the sea resumed its angry attack. Bestell was once again forced to first reduce speed, and then heave-to.

For more than two hours the *Ainderby* rode the sea, sliding awkwardly from crest to trough, uncomfortable, vulnerable, but as safe as good seamanship could make her. Then, without warning, she slipped into a trough so deep that the sky was completely blotted out. Those on the bridge watched horror-stricken as a giant wave, its crest frothing white, reared up to mast-top height and then pounced with a triumphant roar. The *Ainderby* went down groaning and shuddering under the weight of thousands of tons of green water and it seemed she would never rise again. But rise she did, slowly and determinedly, shrugging aside the might of the great Atlantic. Her wounds, however, were grievous.

At the same time, 150 miles to the east, the *Millpool* was fighting her own lonely battle with the enraged ocean. On her bridge, a gaunt-faced Captain Newton managed a wry smile as he read the message handed to him by his wireless operator: *From s.s. Ainderby 53° 14' N 41° 20' W No.1 hatch forward and iron bulkhead stove in. Bridge partly wiped away. Chief Officer injured. We are unable to heave to.*

If anything, the *Millpool* was in an even more desperate situation than her cousin. Earlier in the day, her forward hatch had been breached by the sea and Newton had been obliged to turn and run before the storm. She was now heading back towards Ireland, down

Widow-Maker

Storm force in the North Atlantic

(Photo: Captain J. Thomson)

by the head through the water in her forward hold, and riding the mountainous seas like a great, ungainly surf boat. As each sea raced up astern of her, filling the air with flying spray torn off its over-hanging crest by a wind in excess of eighty knots, the ship was in constant danger of being overwhelmed. Yet, always at the last minute it seemed, she was able to lift her old fashioned stern high and ride up on the back of the wave and down into the following trough, her propeller racing and her decks streaming water. She was a brave ship, but Newton feared it must be only a matter of time before she faltered in her stride and stumbled in the path of the advancing seas.

The agony of the *Millpool* was not prolonged. A few hours later, the American coast station, Mackay Radio, picked up the following message: *SOS....from s.s. Millpool 53° 30' N 37° 10' W. After hatch stove in, main topmast gone, three men injured. Driving helplessly before gale. Using temporary aerial....SOS.*

The plaintive cry for help was also heard by the *Ainderby*'s oper-ator, but Bestell could offer to Newton no more than his heartfelt sympathy, for his own ship was also in mortal danger. The rogue sea that had laid open the *Ainderby*'s No.1 hatch had also smashed the forward bulkhead of her shelter deck, so that she was wide open to the sea. Water had swept along the length of the shelter deck, cascading down into the holds and into the stokehold, threatening to douse the boiler fires. For a while, it seemed the ship must go, swamped by the sea flooding unchecked through her hull, then, with a supreme effort, Bestell had brought her around so that she was stern-on to the sea. Now, with her pumps working at full capacity and coping with the ingress, she was temporarily out of danger. Two ships, the Cunard liner *Antonia* and the cargo steamer *Trematon*, were standing by her. This gave some comfort to Bestell and his crew, but as seamen they were well aware that, should the *Ainderby* founder in such weather, the other ships could do little to save their lives.

Similar help was also on the way to the *Millpool*. Following her distress message, another Cunard liner, the *Ascania*, and the cargo ship *Beaverhill*, both eastbound across the Atlantic, were making all possible speed towards the position given by the stricken tramp. The *Ascania*, a ship of 14,000 tons, kept wireless contact with the *Millpool* throughout that day and into the night, but the distress signals grew fainter and fainter until, at 02.00 GMT on the morning of 3 October, they faded altogether.

The rescue ships reached the last position given by the *Millpool* just after dawn on the 3rd They found only an empty expanse of angry sea. For the next twelve hours both ships, themselves at considerable risk in the huge seas, quartered the area, sending up rockets and calling on the *Millpool* to give her position. Nothing was seen or heard. At least a dozen other ships later joined in the search. They found nothing; no wreckage, no lifeboats, no bodies. The *Millpool* and her crew had disappeared off the face of the sea forever.

To this day, the fate of the *Millpool* and her twenty-six-man crew remains a mystery, but speculation as to how she met her end is not difficult. In her distress message she reported her main-topmast gone and her after hatch stove in, so it is highly probable she was overtaken and pooped by a rogue wave similar in size to that which damaged the *Ainderby*—it may even have been the same wave. The consequences of being pooped will have been catastrophic and, in addition to the damage she declared, it is almost certain the after bulkhead of the *Millpool*'s shelter deck caved in under the weight of water. The sea then had free access to the heart of the ship, destroying her reserve buoyancy, creating negative stability, and possibly extinguishing her boiler fires. As she was already running before the storm, there was nothing Newton could have done to save her. She must simply have rolled over and been swallowed up by the sea.

The *Ainderby*, being slightly larger and younger than the *Millpool* by nineteen years, survived the terrible ordeal of the winter of 1934. She limped back into Swansea a week later, her decks and accommodation in a shambles, her deck plating cracked across the breadth of the ship amidships, and with a foot of water in her holds. Captain Bestell and his crew were tired, physically and mentally bruised, but unbeaten. Ten days later, after hurried repairs, they once more set out to challenge the North Atlantic. This time the *Ainderby* reached Montreal without mishap. Her end was not to come until seven years later, and then not by the hand of the sea, but by a German torpedo. She still lies, along with so many of her kind, in a grave 120 miles to the north-west of Bloody Foreland.

The winter of 1934, which had begun with such sudden fury in that late September, raged in the North Atlantic almost unabated until the end of December, with violent storm following violent storm so closely that the ocean was forever in a frenzy. Apart from the *Millpool*, three other British tramps foundered with heavy loss of life and reports of ships being swept by hundred-foot waves were common. These reports may have been subject to some exaggeration, but certainly the wave that hit the Japanese ship *Victoria Maru* in early December must have been a monster. When she staggered into Cardiff, her entire bridge superstructure and funnel had gone, along with her master, chief officer and third officer. The British ship *Monkleigh*, in difficulties 770 miles west of the Scillies, lost her mainmast, most of her deck cargo of timber, and suffered severe damage to her superstructure. Ships were flung ashore on the Atlantic coasts of Spain and Portugal and, for almost three months, cries for help jammed the wireless waves from Cape Hatteras to the Faroes and from Newfoundland to the Canaries.

29.   And Again to War

Truro - 1939

The Second World War was only eleven days old when the British steamer *Truro* left the Firth of Forth, bound for the Norwegian port of Devanger, near Bergen. She was unarmed and carried no radio—an innocent participant in a war that was eventually to engulf half the civilised world and destroy the core of Britain's merchant fleet.

To forty-six-year-old Captain J.E. Egner, master of the *Truro*, the war to date had amounted to little more than a thoroughly unwarranted interference in his God-given mandate to command and navigate his ship in a manner dictated only by his experience and expertise. He had already felt the bureaucratic might of the Admiralty, having been ordered to call at the port of Methil to receive his routing orders for the crossing of the North Sea. To a man who was as familiar with this sea as he was with his own back garden this seemed an unnecessary waste of time, to say the least.

The 974-ton *Truro*, built at Aberdeen in 1922, and owned by Ellerman's Wilson Line of Hull, was only a tiny cog in the great wheel of the Ellerman shipping empire, whose trade routes stretched to the four corners of the globe. A bluff-bowed, overgrown coaster—as she was regarded by many—she was a regular trader between the east coast of Britain and ports in Scandinavia and the Baltic, covering the well-trodden path across the North Sea on a weekly basis. Her home port was Hull, Captain Egner and his crew of thirty-two lived in Hull, and, more often than not, she ended up in the Humber at the completion of each voyage. For Egner and his men this was a most satisfactory arrangement. However, as always, there was a price to be paid. In winter it was a hard run, with the North Sea often swept by fierce gales, which churned this shallow sea into a frightening maelstrom, meting out savage punishment to the little *Truro* as she went about her business. Then, at the end of the outward passage, there was ice, snow, and the bone-chilling cold that no multiple layers of clothing could keep at bay. The summer months were perhaps more comfortable, but no less hazardous, for the curse of fog, dense and blinding, was frequently with them. Small, underpowered and equipped with the absolute minimum of navigational aids, the *Truro* was not a ship for the faint of heart at the best of times.

Widow-Maker

Having been duly briefed by the Naval authorities, the *Truro* sailed from Methil at 14.00 on 14 September 1939. Two hours later, she had left the shelter of the Firth of Forth and was burying her bows in the first swells of the open sea. The weather was fine and clear, with no more than a fresh breeze and Captain Egner was confident that the two-day passage to Norway would be an uneventful one. Methil had warned him to be on the lookout for U-boats, but he was inclined to think the Navy was making a song and dance about nothing. In Egner's opinion, which he expressed to Second Officer Morrell, who stood beside him on the bridge as they headed out to sea, if the Germans had any sense, they would be out in the Atlantic looking for the big ships. In any case, the immediate enemy for the *Truro* was fog. There was, again in Egner's opinion, the smell of it in the air.

Egner was correct in his supposition that the Germans would be better occupied in the deep waters of the Atlantic. Unknown to him, the U-boats had, in fact, been out there in force since the third week in August, waiting for the signal to begin hostilities. When this came, they had wasted no time, sinking seventeen British merchantmen in the first ten days of the war. The situation in the North Sea was less threatening, the few U-boats operating in the area had found only one victim in that period.

The fog Egner had forecast did not materialise, neither did the enemy, and on the evening of the 15th the *Truro* was more than halfway across the North Sea, with just 120 miles to go to the Norwegian coast. As the sun dropped below the horizon and the long northern twilight began to draw its reassuring cloak around his small and vulnerable ship, Egner relaxed in his cabin.

On the bridge, Chief Officer A.W. Johnson, who had the watch, paced the starboard wing, stopping occasionally to run his binoculars over the horizon. He, too, welcomed the coming of the night and was reassured by the fact that the *Truro* was apparently alone on an empty sea. Then he glanced astern and froze.

The frenzied shriek of the voice-pipe whistle brought Egner tumbling out of his armchair. Seconds later, at Johnson's request, he was racing for the bridge ladder.

The submarine was about two miles off on the starboard quarter, trimmed down and appeared to be shadowing them. Egner had no way of knowing if this was the enemy, but he was not in the mood to take chances. He brought his ship sharply round to the north, putting the submarine right astern, and called on the engineroom for maximum revolutions. His plan was simple—and being unarmed, the only one open to him—he would run away, hoping to escape under the cover of darkness.

U-36, the *Truro*'s pursuer, was a Type II craft of 250 tons displacement, being in the eyes of the German Navy as insignificant as the *Truro* was to her big sisters who sailed the deep waters. She was one of Admiral Dönitz's original fleet of coastal submarines, built well before the outbreak of war and with a very limited operational range; hence her presence in the North Sea. For her commander, Kapitan-Leutnant Wilhelm Frolich, this was his first confrontation with the enemy, and he intended to play the game according to the rules laid down by the Prize Ordinance. This unrealistic piece of international legislation, enacted by the League of Nations, stipulated that a submarine must first stop a merchant ship and allow her crew to take to the boats before sinking the ship.

For the *Truro*, escape was, of course, impossible. The U-boat, running on the surface, had the legs of the small cargo ship, even though her stokers worked like men possessed to keep the boiler furnaces roaring. Steadily, the distance separating pursuer and pursued shortened, and soon U-36 was abeam to port of the *Truro*, her deck gun manned and pointing menacingly. Her signal lamp flashed the order to stop and abandon ship.

Grim-faced, Egner stared down the barrel of the U-boat's gun from his bridge. Given a gun of his own, however small, he would have been tempted to make a fight of it. Had he not fought the sea all his life, no matter how great the odds? But his cunning and navigational skills would be of little use against this enemy. He could conceivably continue to run, but sooner or later would come the hail of shells or the silent torpedo. The end result would only be more grieving widows, more fatherless children in the port of Hull. With a hopeless shrug Egner walked into the wheelhouse and rang the engineroom telegraph to stop.

In order to gain precious time, Egner ordered Second Officer Morrell to contact the U-boat by semaphore, if possible feigning confusion and misunderstanding. Meanwhile, he directed Chief Officer Johnson to stock the lifeboats with blankets, cigarettes, spirits, and all the tinned food he could lay his hands on. Having no radio on board, he was unable to send an SOS and there was no telling how long they might be adrift in the boats.

The U-boat was now signalling insistently for them to abandon ship, adding that the captain must bring all his papers with him when he left. Egner's answer to that was to gather up all his confidential papers and books and carry them below to the stokehold, where he tossed them into the dying flames of a boiler furnace.

With the shadows of night drawing swiftly in, the *Truro*'s two lifeboats were lowered, Egner taking the starboard boat and Johnson the port one. The evacuation was orderly and unhurried, but there was a moderate swell running and Egner's boat was slammed against the ship's side and slightly damaged. The only casualty was the *Truro*'s chief engineer, who bruised his ribs when falling from the deck of the ship into the sea.

As Egner's boat pulled around the bow of the *Truro*, the U-boat came into full view. She was about 150 feet in length, with a small but deadly looking gun on her fore casing and a large instrument abaft the conning tower resembling a range finder. There were no rust streaks on her grey paint and her only identifying mark was a red swastika painted on the side of her conning tower. While Egner was mentally photographing the enemy, Morrell, who was in the same boat, was busy with his camera, making a more permanent record of the submarine's appearance. Fortunately for him, the Germans did not appear to notice his activity.

The submarine now hailed the lifeboats, asking for the captain to come aboard with his papers. Egner, suspicious, yet curious to meet the man who was holding his ship at gunpoint, ordered his men to pull for the U-boat. The only papers he carried with him were the ship's articles and certificates, which could be hardly regarded as being of a secret nature.

The boat bumped alongside the after end of the submarine and Egner, clutching his bundle of papers, was helped aboard by two German seamen. He was then escorted to the conning tower, where he came face to face with Wilhelm Frolich, a man in his early thirties with a sallow complexion and several days growth of beard on his chin. Frolich was polite, almost apologetic, when he explained to Egner that it would be necessary to sink his ship. Not expecting anything less, Egner shrugged and handed over his papers. No one would be more aggrieved than him at the sinking of the *Truro*.

Frolich gave the papers a cursory examination and then handed them back to Egner. He then enquired if the captain had sent out an SOS and was somewhat surprised when Egner admitted that his ship did not carry a radio. The conversation became less strained, and it was Egner's turn to be surprised when the German asked for his help in fixing the submarine's position, which had been in some doubt for two days past. Having personally taken sun sights earlier in the day, Egner took a great delight in giving the German Navy a lesson in navigation.

Egner was now invited, not ordered, to enter the submarine, but it was with some misgivings that he lowered himself through the conning tower hatch and climbed down into the control room. He had heard rumours that the Germans were in the habit of making prisoners of ship's captains. Was he to end up in a prisoner of war camp?

Whatever the Germans' intentions, they showed no animosity towards Egner. It seemed that the whole crew of the U-boat—twenty-five or thirty men—had crowded into the control room, agog with curiosity. They were all young, fresh-faced and eager to try out their limited English on the bewildered shipmaster. He was not to know that this was their first sight of the enemy, U-36 having been, until then, in contact only with neutral Norwegian ships. While answering the questions fired at him, Egner gained confidence and took the opportunity to look around him, taking careful note of the layout of instruments and equipment. The Admiralty would welcome any such information—should he be allowed to go free.

When they returned to the conning tower, Frolich expressed a genuine regret that his country should be involved in a war with Britain, a sentiment with which Egner heartily agreed. As seamen, neither man could see sense in the wanton sinking of ships which the war would undoubtedly demand. The bond between the two men became firmer. They exchanged names and addresses, agreeing that they should meet after the war, which Frolich confidently forecast would not last more than another two months. Without prompting, the commander now offered to use the U-boat's radio to send out and SOS, so that the *Truro*'s lifeboats would not be long adrift before help came. Egner accepted gratefully and asked for additional water for the boats. As the U-boat was short of water herself, Frolich could offer only two dozen bottles of beer. These were handed down to the waiting survivors, who accepted them with acclamation. A bucket was also lowered to Egner's damaged boat to help with the bailing.

Feeling that the situation had become completely detached from the realities of war, Egner shook hands with Frolich and made to leave the conning tower. As he put his foot on the first rung of the ladder, a heavy hand on his shoulder stopped him. In a complete reversal of his previous attitude, Frolich now informed Egner that he was to be made prisoner and taken back to Germany.

The dumbfounded Egner at once refused to stay, pointing out that his place was in the boats with his men. A heated argument between the two captains followed, but in the end Frolich relented. He agreed to release the Britisher if he would sign a paper declaring he would not go to sea again until the war was over. The prospect of such an undertaking, which had a Napoleonic ring to it, did not appeal to Egner. He pointed out to Frolich that he was a master mariner and could not, under any circumstances, give up his profession. But the commander was adamant. If Egner did not sign the paper, he would be taken as a prisoner of war. Frolich now also demanded that the *Truro*'s chief and second officers be brought aboard to sign the same declaration.

Johnson and Morrell were called aboard the submarine and clambered up into the cramped conning tower, mystified but curious. Frolich once more explained the terms under which all three could gain their parole and produced a printed document, which he translated from the German and offered to the two men for signature. The two officers flatly refused to sign, and, for a while, it seemed that the entire navigation department of the *Truro* would be whisked off into captivity. Then Egner made a quick decision. The whole thing was so ridiculous as to be laughable. No one could ever hold them to a promise of this nature made under duress. Furthermore, the document Frolich offered was in German, a language which he and his officers could not understand. With a slight

shrug of his shoulders he signed, indicating to the others to do likewise. Surprisingly, Frolich accepted the sudden surrender without
question, and, after a final handshake all round, Egner took his officers back to the lifeboats.

As the boats were pulling clear of the submarine, Egner heard
a muffled thump and he knew his ship was doomed. Silently, he
watched the torpedo feather its way across the intervening water to
explode with a flash and an angry roar, tearing open the *Truro*'s
defenceless hull midway between her No.2 and 3 holds.

The little ship, a survivor of seventeen years of the worst that
Europe's northern seas could throw at her, did not die easily. Frolich
manned his deck gun and opened fire, but, even though the range
was less than half a mile, only one hit was scored. The German commander was then forced to use another of his precious torpedoes to
finish the job. The torpedo ran true, hitting the *Truro* in way of her
boiler room. She blew up and sank within two minutes.

Having disposed of the British ship, Wilhelm Frolich now
showed amazing compassion to her crew. He called the two lifeboats
back alongside and informed Egner that he had sent out an SOS,
using the *Truro*'s call sign. Until help came, he would take the boats
in tow.

And so they set off, with the U-boat motoring quietly on the
surface, and the lifeboats strung out behind on a long tow line, for
all the world like a mother hen leading her chicks to safety.

After about half an hour, Frolich stopped and allowed the boats
to come up to him. He pointed out the lights of a ship to port and
fired a series of red distress flares to attract the unknown vessel's
attention. When he felt he had done so, the German commander
wished Egner and his men good luck, cast off the tow rope and
motored off into the night.

As soon as the U-boat was out of sight, swallowed up in the
darkness, Egner turned his attention to the approaching ship, which,
as it was showing lights, he assumed to be neutral. The lifeboat distress flares were broken out and burned, but, although the ship came
within two miles of the boats, it did not stop, although it could
hardly have failed to see the flares. The rest of the horizon was empty
as far as the eye could see, and Egner realised he must now attempt
to sail the boats back to the British coast. The nearest point, the coast
in the region of Aberdeen, was about 115 miles away; forty-eight
hours sailing, if the weather did not deteriorate—and there was no
guarantee of that.

The two boats sailed westwards throughout the remainder of
the night, steering by their dimly-lit compasses and striving to keep
in sight of each other. At about 08.30 on the morning of the 16th,
an aircraft passed low over the water, about five miles away. Not
knowing, or caring, whether the plane was friend or foe, the survivors stood up in the boats shouting and waving. But it was no

good. The aircraft continued serenely on its course, giving no sign that the boats had been sighted.

The sun climbed towards its zenith and still the sea around them remained stubbornly empty. The complete absence of fishing trawlers worried Egner, for this part of the North Sea was normally well populated by fishermen. He began to wonder if they had all run for shelter before an advancing gale; it was most unlikely that the weather would hold fair for much longer. Then, in the late afternoon, smudges of smoke were sighted on the horizon to the west, and it seemed they had found the fishing fleet at last.

Darkness fell on this the second day of their ordeal, and, although they sailed steadily westwards, the reassuring pencils of smoke drifting skywards from the horizon came no nearer. The night dragged on, they were cold, tired and morale was flagging. Midnight passed, and the next day, Sunday, was upon them, when, suddenly, they found themselves among a fleet of trawlers.

Egner galvanised his men into action. The oars were shipped and the boats pulled hard for the nearest trawler, burning distress flares as they went. To their complete surprise, the fisherman put his stern to them and made off at speed like a frightened rabbit. The same thing happened time and time again as the boats, burning their rapidly diminishing stock of flares, attempted to approach the nearest trawler. The farce was rapidly turning into a tragedy, for it was obvious to Egner that the fishermen had mistaken his boats for the enemy and were in mortal fear of being stopped. There remained only one solution. If the fishermen would not voluntarily rescue them, then they must be made to do so.

Egner consulted with Johnson, and they each selected a trawler to shadow and approach silently. It was hard, painstaking work, but the plan succeeded and two Belgian trawlers suddenly found themselves boarded by a gang of dirty, unshaven and desperate British seamen, who must have put the fear of God into them. Fortunately, there was no violence, and when the *Truro*'s survivors had explained their predicament to the Belgians, they were treated with great kindness. Egner and his men were landed at Aberdeen later that day, having spent thirty-three hours in the lifeboats.

The crew of the *Truro* were early victims of a war at sea that had not yet degenerated into a vicious killing match. In Wilhelm Frolich they had met with a U-boat commander who, although dedicated to taking the war to Germany's enemies, did so with compassion and regard for human life. In the years that were to follow, there were few of his kind in evidence.

Following her meeting with the *Truro*, U-36 sank the Swedish steamer *Silesia* off the coast of Norway on 25 September, but that was to be her last victory. Two months later, she was sunk in the North Sea by His Majesty's submarine *Salmon*. Her war had been a short and unproductive one.

30   A Brush With a Condor

Nestlea - 1940

The thunder of the rainy season was still reverberating around the hills behind Freetown when, on the morning of 26 October, 1940, a long line of heavily laden merchant ships filed past Cape Sierra Leone into the open sea. Once clear of the cape and in deep water, the ships of Convoy SL 53 formed up under the watchful eye of their escorts and began the long voyage north. For the second time in a quarter of a century Britain and Germany were at war and the Atlantic was once again a major battlefield.

In the ranks of SL 53 was the 4,274-ton *Nestlea*, a nineteen-year-old coal-burner owned by J. Morrison & Sons of Newcastle. Commanded by Captain W. McPherson and carrying a total crew of thirty-eight, the *Nestlea* was weighed down with 7,150 tons of manganese ore consigned to Workington, on the north-west coast of England.

The *Nestlea* had seen her best days tramping the trade routes of the world between the wars, efficiently, economically, and with considerable profit to her owners. Now she was old and tired, and with the convenient blind eye of wartime turned on her load line, grossly overloaded. Although the convoy's designated speed was only a modest seven and a half knots, McPherson knew his ship would be hard pressed to keep up with the others. Furthermore, the route laid down for the convoy, a long reach out into the Atlantic and north to latitude 57 degrees, before turning in to enter the Irish Sea by the North Channel, was not to his liking. This diversion, while no doubt necessary to confuse the enemy, added another 500 miles to the passage, an extra three days steaming at the convoy's best speed. It was doubtful if the *Nestlea*'s coal bunkers would run to this. As to the enemy itself, McPherson did not give much thought. The *Nestlea* was armed with a four-inch anti-submarine gun and a twelve-pounder to fight off attacking aircraft. She would give a good account of herself if called upon to do so.

Under blue skies, and with the north-east trades blowing fresh, the convoy skirted the Cape Verde Islands, passed 300 miles to the west of the Canaries, and then steered due north to pass midway between Madeira and the Azores. It was a fair weather passage without a sign of the enemy, a passage to promote peace of mind. If

McPherson and Chief Engineer Narne were worried about the
Nestlea's rapidly emptying bunkers, they kept it to themselves.

On the morning of 12 November, SL 53 was abreast the Bay of
Biscay, having averaged seven knots since leaving Freetown. With
less than a thousand miles to steam, journey's end was only six days
away, and this showed with a general lifting of morale in all the
ships. Even McPherson and Narne were seen to have given up their
daily calculations of bunkers remaining and walked with a new
spring in their step. Then, all too soon, the party was over.

Later that day, the skies clouded over, and by nightfall it was
blowing a gale from the north-west, a not unexpected development
in this area. During the following twelve hours the wind increased
further, and the sea became like foam-flecked mountains. Steaming
into the teeth of the wind, and sliding crazily from trough to crest,
many of the heavily laden merchant ships experienced great difficulty in keeping station. The once orderly convoy became an uncoordi-
nated rabble. The *Nestlea,* with her elderly engine labouring hard and
her decks continuously awash, was making particularly heavy weather of it.

When in latitude 50° North, and 660 miles due west of Land's
End, intense U-boat activity reported in the path of the convoy
resulted in an alteration onto a more northerly course. This brought
the heavy seas more abeam, and the *Nestlea,* having an abnormally
low centre of gravity due to the huge weight of ore low down in her
holds, developed a heavy, shock-like roll. In order to avoid serious
damage to his ship, McPherson was forced to reduce speed.
Eventually, the steamer was down to three knots and straggling
astern of the convoy.

It was not long before one of the escorts came fussing around
the *Nestlea,* demanding that she increase speed, if only for her own
safety. McPherson was well aware that what the Navy was asking of
him was an impossibility but he was obliged to make one more
effort. Much against Chief Engineer Narne's better judgement, revolutions were increased. What followed was inevitable. The ship
surged forward, slamming her blunt bows into the oncoming waves,
attempting to make her way by brute force. Then she hit the face of
the notorious seventh wave, and with a shuddering crash came to an
abrupt halt, with a thousand tons of green water sweeping over her.
When she reappeared out of the sea again, like a surfacing submarine, the port side of the *Nestlea*'s bridge was crumpled, and she had
lost two of her lifeboats. Enough was enough, and McPherson signalled to the commodore that he was dropping out of the convoy.

Before an hour passed, the *Nestlea* was alone on that desolate,
storm-tossed sea. With the wind and sea on the port bow, and her
engine turning only sufficient revolutions to maintain steerage way,
she rode each advancing wave awkwardly, but without doing further
damage to herself. Although there was great danger in the area from

marauding U-boats, McPherson accepted that the immediate threat came from the sea, and he must first ride out the storm. Later, when the weather moderated, he would push the *Nestlea* to her utmost limits in order to cover the seven-hundred or so miles to the safety of the North Channel in the shortest possible time. It was then that a grim-faced Chief Engineer Narne came to the bridge to report only four days supply of coal remaining in the bunkers.

McPherson was now faced with a decision that could mean life or death for his ship and crew. The barometer was still falling, and every hour the *Nestlea* laboured in the heavy seas making little or no forward progress was eating into her meagre stocks of coal. If he continued to the north, even if the weather did moderate, the ship would run out of fuel and lie drifting helplessly long before she reached the North Channel. The U-boats would make short work of her then. The English Channel and the St Georges Channel were both blocked by minefields, so a port of refuge in southern England or Wales was out of the question. The only option remaining was to put the weather astern and head due east for the neutral harbour of Queenstown, in Southern Ireland. There was always the possibility the Irish might intern his ship, but it was a risk he must take. He gave the order to put the helm over.

If anything, the *Nestlea* fared worse with the wind and sea behind her. The huge seas rolling in on her from astern made steering a matter of fine judgement. A few degrees off course and a wave would catch her on the quarter, slewing the stern around so that she ended up wallowing broadside on in the trough with her hard-pressed engine racing to regain steerage way. When, on the morning of the 18th, a grey light in the eastern sky announced the dawn, she had reached a position a hundred miles west by south of Cape Clear, the south-western corner of Ireland. The wind was force nine from the west, the clouds down to mast-top height and the visibility reduced by rain to less than half a mile. Queenstown lay another 150 miles to the east, the patent log showed a speed of only two knots, and the *Nestlea*'s firemen were scraping the far corners of the bunkers. Yet McPherson was still confident he could bring her safely into port. In his preoccupation with the sea he had forgotten the other enemy.

The big, four-engined aircraft swooped out of the clouds from the south-east, the noise of its engines all but drowned by the clamour of the storm. The *Nestlea*'s lookouts were caught completely unawares, but McPherson, keeping vigil in the starboard wing of the bridge, had a good sight of the enemy before diving for cover. The black crosses on the aircraft's wings were plainly visible, as were the bristling gun turrets and the gondola-like structure beneath the fuselage. It was a long range Focke-Wulf Condor, coming in guns blazing. The huge aircraft roared overhead, its bullets ricocheting off the *Nestlea*'s steel superstructure.

Bernard Edwards

The Focke-Wulf circled lazily astern before coming in for its second attack. By this time, the *Nestlea*'s twelve-pounder had been hastily manned, and the gun opened up, firing as fast as its gunners could load. Unperturbed, the enemy plane dropped down to about two-hundred-feet and came in from astern, flying through the bursting shells unharmed.

McPherson had returned to the open wing of the bridge, and took cover behind the bulwark as the huge black shape, its engines rising to a screaming crescendo, swooped down on the ship like a manifestation of the great predatory bird for which it was named. Lines of tracer arced downwards from the gun turrets beneath the plane and McPherson ducked as a hail of bullets rattled the decks. He looked up just in time to see a black shape drop from the open bomb doors and curve down towards the bridge.

The bomb fell short of the bridge, smashing through the engine-room skylight and dropping thirty feet, before exploding on the floor plates with devastating effect. The *Nestlea*'s main engine was reduced to a heap of scrap, a hole was blown in her bottom and the sea poured in. By sheer good luck, only two men of the watch were injured. They were quickly evacuated.

When the bomb hit, McPherson's immediate reaction was to put the helm hard over in order to bring the *Nestlea*'s head up into the wind while she still had way on her. The move was in vain. The ship was already dead in the water and swinging beam-on to the seas. She fell into the trough and lay there taking the full brunt of the breaking waves.

The Focke-Wulf had meanwhile flown off to the east, and McPherson dared to hope he was to be left in peace to attend to his crippled ship. It was not to be. The enemy soon returned, his machine-guns hammering out an evil chorus. The *Nestlea*'s twelve-pounder opened up again, but as before, the Focke-Wulf came on unharmed. This time the bomb, aimed with remarkable accuracy, exploded in the steamer's boiler-room, completing the destruction of her engine spaces. The scream of high-pressure steam escaping from broken pipes added to the horror of the scene. Fortunately, the area had already been cleared and there were no more casualties.

A lull of about half an hour followed, during which the Focke-Wulf circled on the horizon to the north-west, obviously loitering to see if the two bombs had been sufficient to finish off the *Nestlea*. This gave an opportunity to replenish the twelve-pounder's stock of ready-use ammunition, and to assess the damage to the ship. The *Nestlea* would never move under her own power again, but she was a tough old ship, and appeared to be in no danger of sinking. Radio Officer Willis, who had been at the key transmitting distress signals from the commencement of the attack, informed the shore of the situation.

The German pilot, having concluded that his job was not finished, came in for a fourth attack, flying at a height of about 250 feet. As before, the plane approached from astern, raking the helpless ship with its machine-guns. Two more bombs were dropped, and this time they appeared to be larger. One landed aft, wrecking the accommodation there, while the other fell in the sea close to the starboard bow, the explosion shaking the *Nestlea* violently. As the aircraft flew away, it was hit by a shell from the twelve-pounder, which despite the machine-gunning and the spray sweeping over the ship, maintained a steady rate of fire. Although the Focke-Wulf did not appear to be seriously damaged, its pilot had clearly had enough, for the plane banked sharply away and roared off towards the east. It did not return.

It was now possible for McPherson and his chief officer, G.H. Nicholas, to survey the damage to the ship. It was far worse than they had at first imagined. The engine-room, stokehold and No.5 cargo hold were all holed below the waterline and flooding rapidly. Amidships, the seas were breaking clean over the deck. The *Nestlea* was sinking, and much as it grieved him to do so, McPherson had no alternative but to order his men to abandon ship.

Of the four lifeboats the *Nestlea* carried, two had been smashed by heavy seas when she was attempting to keep up with the convoy, and one of the others was found to be damaged by the bomb blast. However, with the ship so low in the water, the two boats were launched without further damage. McPherson took the starboard boat, with twenty-one men, while Nicholas and fifteen men got away in the damaged port boat.

McPherson ordered both boats to heave-to once they were clear of the ship, for he still entertained a faint hope that the *Nestlea* might survive. She was a sad sight, her decks awash amidships and her bow and stern both beginning to angle upwards, as though her back would soon break. Rising and falling on the mountainous seas, the two boats held their position for twenty minutes or more. Then they slipped into another deep trough, and when they soared skywards again on the crest, the *Nestlea* was gone. She had entered her grave as quietly and unassumingly as she lived her long life.

His ship gone, McPherson now addressed the problem of saving her crew. The nearest land, the coast of County Cork in the region of Bantry Bay, was some eighty miles to the east-north-east, but there was no shelter there from the weather. He decided to continue on for Queenstown, another sixty miles eastward, where a landing could be made. After a brief consultation with Nicholas, McPherson gave the order to hoist sails and set course to the east.

The bid to make the land was doomed from the start. Although ship's lifeboats are designed to sail best before the wind, in this case, the sea was too rough even for this. After an hour, during which both boats were almost swamped, it was decided to heave-to and stream sea anchors to await a moderation in the weather.

Bernard Edwards

A long, demoralising night followed. The boats tossed like mad things in the rain-lashed darkness, their crews so weakened by sea-sickness that they cared neither whether they lived or died. They sat huddled together on the thwarts, up to their knees in icy water, with no strength or inclination to bail. At some time during the night, McPherson's boat lost its sea anchor and drifted away. When daylight came on the 19th, there was no sign of the chief officer's boat.

A little before sunrise, the sound of aircraft engines approaching from the south-east brought the drooping heads erect. But when the all too familiar shape of a Focke-Wulf came in sight flying low, exhilaration turned to fear. But the German aircraft ignored them, flying on out into the Atlantic in search of larger prey.

For another five hours, as the sun, hidden behind the thick cloud, climbed to its zenith, the boat drifted aimlessly at the mercy of the wind and waves. McPherson tried in vain to rally his men, but they had lost all hope. When aircraft engines were again heard approaching, few heads were raised, until it was seen that this was a British plane. Then, they stood up and cheered. The aircraft circled low over the boat, waggled its wings, and then flew off to the east. Unknown to the survivors, they had already been sighted on the previous afternoon by another aircraft, and a watch was being kept on them until a ship was available to rescue them.

New life surged through the boat. The sails were hoisted and men set to with a will to bail the boat dry. At this time, although they were not aware of it, they were thirty-six miles to the south of Cape Clear, having drifted easterly before the wind at a rate of about three knots since leaving the *Nestlea.*

The rescue they expected hourly did not come that day, and the survivors entered the next night with hopes again failing. There was no improvement in the weather, and the monotonous task of bailing went on, flagging as the long hours passed. Then, at about 10 o'clock, the lights of a ship were seen and pandemonium broke out in the boat. There was a rush to find the distress flares and rockets, but as the boat's lockers had been under water for most of the time, these all proved useless. The only dry article in the boat was the scarf around McPherson's neck. This was soaked in paraffin and set alight, a primitive but traditional distress signal known as 'flames on the vessel'.

The flames had an immediate effect on the ship, but hardly that desired. She doused her lights and steamed off in the opposite direction at speed, possibly believing she had fallen in with a surfaced U-boat.

Two hours later, the lights of another ship were sighted very close by. The improvised flare was again lit, and when again the ship put out her lights and made to steam off, the desperate survivors set up such an angry chorus of shouts that she stopped and then moved towards the boat. She turned out to be the Belgian trawler *Ibis II.*

Widow-Maker

McPherson and his men were in an advanced state of exhaustion when they were taken on board the trawler. Their boat, which had kept them afloat for thirty hours, was by this time so damaged that it was cast adrift to sink in its own time. The survivors were landed at Swansea on the morning of 21 November, where they were delighted to learn of the rescue of Chief Officer Nicholas and his crew by a British trawler working off the west coast of Ireland.

Bernard Edwards

31   A Rare Catch

HMS *Lady Shirley* - 1941

On his first tour of operations in command, in the spring of 1941, Kapitän-Leutnant Wilhelm Kleinschmidt sank 20,000 tons of Allied shipping. This was a most credible opening score for a man who was not a professional submariner, and at thirty-four somewhat over-age to be commanding a U-boat. Before Adolf Hitler embarked on his foolhardy bid to conquer Europe in 1939, Kleinschmidt was a merchant service career man, dedicated to the safe delivery of cargoes, rather than their destruction. However, like most gamekeepers turned poacher, he had taken to his new role with enthusiasm and dedication. In U-111 he had found a weapon that matched his zeal.

A Type IX trans-ocean boat of 740 tons displacement, U-111 was a product of the Deschmag Yard in Bremen, commissioned in Kiel at the end of 1940. She had a diving depth in excess of 330 feet, a maximum surface speed of 18.3 knots and a range of 16,300 miles at ten knots. Her crew numbered fifty-two and she was armed with nineteen torpedoes fired through four bow and two stern tubes, a 105 mm gun on deck forward, a 37 mm anti-aircraft cannon aft, and two 20 mm cannons in the conning tower.

U-111 set out from La Rochelle on her second voyage in August 1941 with orders to probe the lower reaches of the North Atlantic for targets. Kleinschmidt had with him as a passenger in the boat Fregatten-Kapitän Hans-Joachim Heinecke, who was on board to study tactics before taking over his own U-boat. Although the two men were old shipmates and contemporaries, Heinecke was considerably senior in rank, which put Kleinschmidt at an awkward disadvantage, the junior man feeling obliged to produce results at all costs. That this would sometimes involve taking unwise risks was inevitable, and as he was to be married at the end of the tour, Wilhelm Kleinschmidt had the understandable inclination to avoid the game of chance.

As it turned out, on the outward passage from the Bay of Biscay targets were few and far between. U-111 was 3,400 miles out from her base, and within 300 miles of the coast of Brazil, before, on 10 September, she fired her first torpedo. The 5,719-ton Dutch motorship *Marken*, sailing alone and unsuspecting, gave Kleinschmidt an

Widow-Maker

excellent opportunity to demonstrate his prowess before Fregatten Kapitän Heinecke. Encouraged by this success, Kleinschmidt moved further south, but ten more days of empty horizons were to pass, before he came across the *Cingalese Prince*.

On 20 September, 1941, the 8,474-ton *Cingalese Prince*, direct descendent of the *Belgian Prince*, sunk by U-44 in another hemisphere and in another war, was 250 miles south-east of St Peter & St Paul Rocks, bound from the UK to South American ports. She was in a little frequented part of the South Atlantic, where, up to that time, no ship had been sunk by a U-boat. Her master, Captain Smith, was therefore justified in thinking that, for a while at least, his ship had escaped the attentions of the dogs of war. His optimism was sadly misplaced. Soon after U-111's torpedo struck, the *Cingalese Prince* went to the bottom, taking Smith and his crew of fifty-seven with her.

Encouraged by his good fortune, Kleinschmidt cruised in the area for some days, but he was unable to repeat his success. He decided to cross the Atlantic to West African waters, where the pickings were said to be good.

Convoy SL 87 sailed from Freetown on 14 September, bound for the UK. It consisted of twelve British merchant ships, escorted by two old sloops, a corvette and an ex-American coastguard cutter. The merchantmen, all deep laden with sorely needed foodstuffs and timber, were slow-moving, and their escort far from adequate. A pack of four German submarines, U-67, U-68, U-103 and U-107, sighted the convoy on the 19th, when it was to the west of the Cape Verde Islands, and fell in behind it, seeking the opportune moment to attack. This did not arise until three days later, when in the early hours of the 22nd, U-68 torpedoed the 5,302-ton *Silverbelle*, carrying a full cargo of sugar from Mauritius. For the next forty-eight hours, the U-boats harassed the convoy, running rings around the escorts, and sinking six ships totalling 28,000 tons. The *Silverbelle*, although badly damaged, did not sink and was taken in tow by the Free French sloop *Commandant Dubac*.

On 27 September, the 6,000-ton ocean boarding vessel HMS *Maron* left Gibraltar, bound for the Canary Islands, escorted by the armed trawlers *Lady Shirley* and *Erin*. When, on the 29th, the small convoy was nearing the Canaries, the *Lady Shirley* was ordered to detach and proceed at all speed to rendezvous with the *Commandant Dubac* and her tow, and to escort them to Las Palmas.

The *Lady Shirley*, built in 1937 for Jutland Amalgamated Trawlers of Hull, was a typical East Coast trawler. Of 472 tons gross, she was a broad-beamed coal burner, with a top speed of ten knots and a large bunker capacity capable of sustaining her on long voyages to the White Sea and Icelandic waters. Soon after the outbreak of war, along with many of her sisters, she was drafted into the Royal Navy. Her trawl winch was ripped out, her fish hold converted to mess decks, and she was armed with a four-inch gun, two point fives and two Hotchkiss .303 machine guns, asdic equipment and depth charges. In early 1941, she joined the Seventh Anti-Submarine Group, operating out of Gibraltar. Appointed to command was thirty-six-year-old Lieutenant-Commander Arthur Callaway, RANVR, an anti-submarine specialist, who brought with him a fellow Australian, Lieutenant Ian Boucaut, as first lieutenant. The *Lady Shirley*'s navigating officer was twenty-four-year-old Temporary Sub-Lieutenant Frederick French, RNR, and her signals officer Acting Sub-Lieutenant Allan Waller, twenty, while the majority of her twenty-two petty officers and ratings were ex-trawlermen. Callaway ran the ship in a relaxed manner, but he spared no man when it came to the efficiency of the guns and anti-submarine equipment.

When, on the 29th, the *Lady Shirley* peeled away from *Erin* and *Maron* to head south to rendezvous with the *Commandant Dubac*, U-111 was 300 miles south-west of the Cape Verde Islands and making towards the Canaries. Having been too late to join in the attack on Convoy SL 87, Kleinschmidt was hurrying towards the unmarked Atlantic crossroads between the Azores and Madeira. It was here that so much of Britain's vital shipping to and from the Cape and the Americas converged and crossed paths, and there would be ample opportunities for U-111 to expend her stock of unused torpedoes.

Kleinschmidt's hopes of increasing his abysmally low tonnage for the voyage were ruined when, later that day, he received orders to transfer his remaining torpedoes to U-68, and then return to base. Anxious though he was to return home, and with the added incentive of a bride waiting for him, Kleinschmidt was loath to hand over his weapons while he was so far from base. He could not, of course disobey an order from Admiral Dönitz, so he compromised by handing over most, but not all of his torpedoes to U-68 when he met her south of the Canaries. He then proceeded towards La Rochelle, still on the lookout for likely targets.

The *Lady Shirley* reached the arranged rendezvous with the *Commandant Dubac* and *Silverbelle,* some 300 miles west-south-west of Tenerife, on 1 October. She then commenced to sweep east and west in search of the sloop and her tow. It was a lonely beat, but the weather was fine, with warm sunshine, a light north-easterly breeze and unlimited visibility. Steaming at an undemanding eight knots, with lookouts posted and guns' crews handy, the *Lady Shirley* took time off from the war. For Coxswain Bill Mackrill it was an ideal opportunity to detail work parties to catch up with some long overdue maintenance on deck, and he used it to full advantage.

The unofficial holiday lasted for three days, with no sign of the French sloop and her tow. Lieutenant-Commander Callaway was on the point of breaking radio silence, when, at 08.40 on the morning of the 4th, the lookout in the crow's nest reported a ship hull-down on the horizon. Lieutenant Boucaut, officer of the watch at the time, could see nothing from the trawler's bridge and climbed the mast for a better view. There was certainly an object on the horizon to the north, but it was no more than a shimmering speck of grey. Boucaut returned to the bridge and called the captain.

Callaway studied the horizon through his binoculars for some time, and then erred on the side of caution. It was possible they had at last found the missing ships; on the other hand they might be looking at the conning tower of a submarine. He assumed the worst, and brought the trawler round onto a northerly course, heading directly for the unidentified target. Coxswain Mackrill switched on the asdic and began to sweep ahead.

A few minutes later, the target disappeared from sight. Callaway's suspicions were now fully aroused. He ordered Mackrill to continue sweeping and rang for more speed. As the *Lady Shirley* lifted her skirts, Callaway and Boucaut carefully examined the horizon through their binoculars, but it remained deceptively empty. Meanwhile, word of the sighting had spread throughout the ship, and men quietly left their work and edged nearer to the guns.

At 10.04, Mackrill reported a contact off the port bow at 1,800 yards, and the ship came alive. The alarm bells shrilled, Callaway rang for emergency full speed, and there was a flurry of activity on deck as men threw down their paint brushes and went to their action stations. Within a few minutes the *Lady Shirley* was closed up and vibrating wildly as her engine worked up to maximum revolutions. Callaway, an acknowledged expert in the field, took over the asdic, Boucaut had the con on the bridge, Sub-Lieutenant French went forward to the four-inch and Sub-Lieutenant Waller ran aft to supervise the depth charge party.

The asdic bridge recorder was out of action, and it was necessary for Callawsay to time each returning echo with a stopwatch. But the contact was firm, drawing nearer, and veering from bow to bow as it tried to shake off the *Lady Shirley.* It was without doubt a U-boat running way.

At last Callaway judged they were in a favourable position to attack, and he gave the order to fire a full pattern of five depth charges from the throwers and rails aft. By this time, the trawler had worked up to a rattling eleven knots, but this was not fast enough to save her from the effects of 1,500 pounds of TNT exploding close astern. The blast lifted her clean out of the water and slammed her down again, sending her unsuspecting crew sprawling.

There was a stunned silence, then wild cheering broke out as the bows of a submarine reared up out of the sea 500 yards off the port quarter. This was followed by a conning tower, then casings spewing water. She was huge, completely dwarfing the diminutive *Lady Shirley.* But as the U-boat's conning tower hatch clanged open, the trawler was heeling over, coming round under full helm to ram. Callaway passed the order for all guns to open fire as they came to bear.

U-111's gun's crew came tumbling out of the conning tower and ran for the 105 mm on the forward casing, only to be caught in a withering stream of tracer as the two Hotchkiss guns on the trawler's bridge opened fire. The two point fives aft joined in, spraying the U-boat's conning tower with heavy calibre bullets. Then the four-inch came to bear, and Sub-Lieutenant French opened fire with semi-armour piercing shells.

The sheer ferocity of the *Lady Shirley*'s attack gave U-111's crew little time to organise a defence. Her heavy gun barked once, and then fell silent. But the trawler was not to escape unharmed. The two 20 mm cannons on the U-boat's coning tower opened up with deadly accuracy, concentrating on the *Lady Shirley*'s bridge and her forward gun. Seaman Leslie Pizzey, gunlayer of the four-inch, was hit in the stomach by an explosive bullet and died instantly. His place was immediately taken by Sub-Lieutenant French and the gun continued to fire. On the bridge, Signalman Warbrick went down at Callaway's side with a smashed thigh bone, while the men manning the Hotchkiss guns, Seaman William Windsor and Sidney Halcrow, were hit, Halcrow being badly wounded. Both men continued to fire their guns.

With no more than two-hundred yards of water separating them, the little trawler and the U-boat slugged it out, round for round. The German's 20 mm cannons, firing high explosive and tracer, wreaked havoc aboard the trawler, riddling her bridge and superstructure, shattering the bridge windows, ripping up the deck planking, and reducing the ship's only lifeboat to matchwood. A fire was started in the provision room and a shell smashed the deck steam line, adding clouds of high-pressure steam to the bedlam.

U-111 was faring even worse. The *Lady Shirley*'s four-inch had found the range, the fourth, fifth and sixth rounds scoring direct hits on the submarine's pressure hull, and the next two either hits or near misses. French then switched to shrapnel, with the object of silencing the U-boat's gunners. This was achieved, and when two more rounds from the four-inch slammed into the submarine, her crew threw up their hands in surrender. They had put up a brave fight against a smaller, but superior enemy.

When Wilhelm Kleinschmidt first sighted the *Lady Shirley*, he took her to be a cargo vessel, slow and vulnerable, the sort of victim he had held back his torpedoes for. He went to periscope depth for the attack, and was in position to fire, when his quarry suddenly charged at him. Depth charges exploded around the U-boat while she was still at periscope depth with devastating effect, and Kleinschmidt momentarily lost his head. First he gave the order to surface, then changed his mind and decided to dive deep. Order, counter-order, led to confusion, as it invariably does, and the U-boat porpoised to the surface, out of control. Kleinschmidt led the way up through the conning tower hatch, and must have been the first caught in the hail of fire from the *Lady Shirley*'s machine-guns. He fell back into the control room mortally wounded, leaving a young woman in Germany to grieve for a wedding that would never be.

The U-boat's gun crew, who followed Kleinschmidt up through the hatch, reached the casing safely and ran for the 105 mm gun. They were an enthusiastic crew, and had the gun loaded and trained on the enemy within a few seconds. Unfortunately, in their eagerness to open fire, they omitted to first remove the watertight tampon from the end of the gun barrel. When the gunlayer pulled the trigger, the gun exploded killing or wounding all those around it. From that moment on, with her only heavy gun out of action, U-111 was fighting a battle she could not hope to win.

When Kleinschmidt was cut down, his passenger, Hans-Joachim Heinecke, took over. However, as U-111's crew was already surrendering, the first, last, and only act of the fregatten-kapitän's short-lived command was to order the vents to be opened to scuttle the boat.

Seeing that the U-boat was clearly finished, Callaway ordered his guns to cease fire, and an eerie silence settled over the scene. The action, seemingly unending, had lasted just twenty-three minutes. Callaway watched, the tension slowly draining from him, as the submarine settled quickly by the stern and sank in a flurry of escaping air. Her crew was left struggling in the water.

Only when the numbers of Germans being unceremoniously hauled aboard the trawler became evident did Callaway realise the gunfight had been merely the prelude to his troubles. Kleinschmidt had gone down with his boat, as had seven others; two were injured, one very severely, but forty-three young, tough and extremely fit German seamen had been rescued. As to the *Lady Shirley*, one man was dead and three were wounded, leaving only twenty-four men to run the ship and mount guard over a body of prisoners greatly outnumbering them. Gibraltar was over 1,000 miles away, the trawler was running short of coal, and her only lifeboat lay in ruins. It was a situation fraught with all kinds of nasty possibilities.

Callaway's first sad duty was to commit the body of Seaman Leslie Pizzey to the deep. This he did that same afternoon. In the evening, Hans Ruskens, whose legs had been shattered in the action, also died, and was buried next morning with full honours. His shipmates were confined to the trawler's wardroom, the only compartment on board large enough to hold them. During the next four days, as the *Lady Shirley* headed for Gibraltar at full speed, four men, armed with rifles and grenades, kept watch day and night on the Germans. Boatswain's Mate Gerhard Hartig made an attempt to organise a breakout, but the others were content to bow out of the war. Twelve hours out of Gibraltar the *Lady Shirley* was met by the destroyer *HMS Lance* and Callaway's problems were solved.

Honours were deservedly heaped upon the *Lady Shirley*. Lieutenant-Commander Arthur Callaway was awarded an immediate DSO, Lieutenant Ian Boucaut and Sub-Lieutenant Frederick French each earned the DSC. Seaman Halcrow who, though wounded in both legs, refused to leave his post at the Hotchkiss, was awarded the CGM, while six other ratings were given the DSM and five were mentioned in dispatches.

As soon as her damage was made good, *the Lady Shirley* returned to active service. On the night of 11 December, 1941, she was carrying out an anti-submarine sweep in the Straits, in company with three other armed trawlers, when they ran into a heavy rain squall. When the rain cleared some twenty-five minutes later, the *Lady Shirley* was missing. No explosion had been heard by the other trawlers and no wreckage or bodies were ever found. The *Lady Shirley* was later claimed by U-374, which had been in the area at the time but, as this boat was sunk by a British submarine a month later, her claim could not be substantiated. A theory was advanced that a time-bomb was placed on board the *Lady Shirley* before she sailed from Gibraltar by a Spanish agent working for the Germans, but this also was never proven. Whatever her end—and Callaway and most of the original crew went with her—the *Lady Shirley* reserved for herself a very special place in British maritime history.

32   The Eleventh Hour

Ondina & HMIS *Bengal* - 1942

On the morning of 11 November, 1942, while flags around the cenotaphs of a beleaguered Britain dipped in homage to those who had made the supreme sacrifice, two ships, one British and one Dutch, prepared for battle in the lonely reaches of the South Indian Ocean. Theirs was not to be a day of glory; of creaming bow-waves and thundering broadsides, but a desperate struggle for survival against impossible odds.

The 14,000-ton Dutch tanker *Ondina* had sailed from Freemantle on 5 November, escorted by the 650-ton Royal Indian Navy minesweeper *Bengal*, bound for the Indian Ocean island of Diego Garcia. Commanded by Captain Willem Horsman and manned by Dutch officers and Chinese ratings, the *Ondina* was armed with a single four-inch gun mounted on her poop. Her gun's crew, led by Able Seaman Herbert Hammond, RANR, was made up of four Royal Navy ratings, three Royal Artillery gunners and a Dutch merchant seaman gunner. The *Bengal*, dwarfed by her huge charge, was commanded by Lieutenant Commander William Wilson, RINR, and carried British officers and Indian ratings. She had a top speed of twelve knots and her sole armament consisted of a twelve-pounder gun mounted forward. For this gun she had on board only forty rounds of ammunition.

Lt. Cdr. Wilson was not unduly concerned with his lack of fire-power as he pressed north-westwards with the *Ondina* dutifully keep-ing station astern of him. By the autumn of that year, the Indian Ocean had been largely cleared of German surface raiders. A few U-boats were reported operating in the southern approaches to the Mozambique Channel, but that was more than 2,000 miles to the west of the small convoy's proposed route. As for the Japanese, after a determined and very bloody foray against Allied shipping in the early summer, using armed merchant cruisers and submarines, they had long since retired sated to their bases in Malaya. Wilson's only other potential enemy, the weather, had also sheathed its claws. In November, the Indian Ocean is free of cyclones and under the benign influence of the north-east monsoon, which brings with it a season of cloudless, blue skies and zephyr-like winds. However, for a small ship like the *Bengal*, the 2,800-mile passage to Diego Garcia would be no mean feat of endurance. Wilson, although he would have been loath to admit as much, drew great comfort from the presence of the big merchantman lumbering along in his wake.

On board the *Ondina*, Captain Horsman was in a similarly contented frame of mind. Apart from 390 tons of fuel oil—much of it needed to refuel the *Bengal* from time to time—he had nothing more volatile in his cargo tanks than salt water ballast. For a man used to the awesome burden of commanding over the carriage of thousands of tons of high-octane gasoline, this was a pleasant relief indeed. At his tiny escort Horsman cast a somewhat jaundiced eye. The *Bengal* seemed no bigger than the average North Sea trawler, and in the event of a meeting with the enemy, her twelve-pounder pea-shooter would probably prove a very empty threat. But, puny though she might be, the *Bengal* had about her the tight, resolute air of a British man-of-war. Horsman could not help being impressed.

At 11.00 on the morning of the 11th, the two ships were making ten knots and in position 20°S, 93°E, just over the half-way mark on their long passage. The weather was fine, with the sun hot in a clear, blue sky and the sea like a mirror, its glassy surface disturbed only by the ships' bow waves and occasional darting shoals of flying fish. This was the Indian Ocean at its idyllic best.

On the bridge of the *Bengal*, which was keeping station a quarter of a mile ahead of the *Ondina*, the officer of the watch lifted his binoculars and made a slow sweep of a horizon as sharp as a whetted knife. At ten degrees on the port bow he snapped alert. The masts and funnel of a large ship were just lifting above the horizon. He dived for the captain's voice-pipe.

Lt. Cdr. Wilson was on the bridge within seconds and reaching for his own binoculars. Following the pointing finger of the officer, he brought the glasses to his eyes and swore softly. The ship, now hull-up, was a large one—about 10,000 tons, he estimated—and she had the lines of a passenger vessel. In this time and place that could mean only one thing—armed merchant cruiser. Wilson knew she was unlikely to be British.

The unknown ship was heading straight for the *Bengal* and *Ondina* and closing on them rapidly. At eight miles Wilson's worst fears were confirmed. The short, unraked funnel, clipper bows and cruiser stern were all unmistakably Japanese. A few minutes later, he was able to make out the funnel markings of the Nippon Yusen Kaisha (N.Y.K.) Line. No further proof was needed.

Wilson's next actions were quick and decisive. Ordering hands to battle stations, he altered course ninety degrees to starboard away from the approaching enemy, at the same time signalling the *Ondina* to take up position on his starboard beam. No sooner had the *Bengal* put herself between the enemy and the tanker than a second ship came over the horizon, hard on the heels of the first. Wilson's face went white under his tan as he once again lifted his binoculars and

Widow-Maker

m.v. 'Ondina' *in her peacetime colours*
(Photo: L.L. von Munching)

identified the funnel colours of the N.Y.K.

Although Wilson was not aware of it at the time, he was facing the Japanese raiders *Hokoku Maru* (10,438 tons) and *Aikoku Maru* (10,500 tons). Both vessels carried ten 5.9-inch guns, torpedo tubes and spotter aircraft.

On identifying the second ship as a belligerent, Wilson ordered the *Ondina* to reverse her course and make off to the south-east at maximum speed, giving her a rendezvous to keep twenty-four hours later, should both ships still be afloat—and at the time this must have seemed extremely unlikely. He then turned the *Bengal* to face the *Hokoku Maru* and increased to full speed. The diminutive David was rushing to challenge a Goliath more than fourteen times his size.

Perhaps unable to comprehend such audacity, the commander of the *Hokoku Maru* held his fire until the two ships were only 3,500 yards apart, and still closing. When the Japanese did open up, her first shell landed four-hundred yards ahead of the *Bengal*. The British ship's small gun spat back defiantly, but the range was far too great for accuracy.

The *Aikoku Maru* now entered the fight and the sea around the tiny minesweeper became a maelstrom of bursting shells. Yet, by some miracle, the *Bengal* was not hit and stood on, weaving from side to side like the fly-weight she was, but always her bow coming back to face the *Hokoku Maru*. Her gun's crew, all Indian ratings, crouched behind the thin shield of the twelve-pounder loading, laying and firing with determination and precision. Above them, on the bridge, Lt. Cdr. Wilson and his officers settled their steel helmets firmly and steadied themselves against the frantic vibration set up by the *Bengal*'s racing engine. There would be no turning back.

When he received orders from the *Bengal* to proceed independently, Captain Horsman of the *Ondina* was thereby relieved of all responsibility in the action, other than that of saving his own ship. But Horsman, marvelling at the bravery of the British ship as she rounded on the Japanese like a snarling terrier, decided that this was one fight he could not stay out of. His ship was not equipped for an offensive role, but Horsman was confident she could still play her part in the battle, and at the same time, perhaps, save herself.

Instead of altering course 180° and running away from the scene, as instructed by Wilson, Horsman came around only 90°, presenting his stern and already manned four-inch to the *Hokoku Maru*. He did not increase speed. At 8,000 yards, Horsman gave the order to open fire. On the poop, Second Officer Bartele Bakker, officer in charge of the gun, tapped the shoulder of Able Seaman Hammond, who was already crouched over his sight. The four-inch barked and recoiled.

The *Ondina's* first shell screamed over the *Hokoku Maru* to explode 400 yards astern of her. Hammond adjusted the range and the next three shots landed short of their target. The fifth shell scored a direct hit on the after deck of the Japanese raider, causing a violent explosion and hurling the debris of her two aircraft high in the air. A fierce fire, probably fuelled by high-octane petrol, was seen to break out.

The *Hokoku Maru*, still trading shell for shell with the pugnacious *Bengal*, now turned some of her guns on the *Ondina*. Within minutes, the tanker was hit, one of her lifeboats being smashed and her main topmast and wireless aerials brought crashing down. Shells fell all around her, throwing up a curtain of spray that obscured the aim of the four-inch crew, Hammond, showing remarkable coolness, waited for the spray from each salvo to clear before firing his own gun. In this way, he registered five hits in succession on the raider, the fifth shell again striking her after-deck and setting off an even more massive explosion, which appeared to demolish much of her stern section.

The *Hokoku Maru* stopped and began to settle by the stern, but her guns continued to fire.

From the *Bengal*, under fire from both raiders but still unharmed, a great cheer went up at the crippling of the *Hokoku Maru*. It was thought the *Bengal's* twelve-pounder had caused the damage for, in the heat of the battle, it had not been noticed that the *Ondina* had disobeyed orders and weighed in with her four-inch. There is no evidence to confirm which gun caused the explosion on the *Hokoku Maru*—presumably her magazine was hit—but it seems likely the heavier shells of the *Ondina's* four-inch were responsible.

Lt. Cdr. Wilson, even if he had been so inclined, had no time to apportion credits for the victory. Shells were bursting all around the *Bengal* and, inevitably, she was soon hit repeatedly and on fire herself. Wilson was now faced with the critical decision of whether to go on

'Ondina' & 'Bengal' *under fire, with* 'Hokoko Maru'*(on fire) and*
'Aikoku Maru' *in background.*
(From an oil painting)

or pull back. His ship had received considerable punishment and, with only five rounds left for the twelve-pounder, she would soon be defenceless. For the first time since joining the action with the Japanese, Wilson now looked around for the *Ondina*. To his great relief, she had opened up the distance between herself and the raiders to about seven miles and appeared to be escaping to the south-east undamaged.

Wilson decided to break off the engagement and retire under the cover of a smoke screen while his ship was still afloat.

The *Aikoku Maru* gave chase—as Wilson had hoped she would—and, for a further fifteen minutes, continued to fire on the minesweeper. Then she also gave up the fight. When the *Bengal*'s smoke cleared some twenty minutes later, neither raider was in sight and the *Ondina* was hull-down on the horizon, heading south. Wilson was satisfied his commitment to the tanker had been fully discharged.

Unfortunately, the *Ondina* was not in as favourable a position as Wilson had presumed. She was, in fact, in desperate straits, for the *Aikoku Maru*, believing she had sunk the *Bengal*, had gone after the tanker, firing with all guns she could bring to bear. Captain Horsman, down to his last twelve rounds of ammunition, and also convinced the *Bengal* had gone down, dropped smoke floats and rang for emergency full speed on his engines.

The smoke floats failed to hide the fleeing tanker from her pursuer and salvoes from the heavy guns of the *Aikoku Maru* were soon straddling her. The *Ondina*'s four-inch continued to hit back, but it was a contest that could have only one end. The tanker received six direct hits, shells slamming into her forecastle, bridge and after pump room in quick succession. When the news came from aft that all ammunition had been expended, Horsman was left with only one option, and he took it without hesitation. Sending below for two white bed-sheets, he ordered them to be hoisted on the flag halyards. The *Ondina* was offering surrender.

The *Aikoku Maru* ignored the signal and continued firing on her helpless quarry. Horsman now had no alternative but to stop his engines and order his crew to abandon ship. No sooner had he given the last order than a Japanese shell burst on the bridge of the *Ondina* and he was killed by flying shrapnel.

The remaining fifty-six men of the *Ondina*'s crew, most of them unaware of their captain's death, set about abandoning ship. Although the shells continued to burst all around them, there was no panic and, in less than three minutes, all lifeboats and rafts were in the water and pulling away from the ship. Ironically, as the *Ondina*'s men were thus engaged, they witnessed the last of the *Hokoku Maru*, which sank stern first, leaving many men struggling in the water.

What little satisfaction the tanker's men gained from the demise of their erstwhile enemy was soon dissipated by the arrival of the *Aikoku Maru*, which swept down on the *Ondina*, her guns still blazing. At 400 yards, the raider fired two torpedoes, which passed

'Ondina's' gun crew. 2nd Off. Bakker 3rd from right, back row. AB Hammond extreme left, front row
(Photo: L.L. von Munching)

under the lifeboats and struck the *Ondina* in way of her after tanks. She immediately took a heavy list to starboard and began to settle by the stern.

For the shocked survivors of the *Ondina* there was worse to come. In a vile demonstration of man's inhumanity to man, the *Aikoku Maru* now closed the lifeboats and opened fire with her machine-guns. Five of the survivors were wounded, two of them seriously, including Chief Engineer Jan Niekerk.

Mercifully, the raider's fit of revenge was short-lived, and she suddenly sheered off and steamed back to pick up survivors from the *Hokoku Maru*. The tanker men, who had thrown themselves into the water when the machine-guns opened up, now re-boarded their boats and rafts. The wounded were made as comfortable as the circumstances would allow, but for Chief Engineer Jan Niekerk nothing could be done. He died of his wounds and was returned to the sea, which had been his life and his livelihood.

And still the ordeal was not over. After about half an hour the *Aikoku Maru* came racing back, seemingly intent on finishing off the helpless men. Fortunately, this attack did not materialise. The raider swept disdainfully past the boats and, having fired a third torpedo at the *Ondina*, which missed, headed off in a northerly direction and was soon over the horizon.

Questioning glances were now cast at the *Ondina,* which, although listing heavily and down by the stern, was still very much afloat. To the survivors she represented sanctuary in a very lonely ocean. Second Officer Bakker volunteered to take the motor lifeboat back to the ship to investigate the possibility of saving her. With him went Able Seaman Hammond and Third Engineer Hendrik Leys.

Once aboard the tanker, Leys inspected the engine-room and found the main engine and pumps in working order. Apart from being holed and two of her cargo tanks flooded, the *Ondina* appeared to be seaworthy. Working quickly, Bakker, Hammond and Leys flooded sufficient tanks to bring the ship upright and signalled the others to come aboard.

Shortly after sunset, the survivors were all back aboard, with the exception of two Chinese ratings, who were missing and believed killed in the machine gunning. Chief Officer Martin Rehwinkel took command, his first task being to bury Captain Horsman, who still lay on the bridge where he had fallen during the action. Three hours later, after dealing with a fire discovered to be raging in the forecastle store, the *Ondina* was once more under way. She arrived back in Freemantle seven days later on 18 November.

When both ships were safe in port—the *Bengal* having made Colombo—the inevitable inquiries began. Predictably, the actions of the *Bengal* were questioned. In some quarters, she was accused of running away, leaving the *Ondina* to her fate, but there was no hard evidence to back this accusation. The minesweeper had achieved what Lt. Cdr. Wilson had set out to do, and that was to draw the enemy's fire for as long as possible in order that the tanker might be given a chance to escape.

In retrospect, it seems likely that Wilson did the wise thing in breaking off the action when his ammunition was running low. Had he gone back to the tanker's aid, there was little he could have done and the *Bengal* would almost certainly have been pounded to pieces by the guns of the *Aikoku Maru*. Such action by the *Bengal* might also have stirred the Japanese into machine-gunning the *Ondina*'s survivors in earnest—perhaps murdering them to a man.

Criticism was also levelled at Captain Horsman for joining battle with the raiders instead of running away, as he had been ordered to do. But Willem Horsman was no coward and, like any master mariner, he fiercely resented the threat to his ship. His Nelsonian gesture cost him his life but it did result in the sinking of the *Hokoku Maru* and, in turn, undoubtedly saved the little *Bengal* from destruction.

In a war that witnessed so many acts of courage and sacrifice, the fight put up by the *Bengal* and *Ondina* against the might of the two fast and heavily armed raiders went largely unnoticed. As the guns signal the eleventh hour on Armistice Day down the years, there will be few who will remember those who fought, and even fewer who will weep, for those who died in the Indian Ocean on that November day in 1942.

The 'Ondina' *survived the war and was the first tanker to call at the Rotterdam oil terminal when it reopened, 3 June 1945 (Photo: L.L. von Munching)*

33   The Fugitive

Empire Glade - 1942

As the Second World War progressed, Axis naval sources estimated that, in order to bring Britain to her knees, they required to sink 700,000 tons of Allied merchant shipping per month over a long period. By the end of October 1942, they were very near to reaching their goal, having sunk ninety-three ships of more than 600,000 tons. The great majority of these sinkings took place in the Atlantic, and were almost certainly a direct result of a shortage of escorts for Allied ships. At that time, 'Operation Torch', the invasion of North Africa, was under way, with simultaneous landings at Algiers, Oran and Casablanca planned, and involving some 800 merchant ships sailing in convoys from British and American ports. The protection of these convoys was a massive operation which stretched Allied naval and air forces to their utmost limits. Any Allied merchant ship not involved in this gigantic seaborne attack was more than likely to find herself sailing alone and protected only by God and the strength of her own arms. One such was the Glasgow ship *Empire Glade*

The sun had just risen over Table Bay when, at 06.00 on the morning of 6 November, 1942, the *Empire Glade* passed through the breakwaters of Cape Town harbour and lifted easily on the long rollers of the South Atlantic. The coolness of the African night was still in the air but the cloudless blue sky presaged yet another glorious summer day. On the bridge of the ship, Captain George Duff felt the first warmth of the sun on his neck and thought briefly, and without regret, of his native Liverpool, 6,000 miles away, and, inevitably at this time of the year, cold, sunless, and shrouded in fog. He gave an involuntary shiver and turned his thoughts to the voyage ahead. The *Empire Glade* was bound in ballast for the island of Trinidad, where she would load whatever cargo the Ministry of War Transport had scheduled for her. Duff had not yet been let into this secret, but he had no worries about the passage across the South Atlantic. The weather was likely to be favourable and he had complete confidence in his ship and crew.

The *Empire Glade* was a motor vessel of 7,006 tons, built in 1941 at the Barclay Curle yard on the Clyde for the Ministry of War

Transport. Being a replacement ship designed to fill one of the many gaps in Britain's merchant fleet left by an increasingly active enemy, she had been built in a hurry. That is not to say she was shoddily built, but she was somewhat basic in construction. Managed and manned for the Ministry by the Blue Star Line of London, she was commanded by forty-two-year-old Captain George Duff and carried a crew of forty-eight, which included six naval gunners seconded to the ship under the DEMS (Defensively Equipped Merchant Ships) arrangement. Her top speed was twelve knots and she mounted a 4-inch anti-submarine gun and a 12-pounder aft, while her bridge and boat deck bristled with six machine guns and four rocket launchers. She also carried three depth charges on a ramp at her stern, which must have been no more than a morale booster. To have dropped these even at her best speed of twelve knots would most likely have blown her stern off.

Despite the *Empire Glade*'s show of arms, Captain Duff's confident approach to the coming voyage might have been dented had he known of the enemy's activities in the Western Atlantic. A powerful group of U-boats, consisting of U-67, U-129, U-156, U-161 and U-502 had moved in to cover the south-eastern approaches to the United States and the Caribbean. A net had been cast which could prove deadly for unsuspecting Allied ships.

On the morning of 8 November, the *Empire Glade* was almost 600 miles north-west of Cape Town, and making good progress in fine weather. At the same time, some 4,000 miles to the north, events which would effect the Blue Star ship's future were moving swiftly to a climax. Shortly before dawn on that day, 290,000 American and British troops landed on the beaches of Casablanca, Algiers and Oran, and within hours were advancing inland. It was the beginning of the end for Rommel and the Afrika Corps. Already, merchant ships loaded to the gunwales with military stores needed to sustain the advance were queuing up off the beachheads, and many more such ships would be needed throughout the coming months.

Far on the other side of the world, close northwards of the island of Trinidad, a drama on a smaller scale was taking place. The ex-Italian, British manned steamer *Capo Olmo* had been torpedoed by U-67, was damaged and struggling to make good her escape. This she did. As a result, the frustrated commander of U-67, Korvetten-Kapitan Gunther Muller-Stockheim, decided to try his luck further out in the Atlantic, where, through the changing course of events, his path would eventually cross that of the *Empire Glade.*

The *Empire Glade* crossed the Equator on the 23rd in the region of St. Paul Rocks, a barren, uninhabited archipelago lying 550 miles off the coast of Brazil. The weather continued fine, and in the absence of any reports of U-boat activity, George Duff still had high hopes of an uneventful passage.

Four days later, on the night of the 27th, Duff was on the

bridge writing up his night orders when the radio officer handed him a message form. This contained instructions from the Admiralty diverting the *Empire Glade* to Charleston, South Carolina, where she was to proceed with all dispatch to load cargo. The Allies' North African adventure was in urgent need of more supplies.

At 04.00 on the 28th, Chief Officer Glyn Roberts took over the watch from Second Officer Francis Hender. The ship was 640 miles east-north-east of Barbados and zigzagging around a mean course of 320°. Having checked compass, chart and logbook, Roberts chatted to Hender for a few minutes and then bade him goodnight. Hender, who would be back on the bridge for morning sights at 09.00, wasted no time in going below to his bunk. When he had gone, Roberts poured himself a second mug of hot, strong tea and wandered out into the wing of the bridge.

It was quiet in the wing, with only the quick, muted beat of the *Empire Glade*'s diesel engine breaking the silence. The weather had deteriorated a little, with the moon struggling to pierce a thick overcast and showers were blanketing sections of the horizon. However, the wind remained light and only a slight sea and low swell were running. Roberts anticipated a peaceful watch.

In the engineroom Second Engineer Dugald Kinleyside had the watch and was also on his second mug of tea. When that was drained, he would begin his customary round of the main engine and auxiliaries. For the moment, he drank and listened to the pulsating machinery around him. It all sounded as sweet as his tea.

Right aft, in the cramped, airless crews' quarters, cabin boy Leonard Prestidge slept lightly, carried on the wings of a dream back to his home overlooking the estuary of the River Dee. At sixteen, Prestidge had the world at his feet and was content.

On the poop deck, the DEMS gunners on watch sipped steaming mugs of Navy issue cocoa and quartered the dark horizon with questioning eyes. Their whispered talk—it was a night for whispers—was of North Africa and of those less fortunate than themselves who were caught up in the fighting war. Out here, in the broad reaches of the Atlantic, where only the threshing to the *Empire Glade*'s propeller below their feet disturbed the night, the angry crack of gunfire and the screams of the wounded and dying seemed so far away.

But the ocean was not as empty as it seemed. Nine miles ahead of the *Empire Glade*, hidden in a passing rain squall, a long, low shape lurked on the water. U-67, having sunk three ships since damaging the *Cape Olmo* on the 8th, was lying in wait for another victim.

At ten minutes before five, the *Empire Glade* completed the last leg of her current zigzag pattern and Roberts steadied her on course before commencing the next pattern. As he turned away from the compass, there was a bright flash fine on the starboard bow, followed by the sharp crack of a gun; seconds later, a shell whistled overhead.

Bernard Edwards

In this the darkest hour before the dawn, the *Empire Glade* was under attack.

In his cabin directly below the bridge, Captain Duff lay fully dressed on his day-bed, dozing, but as always, subconsciously alert. He was on his feet and rushing for the bridge ladder almost before the sound of the gun had died away. He reached the bridge as the unseen gun crashed out again, but, as on the first occasion, the shell again overshot the ship and exploded harmlessly in the sea to port.

A third shell followed, and this found its mark in the *Empire Glade*'s forward rigging. The wireless aerials came down—no doubt achieving the primary object of the shell; one of the liferafts carried in the rigging was shattered by the blast and a container of red distress flares in the raft was set alight. The ship was suddenly bathed in a brilliant red glow that must have been visible from horizon to horizon.

George Duff felt like a small defenceless animal caught in the headlights of an approaching car. He had no forward mounted guns with which to retaliate, and with his ship giving a good imitation of a Roman candle, it would be useless to turn and run. There was only one possible alternative, and he took it without hesitation. Bringing the gun flashes right ahead, Duff gave a double ring on the engine-room telegraph, indicating he required emergency full speed ahead.

U-67's gunners continued to fire at a rapid rate, the illuminated *Empire Glade* obviously presenting them with a perfect target. Their fourth shot struck the forward end of the ship's bridge, exploding in the cabin Duff had recently vacated. The explosion severed the voice-pipe which provided the only communication between the bridge and engineroom and, by some terrible quirk of fate, also damaged the electrical wiring leading to the morse signalling lamp high up on the signal mast. The bright white light came on and stayed on, despite all efforts to extinguish it. The *Empire Glade*, flares still burning in her rigging, could not have been better illuminated.

With the shells falling all around his ship at the rate of one every ten seconds, Duff was forced to come to terms with his predicament. If he persisted in his attempt to ram the attacker, the *Empire Glade* would surely be blown out of the water within the next few minutes. But he had no intention of giving up the fight. Stopping only to hurl the ship's confidential books overboard in their specially weighted box, he ordered the helm hard to port. It was time to bring his guns to bear.

As the cumbersome merchant ship answered slowly to her helm, swinging in a wide circle, she ran the gauntlet of a fusillade of shells fired by U-67. She was repeatedly hit in the hull and superstructure and one shell slammed into her engineroom. Kinleyside, who had by this time been joined by Chief Engineer John Parker, was thrown to the plates by the blast and both men narrowly escaped injury by shrapnel. So savage and deadly had the attack become that

Duff was forced to consider saving the lives of his crew before it was too late. Reluctantly, he rang the engineroom telegraph and the frenzied beat of the engine slowed and then died away.

By this time the *Empire Glade*'s stern had swung around far enough for her 4-inch gun to bear. The gun's crew, led by Second Officer Hender and Gunlayer Turner, lost no time in opening fire, using the flashes of the other gun as a target.

On the bridge, George Duff, encouraged by the sound of his own gun hitting back, had second thoughts about abandoning the ship. However, Parker and Kinleyside, under the impression that the ship was sinking, had by now shut down the engine and had come on deck, intending to go to their boat stations. Duff called Parker to the bridge and advised the chief that he had a mind to make a run for it. Without hesitation, Parker volunteered to go below and restart the engine. He was followed down the ladder by Kinleyside and seven minutes later the *Empire Glade* was once more under way and working up to full speed. Duff put the enemy's gun flashes right astern and steadied the ship on a course that would take her away from the danger as rapidly as possible.

There was a last exchange of fire between the two ships, the U-boat lobbing two shells wide to starboard of the fleeing merchantman, whose 4-inch replied with four rounds. The liferaft flares had at last burned out, and with her signal lamp extinguished, the *Empire Glade* made off into the darkness using every revolution Parker and Kinleyside could coax from her engines.

It was by now 05.25, and the paling of the horizon to the east indicated that the *Empire Glade* would soon lose the cover of the night. It was Gunlayer Turner who suggested they try using smoke floats to cover their escape. As dawn broke, two floats were put over the stern, creating a most effective screen, behind which the ship was able to escape in a south-westerly direction, keeping to the windward edge of the smoke.

The fierce action with U-67 had lasted just over half an hour, during which time Duff estimated the enemy had fired between twenty and thirty shells at his ship, scoring eight hits in all. An inspection of the damage showed five holes in the starboard side of the hull—all fortunately above the waterline—and extensive but not serious damage to the superstructure. In human terms, five men had been slightly injured and, sadly, the youngest member of the crew, sixteen-year-old cabin boy Leonard Prestidge, had been killed. He was buried in the lonely deeps of the Atlantic, 3,000 miles from the land of his birth.

Having tended to his wounded and buried his dead, George Duff turned his attention to the repair of his ship, for she was still more than 2,000 miles from her destination. For the next forty-eight hours, a team of men led by Chief Officer Roberts worked day and night to patch the holes in the ship's side. It was largely due to their efforts that the *Empire Glade* reached Charleston on the night of 7 December.

Some well-deserved medals were handed out when the *Empire Glade*'s story was finally told. Captain George Duff received the George Medal and Lloyd's War Medal for Bravery at Sea. Chief Engineer John Parker was awarded the OBE, while Chief Officer Glyn Roberts, Second Officer Francis Hender and Second Engineer Dugald Kinleyside received the MBE. In addition, the ship's carpenter, Harry Shakeshaft, and the engineroom storekeeper, Frank Simmonds, were given the BEM in recognition of their unflagging efforts to repair the ship.

There were no medals for U-67. Following her unsuccessful brush with the *Empire Glade*, she was to sink no more ships in this war. On 16 July, 1943, she was caught on the surface in the North Atlantic by aircraft from the US carrier *Core* and sent to the bottom.

34   Indian Ocean Rendezvous

Congella - 1943

On 21 October, 1805, Admiral Horatio Nelson soundly trounced the French and Spanish fleets at Trafalgar, thereby establishing Britain's supremacy at sea for all time—or so it seemed then. When, 138 years later, on Trafalgar Day 1943, Captain Arthur Folster took the *Congella* out of Colombo harbour, Britannia no longer ruled the waves, least of all in the Indian Ocean. Admiral Somerville's Eastern Fleet, forced to retire to East African waters following its defeat by the Japanese in April 1942, had recently returned to Ceylon, but it was of little account. Led by the ageing battleship *Ramillies*, Somerville's command consisted largely of a collection of old cruisers and armed merchantmen.

The 4,533-ton *Congella*, owned by Andrew Weir & Company of London, was herself no youngster. Built for Hamburg America Line in 1914 at the Blohm & Voss shipyard in Hamburg, she was first named *Secundus*, and had served under four national ensigns and eight company house flags in her twenty-nine years in deep waters. She was a twin-screw motorship of early design, and under Andrew Weir was manned by a crew of sixty-six, comprising British officers, Indian ratings and British naval gunners. When she sailed from Colombo, bound for Mombasa and Durban, she was loaded with 8,700 tons of produce and 200 bags of Admiralty mail.

Once clear of Colombo's breakwaters, Folster put the *Congella* on a south-westerly course and rang for full sea speed. In her younger days, the German-built ship would have worked up to twelve or thirteen knots, but her twin six-cylinder diesels were long overdue for retirement, and her bottom was foul. Under the circumstances, Folster was content to settle for a hard-won ten knots, but even in this he was disappointed. Despite the lateness of the year, the south-west monsoon had not yet finished, and the *Congella* was soon battling against a strong westerly wind and rough sea. Noon sights on the first day indicated she was making just a fraction over seven and a half knots, at which rate the passage to Mombasa would take all of fifteen days.

The *Congella*'s shortest route to the East African port lay through the One-and-a-Half Degree Channel, a gap in the long chain of the Maldive Islands near the Equator, thereafter passing 130 miles north of the Seychelles. At the time, there were said to be only one or two German and a half a dozen Japanese submarines at large in the Indian Ocean, and the surface raiders had long since disappeared from the scene. The risk of attack by the enemy was therefore not deemed to be too great. In any event, given the impoverished state of the Royal Navy in the area, the *Congella* was obliged to sail unescorted. However, she was armed with a 3-inch anti-submarine gun, four 20 mm Oerlikons and two twin Marlin machine-guns, and would hit back, given the opportunity.

While there had been no reports of U-boat activity in the area through which the *Congella* would pass since early September, the enemy was never far away. Coincidental with the British merchant ship leaving her berth in Colombo, 1,300 miles to the west-north-west, in the approaches to the Gulf of Aden, the Japanese submarine I-10, commanded by Captain K. Tonozuka, was in search of greener pastures.

I-10, a 2,200-ton, long range submarine, carried a spotter aircraft, was armed with eighteen torpedoes, a 5.5-inch gun and two light machine-guns, had a surface speed of eighteen knots and a range of 16,400 miles. She was a formidable warship, but her record of success to date was not outstanding. Three days after Pearl Harbour, I-10, then commanded by Lieutenant-Commander Y. Kayahara, torpedoed the 4,773-ton Panamanian cargo ship *Donerail* in the Pacific. Her crew of forty-three escaped in boats before she sank, but were machine-gunned on Kayahara's orders. Only sixteen men survived to tell of the atrocity. In the fifteen months that followed, I-10, operating in the Pacific and Indian Oceans, sank only eight Allied merchant ships, totalling 34,000 tons. A German Type VII C operating in the Atlantic would expect to net as much in a single month. Tonozuka took over command in June 1943 and I-10's record showed an immediate improvement. Over a period of four months, casting her net in the eastern approaches to the Gulf of Aden, she sank four ships of 26,000 tons and damaged a 9,000-ton tanker. Then her luck ran out, and for more than two weeks the horizon remained stubbornly empty. Tonozuka decided to move south and east.

The *Congella* passed through the One-and-a-Half Degree Channel in the early hours of the 24th, and altered course direct for Mombasa, which lay 2,050 miles west-by-south. So far, no enemy submarine warnings had been received from Colombo and no diversions recommended, and it appeared to Folster, who was on the bridge for the alteration of course, that much of the danger was past. The weather, on the other hand, was deteriorating steadily. Folster took a last look around the dark horizon and decided to snatch a few hours sleep while he was able.

Considerably refreshed, Folster was back on the bridge in time for morning sights. The wind was blowing force six from right

The 'Congella' *working cargo at an anchorage on the Indian coast before the outbreak of war*
(Photo: A. Duncan)

ahead, with the white horses running riot and the swell beginning to heave menacingly. Overhead, the dark clouds were lowering as Second Officer C.B. Skinner and Third Officer Anthony Rose, sextants ready, waited in vain for a glimpse of the sun. With a sigh, Folster mentally added another half day to his ETA Mombasa.

Two miles off the *Congella*'s port quarter, Captain Tonozuka was also silently cursing the petulant ocean. Since before dawn he had been carefully stalking the British merchantman at periscope depth, and fighting to keep his boat on an even keel in the heavy swell. The gun plainly visible on the *Congella*'s stern, although apparently unmanned, was a constant reminder of the need to stay submerged.

I-10 porpoised once too often, and at 09.30 a lookout fifty feet above the deck in the *Congella*'s crow's nest, caught sight of the conning tower amongst the white horses. He reported to the bridge, but by the time Folster and his officers trained their binoculars on the horizon, the submarine had gone deep. As the *Congella* was then only 180 miles north-west of the Allied naval air base on Addu Atoll, Folster ordered his wireless operator to break radio silence to report the submarine, confidently expecting a patrol aircraft to arrive in an hour or so. But noon came and went, and as the day wore on and the skies remained empty, it became obvious that no help would come from outside. The *Congella,* with her guns manned and extra lookouts posted, held her course, grimly punching her way through the rising seas. It was hot and sultry, the air heavy with moisture borne on the monsoon wind. There was not a man on board, from the lowly Indian sweeper to Folster himself, not aware of the great danger they faced.

Folster was still pacing the bridge, the strain of the long hours of tension showing in his face, when soon after 18.00, the short equatorial twilight abruptly brought an end to the day. The submarine had not been seen again, but as the *Congella* was making only seven knots in the rough seas, it seemed likely the enemy was pacing her, lurking below the waves, waiting for the opportunity to attack. It could be that the cover of darkness would offer that opportunity. Folster gave the order to commence zigzagging.

The low cloud lifted with the coming of night, and a sliver of a moon broke through to cast a faint glow in the sky. There was an air of uneasiness hanging over the bridge, and Folster and Chief Officer John Green, who had taken over the watch from 16.00, found themselves conversing in hushed tones as they swept the horizon with their binoculars. In each wing of the bridge the shadowy figure of a steel-helmeted gunner hovered nervously by the long-barrelled Oerlikon. Right aft, on the poop, the rest of the ship's gunnery team were grouped around the 3-inch, alert and ready for action.

In his cabin two decks below the wheelhouse, Second Officer Skinner, due on watch again at midnight, debated whether to alter his normal routine in the face of the enemy. Skinner, who had joined the ship in Calcutta just a week before, like most keepers of the middle watch, was in the habit of turning in soon after dinner to catch a few fitful hours of sleep before seeing the early hours in on the bridge. Eventually, after fidgeting with the pages of a magazine for half an hour, he placed his lifejacket handy, undressed and climbed into his bunk. The craving for sleep was too strong.

Third Officer Anthony Rose, although blessed with the resilience of youth, could not avoid being affected by the strong feeling of apprehension abroad. He was on the bridge twenty minutes before he was due to take over the watch from the chief officer at 20.00. Having consulted the chart and checked the compass course, he moved out into the starboard wing, where Folster and Green were keeping a lookout. As Rose joined the two men, the first shell from I-10's 5.5-inch gun whistled through the air.

The crash of the shell brought Second Officer Skinner rudely out of his shallow sleep and tumbling from his bunk. He threw on a pair of shorts, picked up his lifejacket, and headed for the deck at a run. As he did so, more shells began to rain down on the ship. I-10 was on the surface, one mile off, and intent on the destruction of the *Congella* in as short a time as possible.

When Skinner reached the open deck, he found the midship section of the ship was ablaze as far forward as No.2 hold. With the stench of burning cordite in his nostrils, he fought his way through the crackling flames to the bridge and there walked into a manifestation of Hell itself. The submarine's first shell had destroyed the fore part of the bridge, the second landed in Folster's cabin, immediately below the bridge, and the third wiped out the wireless room. In the smouldering wreckage of the wheelhouse lay the bodies of Captain Folster, Chief Officer Green, Third Officer Rose and the apprentice of the watch.

Chief Engineer Maclachlan joined Skinner on the bridge, and together they dragged the bodies clear of the wreckage. At first it seemed that all four were dead, then Folster groaned and tried to raise himself. Arthur Folster was still alive, but dreadfully wounded. He had lost an arm and a leg, and there was a terrible gaping wound in his stomach. But he had enough strength to issue one last order to Maclachlan. 'I'm finished Chief,' he gasped. 'Stop the engines and abandon ship.'

Maclachlan went below to the engine-room, while Skinner administered morphine to Folster to ease his dying pains. And there, amidst the blood and destruction, the leaping flames and the exploding shells, the mantle of command passed to the young second officer, the only surviving navigating officer.

The *Congella*, burning furiously, her helm useless, her engines stopped, drifted helplessly, but she was not going down without a fight. On the poop, the 3-inch gun's crew, led by Gunlayer Lewis, were hitting back. Their gun was no match for I-10's heavier calibre weapon, and they were firing blind, aiming at the flash of the enemy's gun. It was a fight they could not hope to win.

Later it was estimated that the Japanese submarine fired fifty shells at the *Congella*, more than forty of which found their mark. When the bridge and midships accommodation were reduced to a mass of smoking, twisted metal, Skinner decided the time had come to save those who still lived. When he mustered the survivors on the boat deck and called the roll, he found twenty men to be missing or known dead, leaving forty-six to be distributed among the lifeboats. The *Congella* carried four lifeboats, two large and two smaller ones, more than adequate under normal circumstances to evacuate her full complement. On that dark, stormy night in the Indian Ocean the circumstances were far from normal, one large boat having been destroyed, one extensively damaged and the two small boats slightly damaged by the shelling. Skinner took charge of one of the latter, and with him were the Seventh Engineer and eleven Indian ratings. Apprentice Ian Clark and nineteen others, including four gunners, crowded into the second small boat, while Chief Engineer Maclachlan, three gunners and eight engine-room ratings crewed the larger, but badly damaged, boat. It was not an ideal distribution, but it was the best that could be done.

Before ordering the boats away, Skinner returned to the bridge, where he found Captain Folster to be still alive, although beyond all human help. Skinner said his farewells, and left Arthur Folster to go down with his ship.

At 20.40, less than an hour after the first Japanese shell came screaming out of the night to explode against the front of the *Congella*'s bridge, Skinner gave the order to abandon ship. In view of the heavy sea running and the state of the boats, this was not an easy operation, but it was accomplished without accident. While rowing clear, Skinner met up with Maclachlan, who reported his boat to be sinking. As his own boat was also leaking badly and required strenuous bailing, Skinner could offer only verbal encouragement.

The other boats were soon swallowed up in the darkness, and to his great dismay, Skinner found himself drifting close to a long, sinister shadow on the water that could only be the enemy submarine. His fears were confirmed when a machine gun opened fire and a line of tracer scythed across the boat. Ordering his men to take cover below the gunwales, Skinner waited for the thud of bullets slamming into the planking of the boat, but it did not come. When he put his head above the gunwale again, the submarine was no longer visible.

In the hours that followed, Skinner kept the boat within about half a mile of the *Congella*, hoping there might be a chance to reboard. But the ship was alight from stem to stern, and burned furiously, until, at about 01.30 on the 25th, the flames were suddenly quenched. The *Congella* had gone.

At daybreak, the horizon was empty as far as the eye could see. The submarine had long disappeared, probably seeking another victim, and of the other boats there was no sign. Skinner feared they might have sunk during the night and spent some hours searching for survivors, but without success, and he assumed the worst. Although it was known that the *Congella*'s radio officer had hammered out an SOS before the wireless room was hit, this had gone unanswered, in which case there was little point in waiting for rescue to come. Without further hesitation, Skinner hoisted sail, and running before the wind, set off in the general direction of the Maldive Islands.

Although the boat was frequently swamped by the following seas, and the men were exhausted by continuous bailing, they had adequate supplies of food and water, and morale was high. At 01.30 on the morning of the 26th, after sailing for thirty hours, the navigation lights of a ship were seen. She was low down on the water, and it was first thought she might be an enemy submarine. The inclination of most of the survivors was to creep quietly away, but Skinner insisted on signalling the unknown vessel with his torch. It was just as well, for she turned out to be the armed trawler HMS *Okapi,* which in response to the *Congella*'s distress signal, picked up by Addu Atoll, was searching for them. The *Okapi* had, in fact, already seen the flickering oil light of the lifeboat's compass binnacle and was steaming towards them. The nineteen survivors, who had sailed 120 miles in an easterly direction, were all aboard the trawler by 02.30, none of them much the worse for their ordeal.

Throughout the rest of that day, the *Okapi* steamed in widening circles, searching for the other two lifeboats, but without success. When darkness fell again, she returned towards Addu Atoll, where Skinner and his crew were landed on the morning of the 27th. It was here that they later learned that two Catalinas had sighted the boat in charge of Apprentice Ian Clark, and in spite of the rough seas, landed on the water to rescue all twenty men. The boat containing Chief Engineer Maclachlan and thirteen others could not be found, and it was assumed it had sunk as a result of the damage sustained in the shelling.

The *Congella's* long and fruitful career, which spanned twenty-nine years and many oceans, came to an end in a lonely part of the Indian Ocean sixty miles north of the Equator. She lies 2,000 fathoms deep, and with her lie Captain Arthur Folster and twenty of his men; thirteen others of her crew have no known grave.

Eight months later, on 2 July, 1944, in another ocean, and off another chain of islands, the Marianas, I-10 was sent to the bottom by the American destroyers *David W. Taylor* and *Riddle.* The *Congella* was her last victim, and so had been avenged.

Bernard Edwards

35 The Replacement

Samtampa - 1947

The pavements of Middlesbrough were still wet from an overnight shower when John Dinsmore, signed on as donkey-man in the steamer *Samtampa*, hurried through the dock gates, kit bag over his shoulder. It was Saturday 19 April 1947, the war had been over for two years, and it was a fine morning. Dinsmore was cheerfully looking forward to the short voyage ahead of him, his good humour somewhat dampened when, having reached the quays, he found his ship had already sailed. The *Samtampa*'s owners, acutely aware of the lack of profit shown by a ship lying idle in port over a weekend, had packed her off to sea in the early hours. Unwittingly, they had done John Dinsmore a priceless service.

By the time Dinsmore made his way disconsolately back through the dock gates, the *Samtampa* had already cleared the Tees and was in the North Sea, heading south-east for Flamborough Head. On her bridge, Captain H. Neane Sherwell had been informed he was a donkeyman short, but was not unduly worried. The passage to Newport Mon., where the *Samtampa* was bound in ballast, would occupy only a little more than three days. In such a short time one man in a crew of forty was unlikely to be missed. Below decks, in the engineroom, Chief Engineer W.B. Atkinson was somewhat less pleased at the absence of one of his watchkeepers, but was not disposed to let such a trifle spoil his day. Atkinson, a Swansea man, was looking forward to a few days in Newport, where the *Samtampa* was to lay up for drydocking and minor repairs. He had plans to spend some time with his family, work and the owners permitting.

When the *Samtampa* passed Flamborough Head the weather continued fine, with a light wind and slight sea, although the visibility had deteriorated. No gale warnings were in operation, but Captain Sherwell, knowing the fickleness of the weather on the British coast, was not fully at ease. His ship, flying light, with only 182 tons of permanent ballast in her empty holds and drawing a mere thirteen feet of water, had almost three quarters of her slab-sided hull exposed to the elements. In a high wind, as Sherwell had learned from bitter experience, she would be hard to handle. But then, one could hardly expect perfection from a Liberty ship.

Widow-Maker

At the height of the Battle of the Atlantic, in the winter of 1942, Britain was losing her merchant ships to the U-boats at the rate of sixty a month, faster than they could be replaced by her hard-pressed shipyards. In desperation, she turned to the USA, then a vast and largely un-stretched industrial powerhouse. The call was for a tramp-style cargo ship, with a large carrying capacity and economic fuel consumption—a hostilities-only replacement ship. The Americans responded with characteristic enthusiasm and soon had eighteen shipyards turning out the new 'Liberty' ship at the rate of nearly two a day.

The Liberty, based on plans drawn up in a Newcastle-upon-Tyne shipyard as far back as 1879, emerged as an all-welded ship of 7,000 tons gross, 420 feet long and 57 feet in the beam. A triple-expansion steam engine, driven by oil-fired Scotch boilers, gave her a service speed of eleven knots. However, her deadweight capacity of 10,000 tons allowed for no fine lines and she was really only a huge, unwieldy barge, vaguely shaped at each end and topped by a single block of accommodation, two masts and a short funnel. For her size, she was grossly under-powered, a failing exacerbated by an insufficiency of ballast tanks. In the light condition, her propeller was not completely submerged and thus lost much of its thrust. This, combined with a large area of hull exposed to the wind, gave her a dangerous tendency to make leeway on a par with the windjammers of another age. A Liberty in ballast was not a ship to be caught on a lee shore in high winds.

For all their failings, the Liberty ships more than proved their worth in supplying a beleaguered Britain in the 1940s. It was said that even if a Liberty survived to bring only one cargo across the Atlantic, she had served her purpose. In the event, more than 2,700 of these replacement ships were built, and many of them, the *Samtampa* being one, were still in service after the war.

Built in 1943 by the New England Shipbuilding Corporation of Portland, Maine, the 7,129-ton *Samtampa* was owned by the Ministry of Transport and managed by Houlder Brothers of London, a company long established in the River Plate trade. Having survived the war unscathed she was about to be handed over to Houlders to replace one of their many wartime losses.

Fog in the North Sea slowed the *Samtampa* down to a crawl and it was late on the morning of the 21st before she began her passage of the busy Dover Strait. As Captain Sherwell had feared, a rapidly falling barometer indicated the spell of calm weather was coming to an end. A few hours after clearing the strait, she was butting into the teeth of a rising south-westerly wind and losing speed with every wave she shouldered aside. Further down the Channel small ships were running for shelter and the 31,000-ton battleship *Warspite*, under tow to the breaker's yard, was reported in difficulties off the Cornish coast.

Bernard Edwards

At 10.00 on the 23rd, after what must have been a long and arduous struggle to round Land's End, the *Samtampa* was sighted off Hartland Point, on the north coast of Devon, and running before a force 8 south-westerly. She was already thirty-six hours late on her original ETA at Newport and likely to be delayed further still. Warnings of severe weather to come had been issued by the Meteorological Office. In the English Channel, the *Warspite* had broken free of her tugs and had been thrown onto the rocks off Penzance by heavy seas.

During the afternoon, the 6,000-ton British cargo ship *Empire Success*, also inbound in the Bristol Channel, was in radio contact with the *Samtampa*. The Houlder's ship reported she was about to heave-to off Foreland Point, near Lynmouth. It was apparent that Sherwell had been forced to abandon all thoughts of proceeding up Channel and was preparing to ride out the storm head to wind and sea. The wind was now blowing near-hurricane force from the south-west and the seas were steep and menacing. The scene was set for one of the worst disasters seen in the Bristol Channel for many years.

Nothing was heard from the *Samtampa* for another two hours, then, at 17.14, the radio officer of the *Empire Success* picked up an anguished cry for help: XXX SAMTAMPA RAPIDLY DRIFTING TOWARDS NASH SHOAL. The Liberty ship, riding high out of the water and with her propeller threshing air each time her stern lifted on the sea, was being blown bodily towards the Welsh coast to the east of Swansea Bay.

Forty minutes later, Burnham Radio, which was monitoring the emergency, heard: HAVE BOTH HOOKS DOWN NOW AND HOPE TO KEEP OFF THE SHOAL BUT DOUBTFUL STILL. The exact position of the *Samtampa* was unknown, but local rescue services, including coastguards at Porthcawl and the Mumbles lifeboat, were immediately alerted. Tugs attempted to leave Swansea harbour to search for the ship but were driven back by heavy seas.

In the clubhouse of Porthcawl's Royal George Golf Club, on the high ground overlooking Sker Point, the club's steward, William Price, was making ready to shut up shop for the day. The gale force winds and driving rain had long since cleared the greens of even the most dedicated golfers. Price was about to lock up when, through a break in the rain, he was astonished to see a large ship looming close inshore, apparently less than a mile off the beach. At that point Price was joined by the station officer of the Porthcawl coastguard. Both men examined the ship through binoculars, establishing that she was stern-on to the shore, with both anchors down and going ahead on her engines in a desperate effort to avoid being driven on the rocks at the foot of Sker Point. The coastguard officer, realising he had found the *Samtampa*, asked William Price for the use of his telephone.

At Mumbles, on the far side of Swansea Bay, Coxswain

Widow-Maker

Gammon took the call and ordered his men into oilskins and life-jackets. Gammon then went outside the boathouse to test the full force of the weather. He was not pleased. In the failing light, the bay was a mass of angry whitecaps. Beyond the headland, the waves would be running high, for the anemometer on the boathouse was showing a wind speed of seventy knots. Gammon rasped at the bristles of his chin and thought back to that black night in 1944, when they had taken off the crew of the Canadian frigate *Cheboque* in similar weather. The war was on then and two of his crew had been over seventy, yet they had done their job—as they would do again tonight, if and when the time came.

What happened on board the *Samtampa* during her last hours will forever remain in the realms of conjecture. Her final messages, received by Burnham Radio, first indicated that her anchors were dragging. Then, her starboard anchor carried away and, twelve minutes later, her port anchor cable parted. Witnesses on shore said they saw men board one of the ship's lifeboats but were unable to see if the boat was launched. Given the sea running at the time, it is highly unlikely any boat could have survived, even if it had been launched.

From his vantage point in the clubhouse, William Price watched horror-stricken as the *Samtampa* was thrown onto the jagged rocks of Sker Point shortly after 19.00. Pounded by huge, thirty-foot waves, she broke her back at once. Her forward section then drifted out to sea about two-hundred yards, before that also broke in two. Within a few minutes of striking, the 423-foot-long ship was in three pieces and, through the rain and flying spume Price could see some of her crew huddled together on the bridge with the waves breaking right over them. Unless rescue came very quickly, they were finished.

The Porthcawl Lifesaving Company now arrived on the scene and set up a breeches buoy apparatus on the beach. A crowd of onlookers gathered around them, willing them on, but all efforts to save the *Samtampa*'s men were doomed from the start.

The wind was blowing straight on shore with such force that those on the beach had great difficulty in keeping their feet. However, the first rocket fired went to the full extent of its 400-yard line but fell short of the wreck. The *Samtampa* was out of reach. More rockets were fired, but a swiftly rising tide was forcing the crew back up the beach, so that their efforts were increasingly in vain. Soon, they were obliged to join the crowd of onlookers, leaning helplessly into the wind, their faces spattered by fuel oil borne on the screaming wind from the ship's ruptured tanks.

Immediately news reached them that the *Samtampa* was dragging her anchors, William Gammon and his crew of seven took the twenty-three-year-old Mumbles lifeboat, *Edward Prince of Wales*, down the slipway and plunged into the foaming maelstrom of Swansea Bay. The sixteen-ton boat, sliding from crest to trough, raced twelve miles up-Channel and for more than an hour searched the shore in the vicinity of Porthcawl but failed to find the *Samtampa*. As visibility was down to just over one mile and darkness was fast closing in, this was not altogether surprising. The lifeboat was not equipped with radio, so Gammon had no alternative but to fight his way back to the Mumbles to gain more information on the wreck. At 19.10, the *Edward Prince of Wales* put to sea again and all contact with her was lost.

When full darkness came, the broken hull of the *Samtampa* could be seen as a ghostly silhouette in the headlights of cars drawn up on the sand dunes backing the beach at Sker Point. All hope for

The broken halves of the 'Samtampa' lying off Sker Point

(*Photo:* Western Mail)

the thirty-nine men on board the ship had been abandoned. Their deaths were accepted as another cruel sacrifice on the altar of the ever-demanding sea, for this is a risk men who earn their living by the great oceans must take.

At first light next morning, the storm-ravaged beach was seen to be thick with oil and scattered with debris from the battered wreck. When the tide receded, the bodies began to come ashore. Ironically, the first to be found was that of Chief Engineer Atkinson, who had come home to his native Wales for the last time.

Police and coastguards waded out to the wreck and, when satisfied there was no one alive on board, began the grim task of recovering more bodies. While they were so engaged, word came through that the Mumbles lifeboat was missing. The search was widened and when the broken shell of the *Edward Prince of Wales* was found half a mile further along the beach, the enormity of the tragedy of the night of 19 April was revealed.

Unseen and unheard, William Gammon and his gallant band of

The symbolic burning of the Mumbles' lifeboat
(*Photo:* Western Mail)

Bow section of the 'Samtampa' *lying off Sker Point*
(Photos: Western Mail)

All that remained of the 'Samtampa' *a year later*
(Photos: Western Mail)

volunteers had given their lives in the fight to save the men of the *Samtampa*.

The court of inquiry into the loss of the *Samtampa* confirmed only what had always been a fact of life for those who sailed in the Liberty ships; in the weather prevailing, the ship had become unmanageable in her light condition. There was much talk of increasing the ballast capacity of these ships, of instituting a 'light loadline'. But, with the passage of time, the disaster off Sker Point was soon forgotten and the Liberty ships continued to wage their unequal battle with the elements for many years to come. The oceans and shores of the world are littered with their broken skeletons.

Bernard Edwards

36   No Way Back

Princess Victoria - 1953

The year 1947, which saw the tragic end of the unsophisticated and vunerable *Samtampa*, also witnessed the birth of a ship of a very different breed. She was the 2,694-ton passenger/car ferry *Princess Victoria*, purpose built by William Denny of Dumbarton for the Stranraer/Larne service.

Sturdily constructed, powerfully engined and equipped with the latest navigational aids, including radar, the twin-screw motor vessel *Princess Victoria* was one of the first drive on/drive off ferries to come into service in European waters. Owned by British Railways, she offered car and lorry drivers a revolutionary means of transport between the United Kingdom and Ireland and proved to be immensely popular from the start. The method of loading and unloading was simple, vehicles driving on or off her open main deck via a ramp at her stern. While at sea, this deck was closed off by a portable bulwark in the form of two steel, hinged doors five feet six inches high. There was no attempt at a watertight closure; it was considered the man-high doors were sufficient to stop any appreciable amount of water being shipped over the stern during the thirty-three mile passage across the North Channel.

Captain James Ferguson, by nature of his calling, was a man who rarely missed the regular BBC weather forecasts for shipping. On the morning of 31 January 1953, over an early breakfast at his home in Stranraer, he listened with care to the detached voice of the announcer warning of severe weather in the Malin area. The wind was in the north-west, promising a rough passage across the North Channel for the *Princess Victoria* that morning. Steering a south-westerly course for Larne, she would be beam-on to wind and sea throughout.

When Ferguson reached the quayside an hour later, it was still dark; ragged clouds raced low across the sky and the cold rain lashed spitefully at his face. It was not an ideal morning to be venturing to sea, but there was a schedule to keep up.

Had Captain Ferguson been the recipient of the mass of satellite-generated weather information on offer today, he might well have hesitated to sail on that foul January morning. The forecasters had correctly diagnosed a depression centred to the north-west of

Widow-Maker

A deep-laden merchant ship in heavy weather

(Photo: Norman Kneale)

Scotland and anticipated the usual winter gales moving east across the country. But what they had failed to spot was a small secondary depression forming on the south-eastern edge of the primary. This secondary was to grow and combine with the isobars of its parent to produce winds of hurricane force, and would sweep rapidly across southern Scotland to the Continent, trailing death and destruction in its wake.

The *Princess Victoria* left her berth in Stranraer at 07.45, having on board, apart from her crew of forty-nine, only 127 passengers, a few vehicles and forty-four tons of general cargo, most of which was carried on the car deck. This was a slack time of the year for both passengers and freight. As the ferry made her way up the three-mile-long Loch Ryan towards the open sea, the wind was gusting strongly but Ferguson still had no reason to anticipate anything more than an uncomfortable passage. When, at 08.30, she left the shelter of the land, it was as though she had steamed straight into the mouth of Hell itself.

Funnelling down the narrow gullet of the North Channel, which separates Scotland from Northern Ireland, storm-force winds had already built up thirty-foot seas with angry, foaming crests. Rain and sleet lashed down and lightning flashed as the small ferry buried her bows deep and staggered under the weight of water that came pouring over her raised forecastle. The cries of startled passengers mingled with the crash of breaking crockery and the thud of falling furniture.

James Ferguson, bracing himself in the starboard wing of the bridge, half-blinded by sleet and flying spray, recognised he had an urgent decision to make. The choice presented to him was not wide. Altering course to port to put the *Princess Victoria* on her south-easterly course for Larne was out of the question. She would then be beam-on to the mountainous seas and would roll her bulwarks under, with disastrous consequences for her passengers and cargo, and perhaps for the ship herself. He must either carry on or go back, but to heave-to with the wind and sea ahead, to hold her riding the crests and plunging into the troughs—as she was now—could only be a short-term measure. She was too near the land and might end up being tossed onto the steep cliffs of Corsewell Point. The sleet had turned to snow, reducing the visibility to a few yards, when Ferguson decided he must return to the shelter of Loch Ryan. He must go back.

There was no time to warn those below—not that it would have mattered. Passengers and crew alike were already hanging on for their dear lives as the ship roller-coasted from crest to trough.

Ferguson waited until she rose on the next on-coming wave and then gave the order for full starboard helm, at the same time slowing down the starboard engine to give more torque. The *Princess Victoria* slid down into the trough, turning as she went with an awkward, corkscrewing movement. By the time the next sea bore down on her, she was stern-on.

Any ship running with her stern to a heavy sea is in a potentially dangerous position in that she is liable to be pooped. If the ship's speed coincides with that of the following sea, the curling overhang of a wave may overtake the ship, smashing down on her unprotected stern, causing considerable damage. The effect of the rudder may be lost and the ship broaches-to with disastrous results. The only way of avoiding such a fate is to slow the ship down, so that she rides the backs of the waves like a huge, powered surfboard. It was this action Ferguson took and, for fifteen minutes or more, the *Princess Victoria* rode purposefully before the might of the storm, heading back for the shelter of Loch Ryan. It seemed that she would succeed, then she faltered in her step and her stern slewed suddenly to port. The next wave caught her on her starboard quarter with a blow that shook her from stern to stem.

It was not until the ship began to list to starboard that Ferguson realised something was wrong. Then a report came from aft that the flimsy stern doors had been smashed in and the car deck was flooded. Had there been sufficient large scuppers in the deck to drain the water away quickly, or a longitudinal bulkhead to restrict the free surface, disaster might have been averted. But, with her stern wide open to the sea, hundreds of tons of water surged onto the car deck with every wave that struck. Her cargo shifted, the list increased and the *Princess Victoria* began to drift out of control. Frantic efforts were made to close the stern doors, but they were badly buckled and would not move.

Ferguson was forced to turn his ship again and head back out to sea. He now had only one ace up his sleeve; the *Princess Victoria* was fitted with a bow rudder for manoeuvring when entering port. It was just possible that, by going astern on the engines and steering with the bow rudder, the shelter of the loch might be reached. As this rudder was kept locked in the fore and aft position while at sea, it was first necessary to send men onto the forecastle head to withdraw the locking pin. The ship's carpenter and two seamen volunteered for the job, but the seas were again climbing over the bow, sweeping the forecastle head, and they failed to reach the rudder pin.

The *Princess Victoria* was now moving slowly out to sea, with a 10° list to starboard and a gaping wound in her stern, through which the sea continued to pour. Ferguson instructed Radio Officer David Broadfoot to send out a call for assistance. The time was 09.46. Two hours had passed since the ferry had left her berth in Stranraer.

Rolling heavily and, through the great weight of water swirling around her car deck, more and more reluctant to return to the upright each time she heeled, the *Princess Victoria* drifted crabwise across the North Channel battered by hurricane force winds and pounding seas. By 10.30, she was four miles north-west of Corsewell Point, water had entered the accommodation and her list had increased to 20°. Ferguson passed the word for lifejackets to be issued to the passengers. In the radio room, David Broadfoot crouched over his key, keeping the outside world informed of the deteriorating situation.

Noon came, with no let-up in the storm. The crippled ferry had drifted past Corsewell Point and was five miles to the west. The list was now so severe it was necessary to rig lifelines for the passengers to climb up to the port side of the entrance hall, where they had been ordered to assemble. It was certain they would soon have to abandon ship. Ferguson, for all the horrendous problems assailing him, kept up a flow of reassuring messages over the bridge Tannoy. His calming influence was largely responsible for the absence of panic.

In response to Broadfoot's courageous work in the radio room, help was now on the way. The Portpatrick and Donaghadee lifeboats had been launched and the destroyer HMS *Contest* was racing south at full speed from her base on the Clyde. But the weather was worsening. The secondary depression, continuing to feed on the primary, was producing winds of up to 120 mph and the North Channel had become a seething mass of angry, marching waves. Squalls of sleet and snow were at times reducing the visibility to zero. The rescue, if it came, would involve a tremendous battle of man against the elements gone wild.

Two hours later, the *Princess Victoria* had drifted to a position she reported as five miles east of the Copeland Islands, just south of the entrance to Belfast Lough. She was still under way but had a 45° list. Ferguson was preparing to abandon ship. Radio Officer Broadfoot remained at his post, the ship's tenuous link with the world on the other side of this ghastly nightmare. The rescue ships were a long time coming.

At 13.54, reluctantly concluding that to delay longer would serve no useful purpose, James Ferguson gave the order to abandon ship. In the terrible conditions prevailing, the ship being almost on her beam-ends with the seas washing over her, this was an operation that could easily have turned into a chaotic rout. The starboard lifeboats were almost in the water, some smashed by the seas and all out of reach. On the port side, due to the severe list, it was impossible to swing the boats out. Fortunately, the officers and men of the *Princess Victoria* were a well-trained and disciplined team. Mustering the frightened passengers as best they could, they cleared away the port side boats ready for floating off when the ship went down. Their plan might have worked but, as they were in the act of embarking the passengers, the *Princess Victoria* gave one last agonised lurch and capsized.

Meanwhile, the Portpatrick and Donaghadee lifeboats, HMS *Contest*, the salvage vessel *Salveda* and the coastal tanker *Pass of Drumochter* were battling their way through the storm towards the position passed to them by Broadfoot. Unknown to them, and to the radio officer, this position was seriously in error—an understandable mistake taking into account the dreadful conditions prevailing on the ferry. When the rescue ships finally reached the spot five miles east of the Copelands, they found nothing. The *Princess Victoria* had, in fact, foundered five miles to the north and one mile to the east. It was only when the coaster *Orchy*, which had courageously set out from Belfast Lough on hearing of the plight of the ferry, ran into wreckage that the real position of the disaster became known. The other ships came racing in answer to the *Orchy*'s call.

Of the 176 passengers and crew on board the *Princess Victoria*, only forty-four were rescued, and most of these survived in the port-side boats which had been prepared for floating off when she went down. Captain James Ferguson and all his officers died, David Broadfoot remaining at his post in the radio room until the sea took him.

It was later established that the *Princess Victoria* went down only five miles from the mouth of Belfast Lough. Had she stayed afloat for another half-hour or so, she would have been in sheltered waters. In the summing up at the subsequent court of inquiry, the learned judge said: 'If the *Princess Victoria* had been as staunch as the men who manned her then all would have been well and this disaster averted.'

As the complex depression of 31 January moved across the British

Isles, it deepened and intensified, spawning winds of unprecedented fury. A sustained windspeed—not a gust—of 125 mph, the highest on record, was logged in the Orkneys. As bad luck would have it, this was also a time of exceptionally high spring tides, and the combination of wind and sea produced in the North Sea storm tides which inundated hundreds of square miles of low-lying eastern England, Holland and Belgium. The death toll rose to over 500, and many thousands were made homeless.

On 6 March 1987, the cross-Channel car ferry *Herald of Free Enterprise* capsized and sank off Zeebrugge with the loss of 188 lives. In this case, the breach of watertightness was not due to the elements but to an appalling lack of good seamanship, in that the ship went to sea with her bow doors open. The opinion of the courts was that the *Herald of Free Enterprise* would not have capsized if she had been fitted with (a) sufficient scuppers to clear the water quickly from her flooded car deck and (b) a longitudinal bulkhead or breakwater to restrict the free surface of water. It would seem that, thirty-four years on, nothing had been learned from the loss of the *Princess Victoria*.

Bernard Edwards

37 An Ill Wind

Dara - 1961

The *Dara* was tired and ageing, one of the 'forgotten fleet' of pilgrim carriers of the British India Steam Navigation Company. Although registered in London, the 5,030-ton motor vessel had not seen her homeland since she came out of Barclay Curle's Glasgow yard in 1948. For thirteen long years, with her sisters *Daressa*, *Dumrah* and *Dwarka*, she had maintained a weekly service between Bombay and Persian Gulf ports, originally carrying Moslem pilgrims *en route* to Mecca and, more latterly, Indian clerks, technicians and labourers, who, with the coming of the oil boom, had moved into the Gulf in large numbers to service the oil fields and build the new Arab cities.

For the *Dara*'s nineteen British officers and 113 Indian ratings, the Bombay—Persian Gulf run was a hard slog. Calling at as many as twelve or fifteen ports in a round voyage of ten days, with no passage between ports much over eighteen hours, there was no time to enjoy the pleasures of sailing under blue skies and in calm waters. The *Dara* was certified to carry, in addition to cargo and mails, seventy-eight saloon and 948 'unberthed' passengers. The latter deposited their baggage and rested their heads wherever space could be found; on the open decks, on hatchtops and in alleyways. When she sailed out of Bombay to begin her circuit of the Gulf, the white-painted motor vessel often resembled a crowded Mississippi riverboat. Every available inch of space on board was packed with heaving humanity, and would remain that way throughout the voyage. At each port she called those who disembarked would be immediately replaced with an equal number shouldering battered suitcases and untidy bundles, all prepared to do battle for a favoured spot in the shade. Babies were born on board, the old and the sick died, but nothing was allowed to interrupt the *Dara*'s tight schedule. In a land with few good roads, a dearth of railways, and at a time when mass air travel was still in its infancy, the *Dara* and her sisters provided the main means of communication between the Gulf states.

Chaotic and hard-pressed as the *Dara* might appear at times, she was a well-maintained, tightly run ship, classed 100 A1 at Lloyd's and periodically inspected to ensure she remained so. Her hull was sound, her engines reliable, and her crew of the highest standard. In order to cope with any emergency, she was equipped with sixteen steel lifeboats with a total capacity of 921 persons, twenty-eight small rafts capable of supporting another 560, lifejackets for 1,350 and the usual standard of fire-fighting gear required for British passenger ships. Fortunately, in all her thirteen punishing years she had never been called upon to use any of this equipment, except at the regular fire and boat drills carried out in accordance with Ministry of Transport regulations.

When the *Dara* left Bombay on 23 March, 1961, she was commanded by Captain Charles Elson, whose senior officers were Chief Officer P.E. Jordan and Chief Engineer G.K. Cruickshank. She had the usual large complement of passengers and was scheduled to call at Karachi, Pasni, Muscat, Dubai, Umm Said, Bahrain, Bushire, Kuwait, Mina Al Ahmadi, Khorramshahr, Basrah, then back to Khorramshahr, Kuwait, Bahrain and Dubai, before returning to Bombay on or about 10 April. This was a longer than usual round trip and a very gruelling itinerary, but Captain Elson and his crew accepted the task with their habitual good grace.

The voyage progressed well until the *Dara* reached Bahrain on the return leg on 5 April. It was hot and humid when she anchored, with ominous, dark cumulonimbus clouds building up to the north. The weather in the southern Gulf at this time of the year is normally placid, with mainly light winds and an almost total absence of rain. It was therefore with some surprise that the *Dara*'s deck crew found themselves called upon to batten down hatches when a storm of frightening proportions broke over the port. Thunder rolled, brilliant forked lightning sizzled all around, the rain came down in torrents and the wind blew in fierce, malevolent squalls. The storm raged all day and was, in the opinion of the locals, the worst in living memory. It was late on the afternoon of the 6th before the *Dara* finished discharging her cargo and, having taken on a number of passengers, sailed for Dubai, her last port in the Gulf.

When she anchored off Dubai at noon on the 7th the *Dara* was almost twelve hours behind on her schedule and Captain Elson was anxious to make up for lost time. Fortunately, the weather had by then moderated and the ship was able to commence discharging her cargo into lighters within a short time of arriving.

In 1961, Dubai was little more than a collection of mud huts surrounding a ruined fort and the sheikh's palace, but big changes were afoot. Oil in large quantities had been discovered offshore and the ruler was anxious to make good use of his new-found wealth. European construction companies had been brought in and a great building boom was in progress ashore. The result was that the cargo anchorage was crowded with ships of all nations, the majority carrying cement and building materials. Anchored very close to the *Dara*—uncomfortably close in Captain Elson's opinion—was the Panamanian-flag cement carrier *Zeus*. Elson, aware that the coarse sand of the sea bottom in the anchorage was poor holding ground, instructed his officers on deck to keep a close eye on the Panamanian.

A sudden darkening of the sky at around 16.00 indicated a rapid deterioration in the weather. Soon, a strong onshore wind was blowing, whipping up a rough sea and short swell, both of which were aggravated by the shallow water. Elson feared a repeat of the Bahrain storm and was concerned at the vulnerability of his ship in the crowded anchorage. However, the *Dara* was at the time very near to finishing her cargo, and, as all passengers were already on board, Elson was very loath to cause another delay by shifting his anchorage.

The captain's hand was forced a few minutes later, when the heavily laden *Zeus* dragged her anchor and drifted down on the *Dara*. Luckily, the Panamanian struck the passenger ship only a glancing blow, bending a few rails on her forecastle head and slightly damaging one of the forward lifeboats. But the warning was enough for Elson.

By this time the weather was turning nasty, with the wind up to force 7 and the sea very rough. Clearly, the *Dara* could not continue to work cargo and there was now a very real risk she would drag her anchor and perhaps run ashore. Elson instructed Chief Officer Jordan to cast off the lighters and heave up anchor. There was no opportunity to land the shore personnel still on board, and when the *Dara* hove up her anchor and headed out to sea, she took with her seventy-four stevedores, officials and visitors. All crew members were on board, as were seventy-six saloon and 537 deck passengers, making a total complement of 819.

Elson's plan was to ride out the storm by taking the *Dara* to the north-west into deeper water at slow speed. Experience told him that the bad weather was nothing more than the tail-end of an equinoctial depression spilling over into the Gulf from the Mediterranean, and would subside as quickly as it had arisen.

It was as Elson had assumed. The storm abated quickly during the night, and by 04.00 on the 8th, the captain decided it was safe to return to Dubai to complete cargo and land the shore personnel. The *Dara* was at that time about forty-five miles north-west of the port; by steaming at full speed, she would arrive back at the anchorage by full daylight. Having turned the ship around and steadied her on her new course, Elson handed over to Second Officer Alexander, officer of the watch, and retired to his cabin. It had been a long and stressful day.

Alexander anticipated a quiet watch. The visibility was good, it was a straight run into the anchorage through deep water, and few other ships were in the vicinity. When the *Dara* was about five miles from Dubai, he had instructions to call Captain Elson, who would then take over for the approach. Given fair weather, cargo work would be completed in an hour or so, and, having landed the shore personnel, the ship would sail for Bombay. Seven hours later, she would be out of the Gulf and there would be time to relax. Thoughts were following a similar train in the *Dara*'s engineroom, where Second Engineer Birrell and Fifth Engineer Durham kept watch over the propulsion machinery. The four to eight watch settled down to await the coming of a new day.

At 04.40, Alexander broke off from pacing the wing of the bridge and walked into the wheelhouse. The sun being still more than an hour below the horizon the darkness was absolute. In the wheelhouse, the only light was a dim glow from the compass binnacle, behind which the shadowy figure of the Indian quartermaster eased the spokes of the wheel from time to time as the ship yawed about her course. As a matter of routine, Alexander checked the compass. Satisfied, he moved away from the binnacle, and at that moment the sleeping *Dara* was rocked by a massive explosion. The compass light went out, the quartermaster was thrown to the deck by the wildly kicking wheel, and the alarm bells of the fire detector set up a strident clamour.

In times of peace, an explosion in a dry cargo ship is a very rare occurrence, and Alexander could not have been blamed if he had panicked. The sudden shock, the darkness and the urgent tone of the bells would have unnerved most men. But the second officer kept a firm grip on himself, groping his way first to the panel of the fire detector, where he hoped to locate the source of the explosion. He was under the impression it had taken place in the engineroom, and was attempting to confirm this when the engine coughed and died.

Deep in the bowels of the ship, the force of the explosion blew the circuit breaker off the main switchboard, thereby plunging the engineroom into darkness. At the same time, the air was filled with particles of asbestos lagging, blown from the pipes of the auxiliary boiler. Dazed and temporarily blinded, Second Engineer Birrell was of the opinion that there had been an explosion of gases in the crankcase. He stopped the engine to avoid further damage.

Captain Elson, who had been dozing in his armchair, reached the bridge as the engine stopped. He took control of the situation at once, ordering the oil 'not under command' lights to be hoisted and sent Alexander below to ascertain the damage. Elson, quite naturally, was also convinced the explosion must have occurred in the engine space and this theory seemed to be borne out when Chief Officer Jordan arrived on the bridge at a run. He reported a fire raging in the first-class smoke-room, which was directly over the engineroom. The flames appeared to be coming through the deck from below. Chief Engineer Cruickshank arrived a few minutes later with a similar report. He also informed Elson that the steering gear was out of action, its hydraulic pipes cut. The *Dara* was dead in the water, without lights or steering and on fire below decks. For a ship carrying a large number of passengers, many of whom were liable to panic, this was a frightening predicament.

By this time, the emergency generator had been started up, providing sufficient light in the engineroom for Birrell and Durham to check around the main engine and auxiliaries. They could find nothing mechanically wrong, and there was certainly no evidence of an explosion having taken place. It was only when they reached the top platform that they came face to face with the reality of the situation. Clouds of dense black smoke were billowing in from the forward tween decks. From behind the wall of smoke came the crackle of flames and the screams of trapped passengers. Birrell ordered his men out of the engineroom immediately.

Both Elson and Cruickshank were still convinced they had an engineroom fire on their hands and, once the area had been cleared, Elson ordered the engine space to be flooded with inert carbon-dioxide gas. The gas seemed to have no effect and attention was turned to the fire now raging out of control in the amidships accommodation. Hoses were rigged, but there was no water; the pumps in the engineroom were stopped and out of reach behind the smoke and flames. The emergency fire pump was accessible but could not be started.

With his ship and all on board now in great danger, Elson ordered his radio officer to send out an SOS and then sounded the emergency signal on the alarm bells, repeating this on the ship's whistle. Unfortunately, this caused blind panic amongst the passengers, who, frightened and bemused, rushed to the boat deck. The fire, like a relentless bird of prey, followed them, and by the time the order was given to abandon ship, most of the lifeboats on the starboard side were unapproachable due to the flames.

The panic worsened, fighting broke out, and the officers and crew striving desperately to maintain a semblance of order in the chaos, were overwhelmed by the screaming mob of passengers. Three overcrowded lifeboats capsized as they reached the water, while others caught fire before they could be swung out. Of the twenty-eight small liferafts stowed on top of the engineers' house, twenty-three were destroyed by flames before they could be thrown overboard. In the space of half an hour, the *Dara* had been turned into a dreadful holocaust, from which it seemed few would escape.

It was fortunate, that when the explosion tore through the *Dara*, the converted tank landing craft *Empire Guillemot* was near by and had seen the flames. Her master immediately brought his ship close to the burning *Dara* and sent away his boats to assist. The Norwegian tanker *Thorsholm* also arrived on the scene, to be followed later by three other vessels. In a brilliant combined operation, these ships rescued 584 persons from the sea and the blazing ship.

One of the last rescue boats to go back to the *Dara* took with it Second Officer Alexander and Cadet Grimwood, who reboarded their ship and saved the lives of fifteen terrified passengers found trapped on the poop deck by the flames. Alexander and Grimwood were later joined by Captain Elson, Chief Officer Jordan, Chief Engineer Cruickshank, Fifth Engineer Durham and five Indian ratings. The emergency fire pump was started and hoses brought to bear on the fires, but the pressure on the water was so poor that the hoses had little effect. When the *Dara*'s oil tanks went up in flames, Elson wisely decided to abandon his ship for the second and last time.

That evening, the Royal Navy frigates *Loch Alvie*, *Loch Ruthven* and *Loch Fyne* arrived and took over the fire-fighting. But even with all the trained men and equipment at their disposal the Navy ships had little success. The *Dara* burned on throughout that night, but she was still afloat next morning. The salvage vessel *Ocean Salvor* then took her in tow with the object of beaching her, but the *Dara*, her upperworks a blackened shell and her engineroom and holds partly flooded, capsized and sank before she reached shallow water.

When the roll was called, it was found that 193 passengers, twenty-one visitors and stevedores and twenty-four crew members had lost their lives when disaster struck the *Dara* early on that April morning in 1961. The cause of the explosion that set her ablaze remained a mystery until divers examined the wreck some months later. They found the explosion had occurred not in the engineroom as suspected, but on the upper deck, in or near the first class accommodation. Further investigations were made and Navy experts concluded that the *Dara* had been sabotaged by persons unknown using a powerful bomb similar in effect to an anti-tank mine.

It may never be known why the *Dara* became the victim of a saboteur's bomb—for there was no apparent motive for the attack. However, at the time she was lost the first signs of religious and political unrest were beginning to emerge in the Gulf. In Oman and Saudi Arabia, Moslem fundamentalists had embarked on their struggle to take control of a land suddenly become rich beyond the wildest dreams of all Arabs by the discovery of huge reserves of oil. Shootings and bombings had become commonplace ashore, and it is suspected, though never proven, that a time-bomb was planted on the *Dara* during the unprecedented rain storm at Bahrain. How, and why, are still matters for debate, but one thing is certain, if the *Dara*'s cargo operations had not been interrupted by the second storm off Dubai, she would have been outside the Gulf when she blew up. In deep, shark-infested waters, and with no help near at hand, the death toll in the tragedy would probably have been doubled.

Bernard Edwards

38   Death at the Varne

Texaco Caribbean - 1971

In the 2nd century AD the Romans built the first two lighthouses in Western Europe, one at Boulogne and the other on the cliffs overlooking Dover. The far-sighted Mediterranean empire-builders realised, even then, that the Dover Strait, western gateway to Europe, was destined to become a navigational headache of the first magnitude.

Today, the Dover Strait is the busiest through-waterway in the world. It also remains one of the most hazardous; a fifty-mile long mariner's nightmare beset by shoals, strong tidal streams and a weather pattern often alternating only between gale force winds and calms with dense fog. In any twenty-four hours, more than 300 deep-sea vessels pass through the strait, while ferries criss-cross its narrowest part at the rate of one every few minutes.

The rebuilding of the shattered economies of Europe after World War II brought about an unprecedented boom in shipping. Traffic through the Dover Strait doubled and then trebled. Inevitably, as in any boom situation, the sharks moved in. Sub-standard ships began to appear on the scene in large numbers, predominately under flags of convenience and manned by men to whom the delicate art of navigation was a closed book.

By the 1960s, more than 700 ships a day were flowing through the narrow bottleneck off Dover and a state of chaos reigned. It was every man for himself, with ships jousting for the right of way, at the same time zigzagging suicidally through the hordes of ferries, fishing fleets and, in the season, the wandering yachts of the newly affluent weekend sailors of Europe. Major collisions, resulting in the loss of ships and men and in the pollution of the Channel on a massive scale, were taking place at the rate of one a month.

In 1967, in a desperate attempt to bring order out of the chaos, a system of 'one-way' traffic was introduced in the Dover Strait. All ships were instructed to keep to the right, those bound up Channel hugging the French coast, and south bound ships keeping to the English side, passing close to Dover, Folkestone and Beachy Head. Down the middle of the Strait ran an imaginary 'central reservation', not to be crossed except in specific circumstances. The scheme, which envisaged orderly lines of ships proceeding safely up and down the Strait in their respective 'lanes', was excellent in conception. Unfortunately, it was not legally enforceable and, while the dedicated professional seamen adhered to the rules, there were many who, either through ignorance or sheer bloody-mindedness, persisted in going their own haphazard way. The confusion grew worse and the number of collisions actually increased. Another four years of anarchy were to pass before the Dover Strait was finally and cruelly shocked into sensibility.

At 03.00 on the morning of 11 January 1971, the tanker *Texaco Caribbean* was approaching the South Goodwin lightship, bound down Channel and heading for the sunnier climes of Trinidad, some 4,000 miles to the south-west. On this cold, murky night, as the tanker moved towards the narrows of the Dover Strait, those on watch on her bridge might have been excused if they were more than a little preoccupied with thoughts that included the delights of the warm, tropical sun yet to come.

The *Texaco Caribbean*, a tanker of 20,500 tons deadweight, was American owned, sailed under the flag of Panama and was crewed by Italians—a typical maritime mongrel. She was an average-sized tanker for her day, the 200,000 tonners spawned by the machinations of OPEC having not yet arrived on the scene. In construction she was of the old, traditional build, with her bridge amidships, beneath which was accommodation for her master and deck officers. Her engineers and ratings lived right aft, over the engineroom. This old-style segregation of the classes on board ship was to soon to prove costly for some.

For Captain Franco Giurini, master of the *Texaco Caribbean*, it had been a long, gut-twisting night, during which he had carefully nursed his ship through some of the most difficult waters in the world. And his ordeal was far from over. Ahead lay the supreme test of a shipmaster's ability, the notorious Dover Strait.

The picture on the *Texaco Caribbean*'s radar screen was a daunting one. Like confetti scattered over the dark void between the clearly etched outlines of the English and French coasts were the tiny, glowing echoes of scores of ships. The smaller echoes, slow-moving and bunched together in clusters, Giurini recognised as fishermen sweeping the rich waters off the Varne and Le Colbart shoals, which for some fifteen miles provide a natural divide between English and French waters. On each side of this divide, a procession of larger echoes indicated the commercial traffic of the Channel, the general cargo ships, the bulk carriers and the tankers. All were, as far as Giurini could ascertain, keeping to their allotted lanes, those bound for the North Sea ports and beyond tucked into the French coast and the southbound ships, like his own, passing between the shoals and the coast of Kent. At regular intervals small, fast-moving echoes traced their way across the radar screen at right angles to the main streams of traffic. These were the ferries linking Ostend, Dunkirk, Calais and Boulogne with the ports of Dover and Folkestone.

It appeared that all was well, with the mariners of the Dover Strait on their best behaviour. Yet Giurini knew that hidden in this tranquil scene might be a number of 'rogue' ships—those who ignored the recommended routes and chose to force their way through the Strait against the flow of traffic, thereby endangering everyone. The most frequent violations of the rules took place on the British side, between the South Goodwin and Dungeness, the area the *Texaco Caribbean* was about to enter.

Another matter weighed heavily on Captain Giurini's mind on that January night. Less than twelve hours before, the *Texaco Caribbean* had completed discharging a cargo of petrol and petro-chemicals at the Dutch port of Terneuzen. She was now in ballast, with her cargo tanks one third full of seawater and two thirds full of a lethal mixture of hydrocarbon gas and air. Modern technology has produced an inert gas system capable of stabilising dirty oil tanks, but the Panamanian did not have the benefit of such an arrangement. She was therefore a floating bomb courting detonation as she made her way down Channel. One spark would suffice to set her off. Franco Giurini prayed for an uneventful passage through the Dover Strait.

At 03.45, the tanker was edging past the Varne lightship, which guards the northern end of the narrow, steep-to shoal that runs parallel to the coast off Dover harbour. The visibility had fallen to less than one mile, shutting out the friendly shore lights and hiding the navigation lights of other ships in the vicinity. Soon, even the red flash of the Varne lightship was swallowed up in the gloom and the *Texaco Caribbean* pushed on in a dark, silent world of her own, with only the regular heartbeat of her engines betraying her presence.

Six miles to the south-west, unseen by those on the bridge of the *Texaco Caribbean*, the 9,481-ton Peruvian cargo ship *Paracas* was also feeling her way through the night. The *Paracas*—whether by accident or design—appeared to be willing to sacrifice all the good fortune that had attended her on her 6,000-mile voyage from South America. As a northbound ship, she should have been on the other side of the Varne Shoal, near to the French coast. Yet she was deter-minedly threading her way through the stream of on-coming ships like a single-minded pedestrian caught on the wrong pavement in the city rush-hour.

Medical opinion has it that, in the small hours of the morning, between 3 am and 5 am, the cycle of human life is at its lowest ebb. Those asleep are said to be as near to death as they ever will be, until their final day comes, while the unfortunate minority who must be awake are at their most vulnerable. So it must have been on the bridge of the *Texaco Caribbean* at 04.00 on the morning of the 11th as the watches were changing. After four tense hours, during which he had not once dared to relax his concentration, it was with some

Widow-Maker

Stern section of the 'Texaco Caribbean'
(Photo: Times Newspapers)

relief that Second Officer Luigi Fegarotta was handing over the watch to Chief Officer Giancarlo Ferro. The tired Captain Giurini, conscious that many more hours would elapse before he could safely leave the bridge, stood to one side while his officers went through the handing over routine. It was then the *Paracas*, hitherto unnoticed among the mass of ship echoes on the *Texaco Caribbean*'s radar screen, was sighted right ahead, bearing down on the tanker at speed. Giurini had less than one minute to take avoiding action.

The time was too short. Even as the *Texaco Caribbean* slowly answered to Giurini's urgent helm order and began to swing away from the danger, the great, flared bow of the *Paracas* caught her squarely amidships, just abaft her bridge-house.

Propelled by the unstoppable momentum of ship and cargo, the sharp stem of the *Paracas* sliced deep into the hull of the helpless tanker. Steel grated on steel and showers of sparks cascaded into the ruptured, gas-filled tanks of the *Texaco Caribbean*. The explosion that followed turned the low-hanging clouds blood red and shattered windows five miles away in the sleeping port of Folkestone.

The shock rolled the *Texaco Caribbean* over on her beam ends, and she split in two, the bow section sinking at once. With it went Captain Giurini and seven of his officers and crew. Those in the stern section were watched over by a more kindly god that night. Several were thrown into the sea by the force of the explosion but the others were able to launch a lifeboat and all twenty-two were later picked up by other ships.

The *Paracas*, although her bows were badly mangled, suffered no casualties. She was later towed to Hamburg for repairs.

When daylight came, all that could be seen of the 20,500-ton *Texaco Caribbean* was an oil slick eleven miles long and 300 yards wide, drifting with the tide off the Varne Shoal. Somewhere beneath this grim marker lay the two broken halves of the tanker.

The race was now on to find and mark the wrecks before they claimed another victim from the undiminished stream of ships passing through the area. During the night of the 11th, Trinity House survey vessels traced and buoyed the stern section of the sunken tanker, but all efforts to find the forward part of the *Texaco Caribbean* failed. With this 300-foot-long hazard lurking somewhere close beneath the surface, the southbound passage of the Dover Strait became a game of Russian Roulette that could only have one result. This came sooner rather than later.

On the morning of the 12th, as a pale, wintry sun began its reluctant ascent from the horizon, the German motor vessel *Brandenburg* passed the Varne lightship outward bound, her blunt bows cutting a foaming swathe through the grey waters of the Dover Strait. The 2,695-ton cargo ship, owned by the Hamburg Amerika Line, carried a total crew of thirty-two, including four wives. Her master and officers were German, her ratings Spanish.

Widow-Maker

Cautiously, the *Brandenburg* skirted the mournfully clanging wreck buoys marking the last resting place of the stern section of the *Texaco Caribbean* and hurried on down Channel, anxious to be free of this sombre place. A few minutes later, she was suddenly brought up short and her bottom sliced open over more than half its length. The missing bow section of the Panamanian tanker had been found.

The *Brandenburg* sank so quickly her crew had no time to launch the boats. Those who were not trapped below were forced to hurl themselves into the sea without even the consolation of a lifejacket. Twenty-one died, including the four women on board. Eleven survivors were brought into Folkestone by some of the same fishing boats that had taken part in the rescue of the *Texaco Caribbean*'s men only twenty-eight hours before.

Following this second tragedy, a furious row ensued, involving Trinity House, the Department of Trade and various authoritative nautical bodies. Accusations and counter-accusations were made and proposals put forward. But no amount of argument could bring back the twenty-nine lives already lost or, seemingly, sort out the worsening traffic chaos in the Dover Strait. For this, the full weight of international law was needed and, as is usual, the nations involved could find little common ground. It was as though there were some who favoured more blood-letting before a full diagnosis could be attempted. They were to have their way.

Meanwhile, Trinity House, in a desperate race against time, had four ships out scouring the Dover Strait for the wreckage of its latest casualty. The *Brandenburg* was eventually found lying in twelve fathoms of water close to the two sections of the *Texaco Caribbean*. The area containing the three wrecks was then cordoned off by buoys, supplemented by a wreck-marking vessel. Passage through the southbound lane of the Dover Strait became more difficult, but it was felt the danger had been safely isolated until salvage work could begin. However, within a few days, observers on shore were watching aghast as ship after ship, all with an apparent death wish, deliberately entered and sailed through the buoyed danger area.

The culmination of this crass stupidity came on the night of 27 February, when the Greek cargo vessel *Niki* paid the ultimate price. Completely ignoring the cordon of green flashing wreck buoys, she steamed at full speed across the sunken wrecks and ripped herself open. The *Niki* went to the bottom in minutes, taking with her all twenty-two of her crew.

Ignorance, apathy and, perhaps, sheer bravado, had in the first two months of that winter of 1971 cost the lives of fifty-one men and women in the Dover Strait. Three valuable ships had been lost, beaches polluted and Trinity House saddled with a bill for more than half a million pounds to clear up the mess. But the message had at last been driven home. Twelve months later, the Dover Strait traffic separation scheme became mandatory on all ships and strict policing of the Strait was begun by the British and French authorities.

The Dover Strait is now a model of orderly navigation, with only the occasional 'rogue' attempting to re-write the rules. Much of the credit for bringing order out of chaos must go to the maritime authorities on both sides of the Channel and to the dedicated professional seamen of Britain and Europe, who set the example for others to follow. The real impetus for change, however, came from the tragic loss of the fifty-one men and women—innocent parties most of them—of the *Texaco Caribbean*, the *Brandenburg* and the *Niki*. Their sacrifice was not in vain.

39   A Large White Elephant

Olympic Bravery - 1976

When the Suez Canal was first opened in 1869 it was pledged by International Convention to: 'always remain free and open, in time of war as in time of peace, to all merchant vessels without flag distinction and will never be subject to the right of blockade'. This decree of the Victorian imperialists held good for almost a century, until in the Six Day War of 1967, Israel inflicted a humiliating defeat on the combined armies of Egypt, Jordan and Syria. In a fit of pique the Egyptians then blocked the Suez Canal from end to end with sunken ships, dredgers, barges and tugs. The waterway remained closed for eight years.

The closure of the canal had a dramatic effect on ships trading between Europe and the East, forcing them to return to the old route via the Cape of Good Hope, and adding anything up to a month to a round voyage. Longer passages led to a call for more ships, and the world's shipyards experienced an unprecedented boom, giving weight to the old adage concerning the ill wind.

By far the greatest transformation took place in the oil tanker market. This was the era of cheap oil, for which there was an ever increasing demand, keeping the wells of the Persian Gulf pumping hard and long. At the time most of this oil was being carried in tankers of around 20,000 tons deadweight, but the closure of the canal made such ships uneconomical. The answer to the 11,000-mile Cape run was the 250,000-ton VLCC (Very Large Crude Carrier), and there was a rush to invest and build. The long established tanker companies, however, were reluctant to expand too quickly, and the 1970s gave birth to a new breed of maritime entrepreneur, the one-ship tanker company. Fifty million dollars borrowed from the banks bought a VLCC, which, carrying oil around the Cape at fifteen US dollars clear profit on every ton, would pay for itself in two years. From then on the returns were immense, as much as four million dollars for a single cargo. It was, of course, a one-way trade, with the ship returning from Europe to the Gulf in ballast, but she would be expected to carry four or five cargoes in a year. The speculative one-ship operators, registering their huge money-makers under flags of convenience to avoid taxes and governmental interference, reaped a rich harvest.

Bernard Edwards

The bubble was pricked in 1973, when the OPEC nations of the Middle East made their bid to dominate the world's economy with a sevenfold increase in the price of oil. The industrialised nations of the West slashed consumption, and the demand for oil slumped overnight, leaving millions of VLCC tonnage without employment. When the Suez Canal reopened in 1975, the bottom fell out of the tanker market, and any VLCC operator who had ignored the signs of approaching disaster was in dire trouble. One such was Kirton Panama S.A.

Kirton Panama S.A. was a shadowy 'brass plate' company set up and registered in Panama as a front for Olympic Maritime S.A. of Monte Carlo, which in turn was part of the huge Onassis Group. This was an arrangement typical of the day, quite legal, but designed to confuse and confound those who would pry too deeply into the affairs of an organisation. Suffice to say, Kirton Panama was formed in 1973 to operate a single VLCC, which it was envisaged would generate a great deal of wealth hauling oil from the Gulf to Europe. Unfortunately for those concerned, the venture was embarked upon too late.

On 31 July, 1973, not being a party to Arab intentions, Kirton Panama placed an order with Chantiers de l'Atlantique of St.Nazaire for a 270,000-tonne steam-turbine tanker. She was to be built to the highest standards of the American Bureau of Shipping, whose surveyors would oversee the building. When she was completed in October 1975, the *Olympic Bravery* was of 277,599 tonnes deadweight, nearly 1,100 feet in length, 170 feet in the beam and was powered by a geared steam-turbine engine developing 32,000 horse power. She was a product of the technological age, with a fully automated engine-room and all the latest navigational aids on her bridge. In short, she was a very large, up-to-date ship, well-suited for long ocean passages. Unfortunately, between the time the contract was placed and the time the *Olympic Bravery* was ready for sea, the need for such ships was past. Her owners could find no employment for her, and were in fact saddled with a huge white elephant, for which they were contracted to pay 52.5 million US dollars. It was then that the arguments broke out between Kirton Panama and Chantiers de l'Atlantique.

In the closing stages of the building of the *Olympic Bravery* her appointed master and chief engineer, Captain Tsioros Efstratios and Marimarinos Antonios, joined the ship. Efstratios held a Liberian master's licence, and Antonios a chief engineer's licence issued by the same authority, both men having previously served in ships similar to the *Olympic Bravery.* Their immediate role was not to take any responsibility for the ship, but to observe and report to the owners. However, in the disputes that followed, both men undoubtedly played a significant part.

Widow-Maker

The *Olympic Bravery* carried out her first sea trials from 15 to 20 October, 1975, sailing from St. Nazaire to Cherbourg. During the evening of the 17th, the ship suffered a complete loss of power, or 'blackout', which was said to be due to the automatic switches of the boilers being wrongly wired. The fault was not regarded as serious, and was apparently easily rectified. This was not so with the excessive vibration said to have been experienced in the VLCC's superstructure when she was steaming at full speed. Kirton Panama declared they were not satisfied with the ship and refused to accept delivery until the vibration was eliminated. There followed a long dispute between Kirton Panama and Chantiers de l'Atlantique that lasted for three months and led to extensive strengthening of the tanker's superstructure and five more sea trials. It was a farcical dispute which some saw as an attempt by Kirton Panama to postpone the day when they would have to take over a ship already regarded as an expensive liability. The charade was played out to the very end, the only real beneficiaries of the prolonged delay being Captain Efstratios and Chief Engineer Antonios, who had more time to get to know their ship.

At long last, on the afternoon of 21 January, 1976, Kirton Panama S.A. accepted delivery of the *Olympic Bravery* at the port of Brest. On that same day, a mortgage of 246,791,000 francs was taken out with a French bank, and the Liberian flag was raised at the stern of the VLCC.

Next morning, the balance of the *Olympic Bravery*'s crew of thirty-three joined the ship. They were all Greek nationals, the officers holding Liberian licenses where appropriate. The 277,599-tonne VLCC, with steam on her boilers and her new paintwork gleaming, was ready for sea. She was not, however, heading for the oil terminals of the Persian Gulf, for despite the strenuous efforts of her owners, no charterer had been found. As she could obviously not remain in Brest without incurring a great deal of expense in the way of port and harbour dues, she was to go to an anchorage in a fjord at Farsund, in southern Norway, where she would lie until the time when a cargo could be arranged, if ever.

Captain Efstratios had planned to sail from Brest at high water on the morning of the 23rd, which would allow for a daylight passage through the narrows of the Straits of Dover, an eminently sensible precaution, considering the size and newness of the ship. The weather was fine and clear, although a north-westerly gale was forecast for the Biscay area, in which case Efstratios was anxious to gain the shelter of the English Channel as soon as possible.

At 06.40, with the first grey light of approaching dawn challenging the yellow glow of the dockside lamps, the *Olympic Bravery* was ready to cast off. Her engines were on standby and tugs were made fast fore and aft, when she experienced a complete power blackout. The fault was again related to the boiler switches and was rectified without much difficulty, but meanwhile the ship had missed the tide and the sailing was postponed.

The *Olympic Bravery* finally left her berth in Brest at 18.48 that day. She had on board 1,249 tons of fuel oil, 443 tons fresh water and her ballast tanks were partially full, giving her a maximum draught of 29 feet 6 inches. Once she cleared the shallow waters of the harbour, it was intended to fill all ballast tanks for the 800-mile passage to Farsund. As forecast, the weather had deteriorated, and it was blowing gale force 8 from the north-west when she left the berth. The conditions prevailing, aggravated by the darkness, were not those under which a prudent master would wish to take a new 270,000-tonner to sea, but having set in motion the considerable machinery to unberth, Efstratios was reluctant to postpone the operation yet again. The tugs eased the ship away from the quay, and she was clear of the dock by 19.45. She moved into Brest Roads and began the lengthy process of adjusting her magnetic compasses and calibrating the radio direction finder.

It was 00.50 on the 24th before the *Olympic Bravery* was in all respects ready to proceed to sea. Her harbour pilot was dropped off Pte St. Mathieu and a course was set to pass fifteen miles south of the island of Ushant, which lies twelve miles off the western point of the Brittany peninsular. When clear of Ushant, she would be free to alter course to the northward, thence east-north-east into the English Channel. The engine-room was ordered to maintain sixty revolutions per minute, giving a speed of eleven knots, well within the capability of a ship that had attained fifteen knots on trials. Allowing for the adverse wind and sea, Captain Efstratios anticipated being clear of Ushant by 04.00.

At 01.00, being then in deep water, Efstratios instructed the engine-room to commence ballasting. The pumps were started and the seawater poured into the tanks. A short while later is was established that the ship was making good a speed of no more than nine knots. She was in fact steaming at a little over half speed, which for a ship of her great size, under the influence of a force 8 and on a lee shore, would seem to be tempting providence. However, Efstratios did not seem unduly concerned.

It was not until 03.00, when the speed had dropped to four knots, that Efstratios became alarmed. The *Olympic Bravery* was by then approaching the south point of Ushant, where the tides and currents are fierce and unpredictable. Chief Engineer Antonios was called to the bridge, and when asked to explain the low revolutions, he complained that the ballast pumps were starving the main engine of steam. As both the tanker's huge Foster Wheeler boilers, operating under a pressure of 900 pounds per square inch, were in use, the explanation was plainly ludicrous, but Efstratios was satisfied. Antonios went below and a slight increase in revolutions followed.

By 05.35 ballasting was completed, the *Olympic Bravery* having

Widow-Maker

on board a total of 105,000 tons of salt water ballast, putting her down to a draught of forty feet aft, with her propeller well submerged. She had by then rounded the south end of Ushant and was some five miles west of the island on a northerly course. It continued to blow a full gale from the north-west, and the great ship was rolling and pitching easily. The night was very dark, with passing rainsqualls, otherwise the visibility was excellent, a number of other ships being plainly in sight. The tanker was making good a speed of about six knots, still dangerously low. Captain Efstratios was on the bridge, and with him were the officer of the watch, Second Officer Poriotis Andrianos, and two able seamen. In charge of the engine-room was Third Engineer Bernardis Panagiotis, who had with him an assistant engineer, a junior engineer and an oiler. Chief Engineer Antonios was resting in his cabin.

On being informed of the completion of ballasting, Efstratios ordered engine revolutions increased to seventy-five. This order was not complied with, and Antonios was called and told to go below to investigate the delay.

The *Olympic Bravery* continued to limp along at a mere six knots, on a dead lee shore, and with a current estimated at one to two knots setting her in towards the rocky shores of Ushant, yet Captain Efstratios did not seem to fully appreciate the great danger she was in. Had he done so, it is presumed he would have hauled out to sea. Ten minutes later, it was too late, for a chain of events had been set in motion that was to lead to the end of this great ship.

At 05.45 the *Olympic Bravery* suffered a sudden blackout, losing all power on her main engine and auxiliaries. The lights went out; the radars, gyrocompass and Decca Navigator failed. Almost at once, the emergency generator cut in, restoring some lighting and essential services, but the ship was dead in the water and drifting. Two red lights were hoisted at the signal mast, indicating 'Vessel not under command', and Second Officer Andrianos broadcast a warning to other ships on Channel 16 VHF. Ten minutes passed before power was restored to the main engine, but Antonios was able to offer only twenty rpm, which was barely steerageway. He reported the cut-out switches on the boilers to be again malfunctioning. Captain Efstratios now began to have serious concern for the safety of his ship.

Over the next one and three-quarter hours another five blackouts occurred, in between which the *Olympic Bravery*'s engine turned over at a maximum speed of twenty-five revolutions, and this never for more than a few minutes at a time. She was, in effect, engineless and drifting towards Ushant at between two and three knots. This mammoth, 52.5 million-dollar tanker, drawing forty feet of water, was only forty miles into her maiden voyage, and was in imminent danger of self-destructing on the very shores that spawned her.

Ile d'Quessant—Ushant to the English—is the most westerly point of France, a steep, craggy island four miles long by two miles wide. Surrounded by jagged rocks, it marks the northern extremity of the infamous Bay of Biscay, and has for centuries been a landmark for ships entering and leaving the English Channel. At the north-western end of the island, on Creach Point, stands one of the most powerful lighthouses in the world, its multi-million candle power light being visible on a clear dark night as far as fifty miles out into the Atlantic. As one of the major crossroads of the seas, in sight of which hundreds of ships pass daily on their separate ways, it is seldom that there is not an ocean-going salvage tug within easy reach of Ushant, ready to come to the aid of a stricken ship.

If, after the *Olympic Bravery*'s first blackout, Captain Efstratios had contacted the 479-ton German salvage tug *Heros*, which he knew to be on station in Brest, all might not have been lost. But Efstratios procrastinated. After the fifth blackout, at about 06.45, he sent Chief Officer Mantis Margaritis and a party of seamen forward to let go the port anchor. The vessel was then in fifty fathoms, an unrealistic depth in which to attempt to anchor in a howling gale. Margaritis dropped the anchor on the bottom and began to pay out the cable, but the drift of the ship was such that, as soon as the anchor took hold, the strain on the windlass was so great that the brakes would not hold. All 210 fathoms of cable ran out from the locker and were lost overboard, Margaritis and his men narrowly escaped decapitation as the end of the cable whipped across the forecastle head on its way out of the hawsepipe.

When it was again safe to return to the forecastle head, Margaritis let go the starboard anchor and paid out to forty-five fathoms. The anchor gripped the bottom, held momentarily, and then began to drag. The shoreward drift of the *Olympic Bravery* continued.

It was only now that Efstratios finally concluded that he must call for outside help, but he still could not bring himself to broadcast a Mayday on VHF or an SOS by W/T. He preferred to go through the ridiculous rigmarole of making a radio-telephone call to the offices of Olympic Maritime, 700 miles away in Monte Carlo. The upshot of this call, which lasted for eleven minutes, was that Olympic Maritime contacted the tug *Heros* in Brest and requested she go to the tanker's aid.

By 07.35, the *Olympic Bravery*'s engine was again running, but only ticking over at a negligible sixteen rpm. The *Heros* had left Brest, and was steaming at full speed towards Ushant, giving an ETA of 09.00. Efstartios was in touch with the tug's master by VHF and had agreed to assistance on the basis of Lloyd's Open Form, which is simply a 'no cure, no pay' agreement. All that was now needed was for the tanker's engine-room to produce a few more revolutions over a sustained period, and perhaps the ship could at least be brought up into the wind and her shoreward drift stopped. It was not to be.

Five minutes later, the seventh and final blackout occurred, and the *Olympic Bravery* again lost all motive power. This time she was so close to the rocks that the thunder of the breaking waves could be clearly heard above the noise of the storm. Efstratios now accepted the inevitable and ordered the boilers to be shut down, the engine-room evacuated and sent his crew to their lifeboat stations.

The 277,599-tonne *Olympic Bravery* was thrown ashore on the north coast of Ushant at 08.07, close in to Creach Point. Her starboard quarter struck first, a sharp fang of rock penetrating her No.7 cargo tank with such force that the heavy tank lid was lifted off. The rock held her and she swivelled beam-on, so that her entire starboard side was soon grinding on submerged rocks, tearing open her shell plating like so much thin parchment. Between the ship and the shore lay a maelstrom of white water, interspersed with black pinnacles of rock, some of them up to sixty feet high.

Another three hours were to pass before the tug *Heros*, after a hard battle against wind and sea, arrived on the scene. By then it was too late for her to do more than stand by and watch the slow death of a great ship.

A number of half-hearted attempts were made to refloat the *Olympic Bravery,* but they were all doomed from the start. She was firmly impaled on the rocks, but rising and falling on the swells with a discordant screech of tortured metal accompanying her slow destruction. Far from moderating, the weather worsened—for this was winter North Atlantic at its worst—and by the 30th all crew and salvage personnel had been taken off by helicopter and the ship was abandoned to the forces of nature which had claimed her.

The Liberian Commissioner of Maritime Affairs held an official inquiry into the loss of the *Olympic Bravery,* at which it was concluded: *'On the evidence that is available, it is not possible to determine the cause of the successive blackouts which immobilised Olympic Bravery off Ushant on the morning of the 24th January, 1976...Accordingly one can only speculate and attempt a choice between possible causes. In all such causes, some concealed act of sabotage could have been responsible. In a case like the present, it could be even suggested that it would have been to the Owners' financial advantage to procure the loss of the ship...'*

The latter suggestion was dismissed out of hand by the court, but no effort was made to explain why a ship built to the highest standards, under expert supervision, and by a very reputable shipyard, should experience such cataclysmic difficulties in the early stages of her maiden voyage. She had undergone no less than six comprehensive sea trials, yet from the time of disembarking the pilot off Pte St. Mathieu her main engine was never able to deliver the required revolutions. This, it was later claimed, was due to the operation of the ballast pumps starving the engine of steam. In view of the size of the VLCC's boilers, this was an excuse that plainly could not be substantiated. As to the continuing blackouts that led to the stranding of the ship, these were almost certainly caused by a malfunction of the automatic control switches on the boilers, as had been demonstrated on two occasions before the ship was handed over by the builders. If this fault could not be rectified at sea, it should have been a simple matter to override the switches and operate the boilers in manual control. There is no evidence that this simple procedure was even contemplated by the tanker's engineers.

The decision to take the *Olympic Bravery* to within five miles of Ushant, one of the world's most notorious graveyards of ships, with a north-westerly gale blowing onshore and an unreliable main engine, must also be questioned. Once clear of Pte St. Mathieu, the whole of the wide Atlantic was open to her, and under the circumstances prevailing, it would have been prudent to give Ushant a very wide berth. The last-minute attempt to anchor was amateurish in the extreme, and doomed to failure. But an even greater omission was to refuse to call for tugs when the first blackout occurred at 05.45. The ship was already in great danger, and a rescue operation should have been initiated without delay. Instead, precious time was wasted by telephoning the office in Monte Carlo, and this procrastination proved fatal for the *Olympic Bravery.*

The astounding conclusion reached by the Liberian court of inquiry into the stranding and loss of the *Olympic Bravery* was that no charges should be laid against any of those who sailed in her, her owners, or her managers. The very untimely end of this great ship must therefore have been attributable to the actions of no man, but to an act of God. Magnanimous though the Almighty might be, it is most unlikely he would agree to accept the blame in this case.

It is of some small compensation that no member of the *Olympic Bravery*'s crew lost his life, but the sorry affair was not to be concluded without casualties. In March of that year, a French Navy helicopter checking for oil pollution from the wreck crashed into the sea and its crew of four was lost.

Various attempts were made to salvage the VLCC, but without success. She was eventually declared a constructive total loss, and the underwriters handed her reluctant owners a cheque for fifty million dollars. In August 1977 it was reported that a Marseilles scrap merchant had bought the wreck for the sum of one franc, but no work was ever done on the ship.

Today, the bones of the *Olympic Bravery* still lie off Creach Point, a monument to a once proud ship that nobody wanted, and whose passing was mourned only by those who underwrote her insurance and the men of Chantiers de l'Atlantique who built her.

40   One for the Record

Venoil & Venpet— 1977

On an early December morning in 1977, the towlines of Kharg Island's powerful tugs sang in unison as, inch by inch, they dragged a huge, deep-laden VLCC from its berth at the Iranian oil terminal. The massive tanker was then slowly canted until her squat bows lined up with the buoyed channel leading out to sea. Her 36,000 horse power turbines rumbled into life and the thin pencil of black smoke reaching skywards from her funnel thickened and began to drift astern. High on the bridge of the tanker, Captain Shing-Pao Zia leaned out over the rail and drew a nervous breath as the propeller took a grip on the shallow water, sending clouds of disturbed mud and sand eddying up around the stern. Zia, who was making his first voyage in command of a VLCC (Very Large Crude Carrier), had good reason to feel apprehensive. The 334,030-ton *Venoil*, 1,115 feet long and 176 feet in the beam, was loaded to her maximum draught of eighty feet with 307,045 tons of Iranian crude. Her destination, Point Tupper, Nova Scotia, lay almost 12,000 miles away, on the edge of the Canadian pack ice.

At her loaded speed of thirteen and a half knots, it would take the *Venoil* almost forty-eight hours to steam the length of the Persian Gulf. By reason of her deep draught (she was drawing over thirteen fathoms of water) this would be a passage fraught with danger. The Gulf, once famous only for its pirates and pearls, is strewn with coral banks, more than one third of its area having a depth of less than twenty fathoms. In the deep-water channels traffic is heavy and oil rigs and drilling platforms, many of them uncharted and unlit, abound. Once through the Straits of Hormuz, life would be easier for Captain Zia. The *Venoil* was too big and too heavily loaded to pass through the Suez Canal and her only route to Nova Scotia lay via the Cape of Good Hope, a long, tedious voyage occupying up to five weeks but, for the most part, in deep water and favourable weather.

The sun, which shone down so brilliantly on the *Venoil* as she left the bustle of Kharg Island astern, was then only just rising on her sister ship. Far on the other side of the African continent, the 333,935-ton *Venpet* was in mid-Atlantic, returning to Kharg Island in ballast after delivering a cargo to Point Tupper.

With the exception of the slight difference in deadweight tonnage, the two VLCCs were identical in all respects. Built in 1973 at Nagasaki for the Bethlehem Steel Corporation of America, they were, as a matter of economic convenience, registered in Monrovia and flew the Liberian flag. They had been launched at the height of the oil boom, when charter rates were as much as eight times the cost of transportation of oil. As soon as they were ready for sea, they had been taken on a long-term charter by the Gulf Oil Corporation and placed on the Kharg Island-Point Tupper run. Each tanker carried a Taiwanese crew of forty, the masters and officers holding Liberian licences. Navigational equipment in the ships was of the highest standard and included Decca Navigator, which is capable of accurately fixing a ship's position to within fifty yards.

Commanded by Captain Chung-Ming Sun, the *Venpet* had sailed from Point Tupper on the evening of 19 November. There had been no time to clean and gas-free her tanks following the discharge of her last cargo. This operation Captain Sun intended to carry out in the Indian Ocean, where the warmer water would make it easier. Meanwhile, the dirty tanks had been filled with an inert gas to combat the threat of explosion posed by the remaining hydrocarbon gases.

It had been planned to make the long voyage to the Persian Gulf without interruption. However, the *Venpet*'s main radio transmitter had failed shortly after sailing, forcing Captain Sun to schedule an off-limits call at Cape Town, where a helicopter would be standing by to fly out radio technicians and spares. Sun was fully justified in initiating this action—costly though it might be—for in the world of the oil charter markets good communications between ship and shore are of paramount importance. A working radio would also be useful to contact and exchange intelligence with the westbound *Venoil*, which Sun expected to meet somewhere off the coast of South Africa.

The *Venpet*'s passage across the South Atlantic passed without incident and, at 10.00 on the morning of 15 December, a rendezvous was made with the helicopter off Cape Town. Two radio technicians were landed on the tanker and at once set about repairing her faulty transmitter. In order to avoid delay to the passage, it was arranged that these men would be taken off by launch when the *Venpet* passed Durban, some three days later.

Cape Agulhas, the southernmost point of Africa, was rounded at about 16.00 that afternoon and Captain Sun, with the projected off-limits call at Durban in mind, shaped his course to pass to the north of the Alphard Banks, an extensive area of shoals lying some thirty miles off the coast and forty-five miles east of Agulhas. In doing so, Sun was ignoring a South African recommendation that all ships on the coast 'keep to the right', eastbound ships passing further south than those westbound. After passing the Alphard Banks, the *Venpet* was therefore directly in the path of westbound vessels—and there were many of these in the oil-boom days of the late 1970s. But, given that the *Venpet* was equipped with two good radars and summer at the Cape promised blue skies and clear visibility all the way, Sun did not anticipate any navigational difficulties.

Running south at the height of the balmy north-east Monsoon, the *Venoil*'s passage down the Indian Ocean had been pleasant and trouble-free. On a daily basis her radio officer had been attempting to make contact with the *Venpet*, but without success. By the morning of the 16th, the *Venoil* was to the west of Port Elizabeth and Captain Zia was puzzled by the continued lack of word from the *Venpet*, which by now he expected to be close at hand.

In compliance with South African regulations for loaded tankers, the *Venoil* was steaming at a minimum distance of twelve miles off the coast. The weather was fine, with a clear blue sky and a breeze so light it barely disturbed the oily calm of an even bluer sea. Visibility was excellent. There was, however, an ominous, damp chill in the morning air. It did not occur to Second Officer Jen-Tsao Yang, who had the watch on the bridge, that a dangerous mix of the elements was at work. Zia, when he came to the bridge, also failed to recognise the warning signs. With a quick look around the empty horizon, he set a course of 267°, which would take the *Venoil* to the north of the Alphard Banks and twelve miles south of Cape Agulhas.

Over the horizon, sixty-seven miles to the west, the *Venpet* was in similarly idyllic weather and steaming at full speed on a course of 084°. Unknown to each other, the two 330,000-ton sisters were lined up on almost directly opposite courses and closing at a combined speed of twenty-seven knots.

Third Officer Burt-Chao Chang took over the bridge of the *Venoil* at 08.00. By then, the volatile mixture of low temperature and high humidity had been sufficiently stirred by the gentle breeze and the once sharp horizon was blurring. Soon, the visibility was down to seven miles and occasional fog patches were rolling in on the deep-laden tanker as she pushed steadily westwards. During the next hour, Captain Zia paid several visits to the bridge but ignored the obvious deterioration in the visibility. His prime interest lay in calculating an accurate ETA off Cape Town where, on the following morning, the *Venoil* was to rendezvous with a helicopter bringing mail and fresh provisions—a welcome morale booster for the crew at the halfway point of the voyage.

At 08.45, Third Officer Chang drew Zia's attention to an echo on the radar screen fine on the *Venoil*'s port bow at twenty-two miles. This appeared to be a large ship approaching from the west on a parallel and opposite course. Twenty minutes later, the echo of the other ship was down to thirteen miles and the bearing on the bow had opened by only two degrees. Neither Chang nor Zia thought it necessary at this point to take avoiding action.

On the bridge of the eastbound *Venpet*, Third Officer Jan-Syi Ju had the watch. From the time he had taken over, at 08.00, the visibility had been falling steadily and now stood at about seven miles. The radar screen showed the echo of a large ship ahead and two or three degrees on the *Venpet*'s starboard bow. Ju did not consider the circumstances warranted calling Captain Sun, who had not yet appeared on the bridge that morning.

At 09.10, the *Venoil* suddenly ran into dense fog, which had been forming in the cold air since shortly before sunrise. Within the space of a few seconds, the long foredeck of the VLCC had all but disappeared from sight and the great ship was sliding through a silent world of opaque whiteness disturbed only by the high-pitched whine of her turbines. A glance at the radar showed Captain Zia that the other vessel was now at eight and a half miles, with very little change in the angle on the bow. With a non-committal shrug of his shoulders, he turned away from the radar and informed Chang he was going below to consult with the radio officer on ship to helicopter communications.

Left alone on the bridge, Third Officer Chang studied the radar screen intently and, at long last, decided the other ship was shaping to pass dangerously close. After some hesitation, he altered course five degrees to starboard, intending to pass port to port.

On the bridge of the *Venpet*, also now in dense fog, Third Officer Ju was likewise at last becoming concerned for the safety of his ship. Unlike Chang, he judged a starboard to starboard passing would be in order and made an alteration of five degrees to port. A deadly game of blind man's buff, with two 330,000 tonners participating, had begun.

Over the following twenty minutes, each ship made a number of small alterations of course, the westbound *Venoil* always to starboard and the eastbound *Venpet* always to port. On their respective bridges, Chang and Ju were each convinced they were altering away from the danger. In fact, the giant tankers, both steaming at full speed and hidden from each other by the fog, were locked into what is known in nautical parlance as a 'culminative turn'—a manoeuvre which could only end in disaster.

At 09.30, with the radar echo of the other ship so close it was merging with the sea clutter at the centre of the screen, Chang ordered full starboard helm in a last desperate attempt to swing the *Venoil* away from the danger he could not yet see. It was too late. The whiteness of the fog ahead slowly darkened, and then abruptly parted to reveal a great, slab-sided, rust-streaked hull looming in the path of the *Venoil*'s bows.

The *Venoil* crashed into the starboard side of the *Venpet* and, with her protruding bower anchor acting like a sharp-pointed horn, ripped open her sister from amidships to her engineroom. Showers of brilliant sparks shot into the air to fall lazily back onto the thousands of gallons of oil spurting from the ruptured cargo tanks of the *Venoil*.

The supertanker 'Venoil' on fire off Cape Aghulas

(Photo: Trace Images)

Soon, both ships and the sea around them were a mass of leaping flames.

Fortunately for the crews of the Liberian tankers, two British ships, the *Jedforest* and the *Clan Menzies* were close by. With the aid of a helicopter from a nearby oil rig, all but two of the eighty-two men on board the burning ships were rescued. Those who died, the chief fireman and second cook of the *Venoil*, lost their lives when they jumped into the blazing sea.

Salvage tugs sent out from Cape Town eventually extinguished the fires and took the crippled VLCCs in tow. But little could be done about the 26,000 tons of crude oil that poured into the sea from the *Venoil*'s ruptured tanks. For many weeks after the collision, an oil slick six miles by two miles drifted off the beautiful holiday beaches of South Africa's famed Garden Route coastline, causing pollution on a huge scale.

The *Venoil/Venpet* clash should never have happened. It was a classic example of the misuse of modern technology by those who neither understand it nor have the ability to control it. Even though they had been in sight of each other on radar from twenty-two miles, at no time did either of these sophisticatedly equipped ships make a bold alteration of course away from the other. If only one of them had done so the disaster would have been avoided. Furthermore, at no time during the forty-five-minute run-up to the collision did the two tankers attempt to contact each other on VHF radio. This they could easily have done and come to an agreement on the avoiding action each ship would take. When in fog, with visibility down to fifty yards, neither vessel reduced speed or sounded fog signals, thereby ignoring the basic international rules governing the navigation of ships in poor visibility.

It may be argued that Third Officer Chang of the *Venoil*, and Third Officer Ju of the *Venpet* were inexperienced junior officers and might be forgiven for a lack of appreciation of the developing situation. But the same cannot be said for Captain Zia and Captain Sun. Both these men, and Captain Zia in particular, must have been well aware of the mounting danger to their vessels yet, for some inexplicable reason, both chose to ignore this danger. When the *Venoil* and *Venpet* finally ran headlong into each other, Captain Zia was drinking tea in the Chief Officer's cabin, while Captain Sun was ensconced in the chartroom oblivious to the drama being played out in the *Venpet*'s wheelhouse, only a few feet and a bulkhead away from him.

After lengthy and costly repairs, the *Venoil* and *Venpet* returned to service, only to disappear into obscurity when the oil boom self-destructed a few years later. Today, they are remembered only by an entry in the Guinness Book of Records, where they are accorded the distinction of being participants in the world's largest ever collision.

The damaged stern of the supertanker 'Venpet'

(Photo: Trace Images)

Bernard Edwards

41   The 76-Million-Gallon Oil Slick

Aegean Captain & Atlantic Empress - 1979

In the 18th century, the Caribbean island of Tobago, twenty-five
miles north of Trinidad, was little more than a pirate's watering
hole, often playing host to the infamous 'Calico' Jack Rackham
and Edward 'Blackbeard' Teach. Today, its luxury hotels and silver-
sand beaches cater for nothing more threatening than clusters of
America's sun-seeking tourists. When, in the late afternoon of 20
July 1979, the 210,257-ton supertanker *Aegean Captain* passed off
the northern shores of the island, heading eastwards into the
Atlantic, it is unlikely the affluent on their sun-loungers gave her
more than a cursory glance. Had they but known the threat this ship
was to pose to the island only a few hours later, the tranquillity of
their afternoon would have been rudely shattered.

The *Aegean Captain*, was loaded to her marks with 200,000 tons
of crude oil, shipped at Bonaire in the Caribbean and destined for
Singapore, 11,000 miles and two oceans away. Owned by the
Quadrant Shipping Company of Monrovia and flying the Liberian
flag, the 1,066-foot-long tanker carried a mainly Greek crew of thirty-five. On her bridge as she steamed alongside the palm-fringed
beaches of Tobago, was her chief officer Mr S. Laoudis, and at his side
Fourth Officer Piscopianos. The weather was fine, with a fresh easterly breeze carrying away the heat of the day, but on the horizon
ahead loomed a line of towering cumulo-nimbus, heavy with rain.
The ship's helm was in automatic pilot and one of her radars was
operating on the twelve-mile range.

Thirty miles to the south-east, on the other side of the rain
clouds, the 292,666-ton *Atlantic Empress* was heading in to make her
landfall off Tobago. Loaded with 307,000 tons of naphthalene from
the Persian Gulf, she had just over 2,000 miles to go to her port of
discharge, Beaumont, Texas. Owned by the Branco Shipping
Company of Monrovia, she carried a crew of forty, including three
officer's wives. All were Greek nationals. Her cargo of naphthalene
was classed as 'dangerous', having a flash point of below 23°
Centigrade—the flashpoint of an oil being the lowest temperature at
which vapour given off by the oil will explode when a flame is
applied to it. With the air temperature in the area being close to 32°
Centigrade, the *Atlantic Empress's* cargo was therefore in a highly

volatile state.

The officer of the watch on the bridge of the *Atlantic Empress* as she approached the land was not, as would be expected in the circumstances, her chief officer. In sole charge of the navigation of this 1,139-foot-long, deep-laden vessel was her forty-seven-year-old radio officer, Zacharis Anagnostiadis who, while he was said to take an interest in navigation, had no training or qualification in the subject. The ship's helm was in automatic and one radar was switched on and scanning on the forty-eight-mile range, in which mode it would be extremely difficult to detect ships close by. At frequent intervals, Anagnostiadis would leave the bridge to attend to his other duties in the radio room. During his absences, the ship was left in the hands of the able seaman on bridge lookout.

When the sun went down, shortly after 18.30, the tropical night closed in quickly, and it should have been obvious to those on the bridge of the *Aegean Captain* that the visibility would soon be restricted by rain. No other ships were visible on the radar screen, but the rainsqualls ahead were showing as a dense white curtain several miles thick, through which the radar pulses could not penetrate. The warning was clear that the tanker was moving towards a potentially dangerous situation. The course of action to be taken in such a case is clearly laid down by the International Collision Regulations, which state: *'Every vessel shall proceed at a safe speed adapted to the prevailing circumstances and conditions of restricted visibility. A power-driven vessel shall have her engines ready for immediate manoeuvre'*. The *Aegean Captain* continued to press on at full speed and Chief Officer Laoudis took no action to warn the engineroom. Nor did he use the anti-clutter controls of the radar to attempt to pierce the approaching wall of rain.

Some fifteen miles away, the *Atlantic Empress* was already in rain; as yet only a fine drizzle, but the visibility was falling steadily. Radio Officer Anagnostiadis, like his opposite number on the bridge of the *Aegean Captain*, took no action, other than to, once more, leave the ship in the hands of the lookout while he attended to unspecified duties in the radio room. When Anagnostiadis returned to the bridge, the naphthalene tanker's radar, which remained on the forty-eight-mile range, was showing a faint outline of the island of Tobago near the outer edge of the screen. The white clutter at the centre of the screen, caused by the advancing rainsqualls, effectively obscured any target which might have been within ten miles of the ship. Anagnostiadis made no move to switch to a shorter range, which would have been more revealing.

In the officers' accommodation below the bridge of the *Atlantic Empress*, the scene was reminiscent of a small community ashore settling down for an evening's relaxation after the day's work. Dinner was over and most of the off-duty officers had retired to the lounge to watch a film. Chief Officer Psilogenis and his wife sat side by side engrossed in the film. Captain Chatzipetros, uninterested in the Hollywood offering, had found a willing opponent in Second Engineer Laspitis and the two men were huddled over a backgammon board in the officers' smoke-room. Meanwhile, the 292,666-ton *Atlantic Empress*, with her seventy-million-gallon lake of highly volatile spirit, moved on through the night at fourteen knots, watched over only by her radio officer/navigator.

At 18.45, Second Engineer Laspitis returned to the engineroom and Captain Chatzipetros was left without a backgammon opponent. He decided to pay a visit to the bridge. Entering the wheelhouse, he first occupied himself in fixing the vessel's position by radar, using a bearing and distance off Tobago. Having done this, he idly flicked up and down the radar ranges, checking for the presence of other ships. On the three-mile range, the screen was completely obscured by rain clutter and Chatzipetros gave up the quest in disgust. He then left the wheelhouse to join Radio Officer Anagostiadis, who was standing alone in the starboard wing, the lookout having gone below for a coffee break.

It was now 19.00 and the rain was thickening, severely restricting the visibility. Anagnostiadis had not yet reduced speed, nor had he seen fit to warn the engineroom. Once he had acquainted himself with the situation, Captain Chatzipetros likewise decided no precautionary action was necessary. The two men stood side by side, chatting amiably and occasionally peering into the blackness of the night.

Three miles away, the *Aegean Captain* was in a blinding rainstorm, with visibility down to less than half a mile. On her bridge, the routine had not changed. The radar screen was completely obscured by rain clutter, but Chief Officer Laoudis had not reduced speed, was not sounding the ship's whistle as required by the collision regulations, and he had not yet called the master to the bridge. The 200,000-tonner ploughed on unseen and unseeing.

At a few minutes past 19.00, Captain Chatzipetros, still chatting with Anagnostiadis on the bridge of the *Atlantic Empress*, suddenly became aware of the lights of another ship showing dimly through the rain fine on the starboard bow. For a few seconds, Chatzipetros froze, then he hurled himself into the wheelhouse, an anguished prayer on his lips. Quickly, he knocked the helm out of automatic and put the wheel hard to port. It was too late. The *Aegean Captain* and the *Atlantic Empress*, totalling between them almost three quarters of a million tons weight, crashed into each other at a combined speed of twenty-eight knots.

The holocaust that followed enveloped both ships. Oil poured from the ruptured forward tanks of the *Aegean Captain* and this was immediately ignited by the burning naphthalene spurting from the huge gash in the hull of the *Atlantic Empress*. Soon, the giant ships and the sea around them were enveloped in roaring flames. Men cried out in fear, women screamed.

Reaction aboard the *Aegean Captain* was fast. Radio Officer Haralobos, who was at his correct post in the radio room, rapped out an SOS even as the order was given to abandon ship. A lifeboat and a life-raft were launched on the port side, away from the flames, and the crew were evacuated within a few minutes of the collision. Only one man, the ship's electrician, was lost.

On the *Atlantic Empress*, which now resembled an enormous funeral pyre, chaos reigned. Captain Chatzipetros was trapped on the bridge by the flames but gave the order to abandon ship over the public address system. His crew, with the exception of two engineers who had been killed in the initial explosion, rushed to the boat deck. As no boat drill had ever been held on board the tanker, the ensuing struggle to launch a lifeboat was doomed from the start. When the boat did hit the water crowded with thirty-seven people, it began to sink, for the drain plugs had not been replaced before lowering. By the time this was rectified, the boat was half-full of water, adding to the misery of the frightened wretches it held. And their nightmare had only just begun. In the panic to get away, no one had thought to stop the ship's engines and the forward momentum was such that it was impossible to slip the lifeboat's falls. The waterlogged craft was dragged along by the burning tanker, unable to break free. When the burning oil on the water began to creep up from astern, slowly overtaking the boat, the survivors took to the sea, hoping to swim clear. By the time the rescue ships arrived, only fourteen were still alive, the rest having been drowned, burned alive or taken by sharks. Captain Chatzipetros, although badly burned, survived. Zacharis Angnostiadis perished.

When dawn came next day, the two super-tankers were locked together and still burning furiously. They were only seven miles off Tobago and drifting towards the island. Drifting with them was an oil slick fifteen miles long and three miles across, estimated to contain 76.2 million gallons. After a grim fight, salvagemen separated the burning ships and the fire on the *Aegean Captain* was extinguished. She was towed into port, only to be declared a total loss and written off as scrap. The *Atlantic Empress* burned on for another two weeks, before blowing up and sinking in deep water. To the great relief of those ashore, a benevolent wind steered the oil slick away from the beaches of Tobago and the island's lucrative tourist industry continued to flourish.

Three thousand miles to the east of Tobago, in a back street in the Liberian port of Monrovia, the brass plates of the Quadrant and Branco shipping companies were quietly removed, for they had both lost their only ship. But the demise of Quadrant and Branco went unnoticed. Monrovia, a run-down, pseudo-American port of 150,000 inhabitants, is home to no less than 2,500 separate shipping companies, one for every sixty of its abysmally poor people. Fanciful names like All Oceans Shipping Co., Carnival Carriers Inc. and Golden Fortune Steamship Inc. fill the pages of Monrovia's phone book, conjuring up an image of a shipping Eldorado once enjoyed by the Liverpools of the Western World. But, contrary to expectations, seldom is the heavy chink of gold dollars heard in this land of the freed slaves. Liberia, which has fifty-two million tons of merchant shipping registered under its flag—nearly six times that under the Red Ensign—is the poorest country in West Africa.

42   The Return of the Pirates

Salem - 1980

In January 1722, off the coast of West Africa, Bartholomew Roberts, the most successful pirate of all times, died as he had lived, hurling his ship against a vastly superior foe. The death of Roberts, and the subsequent mass hanging of his crew at Cape Coast Castle, signalled the end of organised piracy in African waters—or so it was thought.

Two hundred and fifty-eight years later, on the morning of 17 January, 1980, the 275,333-ton super-tanker *British Trident* was steaming north ninety-four miles off the coast of Senegal. At 10.50 her lookout sighted a pall of black smoke low down on the horizon and the tanker altered course to investigate. An hour later she was in sight of a large Liberian-flag tanker, which appeared to be burning fiercely. As the *British Trident* moved in, the other ship lifted her bow and slipped beneath the waves, leaving only two crowded lifeboats in her wake.

Without hesitation, Captain Robert Taylor, master of the *British Trident*, stopped his vessel and sent away a rescue boat. This soon returned with the sunken Liberian's lifeboats in tow and containing the entire crew of twenty-four of the unfortunate ship. It seemed that what might have been another ghastly maritime tragedy had been averted by the timely arrival of the British tanker.

The tale told by the crew of the sunken ship, the 213,928-ton tanker *Salem*, was a harrowing one. Their ship, they claimed, had been on passage from Kuwait to Italy with 193,000 tons of crude oil when, shortly before 04.00 on 16 January, an explosion occurred in the pump room, which resulted in the engineroom flooding. The order was given to abandon ship and all crew members had taken to the lifeboats by 04.30. For the next thirty-two hours they drifted in sight of their ship and watched helplessly as she burned. The end finally came at 09.00 on the 17th, when a violent explosion ripped the bottom out of the *Salem* and she began to sink.

With all the survivors safely on board, Captain Taylor made for Dakar to land them, but he was already having misgivings about his passengers, a mixture of Greeks and Tunisians. When taken on board the *British Trident*, they appeared to be in remarkably good spirits for men who had been through the trauma of abandoning a burning tanker, followed by thirty-two hours adrift in lifeboats, even though the weather was mercifully calm. Furthermore, there was not a smudge of oil or dirt on any of them and they were dressed in their best 'shore-going' clothes. It was also clear to Taylor that the evacuation of the sinking ship must have been a most leisurely affair, as the survivors seemed to be carrying most of their personal possessions, including large amounts of money and duty-free cigarettes in suitcases, boxes and briefcases. The lifeboats were also well stocked with food over and above the standard emergency rations—someone had even found time to make sandwiches. As to the ship's papers, all these had been saved, except the vital log book, which should have described events leading up to the sinking. There were many eyebrows raised on board the *British Trident* as she headed for port.

Then there was the question of the oil slick—or lack of it—left behind by the *Salem* when she sank. Taylor estimated the slick to be three miles long by half a mile across and of very thin consistency. For a ship reputed to have been loaded with 193,000 tons of Kuwaiti crude oil, her sinking had caused very little pollution. This led the British master to wonder why it was that no distress message from the *Salem* had been picked up either by shore stations or the *British Trident*'s radio officer until the two ships were in sight of each other and only twenty-six minutes before the Liberian ship sank. The *British Trident* carried the most up-to-date VHF, W/T and R/T radio equipment, all of which was manned or monitored on a twenty-four hour basis, yet the first, and only, SOS had been heard from the *Salem*'s lifeboat transmitter. A chance remark by one of the Liberian's crew confirmed Captain Taylor's growing suspicions. The tanker had left her loading port, 9,000 miles away in the Persian Gulf, thirty-eight days before she sank. It did not require an expert navigator to calculate that the tanker had 'lost' ten or twelve days on her run around the Cape.

A few days later, when questioned by the authorities in Dakar, a Tunisian crew member of the *Salem* claimed that her cargo of crude oil had been unloaded in Durban and the ship deliberately scuttled in deep water to avoid discovery of the loss. This set in motion an investigation that was to last five years and involve in its intricate web so many parties in so many different countries it was almost impossible to sort out the innocent from the guilty. The *British Trident* had stumbled upon the biggest shipping fraud in history, a fraud motivated by greed, which also served dubious political ends.

In 1979, in an attempt to influence the South African government to end apartheid, the United Nations imposed an international oil embargo on that country. The Arab states of the Persian Gulf, from which most of South Africa's oil flowed, readily agreed to adhere strictly to the embargo, and it seemed likely the South African economy was doomed to grind to a halt within months. But, like all sanctions ever imposed, this was one made to be broken. The

Widow-Maker

Supertanker 'Salem'. *Photo taken when she was sailing under original name* 'Sea Sovereign'
(Photo: Source unknown)

South Africans, rich in gold and diamonds, had the money to pay for the oil—well over the odds, if necessary—and they were not about to see their country wrecked by a mere UN directive. The back-street offices of shady oil brokers in Europe and America began to hum with clandestine activity and, before long, the barely interrupted flow of crude oil to the refineries of South Africa had resumed. False declarations, forged cargo manifests and secret sales of oil on the high seas became the popular game of the day. In a seventeen-month period between 1979 and 1981, one Danish tanker company alone supplied a fifth of South Africa's oil needs.

On to the scene in December 1979 came a 213,928-ton VLCC (Very Large Crude Carrier), owned by the obscure Pimmerton Shipping Company of Monrovia and flying the Liberian flag. She entered the Persian Gulf bearing the name *South Sun*, but before she went alongside her loading berth at Kuwait, her name was changed to *Salem*, while her owners became the equally obscure Oxford Shipping Company of Monrovia. The groundwork had been laid for a gigantic sanctions-busting fraud.

When the powerful Kuwaiti tugs gently eased her alongside the berth at Mina Ál Ahmadi, the *Salem*, although owned on paper by Oxford Shipping, was on 'bareboat' charter to a company trading in Zurich under the name Shipomex. The terms of a bareboat charter are that the charterer hires the vessel for a specified period, appoints the master and crew, and pays all running expenses. Shipomex was, then, to all intents and purposes, the temporary owner of the *Salem.*

Appointed by Shipomex to command the *Salem* was a forty-three-year-old Greek, Captain Dimitrios Georgoulis. With him came Chief Officer Andrea Annivas, Chief Engineer Antonios

Kalomiropoulos, eleven other Greek officers, and ten Tunisian ratings. The *Salem* left Mina Al Ahmadi on 10 December, loaded with 193,132 tons of Kuwaiti crude oil destined, according to the cargo manifest, for Italy. The ship was said to be fully seaworthy, her hull being insured for £10.6 million and her cargo for £24.7 million, all carried on the London market by Lloyd's. She was too deep to go through the Suez Canal, her only route to Italy being via the Cape of Good Hope, a distance of 12,000 miles. At some time on the passage southwards through the Indian Ocean, the owners of her cargo, Pontoil of Lausanne, sold the oil to Shell International Trading of London for £25 million. The destination of the cargo was not changed in the course of this quite legal transaction.

Dimitrios Georgoulis and his motley crew of Greeks and Tunisians were a far cry from the swashbuckling Bartholomew Roberts and his men, who haunted the Gulf of Guinea two and a half centuries earlier. They carried neither pistol nor sword, nor did they prey on other ships. However, they were playing a variation of the same old game. Twelve days after clearing the Straits of Hormuz, aided by his crew, who had all been promised large bonuses to be paid in Swiss francs, Georgoulis took the ship into the South African port of Durban. Here the *Salem* was secured to a single-point mooring buoy, and in conditions of great secrecy, discharged her cargo of crude into the storage tanks of Sasol, the South African national oil company. On completion of discharge, the *Salem's* empty cargo tanks were filled with seawater, so that to any inquisitive eyes she would appear to be still fully loaded when she sailed from Durban.

Quite obviously, Georgoulis could not arrive at his destination in Italy with tanks full of worthless seawater, so the second part of the devious plan was put into action. The *Salem* proceeded around the Cape, and then northwards until she was 120 miles south-west of Dakar, Senegal. In this region, where the regular shipping lanes pass, the sea bottom plunges to over 2,000 fathoms, more than deep enough for even a ship as large as the *Salem* to sink without trace. Georgoulis was not, however, prepared to put the lives of himself and his crew in jeopardy. When in position, he stopped the *Salem* and waited for another ship to come along. As the masts and funnel of the *British Trident* lifted over the horizon, he set fire to the *Salem*, placed scuttling charges in her engine room and took to the boats. Once away from the burning tanker, the portable lifeboat transmitter was used to send out an SOS. It was a plan fraught with a certain amount of danger, but it might well have succeeded, had it not been for the suspicions of Captain Robert Taylor of the *British Trident*.

When Lloyd's, the insurers of the *Salem* and her cargo, received word of the deliberate sinking, Scotland Yard's Fraud Squad were called in. Lengthy inquiries followed, which resulted in warrants being issued for the arrest of Frederick Soudan, a Lebanese-born resident of Texas, said to be the owner of Oxford Shipping, Anton

Reidel, a Dutch businessman, Johannes Jurgen Locks, a company director of Frankfurt, and Captain Dimitrios Georgoulis. They were charged with conspiracy to defraud the underwriters of the value of the tanker and to defraud the consignees of the oil, Shell International, of the £25 million it paid for the *Salem*'s cargo. Unfortunately, as conspiracy is not normally an extraditable offence, none of these men could be brought to justice in a British court.

It was a stroke of bad luck for Georgoulis and his chief engineer, Antonios Kalomiropoulos, that they were detained in Dakar by the Senegal authorities on a charge of polluting the seas. The Liberian government, fearing its already tarnished reputation as a flag of convenience host might be irrevocably damaged, requested the extradition of the two seamen. Diplomatic strings were pulled, and the men were deported to Liberia in early March to face trial. If proven guilty of fraud, they would have been liable to spend ten years in a Liberian jail, a prospect which appealed to neither of them. The trial went on for some months, then fate intervened again. Liberia suffered a military *coup*, the country was thrown into confusion, and Georgoulis and Kalomiropoulis were set free. During the course of the trial, however, it had been established that Georgoulis had not been qualified to command the *Salem.* He was not in possession of a foreign-going master's certificate, either Greek or Liberian, although he claimed to have commanded small ships in the Mediterranean for some years. He also claimed to have a foreign-going first mate's certificate, but was unable to produce proof of this. Before the trial ended so abruptly, it came to light that the captain had been involved in three other cases of cargo theft involving considerable sums of money. Dimitrios Georgoulis was an experienced pirate.

The investigation into the loss of the *Salem* and her cargo dragged on and was eventually to involve a host of shadowy figures, six governments and as many police forces. In May 1984, Frederick Soudan was arrested in the United States and brought to trial in the following year. He was convicted and sentenced to thirty-five years in jail. Anton Reidel stood trial in a Dutch court in 1985, but was acquitted on all charges. Johannes Jurgen Locks also went free.

In February 1986, Dimitrios Georgoulis was finally brought before a court in Athens and found guilty of cargo fraud, endangering the lives of his crew and causing a shipwreck. He was jailed for twelve years. Antonios Kalomiropoulis, who confessed to being a party to the conspiracy, received a sentence of four years.

As to the unfortunate *Salem*, lying 2,000 fathoms deep in her dishonourable grave off the coast of West Africa, she also earned a place in the Guinness Book of World Records, being awarded the accolade of 'The Fraud of the Century'.

43   A Bridge Too Far

Derbyshire - 1980

The morning was bright and sunny when, on 11 July, 1980, the 169,044-tonne ore/bulk/oil carrier *Derbyshire* sailed from Seven Islands, on the St. Lawrence River, bound for Kawasaki in Japan. In her cavernous holds she carried a cargo of 157,447 tonnes of iron ore concentrates; ahead of her lay a voyage of 15,320 miles via the Cape of Good Hope and the Singapore Strait. It was estimated that, steaming at an economical speed of ten knots, the *Derbyshire* would arrive in Japan around 13 September. Many of her crew of forty-one, commanded by Captain Geoffrey Underhill, and including two officers' wives, were due for leave on arrival Japan. For them, the long passage could not pass quickly enough.

Built in 1976 by Swan Hunter and owned by the Bibby Line of Liverpool, the *Derbyshire* was equipped with the most up-to-date navigational aids, including two radars and satellite navigator. She was powered by a 30,400 horse power Burmeister & Wain engine of proven reliability and was one of a class of ships designed to fulfil a long felt need of the oil tanker operators, who were unhappy that their highly specialised and expensive vessels spent a great deal of their time running empty to the oilfields. The oil/bulk/ore carriers, or OBOs as they became known, were constructed with large, uncluttered holds, flanked on each side by oil cargo tanks. The optimum aim was for the ship to carry oil in her side tanks on one leg of the voyage and ore in her holds on the return passage, thereby earning freight for every hour spent at sea. Although the ideal balance was not always achieved, the OBOs did offer their owners a much greater flexibility in their choice of cargoes.

Twenty-seven days after leaving Seven Islands, the *Derbyshire* passed Cape Town, where she received fresh provisions and crew mail by helicopter. Once around the Cape of Good Hope, she moved into the Indian Ocean and set course to pass to the north of Sumatra. From that point she would run south-eastwards down the Malacca and Singapore Straits, and then into the South China Sea. It was the shallow waters of these straits that would present Captain Underhill with the first major challenge of the voyage, for his huge, unwieldy command was drawing in the region of fifty feet. However, his officers were well qualified and experienced and his navigational equip-

'Derbyshire' *This photograph shows her while sailing under*
her original name—'Liverpool Bridge'

ment of the best, so he had few qualms. When Singapore was astern,
the only real danger in the offing lay mainly in the South China Sea,
where the typhoon season would then be at its height. But here the
great size of the ship would be to her advantage. The *Derbyshire* was
964 feet long and 145 feet in the beam, a floating colossus quite
capable of standing up to the worst the elements might have to
throw at her.

True to form, when the *Derbyshire* was halfway across the South
China Sea, Japanese weather stations warned of a tropical depression
forming over the Caroline Islands, 1,200 miles east of the
Philippines. The depression would present no great hazard in its
early days, being similar in intensity to the gales that cross the
British Isles in winter. But Underhill was well enough versed in the
ways of the East to recognise this seemingly innocent area of low
pressure as the precursor of much worse to come. Sucking up energy
from the vast area of open water over which it moved, and inflamed
by the rising currents of warm air emanating from small islands and
coral reefs, the depression would first become a storm, and then a
typhoon, the Chinese 'Big Wind'. Being much smaller in diameter

than an Atlantic depression, a typhoon is that much more violent, often having winds of over 100 knots near its vortex, accompanied by mountainous seas and torrential rain. The course of a Pacific typhoon is more or less predictable, the eye of the storm usually moving first west-north-west at about ten knots towards the Philippines, then into the South China Sea to strike the Chinese mainland in the region of Hong Kong. Alternatively, the typhoon may re-curve before reaching the Philippines and sweep back to the north-east parallel to the coast of Japan.

When he received news of the embryo typhoon, Captain Underhill consulted his charts and calculated that, at his present speed of ten knots, and assuming the storm did not re-curve, the *Derbyshire* would meet it head-on in restricted waters between Luzon and Taiwan. This was not an inviting prospect. Accordingly, Underhill increased speed to twelve-knots to pass ahead of the storm. His action was proved correct when, at 11.00 on 4 September, the Ocean Routes Service advised him that the tropical depression was still moving west-north-west at ten knots and forecast to intensify. At her increased speed, the *Derbyshire* would pass about 200 miles off the eye of the storm when she was to the north of Luzon. This was close enough, but an acceptable risk.

Then the unpredictable happened. Typhoon Orchid, as it was named late on the 4th, re-curved and began to move north-north-west towards Okinawa. Had Orchid speeded up after re-curving, which is usually the case, the *Derbyshire* would have been quite safe moving along in the wake of the storm, adjusting her speed to keep out of range of the strongest winds. What followed is largely a matter of conjecture, but it seems that Orchid kept pace with the *Derbyshire* as she entered the Pacific. The great ship and the typhoon were moving relentlessly towards an unplanned rendezvous.

On the afternoon of the 9th, Underhill reported he was 300 miles south-east of Okinawa: '....WITH VESSEL HOVE TO IN VIOLENT STORM, WIND ENE FORCE 11; WAVE HEIGHT 30 FT; CONTINUOUS RAIN...' Three hours later, he informed his owners: 'NOW HOVE TO DUE TO SEVERE TROPICAL STORM: ESTIMATED TIME OF ARRIVAL KAWASAKI 14TH HOPEFULLY.' From then on there was complete silence, but no real anxiety was felt on shore for the ship's safety. She was considered too big to be in serious danger.

It was only when the *Derbyshire* failed to reach Kawasaki on the 14th, and an impatient consignee demanded to know the whereabouts of his cargo, that suspicions were aroused. Attempts were made to contact the ship by radio, but there was no reply. At daylight on the 15th, the Japanese Maritime Safety Agency organised an air and sea search along the ore carrier's planned course and in the area where she had last been reported. Orchid had by then swept across Honshu and into the Sea of Japan, but the heavy seas she left in her wake hampered the search. It was not until the 18th that a Japanese aircraft sighted a large oil slick near the *Derbyshire*'s last reported position. There was no wreckage and no sign of lifeboats or survivors. The worst was now accepted, and the thirty relief crew members and four officers' wives, including the wife of Captain Underhill, who had been waiting in Tokyo to join the ship, were quietly flown back to the UK. There would be no glasses raised, no joyous reunions for the *Derbyshire*.

Twenty-four hours passed and a Japanese search vessel reached the oil slick and reported oil welling up from below the surface. Samples of the oil were gathered and later compared with samples of bunker oil taken by the *Derbyshire* when she last refuelled in New York. The results of the tests were not conclusive, but the two oils were similar enough for it to be assumed they had both come from the same source. Another five weeks went by, then a Japanese tanker sighted an empty lifeboat drifting off the Philippines, 700 miles west-south-west of the search area. As the weather was still rough, the waterlogged boat could not be recovered, but the name *Derbyshire* and the port of registry Liverpool could be clearly read on the boat's sides. This was the only trace ever found of the 169,044-tonne *Derbyshire*.

It may never be known what catastrophic event overwhelmed the *Derbyshire*, for her crushed remains lie 6,000 fathoms deep in the Pacific, and there is no one left to tell of her last hours. An inquiry held by the Department of Trade in London reached the weighty conclusion that, in the absence of wreckage or survivors, the cause of the loss of the bulk carrier could not be established. On the basis of this finding, the Public Inquiry called for by the bereaved relatives of the *Derbyshire*'s crew was resisted. The Department recommended that research be carried out to establish the cause of the loss, but that was all. The relatives were not satisfied with this pronouncement and the fight for the truth continued in and out of the courts.

Four years later, on Tuesday, 18 November, 1986, the Minister of Transport dictated a letter to all interested parties declaring the *Derbyshire* incident finally and irrevocably closed. There was, he stated, no evidence to support holding a Public Inquiry; the forty-four missing men and women must be allowed to rest quietly in their watery grave. The Minister was not to know that, even as he dictated the letter, events happening in the Atlantic were about to blow his case sky high.

The 18th November was a bad day in the North Atlantic. With a deep low centred over Iceland, and a vigorous secondary depression tracking eastwards around the periphery of this low, winds to the west of Ireland were up to hurricane force and mountainous seas were running. Caught in this devil's cauldron, the 169,080-tonne ore/bulk/oil carrier *Kowloon Bridge* found herself running into serious difficulties. Loaded down to her marks with 160,000 tonnes of iron ore from Seven Islands, and bound for the Clyde, she had been bucking heavy seas throughout her Atlantic crossing. When, to the southwest of Ireland, the 970-ft-long vessel began to show signs of breaking up, her master, Captain S.T. Rao, decided to run for a port of refuge.

On the morning of the 20th, the Dutch-owned, Hong Kong-flag *Kowloon Bridge*, manned by Indian officers and Turkish ratings (a typical flag of convenience mongrel) anchored in Bantry Bay, a deepwater fjord in south-west Ireland. Surveyors who rushed to the scene discovered serious fractures in the deck of the giant bulk carrier immediately forward of her tall bridge structure. This more than justified Captain Rao's decision to seek shelter. It also opened up a can of wriggling worms which had remained tightly closed for four years, for it was revealed that the *Kowloon Bridge* was a sister ship of the *Derbyshire*.

It then came to light that, in the winter of 1982, the 169,428-tonne *Tyne Bridge*, another sister of the *Derbyshire*, had been abandoned by her crew in a storm in the North Sea. Fortunately, the *Tyne Bridge* did not sink, and after she had been towed into port an examination showed massive cracks in her deck plating, just forward of the bridge, the most vulnerable point in the vessel's hull. She had been very near to breaking in two.

It was now evident that the pedigree of the 'Bridge' class of ore/bulk/oil carriers required close scrutiny, and to do this it was necessary to go back fifteen years. Between 1971 and 1976, the renowned Swan Hunter yard in Middlesbrough built six OBOs in this class, all supposedly identical. However, it was now discovered that after the completion of the first ship, alterations were made in the approved plans with regard to the construction of the watertight bulkhead immediately forward of the bridge. This change was incorporated in the five other ships built, amongst which were the *Tyne Bridge,* the *Kowloon Bridge* and the *Derbyshire* (built as the *Liverpool Bridge*). Continuity of strength was sacrificed in the interests of economy by cutting the fore and aft bulkheads of these ships where they met the athwartships bridge front bulkhead. This created a crucial weakness in the longitudinal strength of the ships. It was also disclosed that a lighter grade of steel had been used in the building of the *Tyne Bridge*, and it seems highly likely that those who followed after her had suffered a similar economy.

All but one of the 'Bridge' class, it seems, had dangerous weaknesses, and, from the evidence gathered, it must be argued that the *Derbyshire* was not strong enough to withstand Typhoon Orchid. The continuous flexing of her 970-ft-long hull in the huge swells had caused her to break in two at her weakest point, which, due to the cutting of the longitudinal bulkheads, was just forward of the bridge. The stern part of the ship, which housed the heavy propulsion machinery, and on which the bridge and accommodation blocks stood, would have gone to the bottom in seconds, thereby accounting for the lack of any distress message.

The *Kowloon Bridge*, it appeared, had been narrowly saved from a similar fate by the decision of her master to take shelter in Bantry Bay. Unfortunately, the story did not end there. Bantry Bay lies open to the south-west, and when the wind shifted into that quarter, as it inevitably does, the anchored ore carrier was once again in danger. At 08.00 on 22 November, three days after her arrival, the *Kowloon Bridge* snapped her anchor cable. Captain Rao deemed it wise to put to sea again, rather than risk colliding with other ships sheltering in the bay.

It was with some difficulty that Rao took the *Kowloon Bridge* out of Bantry Bay, but his real troubles began when he reached the open sea, where the storm that had forced him to take refuge was still blowing unabated. At 14.23, Rao reported he was off Mizen Head, was battling against force 10 winds, and had already lost one of his inflatable liferafts overboard. Nine hours later, the *Kowloon Bridge*'s rudder carried away and, unable to steer, she was completely at the mercy of the great seas running in from the Atlantic. In response to her Mayday call, two RAF helicopters scrambled, and at 01.20 on the 23rd, Rao and his crew of twenty-seven were plucked to safety. The Sea King crews who risked their lives to bring off the rescue reported 75 mph winds, with the rudderless ore carrier rolling wildly in a mountainous, eighty-foot swell.

Left to her own devices and—such had been the panic to leave her—with her engines still running, the *Kowloon Bridge* sailed on through the fury of the storm for another twenty hours before finally running onto the Stags Rocks, near Baltimore on the wild coast of County Cork. She remains there to this day, a poignant reminder of the men and women of the *Derbyshire,* for whom there had been no rescue.

The years rolled by, but the relatives of those lost in the *Derbyshire* refused to accept that the ship had simply been overwhelmed by the power of the sea. The *Derbyshire Families Association*was formed and, supported by the seamen's union, it campaigned ceaselessly - but without success - for a government funded search for the wreck. But no significant progress was made until 1994, fourteen years after the loss of the *Derbyshire.* Then, despairing of the stubborn refusal of the politicians to act, the International Transport Workers Federation put up $500,000 to finance an expedition to probe the Pacific for the last resting place of the bulk carrier. In a seven-day-long underwater search covering 500 square miles of the ocean, the remains of the *Derbyshire* were finally found and identified two miles down and near the position of the oil slick seen after the ship disappeared. Predictably the money ran out before any serious investigation of the wreckage could be made, and other than the laying of a memorial plaque on the *Derbyshire's* forecastle head, nothing else was achieved.

It was not until the summer of 1997 that a newly-elected British government, anxious to show its caring face, authorised a $4.5 million underwater examination of the wreck. Woods Hole Oceanographic, who conducted the two-month-long investigation, took 137,000 underwater photographs, which were then evaluated by Department of Transport assessors. Their conclusions, published in March 1998, were far removed from those the *Derbyshire Families Association* had hoped to hear. In the opinion of the expert assessors, the *Derbyshire* was not lost through in inbuilt structural weakness searched out by the power of the sea, but through the negligence of the crew.

The probing eye of the Woods Hole's underwater camera had found an open hatchway near the sunken bulker's bow, this being clearly identifiable as the entrance to her forepeak store. The inference drawn was that this hatch had been accidentally left open, and the mountainous seas breaking over the bows during the typhoon had quickly flooded the forepeak store. This resulted in the ship taking a bow-down attitude, allowing subsequent seas coming aboard to land further aft, leading to the dislodging or smashing of the hatch covers of the forward holds. Progressively working from forward to aft, each hold was breached and flooded in turn. Eventually the *Derbyshire* simply sank under the weight of water she had taken on board.

This theory was most convenient, in that it exonerated everyone except the *Derbyshire* crew members, who were unable to defend themselves. It does not, however, explain why, if the sinking of the great ship had been a gradual process, as inferred, she failed to send out an SOS, or why the wreckage was found to be strewn over the ocean bed in some 2000 pieces. In fact, having put the loss of the *Derbyshire* down to an open forepeak hatch, the assessors went on to describe what they had seen through the underwater camera's lens as 'a picture of almost total destruction, with parts of this huge ship ripped apart, lying torn and crumpled on the sea bed'.

To this day, the loss of the 169,000-ton *Derbyshire* has not been satisfactorily explained, nor it seems will it ever be.

44   A Lamb to the Slaughter

Pacific Charger – 1981

The delicate cherry blossoms of Kyushu were in full bloom when, on 24 April 1981, the 10,242-ton bulk carrier *Pacific Charger* first wetted her keel in the blue waters of the ocean for which she was named. Built by Sasebo Heavy Industries, she had been constructed and equipped to the highest specifications of the Nippon Kaiji Kyokai, Japan's equivalent of Lloyd's Register. Her powerful diesel engines, which gave her a speed of 151/2 knots, ran sweetly and her paintwork shone. The *Pacific Charger* was a ship full of pride but destined to be dragged down into the very depths of ignominy by the complicated web of financial intrigue in which she found herself caught.

Delivered to the order of Ocean Chargers Ltd of Monrovia, a 'brass plate' subsidiary of the Kansai Shipping Company, the *Pacific Charger*, although Japanese-built and owned, took to the water under the flag of convenience of Liberia. Within days of her delivery, Ocean Chargers chartered her back to Kansai Shipping, who in turn contracted her to Crusader-Swire of Hong Kong to be engaged in their regular service between Japan and New Zealand. Further to cloud an already blurred situation, Kansai then appointed the Harmony Maritime Company of Taiwan to manage the ship. Harmony Maritime handed over the recruitment of the ship's crew to the Union Maritime Company of Taiwan and the Ocean Services Company of Hong Kong. The former was asked to supply Taiwanese officers and the latter Burmese ratings. By the time the ship sailed from Sasebo, no fewer than six different companies and five nations were involved in the destiny of the *Pacific Charger*.

Appointed to command the *Pacific Charger* on her maiden voyage was 57-year-old Captain Chiou Ruey Yang. Chinese-born Chiou had spent twenty-two years in fishing-vessels and small coastal ships before being awarded, without examination, a Taiwanese ocean-going master's licence. On the strength of this licence, plus the payment of $20 US, he subsequently obtained a Liberian master's certificate and was therefore, in the eyes of the international marine community, qualified to command any deep-sea ship under the Liberian flag. He had no radar training, and his knowledge of English, *lingua franca* of the sea, was extremely limited.

In comparison, the master of a British ocean-going merchant ship must hold a British foreign-going master's certificate, which he mat gain only after serving at least seven and a half years at sea. The examinations for this certificate, which cover all aspects of navigation, seamanship and ship-management, last a gruelling five days, and a seventy percent pass-mark is required. Particular attention is paid to the operation and application of radar and other electronic navigational aids. It is normal that, after obtaining his master's certificate, a man will serve another ten or twelve years as watch-keeping officer, finally gaining his command, if he is judged suitable, with at least twenty years experience of deep-sea sailing behind him.

Captain Chiou's deputy in the *Pacific Charger* was First Mate Chang Yung Chung, aged forty-three, who had previously sailed as first mate in Liberian and Panamanian ships. He held a Liberian first mate's certificate issued on the strength of of a Taiwanese third mate's licence. The ship's navigator was Second Mate Kao Hing Ho, aged fifty-one, an ex-boatswain. Kao had a Liberian second mate's certificate for which he had paid $40 US. Completing the *Pacific Charger's* compliment of deck officers was a 24-year-old third mate who had spent only eighteen months at sea and held a Taiwanese coastal third mate's licence. Like Captain Chiou, none of these officers had any formal radar training.

In charge of the ship's engine-room was a 54-year-old chief engineer who had served as a petty officer in the Chinese Navy. He claimed to hold a Taiwanese chief engineer's licence. His first assistant engineer held a Liberian certificate issued a few days before he joined the ship, supposedly on the production of a Taiwanese engineer's licence. The second assistant engineer had thirty years experience at sea as an engine-room rating. He had passed no examination but had been able to obtain a Liberian first engineer's certificate shortly before joining. Of the ship's third assistant engineer little is known, other than that he had no paper qualifications.

The *Pacific Charger's* Burmese ratings appear to have been of indifferent ability. However, if they had been well officered, this would have been of little consequence. It later came to light that these seamen, although signed on articles at International Transport Federation rates of pay, had also signed a second set of articles agreeing to accept substantially less money. This could well have accounted for a certain lack of motivation amongst these men.

This was the state of the *Pacific Charger* when she completed loading at Yokohama and set off on her 5,000-mile voyage to New Zealand. She was a new ship, well found, correctly loaded and seaworthy in all respects, except one—the competency of her master and crew was seriously in doubt.

Widow-Maker

Wellington, capital city of New Zealand, lies at the south-western end of the North Island. It has a fine natural harbour, whose entrance is unfortunately open to the turbulent winds that plague the Cook Strait all year round. In the early hours of the morning of 21 May 1981, a vigorous south-south-easter was roaring through the heads, kicking up angry white horses on the waters of the outer harbour.

Peering out of the rain-swept windows of the signal station on Beacon Hill, the deputy pilot, Captain Smith, cursed the ship that had chosen such a morning to arrive. He had no details of the *Pacific Charger,* other than that she flew a Liberian flag and had come from Japan via Auckland, but he was of the firm opinion that her master would be well advised to wait for daylight before approaching the port. The entrance to the harbour, between Pencarrow Head and Barrett's Reef, is no more than one and a half miles wide and swept by strong tidal streams; no place for a stranger to be testing his mettle on a dark, stormy night. However, the *Pacific Charger* had requested a pilot for 03.00, and Smith would be obliged to make every effort to bring her in.

Shortly after 01.00 the *Pacific Charger* was south of Cape Palliser, at the eastern end of Cook Strait, with thirty miles to go to the Wellington pilot station off Pencarrow Head. It was a black night, lashed by rain squalls borne on a gale-force south-south-easterly wind. A rough sea and heavy swells racing in on the port quarter gave the ship an uncomfortable, dipping, rolling motion. On the bridge, Second Mate Kao had been joined by Captain Chiou. Neither man was familiar with Cook Strait, and they viewed the task ahead with some apprehension. On such a foul night it would not be easy to find, let alone enter, Wellington Harbour. Now would have been the time to turn around, to steam back out to sea to await daylight or a moderation in the weather. Unfortunately Chiou, although he had been in command for a number of years, did not fully appreciate the difficulties facing him. He elected to carry on, navigating on a small-scale ocean chart and with only a vague idea in his head of the intricacies of the entrance to the outer harbour of Wellington. He did not see fit to make use of the large-scale charts of the Cook Strait or to consult the Admiralty Pilot book, both of which were on board.

At 02.00 the *Pacific Charger* was ten miles off the Wellington pilot station and pressing on in a strengthening wind and falling visibility. Captain Chiou was hunched over the radar while Second Mate Kao, having abandoned all pretence at being the ship's navigator, was keeping a lonely lookout in the wing of the bridge. At the wheel was Quartermaster Soe Tint, who had no experience of steering the ship in restricted waters. There was still time to abort the approach, but Chiou was not of that mind. Unclipping the handset of the VHF, he called Beacon Hill and confirmed his ETA as 03.00.

By this time the Wellington pilot, Captain Smith, was already aboard his launch and outward bound for the pilot station off Pencarrow Head. Conditions in the outer harbour were bad, the small but powerful pilot launch having great difficulty in making headway against the wind and sea. Smith called the ferry *Aramoana*, which he knew to be in the Cook Strait, and learned from her that storm-force winds were blowing in the strait. It was clear to Smith that it would be too rough to board the *Pacific Charger* outside the heads. He contacted Chiou on VHF and voiced his fears, hoping that the captain would agree to stand off, at least until daylight. In his broken English Chiou replied that he intended to enter the harbour on arrival and would follow the pilot launch in if Smith could not board. Under the circumstances, Smith considered this was perhaps the best compromise he could achieve.

To the south-east of Pencarrow Head conditions were even worse than the *Aramoana* had reported. The wind was hurricane force, gusting to seventy knots, and the air was full of flying spray torn from the crests of the angry waves that marched the length of the strait under a low canopy of racing clouds. Rain and spray had reduced visibility to one and a half miles. On the bridge of the *Pacific Charger,* Captain Chiou, alternating between radar and chart and at the same time attempting to keep contact with the pilot launch on VHF, was rapidly losing control of the situation. In the dim light of the compass binnacle, fear showed on the face of Quartermaster Soe Tint as he fought inexpertly to keep the ship on course. The *Pacific Charger* was sheering wildly under the influence of the great seas thundering in on the quarter. Second Mate Kao, crouching in the wing of the bridge, was taking no part in the one-sided battle.

At 02.46 Chiou's hastily plotted radar bearings put the ship close to the south-west of Baring Head and apparently clear to enter Wellington harbour. He reduced speed and ordered Soe Tint to steer due north.

A few minutes later the pilot launch clawed her way around Pencarrow Head, and Smith picked up the *Pacific Charger* on his radar. The Liberian ship was less than a mile off Baring Head and making straight for the shore. Horrified, Smith snatched up the VHF handset and screamed a warning over the air to Chiou. It was too late. The 10,242-ton *Pacific Charger* ended her maiden voyage by driving hard on the jagged rocks at the foot of Baring Head.

Thanks mainly to the magnificent efforts of the New Zealand rescue services, there were no human casualties in the *Pacific Charger's* grounding. The ship herself, although suffering grievous bottom damage, was refloated sixteen days later and towed to Wellington.

'Pacific Charger' *aground off Baring Head*
(*Photo:* Evening Post, *Wellington*)

Bernard Edwards

There can be no doubt that the stranding of the *Pacific Charger* was due to bad navigation and seamanship of her Master, aided by the complete incompetence of the so-called navigator. In view of the weather prevailing at the time, Chiou should not have entered the Cook Strait on that terrible night. His subsequent attempt to enter Wellington harbour, using a small-scale chart and without having fully studied the hazards involved, was sheer folly.

Concerning the Liberian certificates of competency, which enabled Chiou and his officers to take this unfortunate ship on her maiden voyage, it must be said that they were obtained under the most dubious circumstances. They were, in fact, little more than scraps of worthless paper.

When the dust of the courts of enquiry had finally settled, Second Mate Kao Hing Ho, who admitted that his Liberian certificate was fraudulent, gave up his sea-going career and retired to live a less dangerous life on shore in Taiwan. Captain Chiou Ruey Yang merely changed flag. He was last heard of in command of the 28,778-ton Panamanian bulk carrier *Orient Treasury* as she passed through the Suez Canal, bound for Sweden with 27,000 tons of chrome ore, in February 1982. A few days later she disappeared without trace. Piracy is suspected.

45   Programmed to Disaster

Tifoso - 1983

On 17 January, 1983, the 138,823-tonne Liberian registered tanker *Tifoso*, owned by the Clockwork Corporation of Monrovia, sailed from Boston, Massachusetts and headed out into a stormy Atlantic. She was bound for Port Gentil in West Africa.

Once clear of Cape Cod and the Nantucket Shoals, Captain Kyriakis Dimitriadis set course for the Cape Verde Islands, where the *Tifoso* would replenish her bunkers. The distance to go was some 2,800 miles, a passage which she would be expected to complete in eight days.

The weather in the open Atlantic was typical for the winter months, with a long, threatening swell, a rough sea and an unending procession of vicious rain squalls racing in under grey skies. But the huge tanker, in ballast and riding high out of the water, was little affected by the Atlantic's ill humour. Even if she had been, it is likely there would have been few complaints from her crew. Only a few days earlier the *Tifoso* had been in her ninth month of unemployment, seemingly condemned to spend her declining years gathering weed and rust on the Boston waterfront. At that time, she was just another pathetic casualty resulting from a sudden world glut of oil and the subsequent massive surplus of tanker tonnage. More than 340 of her ungainly sisters, totalling sixty-two- million tons deadweight, were similarly rotting away in the creeks and backwaters of the world.

In early January 1983, the *Tifoso* had been born again. Out of the blue came a charter for her to carry 100,000 tonnes of crude oil from Port Gentil, in the Gabon, to Taiwan, and preparations were soon in hand to bring the tanker out of her enforced retirement. A survey was carried out by the American Bureau of Shipping and the *Tifoso* declared seaworthy in all respects for the projected voyage. Her 71-year-old master, Captain Georgios Giannoules, was replaced by a younger man, 45-year-old Captain Kyriakis Dimitriadis, but the elderly Giannoules was not thrown on the beach. When the *Tifoso* left Boston, he sailed in her as Second Officer.

The first in what was to be a series of unexplained disasters struck the Liberian ship in the early hours of the morning of the

Bernard Edwards

18th. The tanker was well clear of the American coast and settled on her south-easterly course for the Cape Verdes, pushing through the darkness at a comfortable and economical speed. Without warning, the 750kW generator providing electrical power for the ship ground to a sudden halt. The regular thump of the *Tifoso*'s engines ceased abruptly, all lights failed and the giant tanker lay wallowing help-lessly in the deep Atlantic troughs.

Chief Engineer Valmas, aroused from his sleep by the eerie silence, pulled on a boiler-suit and dashed for the engineroom. Reaching the generator flat, he found Third Assistant Engineer Eleftheroglou struggling to re-start the big generator. This, Valmas soon discovered, was a hopeless task. The machine, mysteriously starved of lubricating oil, had overheated and seized solid. Fortunately, it was a simple operation to start up the *Tifoso*'s second generator, and she was soon under way again.

The next blow, a near carbon copy of the first, fell almost exact-ly twenty-four hours later. This time Chief Engineer Valmas reached the engineroom to find Eleftheroglou shrugging his shoulders over the second generator. This had been wrecked by a sudden and unex-plainable failure of the stator windings.

Power was once again restored to the helpless *Tifoso* by bring-ing into use her emergency steam-driven generator. But this machine was not designed to sustain a ship of the *Tifoso*'s size on a long pas-sage. It seemed that Dimitriadis had no choice but to make for the nearest port where repair facilities were available. This was Hamilton, Bermuda, which lay handy only 300 miles to the south.

Bermuda, an island some twelve miles by three miles, is ringed by dangerous reefs, with the Great Bermuda Reef in the north extending to nearly seven miles off the coast. To approach from the north, as the *Tifoso* would be obliged to do, is therefore a hazardous operation. It should not, however, have been beyond the capability of an experienced navigator like Dimitriadis.

The tanker had on board no large-scale chart of the approaches to Bermuda and Dimitriadis is said to have drawn up his own chart on plain paper, plotting the various beacons and buoys guarding the Great Bermuda Reef with the aid of the Admiralty List of Lights, which formed part of the *Tifoso*'s navigational library. There was nothing particularly unusual in this. It has long been a common practice for shipmasters faced with the necessity of making a strange port for which they have no proper chart. However, it can be a dan-gerous practice for the less than careful navigator. From time to time, whether by *force majeur* or design, navigational marks are liable to be missing, unlit, or off-station. Fortunately, weekly Notices to Mariners are issued covering any such changes, and it is to these notices the navigator drawing up his own chart must pay particular attention. Before sailing from Boston, the *Tifoso* had been supplied with a full set of such notices. There was no reason, therefore, why the chart constructed by Dimitriadis should have been other than completely accurate.

At 04.00 on the morning of 20 January, the *Tifoso* was sixteen miles to the north of Bermuda, which could then be seen as a diffused glow of light on the otherwise dark horizon. The weather was not good, with the wind gusting to gale force from the north-west and kicking up a rough sea. At times, visibility was reduced by heavy rainsqualls. Captain Dimitriadis was on the bridge, with ex-Captain Giannoules as officer of the watch.

Plotted on the tanker's home-made chart were three light beacons marking the northern edge of the Great Bermuda Reef and the NE Breaker buoy, moored close to the north-eastern extremity of the reef. The lights on the beacons were said by the Admiralty List of Lights to have a range of twelve miles in clear weather. One of the beacons, the NE Breaker, was fitted with a radar responder, a device which positively identifies a navigational mark on a ship's radar screen. Dimitriadis's plan is said to have been to sight the NE Breaker buoy and then shape course to pass to the east of the reef, and thence to a position off St. David's lighthouse, where he hoped to pick up a pilot to guide him into the port of Hamilton.

At 04.08, Dimitriadis had on his radar screen what he later referred to as 'a broken image' of the island. There had been, as yet, no visual sighting of the flashing beacons, which then should have been about seven miles off. He assumed they were temporarily blotted out by rainsqualls. The NE Breaker buoy, which Dimitriadis was making for, was estimated to be just under six miles ahead, but was unlikely to be seen at that distance owing to the heavy sea running.

By 04.15, the atmosphere on the bridge of the *Tifoso* was tense, as the two master mariners and the seaman on lookout strained their eyes to sight the reassuring flash of the buoy, which should then have been only three miles off and 20° on the starboard bow. When, at long last, a flashing white light was seen at 40° on the starboard bow, all three men heaved a great sigh of relief. The NE Breaker buoy had been found.

The wide angle on the bow of the buoy must have indicated to Dimitriadis that the ship was well to the east of her intended track. To correct this he ordered a 10° alteration of course to starboard. At this point, neither the North Rock nor NE Breaker beacons had been sighted, even though the nearer of these two twelve-mile lights should have been no more than six miles off. Likewise, the radar responder of the NE Breaker had not yet shown up on the radar screen.

At 04.40, the 138,823-tonne *Tifoso* steamed straight on to the Great Bermuda Reef, ripping her bottom open from stem to stern.

Had the *Tifoso* grounded on the Great Bermuda Reef, say fifty years ago, her loss would have been put down to an Act of God—and with good reason. It was a dark, stormy night, with uncertain visibility, and she was making her approach to the island without the benefit of a proper chart. However, the art of navigation has progressed a long way since the 1930s.

The *Tifoso*, a ship more than ten times the size of her pre-World War II forbears, was equipped with two radars, a Loran receiver, a radio direction finder and an echo sounder. All these aids to navigation were said to have been in good order when the ship was surveyed prior to leaving Boston. The Loran, an extremely accurate system of hyperbolic radio navigation, would have been capable of fixing the tanker's position to within a fraction of a mile throughout her passage south from Boston. When twenty-five miles, or so, off Bermuda, her radars should have given a clear picture of the outline of the island, enabling Dimitriadis to confirm the Loran position beyond doubt. Closer in, the radar responder on the NE Breaker beacon should have been visible on the radar screen, clearly identifying the beacon. In the unlikely event of further proof being needed, then RDF bearings taken of the Bermuda radio beacon and the depth of water shown by the echo sounder would have confirmed the ship was running into danger. Then why did the *Tifoso* pile up on the reef?

At the court of inquiry held following the loss of the *Tifoso*, the incredible conclusion was reached that Captain Dimitriadis had failed to use radar, Loran, or any other of his navigational aids to fix the position of his ship when approaching Bermuda. Furthermore, it was stated that the NE Breaker buoy, which Dimitriadis had supposedly relied upon during his approach, was in fact no longer there. This buoy had been removed as far back as May 1982 and a Notice to Mariners promulgating the change had been put on board the ship at Boston. It would have been the responsibility of Georgios Giannoules, in his temporary capacity of second officer, to bring this notice to the attention of the Master. Why did he not do so?

When asked by the court to produce the chart he had drawn up for the approach to Bermuda, Dimitriadis said he had destroyed it soon after the stranding. The ship's logbook was saved, but it contained no record of courses steered directly before the *Tifoso* came to grief. The small-scale ocean chart showed that the initial course steered had been directly for the island.

Fortunately, apart from the ship herself, there were no casualties in the *Tifoso* stranding. The tanker landed on the reef in an upright position and remained that way for some days. Her crew was taken off and 700 tons of bunker oil transferred to a barge before she was refloated on 2 February and towed out to sea to be scuttled in deep water.

Even to the layman, the so-called accidental grounding of the *Tifoso* must appear mysterious, if not bewildering. For the seaman, it is impossible to comprehend how a well-found tanker, equipped with all modern navigational aids, and with two experienced master mariners on her bridge, could have blundered into the Great

Widow-Maker

Bermuda Reef. Several important questions cry out for answers. Why was Captain Giannoules suddenly replaced by Captain Dimitriadis shortly before the ship left Boston, and why did the 71-year-old Giannoules then sign on as Second Officer. It is, to say the least, most unusual for a master who has been relieved of his command to remain in the ship in a lower rank. Why, in the space of twenty-four hours—and each time in Third Assistant Engineer Eleftheroglou's watch—did both the *Tifoso*'s diesel generators fail, the second one when the ship was most conveniently situated to Bermuda? And, finally, why did Dimitriadis elect to make a night approach to the reef-fringed island when there was no pressing need for him to do so? These questions were not asked by the court of inquiry and, consequently, never answered.

Built in 1974, at the height of the oil boom, the Greek-owned, Liberian-flag *Tifoso* had made considerable profits for her owners in her heyday. When she joined the ranks of the unemployed in Boston in March 1982, and began to incur costs of thousands of dollars daily for no return, she became a very expensive millstone around her owners' neck. It is indeed strange that at this time—some months before she landed the fortuitous charter and seemed doomed never to sail again—those same owners took out insurance on her for a total of $43 million. It was later estimated that the *Tifoso*'s market value was no more than $7 million. On that dark, stormy night when she found the Great Bermuda Reef with such uncanny accuracy, the *Tifoso* was therefore over-insured to the tune of $36 million. The underwriters paid up without a murmur of dissent.

Whatever the truth of the *Tifoso* stranding, her flag of convenience had served her owners well.

Bernard Edwards

46   Beware the English Channel

Radiant Med - 1984

The English Channel has long been known for its extremes of weather. Facing south-west, it is like a huge, gaping mouth, into which, from time to time, rushes all the pent-up fury of the North Atlantic. In winter, storm force-10 is par for the course; summer is slightly less malevolent, but any easing of the wind is sure to bring down a blanket of dense fog on these tortuous waters. Over 2,000 wrecks litter this 350-mile long navigator's nightmare, baring witness to the folly of those who dared to underestimate the perils of the Channel.

On the night of 22 January 1984, the English Channel was in an ugly mood. Storm force winds, whipped up by a deep depression passing to the north of Scotland, were building up, bringing with them very high seas and driving rain. It was not a night for the unwary to be abroad.

Shortly before midnight the 2,997-ton, Liberian-flag motor ship *Radiant Med*, was off Alderney and clawing her way down Channel in the teeth of the wind. The fourteen-year-old *Radiant Med*, loaded with 5,000 tons of bulk grain and bound for the Congo, was entered in Lloyd's Shipping Index as owned by Maritime Star Shipping Ltd., of Monrovia, and managed by Middle East Agents Ltd., of Piraeus. She carried a total crew of twenty-five, of which her officers were Indian and her ratings Filipino. Her master, Captain A. D'Souza, and her chief officer, Subhas Singh Tanwar, both held Liberian masters' certificates, issued on the strength of their Indian certificates.

For a small ship, deep loaded and facing a passage of 4,800 miles, during which she would be exposed to the full rigours of the North Atlantic in winter, the *Radiant Med* had one dangerous weakness—one that was to be aggravated by a serious underestimation of the power of the sea. Unlike modern ships, which have tight-fitting, hydraulically controlled, steel hatch covers, the watertight integrity of her two cargo holds was dependent on light steel pontoons, over which were stretched canvas tarpaulins. The whole was designed to be kept firmly in place by steel locking bars fitted athwartships, one bar securing each section of pontoons. Under the International Load Line Regulations, this was considered to be a watertight closure.

Unfortunately, over the years many of the *Radiant Med*'s hatch locking bars had gone missing and those still on board could not be correctly fitted due to alterations recently made to the hatch coamings. As a substitute for the bars, D'Souza had concluded that rope nets, stretched over the hatch tarpaulins and lashed down to the deck, would do just as well. While this expedient might have held good in more benign waters, in the Western Approaches in winter it was tempting providence.

When a reluctant daylight came on the 23rd, the *Radiant Med* was thirty miles west of Guernsey and determinedly attempting to punch her way through mountainous seas. As water is incompressible, she was making little progress. In refusing to reduce speed, Captain D'Souza was ignoring one of the basic rules of good seamanship and punishing his ship needlessly. This he was to regret.

The wind had veered more to the west and was gusting force-11 when, at 16.00 that day, Chief Officer Tanwar took over the watch on the bridge. The *Radiant Med*'s engines were still making full revolutions and she was burying her bow deep in the advancing walls of green water, her propeller racing wildly each time her stern lifted high. The air was full of flying spray, torn from the crests of the tumbling waves, and her decks were constantly awash with foaming water, which tugged and plucked with eager fingers at her lightly secured hatches.

At about 17.00, the labouring vessel slammed headlong into a towering wave that had reared up unseen in the darkness, and an avalanche of angry water poured over her bows and thundered the length of her foredeck. To a horrified Tanwar, watching with his face pressed to the glass of the wheelhouse windows, it seemed the ship would never rise again. But rise she did, shouldering aside the sea with a determination born of desperation.

When the welter of tumbling foam had drained from the deck, Tanwar saw that the forward derrick of No.2 hatch had been torn from its stowage position. The long steel boom, suspended from the mast by its topping wires, was scything menacingly across the top of the hatch in an ever-increasing arc.

In response to Tanwar's urgent call, D'Souza came to the bridge a few minutes later and quickly grasped the danger of the situation. The rampaging derrick was to some extent restrained by its heavy lifting tackle, which was lashed to a wooden pallet on the hatch-top. Should this tackle break free, the derrick and its attendant blocks would embark on an orgy of destruction, smashing everything in its path. Most vulnerable—and D'Souza realised this with fear in his heart—were the securing nets and canvas tarpaulins of the hatch-top.

D'Souza now took the only course of action open to him. He brought the ship around until she was stern-on to the seas and ordered the chief officer to take a party of men on deck to secure the derrick. This was really an impossible task, for even with the vessel's stern to the weather, huge seas were still sweeping her decks. Tanwar and his men were forced to withdraw, but not before it had been seen that the heavy derrick tackle was already on the move and tearing the tarpaulins of No.2 hatch to shreds.

With no locking bars in place, it would only be a matter of time before the pounding seas dislodged one or more of the steel pontoons, leaving the hold open to the sea. When he was given this news, D'Souza decided to continue on his present course and run for shelter further up Channel. Unfortunately, the nearest refuge from this storm was 120 miles away, on the eastern side of the Cherbourg peninsular.

At first the *Radiant Med* made good progress to the north-east. With the wind and sea astern, she had ceased to pitch heavily but her decks were still awash at times. She was taking in some water in her forward hold, but the pumps were able to cope. For a while it seemed the danger might be over. Then, late that night, the situation changed dramatically for the worse. A big wave climbed aboard and swept a pontoon hatch over the side. The sea began to pour into No.2 hold.

D'Souza's 'Mayday' was answered by the French Navy frigate *Casabianca*, which was providentially only fifteen miles or so to the west of the stricken ship. The commander of the *Casabianca* assumed on-the-spot control of the rescue operation, under the direction of the Search and Rescue Centre at Cap de la Hague. Also listening in was St Peter Port Radio, which prudently alerted the Guernsey lifeboat.

News that the French Navy was close by brought some comfort to those on board the *Radiant Med*, but the position of the ship was deteriorating rapidly. The wind had shifted to the north-west and was gusting to seventy knots, with thirty-five-foot waves racing up astern, each one threatening to overwhelm the small ship. A second pontoon was washed away and very soon the pumps were fighting a losing battle against the water pouring into the open hatchway of No.2 hold. D'Souza ordered his crew to swing out the lifeboats. In the midst of this frenzied operation the second assistant engineer suffered a heart attack and died. The first act of the tragedy of the night of 23 January had opened.

Shortly before midnight, *Casabianca* was sighted from the bridge of the *Radiant Med*. The frigate was eight miles astern and battling her way towards the Liberian ship, which was now making four knots to the north-east. Conditions were such that there was no question of *Casabianca* lowering a boat, but a helicopter was reported to be on the way from the French mainland. From now on it would clearly be a race against time, for the *Radiant Med* was becoming more and more sluggish in her movements; less willing to rise each time the sea pressed her down.

D'Souza, fearful that his ship did not have long to live, now requested the frigate to close up and make an attempt to take off the *Radiant Med*'s crew. *Casabianca* was reluctant to do so. Her commander suggested that D'Souza increase speed, with the object of making Cherbourg as soon as possible or, if that failed, to beach his ship to the west of the port. The *Radiant Med* was at that time twenty miles west-south-west of Guernsey and steering to pass to the south of the island. Despite the grave risk they knew they were taking, the ship's chief and third engineers went below and increased speed to ten knots.

At 00.52 on the 24th came the bitter news that the helicopter, unable to cope with the extreme weather, had turned back. Ten minutes later, the *Radiant Med*'s steering gear failed and the ship's head fell off until she was beam-on to the sea and rolling helplessly in the trough. D'Souza decided the time had come to abandon ship. He called *Casabianca*, now only two miles off, and asked her to stand by to pick them up.

Due to the water in her hold, the ship now had a heavy list to port and it proved impossible to lower the starboard lifeboat. Likewise, the port lifeboat became jammed in its davits and refused to budge. The inflatable liferaft was launched but, in the confusion of the night, it floated away before anyone could board. At that point, the ship began to sink under them and D'Souza and his men had no alternative but to throw themselves on the mercy of the sea.

D'Souza and Tanwar led the way over the side, hurling themselves into the churning sea, their bodies recoiling with shock as they hit the icy water. When Tanwar came to the surface, he saw that one of the *Radiant Med*'s lifeboats had released itself and was floating close to the sinking ship. He struck out and, after a struggle that all but exhausted him, reached the boat and hauled himself over the gunwale. Four other survivors were already in the boat.

Tanwar's relief was short-lived, for no sooner had he collapsed on the bottom boards than the *Radiant Med* rolled over and her after radio mast crashed down on the lifeboat, causing serious damage. Very soon, the boat was waterlogged and floating only on its buoyancy tanks.

Fortunately for those of the Liberian ship's crew who were still alive, St Peter Port Radio had been monitoring the emergency from the start. When it became apparent the *Radiant Med* was sinking and *Casabianca* was powerless to help, St Peter Port's harbour master took it upon himself to call out the Guernsey lifeboat.

Driving into the teeth of a fifty knot wind, with very high seas and visibility curtailed by rain, the fifty-two-foot Arun Class lifeboat *Sir William Arnold*, with Coxswain Scales at the helm, made good speed and by 03.00 had *Casabianca* in sight. The frigate was hove-to about one mile from the spot where the *Radiant Med* had gone down and had the waterlogged lifeboat in the beam of her searchlight. Coxswain Scales brought the *Sir William Arnold* to windward of the

Guernsey lifeboat 'Sir William Arnold' *returns to St. Peter Port*
(Photo: Guernsey Press*)*

Guernsey lifeboat lands survivors of 'Radiant Med'
(Photo: Guernsey Press*)*

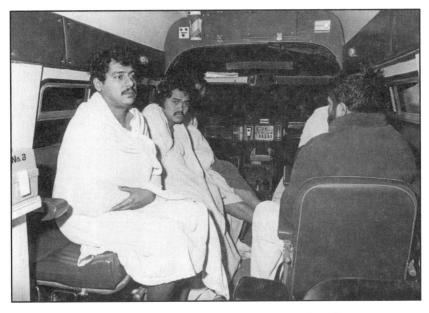

A survivor of the 'Radiant Med' *is brought ashore*
(Photo: Guernsey Press*)*

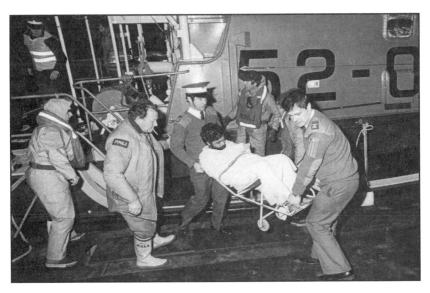

'Radiant Med' *survivors after being landed at Guernsey*
(Photo: Guernsey Press*)*

boat and his men went on deck with their safety lines rigged. In a display of superb seamanship and outstanding courage, the RNLI men snatched Chief Officer Tanwar and eight other half-drowned souls from the grip of the sea.

An extensive search was carried out by other ships and RAF Sea King helicopters, but no more survivors were found. Later, the bodies of Captain D'Souza and fifteen of his men were picked up. At the inquest held in Guernsey, a pathologist stated that all these men had died by drowning within twenty minutes of entering the water, despite being buoyed up by lifejackets. It was assumed that, already in a state of shock, and with their legs acting as involuntary sea anchors, they had drifted face to the wind and had been slowly choked to death by the remorseless seas breaking over their heads.

In the end, it may be said that the *Radiant Med* was a victim of the English Channel in its angriest mood. Yet she need not have been lost. Smaller ships have survived by riding out such a storm, hove-to with the wind and sea on the bow. It was D'Souza's insistence on pressing ahead at full speed in the face of the very severe weather that caused the damage, which eventually led to her loss. With regard to the missing hatch locking bars, this was also D'Souza's responsibility. As master of the ship, he should have insisted that they were supplied and fitted before sailing. But who knows what pressure he was under from those who employed him? The *Radiant Med* was owned by faceless men of indeterminate nationality, registered in Liberia as a matter of economic expediency, and managed in a country where safety takes second place to productivity. She was just another typical example of the prostitution of a flag for profit.

47   The Great Bermuda Reef

Sealuck & *Aguila Azteca* - 1984

On 7 June, 1609 a fleet of nine ships set sail from Plymouth, bound for the new colony of Virginia, on the east coast of North America. In overall command was Admiral Sir George Somers, who sailed in the flagship *Sea Venture,* a vessel of 300 tunnes commanded by Captain Christopher Newport. With Somers in the *Sea Venture* was Sir Thomas Gates, the new lieutenant-governor of Virginia and a number of other officials. It was a brave expedition, with more than 800 people afloat and challenging 3,000 miles of largely unexplored ocean, known to be wracked by the most terrible storms, and, so some said, home to sea serpents and all manner of evil things.

Storms and sea serpents apart, the greatest difficulty Admiral Somers faced on the voyage was a lack of accurate charts and navigational instruments. It was only just over one hundred years since Columbus had defied the sceptics and not fallen off the edge of the earth when he sailed westwards to find a new route to the Orient. Any charts that existed of the Atlantic were largely fanciful sketches drawn by armchair navigators. Latitude was calculated by the use of an astrolobe, a crude forerunner of the sextant, but the results were so inaccurate that an error of 100 miles in the latitude was not considered unusual. The only means of keeping time on board ship was the hourglass, so that the reckoning of longitude, which depends on exact time difference, was beyond the wit of a mariner of the seventeenth century. The speed of the vessel was estimated by tossing a log chip overboard and timing its progress astern with an hourglass. Compasses were imperfect instruments, subject to large and unpredictable errors, so that the course made good was largely a matter of guesswork. The only feasible method of navigating was to sail north or south to the latitude required, and then east or west to the destination.

Admiral Somers' plan was a simple one; to sail south until the island of Madeira was sighted, and then due west to America, ending up, it was hoped, somewhere on the coast of Virginia. All went well until six weeks out of Plymouth, when the fleet ran into the tail end of a West Indian hurricane. The *Sea Venture* was separated from the other ships, and for four days fought a valiant battle with the elements, the story of which inspired William Shakespeare to write 'The Tempest'. The ship was dismasted, her seams opened up, and with her crew manning the pumps continuously, she ran ashore on a submerged reef off an unknown island. And so, quite by accident, the archipelago of Bermuda, a group of 150 uninhabited islands 575 miles east of Cape Hatteras, became Britain's second colony in the Americas.

The art of navigation at sea has moved on apace since the little *Sea Venture* challenged the Atlantic and lost. Voyages of exploration over the years that followed, and the introduction of organised surveys in the eighteenth century, led to the easy availability of detailed and accurate charts. The perfection of the sea-going chronometer in the nineteenth century revolutionised position fixing by sextant, while the magnetic compass was so improved that a true course could be steered to within a degree or two.

The coming of steam, then the internal combustion engine, gave ships, for the first time, a reliable means of propulsion. Then, an explosion in technology, largely brought about by the Second World War, led to a battery of electronic aids that were to bring about radical changes in navigation at sea. The gyroscopic compass, unaffected by magnetic anomalies and always pointing to true north, took much of the uncertainty out of steering a course. The radio direction finder, and later radar, solved most of the problems of coastal navigation and navigation in fog and poor visibility. In the 1950s, Decca, Consol and Loran, hyperbolic radio position fixing systems capable of pin-pointing a ship's position to within fifty yards, and up to several hundred miles from the land, were introduced.

Then, in the 1970s, came the ultimate in navigational tools. Specifically designed as a precision guidance system for nuclear submarines, the US Navy Navigation Satellite System, or Satnav, was made available to commercial shipping. Through a network of satellites orbiting the earth, any ship equipped with the necessary receiver and aerial is now able to plot its position with great accuracy, at intervals of from thirty minutes to two hours depending on her latitude, day and night, in all weathers and in any part of the globe. Modern shipboard navigation requires little skill, other than the ability to read off the latitude and longitude from a digital display and to plot the position on a chart. Satnav has changed the art of the navigator beyond all recognition. It has also, sadly, delivered huge, costly ships into the hands of those who have little knowledge and understanding of the sea.

It was with all the many benefits of modern science and technology to hand that the motor vessel *Sealuck* set sail from Houston, Texas on 8 September, 1984. Owned by East Seas Shipping Ltd. of Valetta, and flying the Maltese flag, the 43,796-ton bulk carrier was loaded with 41,944 tons of grain consigned to the Russian port of Novorossisk, in the Black Sea. She was a seventeen-year-old ship, long past her prime, but equipped with gyro compass, two radars and a satellite navigator, all in good working order. At her maximum speed of twelve knots, the 7,000-mile passage via the Gulf of Mexico, the Atlantic and the Mediterranean, was expected to take some twenty-five days.

In command of the *Sealuck* was 46-year-old Captain Apolonio M. Diego, a graduate of the Philippines' nautical school, with fifteen years in command of foreign-going ships. Diego's chief officer was Eduardo C. Co, who held a Filipino chief mate's licence, and his third officer was 26-year-old Anastacio B. De La Vega, six years at sea and holding a Filipino third mate's licence. The *Sealuck*'s second officer had left the ship at short notice before departure Houston, and with no relief available, Captain Diego decided to sail short-handed on the bridge. Although this was permissible under law, it was not advisable on a long passage, for Diego himself would be obliged to keep a watch, thereby impairing his ability to maintain overall control of his ship.

The weather in the Gulf of Mexico was fair, but the *Sealuck*'s speed was disappointing, and it was late on the 12th before she cleared the Straits of Florida. Diego then set a course of 069°, which would take the ship to a point about fifteen miles north of Bermuda, from whence he intended to follow a single course to the Straits of Gibraltar, passing midway between Madeira and the Azores.

It is normal practice in planning a trans-ocean passage to lay off the courses on a small-scale general chart of the ocean, and when passing near any land to consult larger scale local charts and pilot books for any dangers. Diego, who was on his fourth voyage from the Gulf to the Black Sea, used British Admiralty Chart No.4108 when laying off his courses. This chart has a scale of 1:3,500,000, on which Bermuda is shown in only the vaguest detail, but it was adequate for use in the initial stages of the transatlantic crossing.

The archipelago of Bermuda, of which Bermuda, Somerset, Ireland and St. George's are the principal islands, was first discovered in 1503 by the Spanish navigator Juan Bermudez in the vessel *La Garza*. Bermudez did not land, leaving the islands to be claimed for the British Crown more than a hundred years later by Admiral Somers. The islands, covering an area twenty-five miles by twelve miles, appear to be a series of volcanic peaks similar to the Canaries and the Azores. A submerged reef, extending up to eight miles out to sea, surrounds the whole, forming a shallow lagoon around the islands, with only a few narrow passages accessible to ships. Outside the reef the bottom drops away to 2,000 fathoms. It is recommended that the islands are approached with extreme caution, and any ship not calling should give them a very wide berth.

There was no large-scale chart of Bermuda and its approaches

on board the *Sealuck,* but she did have a copy of Volume 3 of the West
Indies Pilot, which gives comprehensive details of the islands and
their approaches. It is hard to understand why Diego elected to pass
so close to Bermuda when there was no pressing need to do so, but
even more difficult to understand why—as appears to be the case—
neither he nor his watch keeping officers did not bother to consult
the pilot book. After clearing the Straits of Florida, positions were
taken by satellite navigator every two hours marked on a blank plotting chart, and then transferred to Chart 4108.

At 08.00 on the 14th, when about 150 miles west-south-west
of Bermuda, the *Sealuck*'s engine was disabled by a scavenge fire in
one of the cylinders. As she was in open waters and in fair weather,
this was not a serious matter, but the ship lay stopped and drifting
for twenty hours while repairs were made. No positions were taken
while she was stopped, but it must be presumed she drifted to the
north and east under the influence of the Gulf Stream. She was under
way again at 04.45 on the 15th, and when Chief Officer Co obtained
a position by Satnav at noon that day, it was found that the ship was
to the north of her track. Co altered course 11° to starboard and
informed Diego, who approved but did not visit the bridge. The
Sealuck was then some fifty miles to the west of Bermuda.

Captain Diego relieved Third Officer De La Vega on the bridge
at 16.00 to take up the four to eight watch, which in the absence of
a second officer Diego had been keeping since sailing from Houston.
The ship was still steering 080°, although this course had not been
laid down on the chart. Both radars were operating, and a faint outline of Bermuda was showing up on the screens at twenty-two miles.
However, no salient points could yet be clearly enough identified to
fix the ship's position, not that this would have been of much assistance when plotted on the small scale chart in use.

At 16.50, Diego was relieved by Chief Officer Co, and being
satisfied that all was well, went below for his supper. The main island
was then discernible on the radar at nineteen miles, and if a position
had then been plotted, even on Chart 4801, it would have shown
that the *Sealuck* was heading to pass about eight miles off the island.
Not that this information would have conveyed anything to Diego or
Co, for they were both blissfully unaware of the existence of the
Great Bermuda Reef.

Diego returned to the bridge at 17.40, when Co handed back
the watch without having marked the ship's position on the chart.
Ignoring the radar and the fact that the land was now clearly visible
by eye, Diego decided to wait for the next Satnav fix, which was due
at 18.00. It was now approaching sunset, and Able Seaman Alfredo
Bautista reported to the bridge for lookout duties. Diego posted him
in the starboard wing of the bridge, and then went to the chartroom
to stand by the Satnav receiver.

A few minutes before 18.00, Bautista saw what he thought to

be a fishing boat on the port bow. Instead of reporting this to the master right away, Bautista went into the wheelhouse to find a pair of binoculars. When he was thus equipped, he saw that the fishing boat was in fact a lighthouse, and certainly on the wrong side of the ship. In a state of considerable agitation, the lookout man dived for the chartroom to alert Diego. Before he could do so, the 43,796-ton *Sealuck*, steering by automatic pilot and travelling at her full speed of twelve knots, ran straight on to the Great Bermuda Reef.

As Captain Apolonio Diego sadly contemplated the fate of his ship, 1,700 miles to the south-west, the 231,074-tonne VLCC *Aguila Azteca* was breaking away from her berth at the oil terminal of Cayo Arcas, in the southern Gulf of Mexico. The Mexican-flag tanker, commanded by 58-year-old Captain Bernado F. Pena Solana, was loaded with 196,000 tonnes of heavy Maya crude, consigned to Rotterdam. Before embarking on this 5,000-mile voyage, she required to replenish her bunkers, and for this it was necessary for her to go 200 miles deeper into the Gulf to the port of Coatzacoalcos.

At Coatzacoalcos, there was a considerable delay in supplying the 8,000 tonnes of fuel required by the *Aguila Azteca*, and it was 24 September before she finally set off on her voyage. By then she was drawing sixty-three feet of water, or ten and a half fathoms. At such draught, except in a case of absolute necessity, as when steaming through the English Channel, she would be well advised to steer well clear of shallow waters. She would require careful navigating, and to this end she carried two radars and a satellite navigator.

It was Captain Solana's intention to leave the Gulf of Mexico through the Straits of Florida, and then steam parallel to the American coast as far as Cape Hatteras, taking advantage of the north-flowing Gulf Stream. Off Hatteras, where the current sweeps eastwards into the Atlantic, he planned to set course directly for the English Channel. It was a well-tried route, used to full advantage by the sailing ships of another age, and the push of the current astern would ease the strain on the fifteen-year-old tanker's engine.

Before leaving the Gulf of Mexico, Solana was obliged to abandon his planned route by the threatened arrival off Cape Hatteras of tropical storms Hortense and Isodore. He then instructed his second officer, Eduardo Estudillo, to lay off a course direct from the northern end of the Florida Strait to the Channel. Estudillo, a graduate of the Nautical School in Tampico, and with just ten months sea service to his credit, laid off the course on British Admiralty Chart No.2127, a general chart of the North and South Atlantic, having a scale of 1:14,500,000. Other, larger scale charts were on board, but Estudillo ignored them. Neither did he, or Captain Solana consult the West Indies Pilot, which was also available. Both men were, however, aware that the course as laid down on Chart 2127 passed within fourteen miles of Bermuda. This did not cause them any concern, for Bermuda is represented on Chart 2127 by a small dot, and with no indications of any possible dangers given. Although Solana had crossed the Atlantic over one hundred times, he had never been closer to Bermuda than sixty miles, and had no knowledge of the existence of the Great Bermuda Reef.

The *Aguila Azteca* cleared the Little Bahama Bank, at the northern end of the Straits of Florida, early on the morning of the 29th, and Captain Solana—as had Diego seventeen days earlier—set a course of 069°, intending to pass fourteen miles off Bermuda. The weather was fair, with no ill effects being felt from the tropical storms raging to the north. Noon positions were obtained by sextant observations on the 30th and 1st October and plotted on Chart 2127. The Satnav was in use throughout; positions being plotted every watch on a blank plotting chart, but not transferred to the Admiralty chart. Through the medium of the satellite navigator, the geographical position of the tanker was accurately known at all times, although it seems that no one on the bridge took the trouble to relate this to the lie of the land.

Second Officer Estudillo took over the watch at noon on 1 October, and at 12.12 obtained a Satnav fix, which, in terms of latitude and longitude, agreed with the noon position by sextant. Estudillo took further Satnav fixes at 14.02 and 16.00, which he plotted on the blank plotting chart. At some time during the watch he also marked the noon position by sextant on Chart 2127, so he must have been aware that the ship was then approaching Bermuda, yet he did not switch on the radars. The *Aguila Azteca* was at the time of taking the 16.00 Satnav fix only thirteen miles off the land, and had Estudillo taken the trouble to use his binoculars, he would have seen Bermuda on his starboard side. When, just after 16.00, Estudillo handed over the watch to Chief Officer Guillermo Becerra, he remarked, in an apparent afterthought, that the ship would pass Bermuda sometime during the evening, but he did not know when. At this time both radars were switched off, the helm was in automatic pilot and no lookout was posted. It would seem that neither officer bothered to consult the Admiralty chart, and as Bermuda was not marked on the plotting chart in use, they were not aware of the close proximity of the islands.

At about 16.40, Becerra at last noticed the land looming up on the starboard side, and he switched on one radar. He then, at last, took a look at Chart 2127 and was forced to conclude that the ship must be close to Bermuda. Although he did have a vague idea of the reef surrounding the islands, he took no immediate action to haul the ship off the land, preferring to wait for the radar to warm up, so that he would be able to get an accurate position.

Ten minutes later, as Becerra was tuning in the radar, the *Aguila Azteca* steamed onto the Great Bermuda Reef at full speed. Her grounding position was 7.9 miles from the nearest land, and within yards of the spot from which, three days earlier, the unfortunate

Sealuck had been dragged by salvage tugs after a twelve-day operation which involved off-loading nearly 8,000 tons of cargo. The salvage of the *Aguila Azteca* proved to be more difficult, lasting for seventeen days, during which 14,000 tons of her cargo were transferred to another tanker.

The *Sealuck* lived to sail another day, but when the *Aguila Azteca* was examined in dry dock, it was found that the damage to her hull was too great to warrant repair. She was sold for scrap in January 1985.

It would have been unfair to have accused Captain Christopher Newport of negligence or incompetence when he ran the tiny *Sea Venture* onto the Great Bermuda Reef in 1609. His ship was small and at the mercy of the winds; he was sailing on an unknown sea without a chart of any description, and the navigational aids at his command were of the most rudimentary. The same cannot be said for Captain Apolonio M. Diego of the *Sealuck* and Captain Bernado F. Pena Solana of the *Aguila Azteca.* They commanded large, powerfully-engined ships equipped with all the sophisticated technology the late 20th century has to offer. It can only be said that they and their officers were guilty of the most unbelievable complacency and incompetence. The two great ships were being navigated using small-scale charts that were little better than school atlases, and it seemed that no man aboard either ship had bothered to acquaint himself with the dangers surrounding the islands of Bermuda. It was as though they were, like Coleridge's Ancient Mariner, in 'a painted ship upon a painted ocean'. They assiduously plotted, with great accuracy, the positions of their respective ships on blank charts, so that they were at all times aware of their latitude and longitude, yet they had no idea of where they were in relation to the world around them. They were, in other words, baffled by a technology they did not fully comprehend, and yet all were graduates of so-called nautical academies in Mexico or the Philippines.

It is significant to record, that when the Bermudan authorities held official inquiries into the grounding of the two ships, the officers concerned, the ships' owners and the governments under whose flags they were registered all refused to take part. Such was the regard paid to the rule of law at sea.

Bernard Edwards

48   A Large Naval Target

Caribbean Breeze - 1985

The sun hoisted itself slowly over the eastern horizon, turning the unruffled waters of the Persian Gulf from the somber grey of night to an opaline blue. A shoal of tiny, iridescent flying fish whirled into silent flight from the cool depths, while a lone dolphin saluted the new day with a lazy arch of its back that barely rippled the surface of the sea.

On the bridge of the 237,000-ton Liberian-flag tanker *Caribbean Breeze*, Captain David McCaffrey, tired and unshaven, winced as the rising sun struck fire from the wheelhouse windows. Silently, he cursed the malfunctioning boiler, which had reduced his ship's speed to a mere eleven knots during the night. As a result of this, the great, 1,100-foot-long tanker, her white-painted bridge structure towering seventy feet above the waterline, was now in a very exposed position, etched in bold relief against an empty sea and sky.

Some thirty-six hours earlier, the *Caribbean Breeze* had slipped clear of her berth at Mina Al Ahmadi after loading a cargo of 1.8 million barrels of Kuwaiti crude oil. She was drawing sixty-eight feet and at the best of times her two-day passage through the shallow waters of the Gulf would have been hazardous. Now that the Iran/Iraq conflict, bogged down in a dreadful war of attrition ashore, had spilled over into the sea-lanes in earnest, the risks faced by a loaded tanker were awesome. It was March 1985 and, in the previous twelve months, the Persian Gulf had been the scene of vicious attacks on no less than sixty-seven merchant ships, most of them large tankers like the *Caribbean Breeze*. Iraq, desperate to cut off the flow of Iran's oil exports, was flinging Exocets at everything that moved in the vicinity of the beleaguered Kharg Island, while Iran, adopting a grim 'ship for ship' policy, was relentlessly deploying her Phantoms, armed with American Maverick missiles, against ships carrying Kuwaiti and Saudi Arabian oil out of the Gulf. Both sides were making war on neutral ships with impunity.

David McCaffrey, 54-year-old British master of the *Caribbean Breeze*, rasped the bristles of his unshaven chin and reflected on the circumstances that had dragged him into this crazy war. Until two years before, all his working life had been spent in British ships,

starting as a young cadet with the prestigious Blue Funnel Line in
1946. When he had first put up his four gold rings of command, the
future looked secure. Then, when Britain's merchant fleet collapsed
under the weight of cut-price foreign competition, like thousands of
other British masters and officers, he had been forced to 'go foreign'
to keep the pay cheques coming in. He had little dreamed he would
end up in command of a Kuwaiti-owned, Liberian-registered supertanker, a prime target for Iranian missiles, slinking through the
night like a hunted animal, and hiding in friendly waters by day.

On that fine Sunday morning in March, the *Caribbean Breeze*
was approaching a 'safe' anchorage twelve miles north of the lonely
Halul Island, which lies on the edge of the Great Pearl Bank and just
inside the territorial waters of Qatar. There she would seek sanctuary
for the day, before making the final dash for the Straits of Hormuz
and the open sea.

At twenty miles off the island, McCaffrey eased his engines
down to the minimum revolutions compatible with steerage-way.
The tremendous momentum the 237,000 tonner had built up while
steaming through the night would be sufficient to carry her into the
anchorage.

With the two-hundred-foot-high lump of barren rock that was
Halul showing clearly on the radar screen, McCaffrey moved out into
the wing of the bridge and scanned the horizon with his binoculars,
feeling the tension slowly draining away. Then a tiny black silhouette appeared low down in the eastern sky and he froze.

The aircraft swept in and began to circle the *Caribbean Breeze* as
she coasted through the water. McCaffrey's knuckles were white as he
adjusted the focus of his powerful 10 x 50s. The visitor was a large,
four-engined plane, similar to the old British Viscount, but the
Iranian markings were unmistakable.

Following the big aircraft round as it circled persistently
McCaffrey experienced anger, frustration and, momentarily, fear. The
pattern was only too familiar. This was the spotter plane, sent out to
make the identification. Even now, his ship's name and particulars
were being radioed back to base on the Iranian coast, where it would
be quickly established that the *Caribbean Breeze* was carrying Kuwaiti
oil, and therefore in the service of an enemy of Iran. The neutral
Liberian flag would be ignored and the scrambling of a missile-car-
rying Phantom would follow.

McCaffrey lowered his binoculars and pondered his next move.
Had he been in one of Blue Funnel's twenty-one-knot cargo ships, his
course of action would have been clear—a quick dash for the safety
of Qatari inshore waters. Unfortunately, the *Caribbean Breeze* was no
clipper-bowed ocean greyhound. Her maximum speed when loaded
was twelve knots—and it would take her engineers several hours to
work up to that. She was also drawing over eleven fathoms of water,
and to take her close into the coast would be to court disaster. There

could be no running away.

Swallowing hard, McCaffrey re-entered the wheelhouse and reached for the VHF. He first called Bahrain, where two US frigates were based, reported that his ship appeared to be in imminent danger of attack and asked for help. 'Sorry,' the reply came back, 'we can do nothing until you are actually hit.' Shaking his head in disbelief, McCaffrey next contacted the port of Doha, only forty miles away and the base of a small, but powerful Qatari naval force. The reply from Doha was substantially the same. The *Caribbean Breeze* was apparently nobody's problem until she became a casualty.

McCaffrey was now left with only one alternative—he must take his ship into Qatari territorial waters off Halul Island as quickly as possible. There she might be safe from attack. But a 237,000-ton tanker has no brakes, and without the aid of tugs, can only be brought to a halt by gradually shedding her vast momentum. He dare not increase speed for fear of over-running the anchorage and ending up in shallow water.

Another hour passed, with the *Caribbean Breeze* creeping in towards her anchorage, all the while being circled by her unwelcome escort. On the bridge, the tension was mounting. McCaffrey paced the port wing, occasionally entering the wheelhouse to give quiet helm and engine orders. At the chart table, Second Officer Jaffrey maintained a meticulous plot, while Third Officer Finnbar O'Driscoll manned the radar. The Filipino helmsman kept his eyes glued to the clicking gyro-compass.

At 07.30, the big, four-engined aircraft suddenly broke off its patient surveillance and roared away to the east. McCaffrey knew the run-up to the attack on his ship was under way.

The wait was long and agonising, the giant tanker inching her way towards sanctuary, the muted thump of her idling engines the only sound on the still morning air. At 08.00, Chief Officer Stephen Mitchell began the long walk up the exposed foredeck to his anchor station in the bows. The hot sun blazed down out of a cloudless sky, but the sweat soaking Mitchell's thin tropical shirt was ice-cold.

At 08.30, the *Caribbean Breeze* was fifteen miles to the north of Halul Island and only three miles outside Qatari territorial waters. McCaffrey's hopes were now rising. Perhaps the attack would not come after all and, as on any normal morning, he would soon be enjoying breakfast in the officers' saloon below the bridge. Then, as he walked from the port wing into the wheelhouse, his tired brain reviving at the thought of sizzling bacon and eggs, he heard Second Officer Jaffrey's sharp cry of warning.

The Iranian jet came screaming in out of the sun, an ominous black shape detaching itself from beneath the wings before the plane swept skywards again. Seconds later, the 645-pound guided missile crashed into the tall bridge structure of the *Caribbean Breeze* and exploded with a deafening roar. Before the world went black,

McCaffrey saw the armoured glass of the wheelhouse windows shatter like thin ice under a hammer and felt a searing pain in his left arm.

When he regained his senses, McCaffrey struggled to his feet and looked around in horror. The wheelhouse, with all its sophisticated equipment, was now a tangled mass of twisted wreckage. A few feet away from where he had fallen, the steel deck had been peeled back by a giant hand and smoke and flames were pouring up from below. Ugly shards of glass lay everywhere.

McCaffrey's first thought was for his men. Fighting his way through the smoke and wreckage, he found the Filipino helmsman propped up against the after bulkhead, where he had been thrown by the force of the explosion. The man was moaning, but not badly injured. Second Officer Jaffrey was on his knees near the chart table, his hands clasped to his face and blood running through his fingers. He had been blinded by flying glass. Third Officer O'Driscoll, although dazed and cut, was still on his feet and already searching in the wreckage for the first aid box.

It was only when he felt a terrible weakness creeping over him that McCaffrey realised his white uniform was turning scarlet with the blood spurting from a severed artery in his left arm. He was barely conscious when O'Driscoll applied the life-saving tourniquet.

The missile had hit directly below the tanker's wheelhouse, creating a blackened shell out of the once-luxuriously appointed owner's suite. The adjoining radio room was a smoking shambles and fire was sweeping through the accommodation. All communications between the bridge and engineroom had been cut.

The *Caribbean Breeze*, her engines still turning, and with her bridge and its occupants temporarily out of action, continued to slide relentlessly through the water. If the fire in her accommodation did not first ignite the gas given off by her cargo, causing a cataclysmic explosion, then she would surely pile up on the reefs off Halul Island.

McCaffrey, the flow of blood from his shattered arm partially stemmed, moved swiftly and decisively. He dispatched a messenger to the engineroom with the order to stop the engines and, when this was done, sent word forward to Mitchell to let go both anchors.

A cloud of red dust erupted from the forecastle head as the cables rattled out through the hawsepipes and slowly, with the flukes of her huge, high-tensile steel anchors scoring deep furrows in the sea bed, the *Caribbean Breeze* reluctantly, came to a halt. McCaffrey then went below to organise the fire-fighting operation.

It was almost two hours after the attack before a helicopter of the Qatari Air Force arrived in response to the Mayday calls sent out by the damaged tanker's radio officer. By this time, McCaffrey and his team had succeeded in extinguishing the fire in the accommodation. The Captain was now weak from loss of blood, but only when he was satisfied his ship was safe did he hand over command to

Mitchell and allow himself to be flown to hospital with the other injured men. The *Caribbean Breeze* was later taken in tow by salvage tugs and anchored off Dubai for repairs. Two months later, she was back in service.

There can be no doubt that Captain David McCaffrey, by his courageous action and impeccable leadership, saved the *Caribbean Breeze* from total destruction, thereby averting a loss to her owners of in excess of 60 million US dollars. He also avoided massive and widespread pollution of Qatari waters. One would have expected recognition and reward to follow swiftly. This was not to be. At the time of writing, David McCaffrey, partly disabled by his injuries and his career as a shipmaster finished, was still engaged in a prolonged legal battle with his former Kuwaiti employers for adequate financial compensation. It is a battle in which he has precious few allies. Such were the rewards of seafaring in the 1980s.

Captain David McCaffrey, 'Caribbean Breeze'
(Photo: Sunday Express*)*

49 Summer in the Black Sea

Admiral Nakhimov & *Petr Vasev* - 1986

On a warm Sunday evening in August 1986 the *Admiral Nakhimov* let go her moorings for the last time and sailed out from the Black Sea port of Novorossisk, her decks thronged with passengers. The soft glow of the deck lights, the first stirrings of a cool sea breeze and the lazy strumming of the ship's orchestra gave promise of a peaceful end to a long and tiring day. This aged pioneer of cheap sea travel for the masses was continuing in a role she had played, with a few unavoidable interruptions, for sixty-one years. If she sensed she was embarking on the last voyage of her long and eventful career, then she gave no indication. She was as proud and majestic as the day her keel first encountered salt water.

From its inception in 1858, the North-German Lloyd Company of Bremen, operating in the flourishing emigrant trade with its close rival Hamburg America, had built up a reputation for cheap but comfortable crossings of the North Atlantic. At one period, the competition between the two companies was so great that North-German Lloyd was said to be carrying emigrants almost free of charge, at the same time supplying them with free blankets and eating utensils—concessions unheard of at the time. However, both companies were heavily subsidised by the German Government, enabling them to survive a long price-war and prospered into the twentieth century. In 1925, when North-German Lloyd launched the *Berlin,* its fortunes were on the wane.

Built by Bremer Vulkan of Vegesack, on the River Weser, the *Berlin* was a twin-screw, oil-burning steamer of 15,300 tons gross. She was a well found ship, but lacked much of the luxurious outfitting common to most transatlantic liners of the day. Despite these shortcomings, offering a modestly priced cabin class service between Bremen and New York, she gained immediate popularity with the new wave of emigrants fleeing the aftermath of the 1914-18 war. She carried a total of 1,122 passengers, this being reduced to 879 in 1929, when she outgrew the emigrant trade. Two years later she was joined by the 13,450-ton *General von Steuben* and the two ships operated successfully on the North Atlantic run until the mid-1930s, when events in Germany cast a shadow over their future.

When Adolf Hitler seized power in 1933, Germany was a country in deep crisis, bankrupt and on the verge of civil war. Acting with breathtaking speed, the new Chancellor outlawed strikes, disbanded the trades unions, and turned Germany's demoralised labour force into a disciplined organisation dedicated to economic recovery. Wages and prices were strictly controlled, and vast building and construction projects were started which gave people work, wages and a chance to regain their self-respect. There followed an amazing transformation from a country broken by a war lost and a peace that offered no hope into a united nation marching towards prosperity. Much of the outside world, itself in the grip of a dreadful economic slump, looked on in admiration. But too much power concentrated in too few hands led to the total suppression of democracy, the establishment of a police state and the persecution of the Jews and other minorities. When this became apparent, Germany lost all credibility and North-German Lloyd's lucrative transatlantic trade melted away.

By 1938, the *Berlin* had turned into an expensive liability and North-German Lloyd withdrew her from service and laid her up in Bremerhaven. But she was not to lie idle for long. In May 1939, she was taken over by the German Labour Front, a government-controlled body, which in the absence of trades unions, looked after the welfare of the workers, and amongst other things, ran health spas and holiday cruises. The *Berlin* became part of the Kraft Durch Freude (Strength Through Joy) movement, and undertook cruises packed with young, enthusiastic, bouncing men and women. She had become a ship of the people.

The *Berlin*'s new role was short lived. After only two cruises, on 17 July, 1939, off the Baltic port of Swinemunde, she suffered a boiler explosion which killed seventeen of her crew, and she was once again withdrawn from service. On this occasion, however, the liner's unemployment was equally short-lived. War was on the horizon, and the *Berlin* was drafted into the German Navy for service as a hospital ship and stationed in Hamburg.

In 1944, with Germany staggering under the assaults of the Allies, the *Berlin* became an accommodation ship for the Army, being joined by her old companion the *General von Steuben* and another ex-Strength Through Joy ship, the *Wilhelm Gustloff*. In February 1945, while taking part in a mass evacuation of refugees fleeing from the advancing Russians, all three ships were sunk in the Baltic, the *General von Steuben* and the *Wilhelm Gustloff* falling to a Russian submarine, while the *Berlin* hit a mine. The total loss of life in the three ships exceeded 9,000, most of them civilians.

For the other two ships it was the end, but not for the *Berlin*. In 1947, she was seized by the Soviet Union, salvaged, and towed to the Warnow Yard in the then Democratic Republic of Germany. Here, in a long-drawn-out refit lasting eight years, she was largely rebuilt, her tonnage being increased to 17,053 by added accommodation.

Widow-Maker

After being refurbished to a standard that would be regarded in the West as 'adequate but basic', she was handed over to the Black Sea Shipping Company, who renamed her *Admiral Nakhimov*, after a Czarist naval commander killed in the Crimean War.

Up until the 1970s, the *Admiral Nakhimov* operated commercially, cruising between the Black Sea ports of Odessa, Sevastapol, Yalta, Novorossisk, Sochi, Sukhumi and Batumi, a stretch of coast known as the 'Russian Riviera'. Her forty-five-year-old engines still functioned valiantly, but they no longer produced the sixteen knots of her transatlantic days. In the Baltic she cruised at a sedate ten knots, and with her facilities not being up to those being offered by younger ships, she slowly lost her appeal for fare-paying passengers, Soviet or otherwise. So, once again, the aged liner, threatened with unemployment, became a ship of the people. She was handed over to the trades unions, who awarded cruises on board as a reward for diligent work at the factory bench. For an oppressed people living under the grey mantle of Communism, the *Admiral Nakhimov*, superannuated though she might be, offered an escape from life's dreary round. The older the liner grew, the more she became loved by her proletariat clientele.

The *Admiral Nakhimov* was in her 62nd year, and the oldest passenger ship in service anywhere in the world, when she sailed from Novorossisk on 31 August, 1986, with a crew of 346 and 888 passengers. Under the regulations of most other maritime nations she would have long been condemned to the knacker's yard, but the Soviet philosophy was that so long as she floated she was fit for service. Certainly, there were few among her passengers that night—the majority of whom had never set eyes on a ship before—who would find fault with her. The accommodation was reasonably clean, the food adequate, and the State was footing the bill for the three-day cruise. There could be no justification for criticism. Tomorrow they would see the wonders of Batumi; its 250-acre botanical gardens, Museum of the Revolution, Palace of Culture, suphur springs and mud baths. Meanwhile, after a long day sightseeing in Novorossisk, with the temperature in the eighties, few passengers intended to be long out of their bunks. The weather was calm, and although the non-air-conditioned cabins were uncomfortably warm, sleep would come easily.

On the *Admiral Nakhimov*'s bridge, her master, 56-year-old Captain Vadim Markov was as tired as any of his passengers, but until the ship was clear of the approaches to Novorossisk he was not free to join the others below. He yawned and took comfort from the fact that the night was fine and clear, with little other traffic around. To port twinkled the lights of a clutch of fishermen, while a big ship was visible on the starboard bow. Markov examined the steaming lights of the ship through his binoculars and decided she must be one of the many bulk carriers running grain from America. It struck him as ironical that a country as fertile as Mother Russia was obliged to import food from the capitalistic West. But that was for the politicians to worry about. Markov reached for the VHF handset, intending to call the other ship, but before he could do so Novorossisk port traffic control came on Channel 16 to warn him of a ship approaching the port. She was, they informed him, the *Petr Vasev*, inward bound with 41,000 tons of grain, thus confirming Markov's opinion. Bearings were taken of the bulk carrier, and it was soon established that she was converging on the *Admiral Nakhimov*, and unless one or other of the ships altered course, a risk of collision existed.

The International Regulations for Preventing Collisions at Sea, the mariner's Highway Code, clearly states: 'When two power-driven vessels are crossing so as to involve risk of collision, the vessel which has the other on her own starboard side shall keep out of the way and shall, if the circumstances of the case admit, avoid crossing ahead of the other vessel.' In this case, the *Admiral Nakhimov* had the *Petr Vasev* on her own starboard side, and was therefore obliged by international law to keep out of her way. To do this she must either slow down to let the bulk carrier pass ahead, or alter course to starboard to go around her stern. However, not unexpectedly, what applies in the rest of the world does not apply in Soviet waters. Under Soviet maritime law, when two vessels are on a collision course and one is a passenger ship and the other a cargo ship, then the cargo ship must give way. If this rule was adhered to, then the *Petr Vasev*, and not the *Admiral Nakhimov*, was the giving way ship.

In order to avoid any confusion, Markov called the *Petr Vasev* on VHF and asked for her intentions. Captain Viktor Tkachenko, master of the bulker, replied reassuringly that he was aware of the situation and believed the two ships would pass clear of each other without the need for either to alter course. This was not how Markov saw it. His officer of the watch was taking constant compass bearings of the *Petr Vasev* and the bearing was not altering appreciably, a sure indication that the ships were on a collision course. Markov called the other ship again and made known his fears. Again he received a bland assurance that all was well.

Now was the time for Markov to take action on his own initiative, preferably to reduce speed or stop engines to allow the other ship to pass ahead, but he did not do so, preferring to point out to Tkachenko that he should give way. Tkachenko continued to make light of the situation, which led to a heated argument between the two captains conducted through the medium of VHF radio. And so, on a fine, clear night, the two ships, the *Admiral Nakhimov*, 18,000 tons travelling at ten knots, and the *Petr Vasev*, 40,000 tons making fifteen knots, were locked on a collision course, with neither prepared to give way.

Beneath the bridge of *the Admiral Nakhimov*; on the promenade decks, in the saloons and in the cabins, her passengers and most of her crew were totally unaware of the drama being enacted in the darkness of the night. Many of the passengers, exhausted by the day's activities, were already asleep in their bunks. Others, largely the younger ones, remained on deck, where the orchestra still played on, but with rapidly diminishing enthusiasm. Those of the crew not on duty were relaxing in the mess-rooms, or had turned in. Another port was behind them, and another day in the life of the people's ship was drawing to a close. And then without warning, it seemed the world came to an end.

There were a few, those who had paused to lean on the rails and drink in the beauty of the night, who saw the great raked stem of the bulk carrier looming up out of the darkness. They screamed in terror and ran. But, for the majority, the shock of the collision and the sudden heel of the liner were the only indications that all was not well. Then, slowly, the realisation of the dreadful calamity that was upon them spread through the ship, and panic erupted. To add to the chaos, the *Admiral Nakhimov*'s generators then blew up and the ship was plunged into complete darkness. For those caught below decks, lost in the narrow alleyways, or behind jammed cabin doors, there was no hope of survival.

It was three-quarters of an hour before midnight when the *Petr Vasev*, deep-loaded with grain and steaming at full speed, crashed into the starboard side of the *Admiral Nakhimov*, in way of her engine-room. The bulbous bow of the bulk carrier, projecting underwater like a huge battering ram, punched through the sixty-one-year-old liner's paper thin plates, and the flared bow of the carrier followed through, opening up the hull from the main-deck bulwarks to below the waterline.

Captain Tkachenko stopped the *Petr Vasev*'s engine, but instead of holding his ship in the gash in the *Admiral Nakhimov*'s side to minimise the effect of the collision, he went full astern. With a hideous screech of metal on metal, the bulk carrier backed out and water poured into the *Admiral Nakhimov*'s engine-room at the rate of 100,000 gallons per minute. The stricken liner fell heavily to starboard.

Confused and never far from panic themselves, the *Admiral Nakhimov*'s crew made a ragged effort to launch the lifeboats, but there was no time. Eight minutes after the collision, the liner rolled over on her side and sank, leaving hundreds struggling in the oil-covered water. At long last, luck had run out for the *Admiral Nakhimov*, ex-*Berlin*, ship of the people of two nations.

It was fortunate for those in the water that they were only seven miles from the land, and that the port authorities in Novorossisk had been monitoring the two ships on radar. When the frantic Mayday came over the VHF from the bridge of the *Admiral Nakhimov*, the rescue services moved into action without delay. The first rescue boats arrived in the area within ten minutes of the collision, and in under an hour no less than sixty-four craft and ten helicopters were plucking survivors from the water.

The rescue operation continued throughout that night, and for several days afterwards a team of divers worked on the sunken ship, 150 feet down, in the hope that more survivors might be found trapped in air pockets. The work of the divers was in vain. Two of their number lost their lives, and from the wreck of the *Admiral Nakhimov* they brought up only dead bodies.

Of the 1,234 passengers and crew on board the *Admiral Nakhimov*, 423 lost their lives on that tranquil summer's night in the Black Sea. That their deaths were caused by the gross misconduct of those who had charge of the navigation of the two ships is beyond question. The ships were known to be on a collision course from the time the *Admiral Nakhimov* cleared the breakwaters of Novorossisk, but for some perverse reason—was it a fear of losing face?—neither ship was prepared to give way to the other.

In the inquiry held into the collision, it was concluded that there was no logical explanation for the conduct of the two ships' captains. However, justice in the Soviet Union—then moving into the era of glasnost, was swift and harsh. Captain Vadim Markov and Captain Viktor Tkachenko were both arrested and charged with criminal negligence. In March 1987, they were tried before the Soviet Supreme Court in Odessa, found guilty, and each sentenced to fifteen years in prison, plus fines of £40,000. The Soviet Minister of Marine, Timofei Guzhenko, was also relieved of his post, presumably being blamed for a lack of control by his department over ship's captains in general.

50   The New Breed of Seamen

Scandinavian Star - 1990

A ny ship, irrespective of her flag, is only as good as the men who man her. She may be old and poorly financed, but in the hands of dedicated professional seamen she will rarely come to grief. The old British tramps of the 1930s, which ran on the thinnest of shoestrings, proved this beyond a shadow of a doubt. But men like those who sailed the tramps of yesteryear are now an expensive luxury.

On 8 April, 1990, fire broke out in the 7,838-ton passenger/car ferry *Norrona,* bound from the Bristol Channel port of Pembroke Dock to Rosslare, in Southern Ireland. A Mayday was sent out, but meanwhile her crew got on with tackling the fire. By the time firefighters were landed on the ship by helicopter, the *Norrona*'s men had the fire under control, and within an hour it was out. Ten passenger cabins were gutted, one crew member died and twenty-five passengers suffered the effects of smoke inhalation, but the ship was safe. Later, passengers described the actions of the *Norrona*'s British and Irish crew as 'magnificent'. Certainly, the prompt and disciplined response of these men to a serious emergency averted what might have been a major catastrophe. But then they were trained professional seamen of high calibre. The same cannot be said of the crew of the *Scandinavian Star,* which ran into similar trouble twenty-four hours earlier.

The 10,513-ton *Scandinavian Star*, a French-built passenger vessel, had a typical flag of convenience pedigree. Launched in 1971 as the *Massalia* for Nouvelle Cie de Paquebots of Marseilles, she spent twelve years sailing between Marseilles, Casablanca and the Canary Islands with holiday makers. In December 1983, she was sold to the Swedish Stena Cargo Line Ltd., to sail not under the flag of Sweden, but under that of the Bahamas. Renamed *Stena Baltica*, she embarked on her career as a flag of convenience ship. A month or so later, she was taken in for a refit, and emerged at the end of that year as the *Island Venture,* being advertised to run day cruises out of Tampico, Mexico. In March 1988, while under charter to Sea Escape Ltd. of Miami, she was cruising in the Gulf of Mexico, with 1,000 passengers on board, when fire broke out in her engine-room. The ship was badly damaged, but US Coastguard cutters were close at hand and there was no loss of life. However, her owners were severely criticised for poor safety standards on board ship. A month later, after repairs, the *Island Venture* came under the management of Scandinavian World Cruises and underwent yet another change of name, becoming the *Scandinavian Star.* When, in March 1990, the *Scandinavian Star* appeared in European waters, she was still wearing Sea Escape's colours, but was under charter to the Danish Da-No Line, a subsidiary of Vognmands Ruten. She continued to fly the convenience flag of the Bahamas, but her true ownership was cleverly shrouded in a fog of chartering and sub-chartering.

Da-No Line planned to use the *Scandinavian Star* in the ice-free waters of the Skagerrak, running a regular service between Oslo and Frederikshavn in northern Denmark. Several other companies were already operating on this route, catering largely for Norwegians on shopping expeditions to lower-priced Denmark. In order to capture a share of this highly lucrative trade, Da-No put the nineteen-year-old *Scandinavian Star* in for an extensive refit. Her amenities were greatly enhanced by the addition of extra bars, restaurants and a large discotheque, all designed to turn the twelve-hour night crossing into a fun-packed mini-cruise guaranteed to have the customers queuing up at the gangway.

When the *Scandinavian Star* re-entered service at the end of March, she was commanded by Captain Hugo Larsen, a Norwegian. Larsen had under him a crew of ninety-eight, made up of nine different nationalities, the majority being Portuguese and Filipino. No crew could have been less well qualified to man a passenger vessel on a short sea crossing, during which they were bound to be under constant pressure. The men had no common language, either amongst themselves or with the passengers in their care, other than broken English. While they may have been reasonably competent in their various duties, they were given only the most superficial training in emergency routines.

It was a fine, calm evening, with the chill of winter still in the air when, at 18.30 on 6 April, 1990, the *Scandinavian Star*, with 383 passengers on board, sailed from Oslo on her first crossing to Frederikshavn. It was the run-up to the Easter holiday, and the passengers were in a festive mood. From the moment the ship pulled away from the quayside the bars and restaurants did a flourishing business, and the disco throbbed to a wild beat as scores of young couples crowded onto the dance floor. The drink flowed freely, and many of the Norwegian passengers, unaccustomed to such easily accessible alcohol, were soon much the worse for wear. Before the night was far advanced, those with cabins had turned in, while others found comfortable seats in the lounges. Many, however, strictly against international fire safety regulations, dozed off in their vehicles on the car decks, a blind eye being turned on this infringement by the crew. Soon after midnight, with the exception of a few persistent revellers, the ship was quiet. She had by then cleared Oslo Fjord and was in the Skagerrak.

The first hint of danger came at 02.45 on the 7th when a lower deck passenger, apparently very drunk, set fire to his bedclothes. Fortunately the fire was quickly dealt with by a quick-thinking Portuguese barman armed with a fire extinguisher. The incident was reported to the bridge, but no action was taken. Fifteen minutes later, another fire broke out, this time on the lower car deck, right in the bowels of the ship. By the time this outbreak was discovered, it had gone beyond the stage when fire extinguishers would have any useful effect. The plastic panelling of the bulkheads was well alight, and giving off dense clouds of black smoke. The *Scandinavian Star* was then thirty miles south of the entrance to Oslo Fjord, with sixty-three miles to go to Frederikshavn.

Had positive action then been taken by the liner's crew, the fire might still have been contained, or at least held in check. But this was too much to expect. The appalling weakness in the manning of the flag of convenience ship now became all too apparent. Her newly-joined, multi-national crew had never been exercised on board in emergency drill, so few had any idea of how to set about dealing with the fire. There was a great deal of shouting in a multitude of different tongues, and a limited amount of communication in broken English and sign language, resulting in absolute chaos. Fire-doors were not shut, hoses not used, and no concerted attempt was made to move the passengers to a safe part of the ship.

Unchecked, the fire roared through the open car deck, reached a stairwell, and shot up into the accommodation decks. Thick clouds of smoke containing a lethal mix of carbon monoxide and hydrogen cyanide went rolling through the alleyways. Anyone who failed to escape ahead of the fumes was unconscious within thirty seconds, and dead in two to three minutes.

Those passengers lucky enough to reach the open decks, many of them still in their night-clothes, found they had escaped from a charnel house into a madhouse. Any order there might have been before had completely broken down, and passengers and crew, terrified and leaderless, milled around seeking an escape from the smoke and flames emerging from every door and ventilator. Eventually, some semblance of discipline was restored, and at about 03.30, eight out of the ship's ten lifeboats were launched. The boats reached the water safely, but when they tried to get away from the burning ship, the engines of seven of the boats would not start, and the dazed passengers were called upon to man the oars. It was fortunate that the sea was calm and rescue vessels from the nearby Swedish port of Lysekil were by then approaching the scene.

The *Scandinavian Star* did not sink. Shore-based fire-fighters boarded her and brought the fire under control. She was then towed into Lysekil later that day. It was only then that the terrible price that had been paid in the name of economy became evident. Of the 383 passengers that boarded the ship in Oslo for the overnight shopping trip, 158 lay dead, most of them suffocated in smoke-filled alleyways and cabins, or in their cars below decks.

At the Danish court of inquiry held to investigate the disaster, the ship, her owners, her master and her crew were all severely criticised. The court found that many of the *Scandinavian Star*'s fire alarms were not working, escape routes were not properly sign-posted, she had no sprinkler system in the passenger accommodation, and her lifeboats were poorly maintained. In other words, she was not equipped as she should have been for the safe carriage of passengers. It is therefore difficult to understand how, in January of that year, she was issued with a passenger safety certificate by the Bahamas Government, and in February passed inspections by Lloyd's Register and the US Coastguard.

Of the *Scandinavian Star*'s multi-national crew, the court commented that they had made no determined effort to fight the fire, or to organise the evacuation of passengers, until it was too late. They did not close fire doors promptly, and the engine-room was abandoned prematurely. Captain Larsen, although he perhaps did all he could under the circumstances, was found to have committed the cardinal sin of leaving his ship in a lifeboat while some passengers and crew were still trapped on board. Fortunately for him these people were later rescued by helicopters.

Captain Larsen, the ship's Danish owner, Henrik Johansen, and Da-No's managing director, Ole Hansen, were brought to trial in November 1992 accused of breaking Danish maritime safety laws. Larsen denied the charges and claimed that he was being used as a scapegoat by Da-No Line. He admitted that fire and boat drills had not been carried out, that he was aware the majority of his crew had no common language, and that he knew the ship to be unseaworthy. His defence lawyer argued that it he had refused to sail, another master would have been appointed in his place. Johansen was accused by the prosecution of being motivated by profit, and of failing to ensure that faults were remedied and the ship was seaworthy before she sailed. Several witnesses, including the *Scandinavian Star*'s chief officer, said Johansen refused to allow the sailing to be postponed to carry out boat and fire drills. Hansen was accused of attempting to maximise profits by hiring cheap seafaring labour under a flag of convenience.

Two hundred years ago, conditions on board ship for the merchant seaman were so bad that few volunteered to go to sea except misguided romantics, drunks and criminals on the run. Most ratings were recruited under dubious circumstances from dockside ale houses and brothels and shipped out while their wits were befuddled, irrespective of their suitability. Masters and officers were all too often cruel, sadistic, hard-drinking opportunists who drove their men with clubs and guns. Samuel Plimsoll and the passage of the years changed all that, and by the end of the Second World War, a career in merchant ships had become a well-paid, honourable profession. And so it remained, until the 1970s and proliferation of the flag of convenience.

Today, more than one third of the world's merchant shipping is flagged out. Heavy taxation, over-fastidious safety regulations and high crew wages have driven many shipowners to take refuge under one flag of convenience or another. The choice is wide. Panama, Liberia, the Bahamas, Cyprus, Malta, Gibraltar, the Cayman Islands, Mauritius, Madeira and at least half a dozen other countries offer their flags for sale. Even the fiercely nationalistic French have been reduced to registering their ships under the flag of Kerguelen, which is no more than a cluster of barren rocks deep in the Roaring Forties, and home only to flocks of itinerant penguins.

It must be said that many flag of convenience countries insist that ships sailing under their registry conform to the highest standards, with others the flag is a licence to operate outside all governmental control. Furthermore, a shipowner who registers his ship under a flag of convenience is at liberty to employ a crew of any nationality, or mix of nationalities, thereby saving up to one million US dollars annually per ship in manning costs. Once again, the choice on offer is considerable and the restraints few. Koreans, Filipinos, Chinese, Pakistanis, Cape Verde Islanders, and even the new poor of Europe, the Poles, Romanians and one-time Yugoslavs are standing in line to fill the berths vacated by men sacked for being too expensive. The curse of the cut-price seaman, incubated and nurtured under the flag of convenience, is spreading across the oceans unchecked and creeping into national-flag ships. It is estimated that almost fifty percent of the world's merchant ships are carrying some cheap Third World labour, mainly from South-East Asia.

At a conservative estimate, the Far East alone now supplies twenty-five percent of the officers and thirty percent of the ratings for the world's merchant ships. It is possible to ring a number in Manilla and have an entire ship's crew, from master down to galley boy, delivered to any part of the world within a few days. These men will all carry the requisite certificates of competency, but in reality they are likely to be the unemployed of a remote coastal village in the Philippines. The average wage paid is around 300 US dollars a month, and with no hidden extras such as social security, pensions and repatriation costs. For the hard-pressed shipowner struggling in today's cut-throat world the temptation is too great. The consequences can be grievous.

When, as is now common in flag of convenience ships, the crew is a mix of nationalities with no common language, day to day working is full of hazards, and a minor emergency can turn into a major disaster. It was so with the *Scandinavian Star*. The discovery of the second fire led to complete panic among her crew. There was no determined attempt to fight the fire, and if there had been, the men had no training for the job. Even the liner's German chief engineer admitted that he had no idea of the procedure to be followed in the case of fire. And, of course, the ludicrous mix of nationalities and languages exacerbated the confusion. When the fire gained such a hold that a speedy evacuation of the passengers was necessary, then the *Scandinavian Star*'s crew was again found wanting. Only the fortuitously calm weather and the quick response of rescue ships and helicopters avoided an even greater loss of life.

Unlike the 158 innocents who died in her, the *Scandinavian Star* lives on. Following extensive repairs in Southampton, she was bought by Greek owners and renamed *Candi,* under which alias she now continues her career in the Mediterranean.

51 Women and Children Last

Oceanos - 1991

The coastline of South Africa fronting the Great Southern Ocean is rugged, breathtakingly beautiful and as treacherous as any woman consumed with jealousy. Yet, seen from seaward against a backdrop of blue-hazed mountains, the steep, wooded headlands and sheltered bays present a picture of security. Indeed, it is possible to take a ship close inshore, for there is deep water to within a few hundred yards of the cliffs. But great care must be exercised, for there are unpredictable currents setting onshore and the long rollers that sweep up from the turmoil of the Roaring Forties are ever intent on shouldering an unsuspecting ship into danger. Since 1488, when Bartholomeu Diaz first came this way to open up the sea route to the East Indies, countless ships have ended their days on these rocky shores. Their broken and decaying bones, scattered from the Cape of Good Hope to the Umgeni bear witness to man's unchanging habit of ignoring the malicious intent of the sea.

On the evening of 25 February, 1852, HMS *Birkenhead* (see chapter 6) sailed from Simon's Bay, near Cape Town, bound for the Buffalo River, 500 miles to the north-east. Commanded by Master-Commander Robert Salmond, the 1,400-ton, iron-built paddle steamer was forty-nine days out of Cork with reinforcements for British regiments fighting a prolonged war with the Kaffirs. She had on board a crew of 129, a detachment of 489 troops of various regiments under the command of Major Alexander Sefton, their horses and equipment and seven women and thirteen children. Having also replenished her fuel and stores at Simon's bay, the *Birkenhead* was a heavily loaded ship.

Commander Salmond was under pressure to reach the Buffalo River as soon as possible, and so it would seem, he endeavoured to shorten the passage by sailing close to the coast. During the night the unrelenting swell and a local current swept the ship inshore, and soon after two o'clock on the morning of the 26th, the *Birkenhead* sliced open her bottom on an uncharted pinnacle of rock 1 1/4 miles off Danger Point, which lies forty-seven miles eastward of the Cape of Good Hope.

Most of the troops were asleep when the ship struck, and more than a hundred were drowned in their hammocks when the sea poured into the troop decks. On the upper deck, there was chaos as frightened soldiers ran wild-eyed in all directions. Women and children screamed, horses neighed and kicked as the heavily laden ship slowly foundered. There was a rush for the boats, and for a while it seemed that the women and children would be trampled underfoot. Then Major Sefton drew his sword and called on the troops to stand fast. This they did, and Sefton fell them in on deck as though on parade, leaving Salmond and his men to evacuate the women and children. Until their boat was clear of the ship, not a man moved.

A few minutes later, the *Birkenhead* broke her back and sank, taking with her Commander Salmond and sixty-seven of his crew, and Major Sefton and 386 officers and men of the British Army. The gallant action of those who stood fast as the ship went down earned them a hallowed page in the history books, and the 'Birkenhead Drill'—or women and children first—became part of the unwritten law of the sea.

In 1952, one hundred years after the *Birkenhead* went down, the passenger/cargo liner *Jean Laborde* was launched by Forges et Chantiers de la Gironde at Bordeaux. A twin-screw motorship built for the Madagascar service of Messageries Maritimes, the *Jean Laborde* was a 10,000 ton ship with accommodation for eighty-eight first class, 112 tourist and 296 third class passengers. She was a handsome, comfortable eighteen-knotter, and at a time when three out of four passengers bound overseas travelled by ship, she was much in demand.

The *Jean Laborde* served Messageries Maritimes well until the late 1960s, when the overwhelming convenience and speed of air travel dealt the final deathblow to the passenger ship. She was then sold to Constantine S. Efthymiades of Piraeus for service in the Mediterranean, where, under the name *Mykinai,* she began her long decline into genteel poverty. In 1971 she became the *Ancona*, and three years later she went to one of Efthymiadis' subsidiaries, Helite Hellenic Italian lines, for the Australia-Singapore run, being then appropriately renamed *Eastern Princess.* After two years in Far East waters, in 1976, she was bought by the Epirotiki Steamship Navigation Company, also of Piraeus, who had her rebuilt for cruising in the Mediterranean. Her cargo spaces were dispensed with, reducing her gross tonnage to 7,554, and when she came out of the yard she was named *Oceanos.* She was still a fine looking ship, but twenty-four years old, and her hull and engines were no longer of the best.

In July 1991, the *Oceanos,* by now thirty-nine years old, appeared in South African waters on charter to TFC Tours of Johannesburg. She continued to fly the Greek flag and was registered as owned by the Hellenic Company for Seas & Waterways S.A., a subsidiary of Epirotiki. The responsibility for the operation of this veteran liner was somewhat obscure, but she was still classed 100 A1 at Lloyd's, which was either a magnificent tribute to her builders, or a most generous gesture by the surveyors.

The *Oceanos* was under the command of 51-year-old Captain Yiannis Avranias, who had with him a mixed crew of Greeks and Filipinos numbering 183. In addition to her crew, the liner had on board a TFC Tours entertainments staff of twenty-six, which included musicians, comedians, singers and even a magician. Her cruising schedule of Cape Town—Port Elizabeth—East London—Durban in seventy-two hours was a tight one, but the *Oceanos* soon proved popular with South Africans looking for a short holiday with a difference.

Winter on the southern coast of South Africa is comparatively mild and untroubled. However, from time to time, vigorous depressions track in from the Atlantic, bringing with them high winds and rough seas that match the fury of the gales of the high latitudes of the northern hemisphere. The weather was so when, on the afternoon of 3 August the *Oceanos* lay at her berth in East London ready to sail. Out to sea, beyond the breakwaters sheltering the entrance to the Buffalo River, a nasty storm was brewing. Under a leaden sky, black rain squalls moved swiftly across the horizon chased by a cold westerly wind, and the white horses were running free. It was not a good day to venture out on the open sea, and a number of those who had booked passage to Durban had cancelled at the last minute. Others did so when news of the bomb scare leaked out.

About an hour before the *Oceanos* was due to sail, the East London harbour authorities received an anonymous telephone call warning of a bomb on board the liner. Police and bomb squad officers raced to the ship, only to be stopped short at the gangway on the orders of Captain Avranias. As was his prerogative, the Greek captain refused to allow the South Africans on board, insisting that his own security staff were competent to search the ship. Within the hour, he sent word ashore that the ship was clean and he intended to sail on time. Thus Avranias avoided a long delay and kept most of his passengers in ignorance of any danger to the ship—but at what cost?

Unknown to the East London harbour authorities, there was another and more valid reason for holding the *Oceanos* alongside. During the ship's stay in the port, her engineers had been working to rectify a fault in the waste disposal system. The non-return valves between the sewage tank and waste pipes leading into it from the accommodation had been stripped down, and a ventilation pipe passing through the watertight bulkhead between the tank and the generator-room dismantled. As so often happens, what had at first appeared to be a simple repair job turned into a major undertaking. When the time came for sailing, the ventilation pipe and a number of the non-return valves had not been replaced. Not wishing to be held responsible for delaying the ship, the chief engineer kept quiet about his problems, not the least being a four-inch hole in the after watertight bulkhead of the generator-room where the ventilation pipe had been removed.

When she sailed from East London at 15.30 that day, the *Oceanos* had on board a total of 361 passengers. It was not long before many of these regretted having boarded, for as soon as the liner cleared the breakwaters she felt the full force of the incoming swell and lurched heavily. Doors slammed, furnishings creaked in protest and there was the crash of breaking crockery carelessly left unattended. In the main lounge, where the traditional sailing party was in progress, the festive air carefully stoked up by TFC's staff was quickly dissipated as passengers turned pale and grabbed for handholds. The overnight passage to Durban promised to be an uncomfortable one.

On the bridge of the liner, Captain Avranias seemed less concerned with the deteriorating weather than with the necessity to maintain his schedule. To which end, he set his courses to hug the coast at a distance of two to three miles off in order to avoid the full force of the south-west flowing Aghulas Current.

The Agulhas Current has its origins in the equatorial regions of the Indian Ocean. It sweeps southwards on both sides of Madagascar and around the coast of South Africa to the Cape of Good Hope, before joining the Southern Ocean Current in its east to west journey around the bottom of the world. Over much of its length the Agulhas Current averages two to three knots, but between Port Elizabeth and Durban it can reach up to five knots. For ships westbound around the Cape, the current provides a welcome boost, but for eastbound ships the burden is heavy. However, nature is full of compromise, and the Agulhas Current does not encroach inside the hundred-fathom line, so that its effect is not felt when within about three miles of the coast. At this distance off, a counter current flowing north-east at up to one and a half knots is often experienced. It has, therefore, long been common practice for eastbound ships to hug the coast. But, as Commander Salmond of HMS *Birkenhead* found out to his cost, due regard must be paid to the occasional strong on-shore sets and the constant pressure of the swell. The modern vessel, reliably engined and equipped with radar and gyro, is not so vulnerable, but she must always be on her guard.

By 20.00, when the *Oceanos* was four and a half hours out of the Buffalo River, a forty-knot gale was blowing from the north-east and thirty-foot waves marched in from the horizon. Steering into the teeth of the wind, the liner charged headlong at the waves, flinging spray high over her forecastle head. Occasionally, she missed her step and slammed her forefoot into a wall of incompressible water with a crash that jarred every rivet and run of weld in her thirty-nine-year-old hull. Below decks, in the lounges and the dining room, where a few hardy souls were making a brave pretence of eating dinner, there was an air of nervous apprehension. It would have been safer, and infinitely more comfortable, if Avranias had been prepared to reduce speed, but he seemed oblivious to anything but the need to press on.

At around 21.30, a muffled explosion deep in the bowels of the ship was heard. Seconds later, the lights flickered and went out, plunging the entire ship into darkness. The whirr of the air-conditioning fans died, the regular beat of the engines faltered, and then stopped.

The emergency generator cut in automatically, and dim lights came on in the alleyways, but much of the accommodation remained in darkness. An eerie silence, broken only by the thud of a swinging door and the tortured creak of straining bulkheads, descended on the ship. Passengers and crew looked around uneasily, an unspoken fear hanging in the air. It was perhaps just as well they were ignorant of the true facts. The *Oceanos,* at the mercy of a rising gale, was lying dead in the water only two miles off the coast of Transkei, a dark, inhospitable region well named the Wild Coast.

With no way on her, the liner's rudder had no effect, and she swung round until she lay across the swell and beam-on to the wind and sea. Being, like all passenger ships, high-sided and with a tendency to be top heavy, she took on a pendulum-like roll that was both sickening and frightening.

Captain Avranias had no word of the magnitude of the problem in the engine-room, or whether the stoppage was momentary or indefinite. He was well aware, however, that his ship was drifting ashore, and something must be done to stop her. There was no shelter from the storm and the chart showed fifty fathoms of water under the keel—not an ideal situation in which to anchor, but he had no alternative but to try. He therefore sent his chief officer forward with instructions to let go both anchors. Much to Avranias's relief, despite the depth of water and the rocky bottom, the anchors held, and at the full length of their cables brought the liner's bow up into the wind. The rolling eased, and so long as the anchors did not drag, the *Oceanos* was safe.

The respite was short-lived, for soon afterwards a very distraught chief engineer arrived on the bridge. His report to Avranias was an incredible tale of disaster piled upon disaster. At sometime since leaving East London—the engineer could offer no explanation as to how this had happened—the ship had been holed below the waterline on the starboard side. This led to the flooding of the generator-room, with the resultant loss of all electrical power and the immobilisation of the liner's diesel engines. There was nothing that could be done to restore power.

The situation was obviously very serious, but, Avranias consoled himself, all was not lost. The generator-room was sealed off from the rest of the ship by watertight bulkheads, and so long as they held, the inrush of water would be confined to one compartment only. There was no immediate danger of the ship sinking. A brief radio message would be enough to bring powerful salvage tugs racing from Durban to tow the liner away from the coast and into port. Neither the owners nor the charterers would be pleased, but the ship and all on board would be saved.

Avranias was about to put the wheels of rescue in motion when the second bombshell fell. The chief engineer went on to explain about the uncompleted repairs to the waste disposal system, and the ventilation pipe removed and not replaced. Already the water was pouring from the flooded generator-room, through the four-inch hole in the bulkhead, and into the sewage tank, and there was no means of stopping the flow. Had the non-return valves been in place on the tank, then no further harm would have been done. But the valves were lying stripped down on a bench in the engine-room workshop. Once the sewage tank was filled and under pressure, then there was nothing to stop the water backing up the network of drainage pipes from showers, toilets and scuppers into the accommodation. The ship must inevitably flood deck by deck, and so, eventually, capsize and sink. Avranias ordered his staff captain to send out a distress call.

As the first Mayday went out over the VHF, word of the approaching catastrophe spread through the crews' quarters and thoughts immediately turned to self-preservation. Giving no thought to the safety of the 361 passengers in their charge, officers and ratings slipped quietly away towards the boats.

Although the *Oceanos*'s passengers were conscious that something had gone seriously wrong, no information had been passed to them, and they were in complete ignorance of the true state of affairs in the ship. TFC's cruise director, 35-year-old Lorraine Betts, made her way to the bridge, where she found the atmosphere so tense as to be bordering on the hysterical. When she tackled Avranias, it seemed to her that he had gone to pieces and was no longer in command of the ship. After a great deal of blustering, he did admit that there was water in the engine-room, but vehemently denied that his crew were abandoning ship.

Lorraine returned below realising it was up to her to take charge on the passenger decks. With the help of a few Filipino stewards who were still at their posts, she assembled all passengers in the main lounge wearing warm clothing and lifejackets. The pretext was that she was holding a routine lifeboat drill, but in the dim glow of the emergency lights, with the ship ominously quiet, there were few who really believed her. While no one was prepared to contemplate the *Oceanos* sinking, they were all very uneasy.

Meanwhile, in the absence of any reliable information from the bridge, two members of the TFC staff went below to investigate the true state of the ship. They found the lower decks silent and deserted, and already awash in places. The engine-room was in complete darkness, but the thunder of thousands of gallons of water surging from bulkhead to bulkhead with each roll of the ship told its own story. Others went to the boat deck, where a party of officers and ratings, complete with suitcases containing their belongings, were seen to be abandoning ship. They were taking No.1 lifeboat, one of only two fully-enclosed, radio-equipped, motorised boats on board—in other words, the best.

What happened thereafter is confused and subject to accusation and counter-accusation. But it is clear that Captain Avranias and his crew took little active part in the subsequent evacuation of the passengers. It was thanks mainly to Lorraine Betts and her staff of entertainers and administrators that, in spite of the heavy seas running, four more lifeboats were launched. By then a number of ships had responded to the *Oceanos*'s distress calls and were standing off waiting for an opportunity to move in to the rescue. During the night, a total of 344 passengers and crew were picked up by the Panamanian tanker *Great Nancy*, the Polish cargo ship *Kaszuby II,* the Dutch container vessel *Nedlloyd Mauritius*, the Norwegian trawler *Anik* and the refrigerated ship *Reefer Dutchess*. On a dark, wild night, close inshore, it was a superb demonstration of the international brotherhood of the sea at work.

At first light on the 4th, helicopters of the South African Air Force arrived on the scene. The *Oceanos* was lying over on her starboard side, rising and falling on the swell, her foredeck awash and her stern lifting out of the water. On her swimming pool deck at the after end of the ship, over 200 people, mainly passengers, were gathered awaiting rescue. In a brilliant operation lasting seven hours, the helicopters lifted off every person and flew them to the nearby holiday resort of Coffee Bay.

That afternoon, one and a half hours after the last survivors had been lifted off, the deserted *Oceanos* gave one last agonised roll and slipped beneath the waves bow first, taking her shame with her. Of her total complement of 571, not one had been lost, thanks largely to the courageous efforts of Lorraine Betts and her staff of twenty-five, none of them versed in the ways of the sea.

Captain Yiannis Avranias and Epirotiki Lines denied that the passengers on board the *Oceanos* had been left to their own devices, but there can be little doubt that the *Birkenhead* spirit was sadly lacking when the liner ran into trouble. Survivors complained that the crew of the ship had deserted them, and that it was solely due to Lorraine Betts and the TFC staff that any of them had lived through the ordeal. Most of the crew, including the chief engineer, eyewitnesses said, left the ship in the first lifeboats to be launched.

TFC musician Moss Hills said that following the explosion he saw crew members running from the engine-room wearing lifejackets. 'They were bordering on panic.....there were no announcements, no alarms, nothing.' Julian Russell, another of TFC's entertainers, said: 'It was disgusting. The captain, safety officer and other senior crew got off as quickly as they could, so there was nobody to show us what to do during the rescue.'

Many passengers claimed that Captain Avranias abandoned his ship while there were still more than 200 passengers on board. This was confirmed by South African Navy diver Paul Wylie, who was dropped onto the deck of the *Oceanos* to supervise the winching-off of survivors by the helicopters. Wylie stated that Avranias demanded to be taken off first, so that he could co-ordinate rescue operations from the shore. 'He indicated that he wanted to be airlifted off immediately. I told him we were dealing with elderly people and women first and ignored him. As I was helping other people into one harness, I found he had helped himself to the second one and was winched off. I was angry and surprised but we were far too busy to do anything about it.'

Avranias later claimed to have spent the next hours on board a South African Air Force transport aircraft co-ordinating the rescue, but this claim was denied by the authorities. In fact, Avranias landed in Coffee Bay from the first helicopter and there he stayed, taking no further part in the operation. He and his crew later needed police protection to save them from the wrath of the people they had so callously abandoned.

In May 1992, a Greek Maritime Board, held to inquire into the loss of the *Oceanos*, found Yiannis Avranias and five of his senior officers guilty of negligence. The heroes and heroines of that awful night, Lorraine Betts, Moss and Tracy Hills, Julian Butler, Robin Boltman and Piet Niemand, were all recommended for the Wolraad Woltemade Medal, South Africa's highest award for civilian valour. They were men and women; administrators, comedians, singers, musicians, who had no real knowledge of the sea, but when faced with a disaster, rose to the occasion with a courage and determination that matched anything shown aboard the *Birkenhead* 139 years earlier.

As to the *Oceanos*, she lies off the Wild Coast in 300 feet of water, her secret hidden perhaps for ever. Was she the victim of a bomb planted by terrorists? Did she rip open her bottom on an uncharted reef? Or did her old and rusting hull plates simply cave in under the assault of the sea? It is certain that her ultimate end was brought about by the failure of her engineers to complete the repair to her waste disposal system before sailing from East London, and those men must bear that guilt for the rest of their lives. It is fortunate for them that their burden was made lighter by the brave actions of Lorraine Betts and her staff, for without them hundreds would have surely died on that August night off the coast of South Africa.

The 'Oceanos' before plunging to the seabed
(Photo: Associated Newspapers)

Bernard Edwards

52   The Unwelcome Guest

Braer - 1993

The Shetland Islands, an archipelago of some hundred islands and rocks, known to the Romans as 'the northernmost land of the world', are deserving of their bleak reputation. Lying a hundred miles north-east of the Scottish mainland, with nothing beyond but the cold, grey waters of the Arctic, they are open to the full fury of the gales that sweep in from the North Atlantic all year round.

First settled by the Norsemen in the ninth century, and becoming part of Scotland in 1469, for more than a thousand years the Shetlands remained an isolated, self-sufficient community. Its hardy inhabitants lived by the soil and sea, raising sheep and cattle, oats, barley and potatoes, and harvesting the herring and cod that teemed in the cold waters offshore. The two world wars had their effect, the islands being used as an assembly point for North Sea convoys in the 1914-18 conflict, and in the Second World War as a base for clandestine operations against German-occupied Norway. Otherwise, apart from being known as home to a peculiar breed of short-legged pony and a distinctive type of woollen jumper, by and large, the world had passed the Shetlands by. Then, in 1972, the North Sea oil bonanza came in, and the easy-going islanders found themselves unceremoniously bundled into the twentieth century.

Sullom Voe, a huge deep-water sound in the north of the main island, was chosen as the loading terminal for tankers carrying North Sea crude oil to the refineries of the world, and with the tankers came riches undreamed of for the Shetlanders. Overnight, after generations of grubbing a meagre living from the land and sea, well-paid jobs were on offer to all, new roads were laid, new schools built, and previously unheard of leisure facilities provided.

This did not bode well for the Shetlands' role as one of the most wildlife centres in the North Atlantic area. Tens of thousands of sea birds over-wintered in the islands, and the crystal clear waters offshore were home to colonies of seals and otters, along with the abundance of cod and herring that provided a livelihood for many of the islanders. The appearance of 100,000-ton tankers deep-laden with black oil around their shores struck fear into the hearts of those who had for so long lived happily in tune with nature. An environmental disaster of catastrophic proportions was predicted.

The prediction failed to come true. Despite as many as ten tankers a week loading in Sullom Voe, the majority of them flag of convenience ships, the environment remained relatively unsullied, with no lakes of thick oil floating out of the bay on every tide. Furthermore, the tankers maintained a healthy distance off shore, refraining from impaling themselves on the rocks and spilling their noxious cargoes onto the white sand beaches. As the years went by, the Shetlanders came to accept their entry into the world of commerce with good grace. Then, in January 1993, more than twenty years after the oil first came to Sullom Voe, a threat came from a totally unexpected quarter.

On the morning of 4 January 1993, the motor tanker *Braer* lay alongside the Norwegian oil terminal of Mongstad, in Fens Fjord, some twenty miles north of Bergen, preparing for sea. It was not a good morning to be putting to sea; the sky was heavily overcast, the sleet turning to snow, and a stiff breeze was ruffling the iron-grey waters of the fjord, warning of worse to come. The tanker's master, Captain Alexandros Gelis, wished himself anywhere but at sea, however, the *Braer* was down to her winter marks with 84,500 tonnes of light crude North Sea oil, and under charter, bound for the Ultramar terminal at Quebec. Time was money.

The 89,730-ton *Braer*, built in Nagasaki in 1975, was a good example of a flag of convenience tanker of the nineties. Owned by a reputable company, Bergvall & Hudner Shipping Management of Stamford, Connecticut, she was classed by Norske Veritas and registered under the Liberian flag. She had started life as the *Hellespont Pride* of the Invincible Steamship Company, based in Monrovia; now, after nearly eighteen years hard running with the minimum of maintenance, she might still be seaworthy, but she was a ship in decline.

The *Braer's* one obvious weakness lay in the men who manned her, a mix of four nationalities, whose only common language was very basic English. Captain Gelis, his chief engineer and first assistant engineer were Greek, while the rest of the crew were Poles, Pakistanis and Filipinos, the latter predominating. And as if this did not raise enough problems, the *Braer's* men were at war with their employers. Over the previous twelve months, both officers and ratings had lodged complaints against Bergvall & Hudner with the International Transport Workers' Federation alleging they were poorly fed and forced to work long hours without proper payment. They were 'treated like slaves', to quote one complainant. There had been no improvement, and when she lay in Mongstad, the tanker's men were tired and disgruntled.

As his crew went through the motions of preparing the ship for sea, Captain Gelis paced the *Braer's* wheelhouse impatiently, stopping from time to time to tap the barometer and peer out at the grey, lowering sky. The weather forecast was not good. A deep depression in mid-Atlantic was reported to be moving rapidly east-north-east-wards, right into the *Braer's* intended path, and it was certain that her 3,000-mile passage to the Gulf of St. Lawrence would be a stormy one. Given time to spare—which he did not have—Gelis might have opted to go south and enter the Atlantic via the English Channel, rather than strike straight across from Norway. In this way he would avoid the worst of the weather, but would add another 400 miles to the voyage, which he could not afford to do. Reluctantly, Gelis had resigned himself to a rough passage north-about the British Isles, and with this in mind, his crew were now on deck securing anything that might come adrift in heavy weather, not least the four heavy flexible steel pipes used in the transfer of oil, and stowed in a rack forward of the bridge.

The *Braer* left the shelter of Fens Fjord in mid-morning on the 4th, and immediately ran into a rising southerly gale. The Atlantic depression, deepening as it advanced, had moved in quicker than anticipated, and within the hour the tanker was rolling and pitching heavily, beam-on to rough seas and a threatening swell. When darkness closed in at around 15:00—the winter day is short in these high latitudes—with it came driving rain and sleet squalls, seriously decreasing the visibility. Although the tanker was deep-laden, she rode the waves well, and with little traffic around there was no need to reduce speed, despite the indifferent visibility. In all probability, this might have been just another uneventful voyage if, later in the day, the *Braer's* engineers had not decided to shut down the ship's boiler for a 'routine adjustment'.

In common with most of today's motor vessels, the *Braer's* main engine burned heavy fuel oil while at sea, using lighter diesel oil only when manoeuvring in and out of port. As heavy oil is half the price of diesel, this makes sound economic sense. However, there is one difficulty. Before being used in an engine, heavy oil must be first heated to improve its viscosity—hence the need for a boiler in a motor ship. The *Braer* being in high latitudes in mid-winter, her boiler was doubly necessary, and making adjustments which involved shutting it down at sea was courting disaster. And so it proved. When, during the night, work on the boiler had been completed, all efforts to re-ignite the furnace failed. By this time, the heavy oil in the settling tanks had cooled and thickened, and in order to keep the main engine turning over, the engineers were forced to switch to diesel oil.

As the *Braer* made her way across the short stretch of water between Norway and the Shetlands, the weather deteriorated further. The wind was still in the south, and now bringing menacing, foam-crested rollers crashing in on the beam. The tanker lurched heavily from side to side and, having little freeboard, the seas climbed aboard to sweep her decks. She ploughed on through the darkness, salt spray lashing her bridge, her scuppers streaming.

Widow-Maker

At some time during that awesome night, when the *Braer* was in the twenty-two-mile wide channel between the Shetlands and Fair Isle—a turbulent stretch of water known to local fishermen as 'The Hole'—the oil transfer pipes lashed on deck forward of the bridge broke adrift. Each of these steel pipes weighed in the region of a ton, and as they began to charge from side to side on the deck of the rolling ship, they demolished everything in their path.

There was no question of re-securing the runaway pipes in the conditions prevailing, however, if Captain Gelis had seen fit to reduce speed and bring his ship's head round into the wind, it should have been possible to put a party of men on deck. Gelis took no such action, and the *Braer* battled on through the storm with her decks rapidly becoming a scrap yard.

The first indication of trouble came just after midnight, when the tanker was ten miles south of Sumburgh Head, the southernmost point of the Shetlands. Without prior warning, her engine faltered, and then stopped. It picked up again, but the beat was erratic, indicating that something was seriously wrong. The engineer on watch investigated, and found salt water in the diesel oil. The settling tank was drained and refilled. This seemed to solve the problem for a while, but at 02:30 on the 5th, the engine stopped again.

This time, the contamination of the diesel was found to be serious, and the *Braer*'s chief engineer concluded that the diesel tank must be open to the sea. He informed Captain Gelis, and advised him to make for a safe anchorage while he still had power.

Ever conscious of his obligations to the charterers, Gelis was reluctant to make a deviation, but the urgency in his chief engineer's voice convinced him of the need to act. He decided to make for the shelter of the Moray Firth, some hundred miles to the south, and at 04:36 hauled around to port.

With the wind and sea on the bow, the *Braer* rode easier, but within minutes of settling down on her new course, her engine coughed and died altogether. This time it could not be restarted. Then, at 04:40, the generators cut out and the ship was plunged into darkness. With no way on her, the *Braer* fell into the trough of the waves and rolled drunkenly, her decks awash with green water. She was a ship out of control and at the mercy of the elements.

At 05:00, Gelis called the coastguard at Wick, giving the first indication to the outside world of the loaded tanker's predicament.

With dawn still three hours away, the people of the Shetland Islands were rudely wakened to the news that the apocalypse they had feared for so long was at hand. Borne on storm-force winds, a ship carrying 85,000 tons of crude oil was less than ten miles off, and heading for their shores. The Shetland Islands Disaster Plan, which had lain so long on the shelf gathering dust, was hurriedly taken down and activated.

The plan was a comprehensive one, involving the use of salvage tugs, helicopters, and a great deal of oil-containing and dispersal equipment. But, as with so many such plans, much of it was on paper only. Just one helicopter was available, no deep-sea tugs were on hand, and the only oil-fighting gear of any consequence was 600 miles away at the Oil Spill Service Centre at Southampton. It soon became clear that the only real hope of salvation for the Shetlands lay with the *Star Sirius*.

The *Star Sirius*, an oil rig anchor-handling vessel on charter to the Shell Oil Company, had just arrived in the Shetland capital, Lerwick, from sea. At 1,500 tons, and with engines developing 9,000 bhp, she was built for rough weather work, and was strong enough to take the *Braer* in tow. Lerwick Coastguard approached her master, Captain David Theobald, who at once agreed to help. Soon after 07:00, the *Star Sirius* was nosing her way out of Lerwick harbour into the full fury of the weather. Theobald and his crew knew they were about to face one of the greatest challenges of their lives.

Thirty miles to the south, the stricken Liberian tanker lay drifting. Lashed by sixty-knot winds and battered by forty-foot waves, she was by then only five miles off the rocky Shetland coast, so close in to Sumburgh Head that the beam of the lighthouse bathed the ship in light each time it swept round. Conditions on board the *Braer* were as bad as they ever could be. Frightened and wracked by seasickness, the doomed tanker's crew were near to panic as they saw themselves being carried relentlessly towards what seemed like certain death. In a last ditch attempt to save his ship, Captain Gelis lowered both anchors onto the seabed, hoping they would snag and hold her off the rocks. This proved to have little effect. The *Braer* was in forty fathoms, and the deep water continued right up to the cliffs.

At 08:30, in response to the Mayday calls sent out by Gelis, a helicopter arrived overhead. Although the ship was rising and falling up to sixty feet on the huge roller-coaster seas, the helicopter's crew carried out a superb rescue operation, lifting off thirty of the *Braer*'s men. Gelis and three others stayed aboard, hoping for a miracle. With the dawn at last breaking, and the ship less than two miles off the rocks at the foot of Sumburgh Head, Gelis accepted defeat, and called the helicopter back. The four remaining men were taken off, and the *Braer* left to her fate.

Ironically, just as Gelis and his men were lifted off, the *Star Sirius*, accompanied by the deep-sea tug *Swaabie* arrived on the scene. The rescue ships, which had made a two-hour dash against the full force of the storm, were equipped with rocket line-firing apparatus, but there was no one on board the tanker to take their lines.

A further hour passed, during which the *Braer* drifted to within a mile of the shore. Then, the wind suddenly veered to the west and eased slightly. Hopes were now raised that, with the tide running to the east, the ship might be swept clear of the rocks. Seizing the opportunity, Captain Theobald took the *Star Sirius* in close and attempted to nudge the *Braer* away from the land, but the seas were too heavy. He was forced to pull back when his own ship was in danger of being thrown ashore.

A last chance to avoid the impending disaster came at 11:20, when the helicopter returned, flying low under the scudding clouds. On board were Captain Gelis, Jim Dickinson, oil pollution and safety advisor to the Shetland Islands Council, and two Sullom Voe pilots, men skilled in the handling of big tankers. When the opportunity occurred, the four men were dropped onto the *Braer*'s heaving deck, while the *Star Sirius* moved in to fire a rocket line across the ship. But time had run out for the tanker. Although the wind had veered, she was caught by an inshore-running current and drifting against the wind. She was almost on top of an outcrop of rocks off Garth's Ness, close to the west of Sumburgh Head. Gelis and the others were in the act of hauling on board a heavier line from the *Star Sirius* when, with an agonised screech of tearing metal clearly audible above the cacophony of the storm, the *Braer* ripped open her bottom on the rocks, and then settled with oil pouring out of her breached cargo tanks.

The helicopter, which had been standing by, was called in again to lift off the men stranded on the beached tanker, and thus no lives were lost in the failed salvage operation. The *Braer*, however, impaled on the rocks with thick black oil streaking the waves that broke over her, was finished.

The great fear in the minds of the authorities ashore was that the *Braer* would spill the whole of her 85,000 tonnes of oil, and bring devastation to the environmentally sensitive coastline of the Shetlands. Already, when darkness fell that day, dead seals were coming ashore, and the stench of oil was heavy over the land. Next day, the oil-pollution equipment, including booms, vacuum pumps and oil skimmers, arrived from Southampton. On the mainland, six Dakotas fitted for spraying oil-dispersant chemicals were standing by. Unfortunately, during the course of the morning, the wind rose to hurricane force, and the anti-pollution teams were helpless to intervene while the *Braer* continued to spew out her toxic cargo. The white-sand beaches of the Shetlands, their wildlife, and their fishing industry were all in peril.

As had been feared, the *Braer*'s entire cargo of oil leaked out into the sea, despite vigorous efforts to contain it when the weather at last relented. But what the sea had brought about, it then took care of. Local fish and wildlife suffered grievously, but within a few days strong winds and rough seas had dispersed much of the *Braer*'s oil by a process of agitation and evaporation.

Thus, other than the loss of a very large ship and her cargo, for which the owners and charterers were covered for a total of 23.7

million US dollars on the London and New York insurance markets, the consequences of the wrecking of the *Braer* were minimal. As for the unfortunate chain of events that culminated in this casualty, it seems most likely that things began to go wrong in Mongstad on the morning of 4 January, when the tanker's crew were preparing her for sea. On such a bitterly cold morning, even a hardened Scandinavian crew would have had little enthusiasm for the job. The *Braer*'s Filipinos, men from the sun-drenched tropics already disgruntled with their lot, must have found their miserable task beyond them. Under pressure from the bridge to make haste, it is possible that they failed to secure the heavy oil-transfer pipes properly. When, later that night, the pipes broke adrift in the heavy weather, it seems likely that one of them smashed an air pipe of the diesel tank, allowing the sea to pour into the tank. When the *Braer*'s engineer made the decision to shut down the boiler, the ship's fate was sealed.

The oil spill caused by the grounding of the *Braer* was the worst since the *Torrey Canyon* went ashore off the Scilly Isles twenty-seven years earlier, the cost of the clean-up and compensation paid exceeding 21 million US dollars. It is fair to say that this was a disaster waiting to happen. The *Braer* was a ship nearing the end of her useful life, and manned by a mixed nationality crew of questionable ability who were being exploited by an unscrupulous shipowner. All these chickens came home to roost off the Shetlands on the night of 4/5 January 1993.

Widow-Maker

Liberian flag tanker 'Braer' *ashore on the Shetlands*

(Photo: Numast*)*

Bernard Edwards

53   The Weak Link

Estonia - 1994

The 8,000-ton roll-on/roll-off ferry *Herald of Free Enterprise* sailed from Zeebrugge on the evening of 6 March 1987. She was crowded with day-trippers heading for home after a day's tax-free shopping in Belgium; also on board were a party of British servicemen going on leave, and the usual cross-Channel commuters. The evening was fine and cold, with only a light breeze blowing. A fast and uneventful crossing to Dover was anticipated.

The ferry cleared the breakwaters of Zeebrugge harbour at 18:20, and eight minutes later altered course for the open sea. As she did so, she suddenly heeled over and fell on her side. Fortunately, the ship was still close inshore and in shallow water. Rescue craft and helicopters were quick to arrive, but despite their efforts 188 people lost their lives.

A subsequent investigation established that, without doubt, on her final voyage the *Herald of Free Enterprise* had left harbour with her bows doors wide open. When she gathered speed, her bow dipped, and she scooped up the sea onto her open car deck, which was soon awash. With no bulkheads in the hanger-like deck to contain the water, it ran to the low side as the ferry leaned over in altering course. The bow then sank lower, more water came aboard, and the list increased progressively, until the ship lost her stability and capsized—or would have done if she had been in deep water. This disastrous scenario took no more than a few minutes to enact.

The roll-on/roll-off, or ro/ro, first showed its potential on the beaches of Normandy in 1944. Much to the surprise of the German defenders, tank-landing ships of the Royal Navy ran ashore, opened their bow doors, and disgorged squadrons of tanks directly into the battle. Warfare would never be the same again.

It was but a short step from Normandy into the commercial trade. When the dust of war had settled, and labour costs in the docks began to rocket skywards, it became clear that the old, labour-intensive break-bulk cargo system had to go. The way ahead was first shown by Colonel Frank Bustard, who founded the Atlantic Steam Navigation Company in 1946. Bustard bought three surplus tank-landing ships from the Navy, and began operating ro/ro services carrying cars and lorries between Preston and Northern Ireland, and

Widow-Maker

Raising the 'Herald of Free Enterprise'

(Photo: Ian Bowman)

between Tilbury and Antwerp. By 1957, Atlantic Steam was carrying 40,000 vehicles annually, and that same year launched the first purpose-built ro/ro, the 1,300-ton *Bardic Ferry.*

The essence of the ro/ro is that it accepts its cargo on wheels, and leaves it there, and as such it is really an extension of the road system. The drive-on/drive-off principle was ideally suited to the short-range passenger and vehicle trade, and it was not long before ro/ros dominated the ferry scene across the world.

The fate of the *Herald of Free Enterprise* showed in a most dramatic way how vulnerable the ro/ro, with its bow doors and bulkhead-less car deck, was. The tragedy led to the installation of warning lights and video cameras to ensure that bow doors were not accidentally left open. As to the fitting of bulkheads on the car deck to contain any influx of water, this was considered an unacceptable impediment to the drive-on/drive-off concept, and was quietly ignored. The years went by, and with nearly 4,500 ro/ro ferries operating safely worldwide, the painful memories of the *Herald of Free Enterprise* gradually faded. Then the *Estonia* hit the headlines.

The 15,556-ton *Estonia*, built in Germany in 1980, was one of a new breed of ro/ro ferries. Sailing under the Estonian flag, and jointly owned by Nordström of Sweden and Thulin & Estline of

Estonia, she had a capacity of 2,000 passengers and 460 vehicles. She was fitted with a visor-like bow door, which lifted to allow the inner door to be lowered by hydraulic rams to form a ramp. When closed, both doors were secured with stout locks, while the inner door was seated on a heavy rubber seal to maintain watertight integrity.

Employed on a regular service between Stockholm and the Estonian capital Tallinn, the *Estonia* was a popular ship. Among her many attractions were a tax-free supermarket, several bars, restaurants, gifts shops, a swimming pool and sauna below decks, and nightly entertainment. Cheap trips were run from both sides, giving the Estonians an escape from austerity, and the Swedes an opportunity to explore the newly liberated eastern shores of the Baltic. The fifteen-hour crossing in between gave both a chance to relax, and for some, the opportunity to indulge themselves.

The *Estonia* sailed from Tallinn at 19:15 on 27 September 1994, having on board 803 passengers, 186 crew, forty lorries, twenty-five cars, nine vans and two buses. Of her passengers, 520 were Swedish, 163 Estonian, 29 Latvian, two British, and the remainder were Russian, German and Lithuanian.

It was a dark, overcast night, with the wind gusting to gale force as the ferry left the shelter of Tallinn harbour. The weather forecast promised worst to come, but the falling barometer failed to dampen the spirits of the passengers. Cocooned in the luxury of the *Estonia*'s public rooms, they were in carnival mood. The band played, the wine flowed, the restaurants were full, and the supermarket tills rang merrily.

When she reached the open sea, the *Estonia* quickly worked up to sixteen knots, which in view of the weather conditions—it was blowing south-westerly thirty-nine knots with seas up to thirteen feet high—might have been deemed by some to be excessive. Had she been a conventional ship, with a flared bow and low profile, her progress would have been relatively untroubled. But the *Estonia* was anything but conventional; box-shaped, nine decks high, and with most of her hull above water, she was slamming into the short, steep seas awkwardly, and taking severe punishment. This, however, did not appear to trouble those on her bridge, and no effort was made to reduce speed.

At around 20:30, some twenty miles out of Tallinn, the movement of the ship became so uncomfortable that the band playing in the main lounge decided to pack up their instruments and call it a night. This was a signal for many of the passengers to retire to their cabins, leaving only the nervous and the determined drinkers to keep each other company.

The *Estonia*, her accommodation lights dimmed, struggled on through the wild night, forcing her way through the storm, pounding heavily and shipping spray over her bridge as she staggered from wave to wave. By midnight, she was seventy-five miles into the 200-mile passage to Stockholm and crossing the mouth of the Gulf of Bothnia. The incessant pounding of the waves on her bow became worse, but still she did not reduce speed.

At 01:00 on the 28th, Henrik Sillaste, a crew member, was passing through the car deck when with a loud bang the ship hit what appeared to be a brick wall and faltered momentarily before continuing her headlong race through the night. Sillastre went forward to investigate, and was alarmed to find himself up to his knees in water. The sea was pouring in through the inner bow door, which appeared to be partly open.

Sillastre ran to the control-room and called for the engineers to start the pumps, but it was too late. The TV monitor in the control-room showed the car deck to be already awash, and the sea was surging in each time the *Estonia* met a wave. All available pumps were put onto the car deck, but they could not cope with the inflow of water.

The sequence of events that followed was rapid and catastrophic. By 01:15, the *Estonia* had acquired a fifteen degree list to port, five minutes later she was heeled thirty degrees and showing no sign of righting herself. Almost immediately, her four diesel engines cut out and she was left dead in the water, over on her side and drifting helplessly at the mercy of the wind and waves. Her position was approximately twenty miles south of the Finnish island of Utö.

It was only now, with the ship so obviously disabled, that it was thought fit to alert her passengers. Even then, the garbled message given over the public address system in Estonian was not understood by the majority of passengers. This was followed by a coded alert to the crew, and two minutes later, the abandon ship signal was given on the ship's alarm bells. By this time, the *Estonia* had a list of thirty-five degrees to port.

The only distress call to be broadcast by the ferry did not go out until 01:24 and was received by a number of stations ashore and afloat. It ran: 'MAYDAY, MAYDAY. THIS IS *ESTONIA*. TWEN-TY-THIRTY DEGREES HEAVY LIST. POSITIO 59 DEGREES 22 MINUTES.' The message was ambiguous, the position given incomplete, but it was enough to indicate to the rescue services that they had a major disaster on their hands.

When the alarms bells rang, most of the *Estonia*'s passengers were asleep in their cabins, some of them nine decks down. Few of them had been aboard long enough to become familiar with the layout of the ship, which like all large passenger-carrying vessels was a maze of alleyways and stairways below decks. Now, in complete darkness—the generators had failed with the engines—and with the cross-alleyways becoming near-vertical shafts as the list increased, the sleep-dazed, frightened passengers became completely disorientated. Only the fit and young had any hope of escape, and, not surprisingly, panic broke out.

Bernard Edwards

The *Estonia*, her car deck and lower accommodation rapidly flooding, had developed an unstoppable list, which by 01:35 reached eighty degrees. Five minutes later, like the *Herald of Free Enterprise* before her, she fell over on her side, and being in deep water, she then rolled right over.

The stricken ferry carried ten lifeboats and a full complement of inflatable liferafts. The speed at which the list developed prevented any boats from being launched, but some of the rafts, which were self-inflating, floated clear of the capsizing ship. In these lay the only hope of survival for those fortunate enough to reach the upper deck.

Neeme Kaik, an Estonian passenger later told his story: 'I woke up as the ship was heavily tilted. I got dressed as fast as I could and ran out of my cabin to the deck to see what was going on. There was no message on the loudspeaker. I saw people rushing up the stairs to the upper decks. When I reached there, people were grabbing lifejackets.

'There was no activity among the crew and I did not hear any messages. I grabbed a lifejacket and then the boat fell on its left side completely, with the funnel hitting the water. The engines did not work. I managed to jump into a rubber boat with three other people.

'The last we saw of the *Estonia* was the bottom of her hull sliding swiftly beneath the waves.'

Vilho Itaranta, a Finnish passenger, said: 'The ship was listing so badly I had to climb to the other side. I jumped overboard. The first wave smashed me against the ship and I hit my head, but I managed to get hold of a rubber raft while two people were holding on to me, and someone helped me onto the raft.

'It was very difficult to climb onto the raft because it was so high. First a woman held my hand, but she did not have the strength to pull me up because two other men were clinging to me. Finally, a man managed to pull me up. I do not know what happened to the others. There was a metre and a half of water in the raft. We got the roof up but it was partly torn.

'I think we were six on the raft. One man died soon and the girl who had tried to pull me up from the water died one hour before the helicopter got us up after six hours.'

Itaranta was one of the lucky ones. Inflatable liferafts are prone to capsize in a strong wind, and many survivors found themselves aboard a raft, only to be thrown back into the sea when the raft flipped over. Others, who in blind panic had jumped overboard from the doomed ferry, perished in the dark, cold waters of the Baltic.

The close proximity of the land undoubtedly saved many lives that night. Within an hour of the *Estonia*'s Mayday being broadcast, five other ships had arrived in the area, but it was not until first light that helicopters—twenty-six in all, from bases in Denmark, Finland and Sweden, were overhead. By then, weather conditions had worsened considerably, and the rescuers were working in winds of up to seventy knots and twenty-foot seas. Most of the inflatable rafts they found tossing on the waves were empty, and after a search that lasted long into the next day, only 137 survivors and forty-two bodies had been picked up. There would be no more.

Of the 989 souls on board the *Estonia*, no fewer than 852 died, and most of those still lie with the ferry forty fathoms deep in the Baltic. The loss of the ferry would go down in history as the worst maritime disaster in western waters since the *Titanic* sank in 1912.

The fourteen-year-old *Estonia* was a large, well-found ship, conforming to all the safety regulations governing the operation of a vessel of her class, although it was claimed—but never proven—that her inner bow doors were found to be faulty prior to sailing from Tallinn on 27 September. The inquiry into the sinking dragged on for more than three years, allowing for a number of wild theories for the ferry's loss to be advanced. The most bizarre claim was that some crew members opened up the bow doors at sea in order to get rid of a truck containing either drugs or nuclear material following a tip-off that police were waiting in Stockholm to search the ship.

None of these theories proved credible, and were dismissed by the joint Swedish/Estonian/Danish commission of inquiry, which finally issued its 228-page report in December 1997. The *Estonia*'s 56-ton bow visor had been recovered from the sea bottom a mile away from the wreck in November 1994, and from this the inquiry found that the door locks were not strong enough to withstand the force of the heavy seas experienced. The findings of the court were immediately challenged by the *Estonia*'s German builders, Meyer Werft, who pointed out, not without justification, that the ship had been sailing through all weathers for fourteen years, and had experienced no problems with the bow visor.

Much more to the point was the inquiry's finding that the *Estonia*'s speed had been excessive in the weather prevailing. She was being pushed at sixteen knots into very rough seas, and water being incompressible, the visor was subjected to considerable stress. It was in fact estimated that each time the ferry buried her bows in the seas, the impact on the visor was between 600 and 700 tons. One of the basic rules of good seamanship in heavy weather is to slow down and ease the strain on the ship. Had the *Estonia*'s master exercised more caution and reduced speed when his ship began to pound heavily, then this dreadful tragedy might never have happened. Evidence was produced to show that no reduction of speed was made until the ship had, in effect, stove in her own bows against the oncoming seas. It will never be known exactly what transpired on that night, but it is now assumed that when the locks on the *Estonia*'s bow visor failed under the constant pounding of the sea, it was forced upwards and torn off. This caused the inner door to be drawn out, and the sea was scooped up into the car deck. As with the *Herald of Free Enterprise*, the large surface area of water swilling around caused the ferry to lose her stability, and hence to capsize.

Only ten of the *Estonia*'s crew of 186 survived the sinking, and they had been unable to do little to influence events. The inquiry criticised the crew as a whole for lack of positive action throughout, but it must be borne in mind that crewing a ferry has none of the attractions of sailing deep sea. It is the same old routine day after day, night after night, the same stretch of water to cross, the same sheep-like passengers to play nanny to. The work can be boring, and the temptation is to take too many things at face value, to accept that little can go wrong that cannot be fixed when the ship reaches port. And, of course, the commercial pressures are constant and heavy.

The fate of the *Estonia* proved that nothing had been learned from the loss of the *Herald of Free Enterprise*, despite all the publicity at the time. The ro/ro, commercially successful though it may be, still has one great inherent weakness. In order to operate efficiently, its car deck must be free of all obstructions, and that includes bulkheads. A conventional ship is sub-divided by a number of watertight bulkheads, and if the hull is breached, any water that enters can be contained. This is not so with the ro/ro. Water entering the car deck is free to flow from side to side, and creates a virtual centre of gravity. As the ship rolls and the free surface of water changes shape, this centre of gravity moves up and down, which can lead to the ship's resultant centre of gravity rising above her metacentre. In other words, she becomes unstable and liable to capsize. Today, despite all the warnings, roll-on/roll-off ships still sail without divisional bulkheads on their car decks. The next *Estonia* may be one of the 5,000 passenger ferries presently on the drawing board.

54 Malaccan Mayhem

Sun Vista - 1999

With the advent of the jumbo jet, the era of the passenger liner, which for so long had dominated cross-ocean travel, came to an end. The changeover was gradual, but by the beginning of the 1970s the long, lazy days at sea, with gin & tonics served by white-coated stewards, had given way to journeys that were measured in hours, not weeks. In an increasingly affluent world, faraway places soon became, for the first time, accessible to the ordinary man in the street, his wife and his children. It began with the short-haul to the Costa del Sol, and as aircraft became more efficient and fares plummeted, tour operators were able to offer cheap packages ever further afield, to Greece, to Eygpt, to the Americas, to the exotic East.

Inevitably, the novelty of being shoe-horned into a charter jet flying at 35,000 feet began to wear thin. It may well be that the common man had found the means to span the world, but a frenetic two-week package in Disneyland was doing nothing to alleviate the stresses of modern life, from which he was trying to escape. And so the call went out to bring back the days of gracious living.

The cruise liner was the answer. Elegant ships, offering fine accommodation, gourmet food, swimming pools, cinemas, nightly stage shows—all the facilities of a luxury hotel while sailing the oceans in search of wall-to-wall sunshine. The idea soon caught on, and as competition brought prices down, so the demand for berths rose. In the past decade, the cruise market, once the exclusive domain of the rich, has increased five-fold in the United Kingdom alone. World-wide, cruise liners now carry up to eight million passengers a year and the trade is on a steeply rising curve. Shipyards, working to capacity, are unable to keep pace with the insatiable demand for new cruise tonnage. Meanwhile, ships from the past, quietly mouldering away in the backwaters of the world, are being called back into service. The *Sun Vista* was typical of this breed.

The 30,440-ton *Sun Vista*, had a distinguished pedigree, but a somewhat chequered career. A twin-screw, twenty-four-knot ship accommodating 1,104 passengers, she was built in 1963 by Cantieri Riuniti dell'Adriatico of Trieste for the prestigious Lloyd Trestino Line as the *Galileo Galilei*. With her twin-sister the *Guglielmei*

Marconi, she operated a fast service between the Mediterranean and Australia until the summer of 1971, when, with the demand for passages falling off, she began a series of round-the-world voyages. Six years later, bowing to the inevitable, Lloyd Trestino converted her for cruising, and in 1983 sold her to the Greek-flag Chandris Line, who shortened her name to the much more manageable *Galileo*. She served her Greek owners well for fourteen years, being eventually sold on to the Australian-based Sun Cruises, who after a $25 million face-lift, renamed her *Sun Vista*, and placed her under the Bahamas flag. The rejuvenated thirty-six-year-old liner, with 547 passenger cabins on eight decks, offered the last word in luxury, including swimming pools, beauty salons, bars and casinos. But while in her accommodation the *Sun Vista* might resemble a new ship, there could be no escaping the fact that her hull and engines had seen three and a half decades of constant service in a demanding trade. Based in Singapore, she began cruising in Far East waters.

The *Sun Vista* sailed from Singapore on 15 May 1999, having on board 472 passengers, British, Indian and Australian, the majority being elderly. Under the command of Captain Sven Bertil Harpzell, she carried a total crew of 632, of which Harpzell and his six senior officers were Swedish, the rest being Filipino.

The voyage had been advertised as 'A Cruise of a Lifetime'— and little did the *Sun Vista*'s passengers know that it would turn out to be just that. They were promised six days of cruising the Malacca Straits, with a call at Malacca, and then on into the Andaman Sea to the fabulous Thai resort of Phuket. After sampling the delights of this island paradise, which shot to fame in the 1970s when one of its bays was used as a setting for the James Bond film 'The Man With the Golden Gun', she would sail back to Singapore. With the balmy north-east monsoon prevailing, it was to be blue skies and calm seas all the way.

The *Sun Vista* left Phuket on the return leg of her cruise late on the 20th. Her passengers, mellowed by the warm sunshine and pampered by the smiling Filipino stewards, were in a relaxed holiday mood, and totally unprepared for what was to come.

Early on the afternoon of the 21st, the liner was sixty miles south of Penang Island, and just over twelve hours steaming from Singapore. It was a hot, humid afternoon, the sea was as calm as the proverbial millpond, and the spicy fragrance of the distant land was on the air. Some of the passengers were still lingering over lunch, others were at a bingo session in the main lounge, the rest had spread themselves around the pool to soak up the sun. The scene was a familiar one in passenger ships cruising in the tropics.

Sixty-three-year-old Shirley McKieron, the representative on board for Saga Holidays, was one of the first to suspect that all was not well: 'At about 2 pm I saw flames shooting out of the funnel. I reported it to the crew. They told me there was nothing to worry about, and that they were simply cleaning the diesel engine.'

Shirley McKieron's fears were calmed for the moment, but all was not well below. A fire in the *Sun Vista*'s main switchboard had set light to oil in the bilges, and the engine-room was already filling with dense black smoke. Within half an hour the fire was burning out of control and the engines were stopped and engine-room evacuated. The *Sun Vista* drifted to a halt, smoke now pouring from her funnel and engine-room ventilators.

The recommended practice with a serious fire in the engine-room is to seal off the space and flood it with carbon dioxide gas, which should have the effect of smothering the fire. The *Sun Vista*'s CO_2 system was activated but, possibly because the compartment was not properly sealed off, the gas failed to make any appreciable difference. With his CO_2 cylinders exhausted, Captain Harpzell then ordered in the hoses, and water was poured into the engine-room from above.

Meanwhile, Harpzell had instructed his stewards to distract the passengers' attention from the emergency by holding a barbecue on deck, with liberal supplies of free beer. The ruse failed to work, largely because by now everyone on board must have been aware of the seriousness of the situation they faced. The accommodation was in complete darkness, and smoke was seeping through the bulkheads. Dazed and frightened, the passengers ignored the free food and drink, and huddled together on the upper deck looking for reassurance and guidance. Neither was forthcoming.

Attempting to fight the fire with hoses from above proved to be a fatal mistake. The water had little effect on the fierce conflagration, and with all the ship's pumps out of action, the net result was to flood the engine-room, and eventually the lower decks. The *Sun Vista* began to sink.

At 18:30, Captain Harpzell at last accepted that he had lost the battle to save his ship, and ordered the boats to be swung out. At the same time, four and a half hours after the fire was first discovered, he broadcast an SOS.

The sun had by now set, and darkness was fast closing in. But the sea remained a flat calm, the ship was upright, and she had ample lifeboats to accommodate all passengers and crew. In which case, properly supervised, the evacuation should have been a relatively simple and orderly operation. It turned out to be anything but that.

Sixty-two-year-old Tom Bonnard, a British passenger, summed it up: 'It was a nightmare. All the lights on the ship went out, and the next thing we knew we were being herded into lifeboats. But the crew had not got a clue. They were more panicky than the passengers. Our lifeboat's engine failed and we kept drifting back towards the ship.'

Peter Andrews, 76, another Britisher, related how he spent eight hours in a lifeboat before being rescued by a passing cargo ship.

'My lifeboat was overloaded,' Andrews said, 'there were seventy-six people in it when the capacity was forty-five, and the person responsible didn't seem very confident.' Thirty-two-year-old Indian businessman Ram Yalamanchi commented: 'It was a true nightmare. I thought we were all going to die......people were screaming, praying. It was awful, the most terrifying experience of my life.'

The last hours of the *Sun Vista* were indeed handled with unbelievable incompetence. Having bungled the attempt to contain the fire, the liner's crew allowed it to burn for more than four hours before the decision was made to call for help and abandon ship. Then they turned what should have been a copybook evacuation into an astonishing fiasco. Because of the long delay in deciding to abandon ship, the fire was so advanced that the accommodation was filled with smoke, and passengers were unable to go below to collect warm clothing and valuables. And when they finally did take to the boats, it soon became clear that the *Sun Vista*'s seamen were woefully inexperienced in boat handling. Some boats were overloaded, some half empty, engines refused to start, and there was a marked absence of the tight hand of authority needed on such a traumatic occasion.

In the end, the blazing liner having been abandoned to her fate, all 1,104 passengers and crew escaped in eighteen lifeboats and four rafts. Fortunately, the sun had gone down, for many of the passengers were scantily dressed, some in swimsuits, and if they had been forced to spend hours in the open lifeboats under the blazing equatorial sun, they would have suffered greatly. As it was, cold and frightened, they drifted for seven hours, during which time they watched the waterlogged *Sun Vista* sink, before the first rescue ships came along.

The loss of the *Sun Vista* was certainly a maritime disaster that never should have happened, and its roots undoubtedly lay in a largely inexperienced crew having charge of a time-expired liner brought back to life under a flag of convenience. However, more by good luck than good judgement, no one died, and the few injuries incurred in abandoning ship were minor ones. What might well have happened is illustrated by the loss of the *Royal Pacific* in those same Malaccan waters in August 1992.

The 350 holidaymakers who boarded the 13,176-ton Greek-owned *Royal Pacific* at Singapore had been promised two days of 'Champagne Wishes and Caviar Dreams' cruising in the Malacca Straits. The food and drink lived up to the eloquent tour operator's promise, but when the Bahamas-flag liner was hit by a large Taiwanese fishing boat she sank in fifteen minutes.

The collision occurred at 3 o'clock in the morning, when most of the *Royal Pacific*'s 534 passengers and crew were fast asleep. Pandemonium broke out as the crew struggled to launch lifeboats from the blacked-out ship. Several of the wooden boats were smashed against the ship's side, and thirty people lost their lives and seventy

Widow-Maker

The 'Sun Vista' *passengers take to the boats*
(Photo: Numast)

more were injured.

The *Royal Pacific*, began life at Sydney in 1965, built as the *Empress of Australia* for the Australian Coastal Shipping Commission. She was a purpose-built car and commercial vehicle/passenger ferry, and sailed between Sydney and Tasmanian ports for twenty years before being sold to Cypriot owners. Under the name *Empress*, she then operated in the Mediterranean for four years, before she was sold on to Sun Cruises Maritime of Greece, who converted her to a cruise ship, renamed her *Royal Pacific*, and hoisted the convenience flag of the Bahamas.

Contrary to what might be supposed, the *Royal Pacific* and *Sun Vista*—whose separate owners may or may not have been connected—were not regrettable one-off happenings, but part of an increasing catalogue of disasters occurring on the cruise circuit today. Competition in the trade has become fierce, and costs are being cut to the bone, with the result that some tour operators are selling dreams that turn into nightmares.

Operationally, the modern ship differs little from her predecessor of a hundred years ago. The mode of propulsion may have changed radically, and navigation is now an exact science, but strip away all the computer technology—which is, after all, highly dependent on other things functioning well—then everything hinges on the seaworthiness of the ship and the competence of her crew. If she happens to be a geriatric ex-ocean greyhound, sailing under a flag of convenience, with a poorly trained and motivated crew employed only because they are cheap to hire, then minor incidents often become major disasters.

Fire in the engine-room has always been a dreaded scenario at sea. A ship hundreds of miles away from land has no local fire brigade to call upon, and if her crew cannot deal with it effectively, then the fire will consume the ship and drive all on board into the water. Prevention is, of course, always preferable to cure, and if a ship's engine-room is kept scrupulously clean, with no build-up of waste oil allowed, then any fire which does break out is usually minor and easily extinguished. But in order to keep engine-spaces clean and oil-free, sufficient men must be carried in each watch and a strict routine enforced. The modern trend is towards smaller and smaller crews, and, particularly in flag of convenience ships, the cheapest men available are signed on. It follows that the standard of crewing in these ships is such that, either by inexperience, lack of training or lack of motivation, safety is all too often afforded a low priority.

In the case of the *Sun Vista*, her crew appeared not to have the first idea of how to deal with a serious engine-room fire and, in fact, through their ill-advised action in flooding the engine-room, managed to sink their own ship. It was only by the grace of God and good weather that they did not have the lives of many innocent people on their consciences.

The *Sun Vista*'s passengers may have escaped with their lives, but they saved precious little else. Rescued from their boats and rafts by passing merchant ships and Malaysian naval vessels, they were landed in Penang, and later airlifted to Singapore 'barefoot, wearing only singlets and shorts and carrying plastic bags with their toiletries'. In Singapore, Sun Cruises gave each of them $300 to buy new clothes and promised a full refund for the cruise, but there are some things that cannot be recompensed. Thirty-nine-year-old Georgean Stewart, a Scottish nurse, summed it up: 'It was frightening, very frightening. I'm never going to go on another cruise liner.'

The great majority of the cruise liners of today sail under one flag of convenience or another. Panama, Liberia, the Bahamas, Bermuda, Cyprus, Mauritius, Vanuatu, the list of maritime tax havens is growing apace as more and more impoverished nations join the ship registry gravy train. Of the crewing of these ships, NUMAST, the Merchant Navy officers' union, reports: 'While cruise-ship passengers lounge in the sun on deck or plough through sumptuous five-course meals, many crew members are working more than seventy hours a week—sometimes for basic wages as little as $50 a month.

'*Find the perfect job in paradise!*' one cruise-ship recruitment advertisement boasts. But often the reality for cruise-ship personnel is far from the glossy, glamorous life portrayed in the brochures.

The International Transport Workers' Federation says it is concerned at the increasing number of complaints it receives from exploited crew members, on issues such as poor living and working conditions, non-payment of wages, physical and sexual abuse, and racism.

'NUMAST has dealt with an increasing number of complaints from members (officers) in the cruise sector—often relating to poor working conditions, contractual arrangements, or the state of their ships.

'The ITF firmly links the deterioration in cruise-ship pay and conditions to the increase in the number of vessels flying flags of convenience.......Some cruise-ship companies make crew members meet the costs of flights to and from the ship. Some deduct the costs of uniform from wages, and many contracts specify a minimum of seventy hours per week.'

A worrying trend has recently emerged in the Miami-based Carnival Cruise Lines, part of the world's largest cruise company, Carnival Corporation, which owns forty-two ships operating under six different lines, and all registered under flags of convenience.

In July 1998, a serious fire broke out on board Carnival's 70,367-ton *Ecstasy* shortly after leaving Miami with 2,575 passengers and 868 crew. The fire, which started in the crew's laundry, was not discovered until the alarm was raised by other ships which had seen smoke pouring out of the *Ecstasy*'s stern. Fortunately, the liner was still within sight of land, and fire-fighting tugs were soon on hand. The same company's 35,190 *Tropicale* was out of service for five voyages following a fire which started in her engine-room while she was cruising in the Gulf of Mexico with 1,700 passengers on board in September 1999. Just four months later, in January 2000, an engine-room fire in yet another Carnival ship, the 47,262-ton *Celebration*, disabled her and threatened the lives of her 1,586 passengers when 100 miles north-west of Montego.

The spectre of fire at sea now hangs over the cruise ships, which day by day are becoming larger and more luxurious, yet retain this terrible weakness brought about by dumping the old-style seaman and replacing him with the modern cut price sea labourer.

Bernard Edwards

55   Bridge Overload

Norwegian Dream & Ever Decent - 1999

In the halcyon days of shipping, when the sextant and magnetic
compass showed the way, the bridge of a large ocean-going ship
was manned by a dedicated team. The officer of the watch was in
charge, usually assisted by a junior officer or cadet, a seaman was at
the wheel, another on lookout if required, and a third was on call.
The latter made the tea, called the watch, and in between polished
the brass—of which there was plenty around in those far off days.
The ship was in the safe hands of a body of men who were not under
undue stress, and were able to easily cope with most situations that
arose.

However, the march of time cannot be halted, and with the
rapid development of modern technology, so the down-sizing began.
The arrival of the gyro-compass banished the helmsman to the mess-
room, leaving only the ghostly hand of the automatic pilot on the
wheel. Radar dispensed with the lookout man, and as for the junior
officer on the bridge, he was swiftly made redundant by uncannily
accurate satellite navigation and instant ship to ship and ship to
shore communications by VHF radio. The shipowner delighted in a
row of empty cabins.

Much the same thing had been happening in industry ashore,
but here powerful trades unions exercised strict control over the
headlong race to replace men by machines. At sea, no one was watching, and by the early 1990s the dedicated team had gone from the
bridge, replaced by an impressive array of micro-electronics.
Sophisticated anti-collision radars diligently plotted the progress of
nearby ships and gave warning of impending danger, while GPS
(Global Positioning System), monitoring a network of satellites in
space, constantly updated the ship's position to within a hundred
metres. In many ships, one-man bridge operation had become a reality. But, inevitably, there would be a price to be paid for heaping too
much on one man's shoulders.

The 50,760-ton liner *Norwegian Dream* sailed from Oslo on
the evening of 22 August 1999, bound for Dover with 1,740 passengers on board, mainly American. She was on the last leg of a
cruise to the Baltic, that had taken her to St. Petersburg, Helsinki
and Stockholm.

Widow-Maker

Owned by the Norwegian Cruise Line of Miami and registered at Nassau in the Bahamas, the *Norwegian Dream* was technically a flag of convenience ship, but she did not suffer from the shortcomings common to so many flagged out ships. Built in 1992 by Chantiers de l'Atlantique at St. Nazaire, she was a twin-screw ship of twenty-three knots, with bow-thrusters and an ice-strengthened hull. She had been extensively refitted at Bremerhaven in 1998, her passenger accommodation being brought up to luxury cruising standards. Under the command of Captain Robert Teige, with a crew of thirty-nine Norwegian officers and 600 others of various nationalities, she carried all the latest navigational aids and safety equipment. She was, in other words, a first-class ship.

The *Norwegian Dream* cleared the Skagerrak soon after dawn on the 23rd, being scheduled to arrive in Dover twenty-four hours later. It was a fine morning, with a heat haze on the water promising a warm day to come. A few hardy passengers were on deck to watch the sun come up, sad perhaps, that the cosseting they had enjoyed aboard this wonderful ship—for which they had paid in the region of $4,000—was soon to come to an end.

On the bridge of the liner, all was quiet. The babble of the VHF radio was stilled, and only the subdued clicking of the gyro compass, as the automatic pilot applied helm to allow for a cross-current, disturbed the early morning peace. The screens of the two radars glowed softly, the rhythmic sweep of their aerials painting a picture of the sea around. Astern there was land on both quarters, Norway to starboard and Denmark to port. Ahead, nothing more than scattering of tiny echoes indicating fishermen heading out for their grounds. Over the chart table, the recorder of the satellite navigator displayed the changing latitude and longitude as the ship steered to the south-west quickly building up speed.

There was little to demand the attention of the *Norwegian Dream*'s officer of the watch. The ship was in the hands of very competent robots, and as he sipped his mug of scalding hot coffee, he might have been forgiven for feeling somewhat redundant. But this was only the quiet period before the real work began.

At around ten o'clock that night, the *Norwegian Dream*, after an uneventful passage down the North Sea, entered the traffic lanes off the North Hinder, and the testing time was at hand. She had reached the approaches to one of the most congested waterways in the world, the Dover Strait. Of this passage, the Admiralty pilot book has to say:

'The mariner, on entering the Channel, should bear in mind that, owing to the traffic in these narrow waters one of the greatest dangers to its safe navigation lies in the risk of collision, especially in hazy or foggy weather. It is well to remember that, in addition to the vessels following the ordinary track, fleets of trawlers and yachts, there are fast cross-channel vessels plying

between the English and French ports, and crossing the track nearly at right angles.'

The above is a typical piece of understatement by the Admiralty. At a conservative estimate, some 500 ships use the Dover Strait every day. Loaded tankers, ore carriers, old tramps, large container vessels and passengers liners pass north and south bound in uninterrupted streams, while the impatient ferries, sometimes two abreast, cross constantly, using their high speed to weave in and out of the through traffic. The fishermen are a dying breed, but as Europe prospers, they are being replaced by swarms of yachts carrying those seeking escape from a humdrum life ashore. The Dover Strait might now be compared to a busy motorway, bisected at right angles by an equally busy trunk road, and with the added hazard of flocks of sheep straying across the carriageways. Since the 1970s, order has been created out of chaos by the use of traffic lanes—ships sailing outward bound to the Atlantic use the English side of the strait, while those on passage to the North Sea keep to the French side. By and large, this works very well, but there are so many other inherent dangers, fog and poor visibility, sandbanks, wrecks, strong tides, that passage through the Dover Strait in a large ship calls for extreme vigilance.

As the *Norwegian Dream* prepared to enter the southbound traffic lane, the Panamanian-flag container ship *Ever Decent* was leaving the Medway, near the mouth of the Thames estuary, bound east for Zeebrugge, and then on to Japan. The 52,090-ton cargo vessel was also sailing under a flag of convenience, but again, she was a ship with an excellent pedigree. Owned by Evergreen International of Taiwan, one of the world's largest shipping companies, she had been built in Japan in 1997, and was a twenty-five knot motor vessel maintained to the best standards. In her holds, and stacked four high on deck were 3,092 containers, a number of which contained hazardous chemicals. Commanded by Captain Shu, she was manned by a crew of only sixteen men, these being of mixed Taiwanese and Filipino nationality. And herein lay the *Ever Decent*'s only obvious weakness. Although she was within the law, and a crew of only sixteen might be able to handle a 50,000 ton vessel when all goes well, she was very short on numbers to cope with an emergency. She also had the additional problem of having a two-language crew, with all the possible complications that entailed.

The *Ever Decent*'s route to Zeebrugge was a difficult one. Leaving the Thames estuary off Margate, she had to steer first to the north-east to round the top end of the South Falls, a long, narrow sandbank lying outside the Goodwins, after which she must steer south-eastwards, crossing the traffic lanes at the F3 Buoy. This involved running the gauntlet of the north and south bound ships over a distance of ten miles—a highly dangerous undertaking—

'Norwegian Dream' *before collision*
(Photo: Ian Bowman)

before entering the inward-bound traffic lane for Zeebrugge at Hinder 1 Buoy. To assist him in navigating these unfamiliar waters, Captain Shu had on board a North Sea pilot.

At midnight, the *Norwegian Dream* was fifteen miles north-east of F3 Buoy, and approaching the area of greatest risk. F3 stands at a crossroads in the traffic separation scheme. The deep-water routes pass on either side of the buoy, northbound to the south, and southbound to the north, while the routes in and out of the Thames estuary and for Ostend and Zeebrugge also meet here. The buoy also marks the mouth of a funnel formed by the South Falls Bank and Sandettie Bank, which narrows into a gap four miles wide off the Goodwins, through which all deep-draught ships must pass. Given daylight and clear weather, this is a difficult enough gateway for a big ship to negotiate; at night, or in poor visibility, it is every navigator's worst nightmare. On this occasion—a rare one—it was a fine, calm night with good visibility, and by 00:30 on the 24th, the *Norwegian Dream*'s officer of the watch had the flash of F3 Buoy in sight visually fine to port. At least ten other ships were in the vicinity on various courses, and the radar warned that several of these were closing in on him. Ahead and to port, a ship was steering to cross the cruise liner's bow from port to starboard, while on the starboard bow, a very large ship was crossing from starboard to port. These constituted the immediate danger, for the radar's computer was indicating that both were on a collision course with the *Norwegian Dream*.

The Highway Code of the sea—the International

Regulations for the Prevention of Collisions at Sea—lays down quite unambiguously the course of action to be taken in a case like this. It was the duty of the ship crossing from port to give way to the *Norwegian Dream* by altering course or speed to pass astern of her. Likewise, the liner was obliged to do the same for the large ship crossing her bow from starboard. However, the situation was not quite as straightforward as that.

Close on her starboard side, the *Norwegian Dream* had another ship heading in the same direction, which she was slowly overtaking, and was duty bound by the same rules to keep clear of. This precluded the liner from altering course to starboard to avoid the large vessel crossing on her starboard bow, which was, in fact, the *Ever Decent*. In turn, the *Ever Decent* was similarly overtaking a ship on her starboard side, and her ability to manoeuvre was also constrained.

The *Norwegian Dream* was steaming into a trap, which could well have been laid by any cunning examiner in a seamanship test. The rules dictated that she must give way to the *Ever Decent*, yet she could not alter course to starboard to round the container ship's stern for fear of colliding with the ship she was overtaking to starboard. Nor was she able to haul over to port without running into the other ship, which was crossing from that side. And all the while, the *Norwegian Dream* and the *Ever Decent* were moving towards their projected meeting point off F3 Buoy at twenty knots. The alarms were ringing on the anti-collision radars of both ships. A very dangerous close-quarter situation was developing, involving no less than four ships, and the miles were ticking away with the minutes. Someone had to do something, and soon, or it would be too late.

The deadlock was broken at 00:42, when the crossing ship on the *Norwegian Dream*'s port side—then only two miles away—altered course to pass astern of the liner. This was a correct action, but it did restrict the *Norwegian Dream*'s freedom to alter to port. Six minutes later, the ship being overtaken by the *Ever Decent* altered to pass around the container ship's stern.

At this point, the *Ever Decent* called the *Norwegian Dream* on VHF and requested that the liner make a large alteration to starboard to go round her stern. This was the action the *Norwegian Dream* should have taken without prompting, but owing to the close proximity of the other ship on her starboard side, she could not comply. The two 50,000-tonners moved inexorably towards the point of collision.

Unable to sleep, Ned Snyder, a passenger in the *Norwegian Dream*, had come on deck for a breath of fresh air. Leaning on the forward rail of the promenade deck, the 68-year-old Californian sniffed at the cool salt air and drank in the beauty of the night. All around was a carnival of twinkling, flashing lights, the buoys and light vessels that marked the way through the sandbanks and wrecks that litter the approaches to the Dover Strait. Interspersed with them the

Widow-Maker

reds, greens and whites of the ships moving busily up, down and across-channel. An orange loom on the horizon ahead and to starboard was the sleeping coastal towns of Margate, Ramsgate and Deal, to port, on the French side, Calais and Dunkirk made a softer glow. It was a magic night, full of peace and order. Then the world fell apart as the *Norwegian Dream* ran headlong into the *EverDecent*.

Ned Snyder recalled: 'Out of nowhere a huge ship suddenly appeared in front of me and I realised it was going to hit us. I grabbed hold of the rail and there was an almighty cracking sound which seemed to last for ages. It was like a scene out of the *Titanic* movie when the ship crashes into the iceberg. I thought we were going to sink.'

The shock of the two great ships colliding at high speed threw passengers in the *Norwegian Dream* from their beds, windows shattered, decks buckled and loose equipment was flung around. This was followed by the screech of metal on metal as the two great ships swung together and scraped along each other's sides. It was a sound to strike terror in the hearts of the cruise liner's passengers, many of whom were rudely awakened from a sound sleep. Stacey Katz, of New Jersey, was asleep in her cabin below decks, and was flung from her bed and showered with glass as the cabin window caved in. 'I could see another ship passing as it smashed along the side of our ship,' she said. 'I was certain I was going to die. I felt as if the other ship was going to take me with it. There was a huge blast of wind into my room and everything went black.'

Five hours later, the *Norwegian Dream* reached Dover harbour under her own power. She had not been holed below the waterline, but her smart clipper bow was a mess of tangled and torn metal, her starboard bridge wing was crushed and her accommodation laid open. On her forecastle head were five of the *Ever Decent*'s deck containers, catapulted aboard by the force of the collision. Miraculously, only twenty-one passengers and eight crew had been injured, none of them seriously. Largely through the prompt action of Captain Teige and his officers, no panic had broken out on board. 'They were absolutely brilliant,' said Ned Snyder. 'We were all served a full cooked breakfast and English tea as we sailed back to Dover, which we thought was terribly British.'

The *Ever Decent* had not fared so well. She suffered no casualties, but had lost fifteen containers from her deck, was holed below the waterline forward, and flames and smoke were pouring from her deck containers, many of which contained inflammables. Here again, there was no panic, and with his crew fighting the fire, Captain Shu, aided by the North Sea pilot, took his ship into quiet waters off Margate and anchored her. There, with the help of three fire-fighting tugs, the flames were brought under control some hours later.

So ended an encounter that might so easily have turned into a full-scale disaster, with ships sunk and many lives lost. On reflec-

Bernard Edwards

tion, given all the modern aids to navigation available to both ships, it is clearly a collision that should never have occurred.

An inquiry into the incident conducted by the Bahamas Maritime Authority concluded, not surprisingly, that the *Norwegian Dream* was most to blame for the collision. In mitigation, the report of the inquiry stated: 'A concern, which arises from an analysis of this incident, is that the amount of information with which the OOW (Officer of the Watch) has to deal with from time to time can become overwhelming.' This seems like a gross understatement of the position. It must be remembered that this was a 50,000 ton ship travelling at twenty knots, and with just one man on the bridge. Although he had every available navigational aid at his disposal, when faced by a complex manoeuvring situation involving four other ships, at night and in a busy and restricted waterway, he had been unable to cope.

The proverbial straw that broke the camel's back came at a critical moment, when the *Norwegian Dream's* OOW, scurrying between radar and chart, at the same time attempting to identify the relevant buoys and shore lights, was called upon to answer the *Ever Decent's* urgent VHF call. While thus engaged, a seaman came onto the bridge with the ship's garbage book to be signed—a most important duty of the OOW in this environmentally correct age. His attention thus diverted, the officer lost control of the situation.

The wheel has turned full circle in the 200 years since the Honourable East India Company's *Grosvenor* was thrown ashore on the coast of South Africa. The officer of the watch of that ship had little more than his eyes and ears to guide him, and the loss of the *Grosvenor* may be deemed a hazard of the trade. In the case of the *Norwegian Dream*, every conceivable modern navigational aid was to hand, yet, in the end, it was probably this surfeit of technology that overwhelmed the man on her bridge. In the time before the microchip took charge, in ships where only three bridge watchkeeping officers were carried, it was common practice when transiting the Dover Strait, or similar busy waterways, to double the bridge watches. The senior officer was then able to concentrate on conning the ship, while his junior handled navigation, signals and all other aspects of the bridge routine. This was a simple solution to an uncomplicated situation—and it worked. Had the *Norwegian Dream's* OOW been of an earlier generation of seamen, when the pressure became too great he would have disregarded the machines and fallen back on the old maxim 'When in danger with no room to turn, ease her, stop her, go astern.' This being done, it is extremely unlikely that the *Norwegian Dream/Ever Decent* collision would have occurred.

Computer technology now has the upper hand at sea, and as the thinking seaman fades into the background, so the risks of seagoing will increase.

Container ship 'Ever Decent' *on fire with salvage tugs alongside*
(Photo: Numast)

'Norwegian Dream' *in Dover following the collision.*
Dover lifeboat standing by
(Photo: Ian Bowman)

Bernard Edwards

56   The Football Express

"Express Samina" - 2000

Late September in the Aegean Sea is when the long, hot days of summer loosen their grip and give way to the uncertainties of autumn. The once flawless blue sky glazes over, giant anvil-headed cumulo-nimbus threaten the horizon and the wind, quiescent for months past, begins to stir again. It was so in the afternoon of 26 September 2000 when passengers were boarding the island ferry *Express Samina* in Piraeus, the port of Athens.

They came straggling up the stern ramp in untidy groups, loaded down with the mountains of baggage characteristic of the peasantry of the Eastern Mediterranean on the move. Harassed mothers fretted over unruly children, old men and women grumbled, and the young of both sexes eyed each other with suspicion or anticipation. These were the islanders, regular commuters who cared little for the state of the weather, content in the knowledge that this ship would carry them safely home. In their wake came the back-packing gap-year students from the more affluent parts of the world, wide-eyed and seeking a Utopia that no longer exists. It is unlikely that that many of those boarding the Greek ferry on that September afternoon even noticed her general air of dilapidation; even fewer would have been aware of her unsavoury reputation.

The 4,407-ton *Express Samina*, built in 1966 for the French ferry operator SNCM, was one of the oldest passenger-carrying ships still in service in European waters. She was already visibly nearing the end of her useful life when, in December 1999, she was bought for a song by the Piraeus-based Minoan Lines. After a quick check-up in dry dock and a coat of paint all round, she was rushed into service on the 400-mile round trip to the Cyclades islands of Paros, Naxos, Samos, Ikaria, Patmas and Lipsi. Her shortcomings were all too evident from the start of her new career. So much so that even the usually discreet Thomas Cook's 'Greek Island Hopping' guidebook was contemptuous, commenting – *"This dreadful boat is arguably the worst Greek ferry afloat, a large grime bucket with a reputation for running late. For most of the time she has shuddered along: not because of an excess of engine vibrations, but rather with the collective disgust of her passengers thanks to the condition on board. She is definitely a boat to be avoided.'*- With such a reputation so widely broadcast, one has to wonder in which direction the watchful eye of the International Maritime Organisation was turned whenever the *Express Samina* put to sea.

In command of the *Express Samina* was 52-year-old Captain Vassilus Yiannakis, whose professional reputation appears to have matched that of his ship. In the summer of 1989, while in command of another Minoan ferry, the *Nireus*, he first ran her on the rocks off the island of Rhodes, and then sank her—fortunately without loss of life—when attempting to make harbour in Crete. Paradoxically, Yiannakis was held in high esteem by his crew, one of whom, having sailed with him for twenty years, said, 'He knows these waters like the back of his hand. He does not have to look at charts.' In the light of subsequent events, it might have been better if Yiannakis had paid more attention to the charts.

By the time the *Express Samina* left her berth in Piraeus, at five o'clock on the afternoon of 26 September, she had 531 passengers and crew aboard. The passenger list included around 100 foreign tourists, mainly from Britain, Australia, New Zealand, France and South Africa, and a party of eleven doctors from Germany. As she pulled away from the quay, the sky was dark and threatening, with the wind moving up towards force 7, a near gale. Outside the harbour, the sea was heaping up into ugly waves, and the spume was flying. The weather was, in fact, judged to be bad enough for most other ferries due to leave Piraeus that afternoon to cancel their sailings. It must be said, however, that the weather may not have been the primary cause of these cancellations. The highlight of the evening's television broadcasts was the UEFA Champions League match between Hamburg and local team Panathinaikos, a spectacle no red-blooded Athenian would wish to miss.

Captain Yiannakis must have had some good reason for being the exception to the norm, for he had no hesitation in sailing that afternoon. On time, he took the *Express Samina* out through the breakwaters and into the rising wind and sea. His first port of call was the island of Paros, some 100 miles to the south-east, where he expected to arrive at around 10:30 that night. By the time darkness fell, the ferry was battling against force 9 winds and a steep, rough sea, but Yiannakis did not reduce speed. The *Express Samina* ploughed on through the black and moonless night, slamming into each successive wave with a force that set every plate in her ageing hull groaning in protest.

Pushed to the very limit of her endurance, the ferry maintained her schedule, by 10 o'clock being in sight of the flashing light on the Portes Rocks, two seventy-six-foot high pinnacles that guard the entrance tp Paros harbour. Except for a few dejected huddles of back-packers, the windswept upper decks of the ship were deserted, a state of affairs not entirely brought about by the foul weather. In the accommodation, every television set was tuned to the match between Panathinaikos and Hamburg, the outcome of which transcended in importance anything happening outside. The match was nearing its end, and the underdog Athens team was gallantly holding the more powerful German side to a nil-nil draw. Then, at precisely 10:21, Panathinaikos scored, and the *Express Samina* erupted in a frenzy of cheering, back-slapping and whooping that drowned into insignificance the roar of the wind and the crash of the waves. At that point, the ferry was three miles off the Portes Rocks and still moving in towards Paros harbour at her full speed of 17 1/2 knots.

The recollections of what happened next were confused, but it seemed clear from evidence given by a number of passengers that, when the vital goal was scored, everyone on the bridge of the *Express Samina*, including Captain Yiannakis, rushed below to the nearest television set to see the replay. Not surprisingly on that wild night, left to her own devices, the ship crashed headlong into the Portes Rocks.

Having been under way at full speed for five hours, the 4,000-ton *Express Samina* had built up a considerable momentum, and she hit the Portes with the force of an express train hitting the buffers. She bounced off, but the jagged reefs at the foot of the Portes ripped her hull open almost from stem to stern. She fell off into deep water and, as the sea poured into her bowels, she took a heavy list to starboard. Within seconds her generators failed and the ship was plunged into complete darkness, adding to the calamity suddenly visited upon her 500 passengers. Complete chaos ensued, with hordes of terrified men, women and children running blindly in all directions, scrabbling for life-jackets and desperately seeking a way out onto the open deck.

An already catastrophic situation was made worse by the apparent inability of the *Express Samina*'s crew to take charge. 'I went out on deck but nobody knew what to do,' said 34-year-old Michael Beaton from Oxford. 'At no point was an order given to evacuate the ship. People just stood there in the dark trying to make their own decisions on whether or not to jump'. Katrina Stark, 26, a New Zealander, commented: 'There were lots of crew, though mostly old codgers, and once the chaos started you couldn't see any of them. Ordinary people were doing the organising. One group formed a human chain passing lifejackets to elderly passengers who appeared to be too frightened to jump. They seemed to have given up—they were saying the rosary, praying and moaning.' Others reported that crew members told passengers to stay in the accommodation, although by then the ship was clearly sinking. For the foreign tourists, most of whom were unable to understand a word of Greek, ignorance became a life saver. Deaf to the frenzied pleas to stand fast, they fought their way out onto the open deck and jumped into the sea just as the *Express Samina* began her downward plunge.

A few lifeboats were launched, largely through the efforts of a few level-headed passengers who took matters into their own

Widow-Maker

The 'island hopping' ferry 'Express Samina'
(Photo: Numast*)*

Passengers boarding the 'Express Samina'
(Photo: Source unknown)

hands. Two British girls, Katrina Wallace and Nicola Gibson-Hosking, found themselves in one boat with ten other passengers, and thought they were safe. But being without experienced seamen to handle it, the boat was thrown onto a reef and sank. Luckily, all those on board were able to scramble onto the rocks, to which they were left clinging while the waves washed over them. 'We were terrified, cold, just waiting for help,' Katrina Wallace said. 'We could see boats and lights on islands in the distance, but could do nothing but wait.'

When, some twenty minutes after she struck the Portes Rocks, the *Express Samina* capsized and sank, most of her passengers and crew were reported still clinging to the ship. They either went down with her or were thrown into the sea. A forty-knot wind was whipping the tops off the breaking waves, filling the air with spray and foam, and for those in the water clinging to upturned lifeboats or scraps of wreckage there seemed little hope of rescue. Fishing boats were putting out from Patros but with the water becoming colder by the minute for many they would be too late. Then came the miracle. By an amazing stroke of luck, ships of the Royal Navy, on stand by in case of trouble in the Yugoslav elections, were only thirty-five miles to the south. Within minutes of a Mayday being received from the *Express Samina*, nine helicopters from the aircraft carrier *Invincible*, the destroyer *Liverpool*, the frigate *Cumberland* and the Royal Fleet Auxiliary vessel *Fort St George* were racing towards the scene of the disaster. Throughout the rest of the night and into the next morning the helicopters, assisted by a growing fleet of local fishing boats, working under the most appalling conditions, plucked cold and exhausted survivors from the water and from rocky outcrops where they were stranded. Katrina Wallace and Nicola Gibson-Hosking, who had been clinging to rocks for three hours, were winched to safety by a helicopter from HMS *Invincible*.

When dawn broke on the 27th the rescue operation had been downgraded to a hunt for bodies—and there were many of those to be found. When the final count was made it revealed that of the 531 people on board the *Express Samina* when she went down, seventy-nine passengers and three crew had lost their lives. This was said to be the worst accident in Greek waters for thirty-four years and, so it seems, the first maritime disaster ever to be attributable to a television programme.

A preliminary investigation into the cause of the loss of the ferry came up with a finding so bizarre that it defies belief. When the *Express Samina* was on her final run in to Paros, as would be expected, she had a full complement on her bridge. Assisting Captain Yiannakis were his first officer, Anastasios Psychoyos and a junior officer, Yannis Patilas, while a seaman, Panayiotis Gastaglis, was at the helm. However, it appears that these men were not giving their undivided attention to the job in hand, which was to get the ship safely past the Portes Rocks and into port. While conning the ship they were listening with one ear to a play-by-play commentary on the match between Panathinaikos and Hamburg being relayed to the bridge from a television set in the lounge below. When, at 10:21, Panathinaikos scored the crucial goal the ship's helm was switched to automatic pilot and every man on the bridge rushed below to watch the replay of the goal. A number of eye-witnesses confirmed that, when the *Express Samina* hit the rocks, Captain Yiannakis, First Officer Psychoyos, Junior Officer Patilas and the helmsman, Panayiotis Gastaglis, were all huddled around the television in the lounge. Christa Liczbinski, a German survivor, said: 'Everyone was watching the game. I joked with my husband, Who's driving the ship?'

After the event, all four men denied having deserted the bridge of the ferry. Captain Yiannakis claimed he was not even on the bridge in the first place. He said he had been feeling unwell and had gone for a 'little sleep' before entering port. He had overslept and when woken by one of the crew had immediately 'rushed' to the bridge, and had been climbing the ladder to the bridge when the ship hit the Portes. He refused to answer accusations that he had really been watching television at the time of the crash.

First Officer Psychoyos admitted to being absent from the bridge, something he could not really deny, for even before the Panathinaikos goal was scored he had been seen in the lounge 'flirting' with a lady passenger. As soon as he realised the ship was heading for the rocks, Psychoyos said he raced for the bridge and 'grabbed the wheel and turned hard left'. If this is true then the action was far too late.

The 'Express Samina' *piled onto the Portes Rocks at 17 1/2 knots*
(Photo: Source unknown)

Junior Officer Patilas claimed he was 'standing in' for Captain

Yiannakis—presumably while Yiannakis was asleep. When questioned as to why he did not take appropriate avoiding action when the *Express Samina* was heading for the rocks, he could give no satisfactory explanation. The Portes Rocks stand seventy-five feet high and the light on top of one of the northernmost is visible for at least ten miles. If Patilas had been on the bridge he could not have failed to see the danger.

Panayiotis Gastaglis, the helmsman, denied leaving the bridge, and excused his lack of action on the grounds that 'instruments' – radar perhaps? – failed to show the wind had thrown the ship off course, and he did not see the rocks until they were sixty or ninety feet off. The question that must be asked is 'where was Gastaglis when he saw the rocks'? Did he perhaps see them through a window in the passenger lounge?

Wherever these four men were when the *Express Samina* came to grief, their statements suggest they were nowhere near the bridge of the ferry. This was the opinion of the preliminary court of inquiry, held on the nearby island of Syros, which accused them of 'multiple counts of murder with possible malice; causing serious bodily harm with possible malice; violating maritime regulations; violating international regulations on avoiding an accident; and sinking a ship.' The charge was later reduced to 'multiple manslaughter, neglect of duty and violation of maritime principles'. All four were taken to the mainland in irons to await trial.

The reaction of the Greek politicians to the tragedy was strange, summed up by President Apostolos Kaklamanis, who said: 'This accident should at least teach us that Greeks should watch less football on TV'. A disturbing insight into the attitude of the Greek authorities to the operation of the many ferries that ply their waters. Little wonder that to this day the situation has not improved.

The journalist Carole Cadwalladr recently carried out an investigation into the Greek island ferries for the Daily Telegraph. She reported: 'The new ferry on that route from Piraeus to Samos via various Cyclades islands is the *Daliana*. However, 'new' is not an accurate description: the *Daliana* is 31 years old—too old, that is, to operate anywhere else in Europe. Older ferries are not necessarily less safe than new ships, they are no more likely to crash and sink. But sitting in the main passenger lounge of the *Daliana* on the evening sailing from Piraeus to Paros last month (May 2001), I took the advice of the *Samina*'s survivors—and checked the exits.

'A door led from the lounge out onto the deck. But on deck there were no signs indicating which way to go next. The stairs up led to the lifeboats, but there was no way of knowing this. The stairs down led to an open doorway marked "emergency exit" – except that it wasn't. It was the way to the car deck, which had been left unlocked and open throughout the sailing, a practice banned after the sinking of the *Herald of Free Enterprise* in 1987.

Widow-Maker

'There was a strong smell of petrol, layers of white-painted rust were peeling from the wall, a porthole was open just a few feet from the waterline, and the first two fire extinguishers I found were missing pins and did not work.

'Over five days last month I travelled on eight ferries. On seven of the journeys the garage doors were left open and unlocked throughout the sailing; on only one did I hear a safety announcement.

'There were other, more worrying discoveries; lifeboats without engines (on the *Alcacos*); emergency exits were locked (on the *Sappho* and *Express Milos*); 35-year-old lifejackets stamped "Board of Trade 1966" (on the *Appollon* and the *Express Milos*); rubber liferafts in rusty containers showing signs of having perished (on the *Alcacos*); children's lifejackets locked away (on the *Daliana*); adult lifejackets locked away (on the *Artemis*); and stern doors not monitored by CCTV (most ferries).'

While Ms Cadwalladr might be accused of being over zealous in some cases—all lifeboats are not required to have engines, for instance—her investigation confirmed that little had changed on the Greek ferry scene. But nothing she discovered can alter the fact that any ship is only as good as the men who sail her. An old, poorly maintained vessel in the hands of experienced professional seamen can be every bit as safe as the state-of-the-art liner with a crew of disinterested deadbeats. In the *Express Samina* her passengers had the worst of both worlds, and for this many of them paid with their lives.

Bernard Edwards

LIST OF ILLUSTRATIONS
Page

GLOSSARY

Abaft: Behind, in relation to something on board ship.

Abeam: At right angles to the fore and aft line of the ship.

Afterdeck: That part of the main deck abaft the bridge.

Amidships: The middle part of the ship.

Astern: Behind the ship.

Athwartships: Across the beam of the ship.

Barque: Three-masted sailing vessel square-rigged on the fore and main masts and fore-and-aft rigged on the mizen mast.

Beam: Width of the vessel at her widest part.

Binnacle: Pedestal supporting the ship's compass

Boatswain: Senior deck petty officer.

Bower anchor: Main anchor stowed in the bows of the ship.

Bowsprit: Spar projecting forward from the bows which enables ship to carry extra sail.

Breeches buoy: Life-saving apparatus using hawser set up between shore and ship from whichlifebuoy is suspended to carry survivors ashore.

Brig: Sailing vessel with two masts both of them square rigged but having a gaff mainsail.

Broach to: To swing beam on to wind and sea.

Bulkhead: Steel or wooden division between two compartments.

Cant: To turn on an axis.

Clipper: Fast sailing ship built for speed rather than cargo-carrying capacity.

Clipper bow: Raked bow as on clipper ship.

Clutter: Interference on radar screen caused by waves or precipitation.

Coaming: Steel parapet around a hatchway.

Collier: Small ship used exclusively for the carriage of coal.

Conning (the ship): Directing the course to be steered.

Crankcase: Casing surrounding the crankshaft of a ship's main engine.

Crow's nest: Look-out platform situated high on the forward mast.

Cruiser stern: Sloping stem similar to that of naval ship of same name.

Davit pin: Pin securing lifeboat davits while at sea.

Deadweight: Maximum weight of cargo, bunkers, fresh water and stores that can legally be carried by a ship.

Derrick: Boom used for loading and discharging cargo.

Displacement: The weight of water displaced by a vessel.

Dog's leg: Crooked or bent.

Doldrums: Area of light winds and calms near the Equator.

Donkeyman: Senior engine-room rating.

Double bottom: Space between bottom of ship's hull and watertight floor of holds. Used to carry fuel oil or water.

E.T.A: Estimated time of arrival.

Fathom: Six feet or 1.82 metres.

Fine (on bow): Up to about five degrees of arc.

Flag of convenience: Flag which allows registry of foreign ships to avoid irksome legal or financialrestraints in country of ownership.

Fluke: The hooked part of an anchor.

Flush deck: Deck running from forward to aft without interruption of forecastle or poop.

Flying bridge: Open navigation bridge.

Forecastle: Space below deck in the bows of a ship used for crew accommodation or stores.

Forecastle head: Deck above forecastle.

Fore deck: That part of the main deck forward of the bridge.

Forepeak: Ballast or fresh water tank in the bows of the ship.

Freeboard: Distance from the main deck to the waterline.

Gale force: Force 8. Wind speed 34-40 knots (39-46 mph).
Gig: Small open boat.
Gunwale: Point where the hull joins the weather deck.

Halyard: Light rope for hoisting flags.
Hatch board: Portable wooden cover for hatchway.
Hatchway: Opening in deck usually giving access to cargo hold.
Hawsepipe: Pipe through which the anchor cable passes.
Hawser: Heavy wire or rope.
Heave to: To stop the ship at sea.
Hurricane force: Force 12. Wind speed 64 knots (74 mph) and over.

In ballast: Having no cargo on board.

Knot: One nautical mile per hour, a nautical mile being 6080 feet, or the length of one minute of latitude at the Equator.

Larboard: Old name for port or left-hand side of ship when facing forward.
Lead: Weight attached to line used to determine the depth of water under keel.

Leadsman: Seaman who casts the lead.
Lee: The sheltered side.
Lee shore: The shore on which the wind blows.
Lloyd's Register: A body which lays down the rules regarding the building and maintenance of ships.

Main deck: The principal deck of a vessel having more than one deck.
Man-of-war: Armed naval ship.
Master: One who commands a merchant ship.
Mayday: Distress code word used on radio telephone meaning 'I require immediate assistance'.

OBO: Oil/bulk/ore carrier. Large ship built to carry oil or bulk cargo.
Ordinary Seaman: Uncertificated seaman with at least twelve months' sea service

Packet: Small passenger or mail ship.
Paddle-box: Casing covering paddle wheels.
Plimsoll Line: Line painted on side of ship indicating the maximum depth to which she may legally load.
Point (of compass): 11 1/4 degrees of arc.
Pontoon: Portable hollow steel slab for closing hatchway.

Poop: Raised deck at after end of ship.

Pooped: To be overtaken and swamped by wave coming up astern.

Port: Left-hand side of the ship when facing forward.

Quarter: That part of the ship which is halfway between the beam and stem.

Roaring Forties: Belt of strong westerly winds between latitudes 40°S and 50°S.

Schooner: Two-masted sailing ship rigged fore and aft but with square topsails on foremast.

Scupper: Drain at ship's side and in holds to carry away excess water.

Shellback: A seaman of long experience. Usually with reference to sail.

Shelter deck: Deck below the main deck running the length of the ship without dividing bulkheads.

Slab-sided: Straight-sided.

Sloop: Small naval vessel used mainly for auxiliary purposes.

Starboard: Right-hand side of ship when facing forward.

Stator: Stationary part of generator.

Steerage: Communal third-class passenger accommodation below decks.

Steerage way: The minimum speed at which ship's rudder will have effect.

Stern bar: Post at stern of ship to which rudder is attached.

Stokehold: That part of engine-room where boiler furnaces are situated.

Storm Force: Force 10. Wind speed 48-55 knots (55-63 mph).

Tonne: Metric ton of 1000 kilograms.

Torque: Twisting motion of force.

Trade winds: Winds between 30°N and 30°S of Equator which blow consistently from one direction.

Trimmed down: Partly ballasted and low in the water.

Trimmer: Engine-room rating who supplies firemen with coal from bunkers.

Trinity House: Body responsible for the manning and upkeep of lighthouses, lightships, beacons and buoys in the coastal waters of England, Wales and the Channel Islands.

Trough: The hollow between the crests of two waves.

Tween deck: Usually the first deck below the main deck.

VLCC- Very Large Crude Carrier. Usually oil tanker of about 300,000 tonnes deadweight

Notes

For sales, editorial information, subsidiary rights information
or a catalog, please write or phone or e-mail
Brick Tower Press
1230 Park Avenue
New York, NY 10128, US
Sales: 1-800-68-BRICK
Tel: 212-427-7139 Fax: 212-860-8852
www.BrickTowerPress.com
email: bricktower@aol.com.

For sales in the UK and Europe please contact our distributor,
Gazelle Book Services
Falcon House, Queens Square
Lancaster, LA1 1RN, UK
Tel: (01524) 68765 Fax: (01524) 63232
email: gazelle4go@aol.com.

For Australian and New Zealand sales please contact
INT Press Distribution Pyt. Ltd.
386 Mt. Alexander Road
Ascot Vale, VIC 3032, Australia
Tel: 61-3-9326 2416 Fax: 61-3-9326 2413
email: sales@intpress.com.au.